Java EE 6 Cookbook for Securing, Tuning, and Extending Enterprise Applications

Packed with comprehensive recipes to secure, tune, and extend your Java EE applications

Mick Knutson

BIRMINGHAM - MUMBAI

Java EE 6 Cookbook for Securing, Tuning, and Extending Enterprise Applications

First published: June 2012

Production Reference: 1180612

Published by Packt Publishing Ltd.
Livery Place
35 Livery Street
Birmingham B3 2PB, UK.

ISBN 978-1-84968-316-6

www.packtpub.com

Cover Image by Jackson Myers (jax@rice.edu)

Credits

Author
Mick Knutson

Reviewers
Antonio Gomes Rodrigues
Manjeet Singh Sawhney
Deepak Vohra

Acquisition Editor
Andrew Duckworth

Lead Technical Editor
Andrew Duckworth

Technical Editors
Merin Jose
Conrad Sardinha
Mehreen Shaikh

Copy Editor
Insiya Morbiwala

Project Coordinator
Theresa Chettiar

Proofreader
Joanna McMahon

Indexer
Hemangini Bari

Graphics
Valentina D'silva
Manu Joseph

Production Coordinator
ArvindKumar Gupta

Cover Work
ArvindKumar Gupta

About the Author

Mick Knutson, with nearly two decades of experience working in the IT industry in various roles as Enterprise technology consultant, Java Architect, project leader, Engineer, Designer and Developer, has gained a wide variety of experience in disciplines including Java EE, Web Services, Mobile Computing, and Enterprise Integration Solutions.

Over the course of his career, Mr. Knutson has enjoyed long-lasting partnerships with many of the most recognizable names in the Health Care, Financial, Banking, Insurance, Manufacturing, Telecommunications, Utilities, Product Distribution, Industrial, and Electronics industries employing industry-standard full software lifecycle methodologies, including the Rational Unified Process (RUP), Agile, SCRUM, and Extreme Programming (XP).

Mr. Knutson has led training courses and book publishing engagements, authored technical white papers, and presented at seminars worldwide. As an active blogger and Tweeter, Mr. Knutson has also been inducted in the prestigious DZone.com "Most Valuable Blogger" (MVB) group, and can be followed at `http://baselogic.com`, `http://dzone.com/users/mickknutson` and `http://twitter.com/mickknutson`.

Mr. Knutson is exceptional at team building and motivating both at a peer-to-peer level and in a leadership role. He demonstrates excellent communications skills and the ability to adapt to all environments and cultures with ease.

Mr. Knutson is President of BASE Logic, Inc., a software consulting firm focusing on Java-related technologies and development practices, and training for enterprise development.

Mr. Knutson has been a strategic member of Comcast, for Wayne Ramprashad, helping to design and deploy the next generation IVR to align the One Customer Experience and deflect millions in quarterly operational costs. This opportunity helped foster many real world challenges and solutions used indirectly in many of the recipes included in this book.

Acknowledgement

There were several individuals and companies that offered great support in the creation of this book. Rich Highland, Claus Ibsen, and Jonathan Anstey of FuseSource. Atlassian supplied a license of Clover for code coverage. Eviware supported many recipes with a license of soapUI Pro. Jetbrains supplied a license of IntelliJ IDEA editor. MadeForNet supplied a license of HTTP Debugger. Vandyke Software supplied licenses for SecureCRT and SecureFX. YourKit supplied a license for the YourKit profiler.

Visual Paradigm assisted me with the use of their UML modeling suite that was instrumental in writing this book, as well as a powerful tool I have recommended and used on many projects to describe, design and detail all aspects of the software development lifecycle.

Bhavin Parikh assisted in many of the soapUI recipes in this book. Mr. Parikh is a Senior Consultant and Scrum Master, currently employed at Valtech and has more than 13 years of extensive software development experience in OOP, Java, J2EE, web services, database, and various middleware and enterprise technologies. Mr. Parikh holds a Master's degree in Computer Science from Penn State University, and he spoke on data mining at the 13th International Conference on Intelligent and Adaptive Systems and Software Engineering.

Jim Leary of CloudBees assisted with Jenkins and cloud deployment recipes. Mr. Leary has over 30 years of experience in the information technology field. Over half his career has involved working with web-based technologies across a wide swath of frameworks, platforms, and languages. He has held positions as a software developer, manager and architect in a variety of industries including high technology, financial services and energy.

Shawn Northart assisted in Munin and firewall recipes. Mr. Northart moved to San Jose in 2003 after serving various technical support and system administration roles for several ISPs in and around Sacramento. In managed hosting, he honed his system administration skills working with Apache, PHP, and MySQL on the FreeBSD and Linux platforms. He has also worked extensively with designing, implementing, and tuning web-server farms, both large and small, for a number of high-traffic websites.

Justin Zealand assisted with the iOS section in *Chapter 6, Enterprise Mobile Device Integration*. Justin is an independent contractor with over a decade of programming experience in Java-based web systems and more recently native mobile platforms, including iOS and Android. Justin has worked at major companies across a wide range of industries and across many Internet technology disciplines.

Friends and family: I would like to thank my mother for teaching me how to work hard and how one must sometimes make sacrifices to achieve one's goals. I would like to thank my father for giving me the motivation to persevere against all odds. This book would not have been possible without the support of all of my friends throughout the entire process.

About the Reviewers

Antonio Gomes Rodrigues earned his Master's degree at the University of Paris VII in France. Since then, he has worked at various companies with Java EE technologies in the roles of developer, technical leader, technical manager of offshore projects, and performance expert.

He is currently working on performance problems in Java EE applications, in a specialized company.

> I would like to thank my wife Aurélie for her support.

Manjeet Singh Sawhney currently works for a major IT services, business solutions, and outsourcing company in London (UK) as an Information Management Consultant. Previously, he has worked for other global organizations in various technical roles, including Java development and technical solutions consulting. Even though Manjeet has worked across a range of programming languages and technologies, his core language is Java. During his postgraduate studies, he also worked as a Student Tutor for one of the top 100 universities in the world where he was teaching Java to undergraduate students and marked exams and project assignments. Manjeet acquired his professional experience by working on several mission-critical projects serving clients in the Financial Services, Telecommunications, Manufacturing, and Public Sector.

> I am very thankful to my parents, my wife Jaspal and my son Kohinoor for their encouragement and patience as reviewing this book took some of my weekends from the family.

Deepak Vohra is a consultant and a principal member of the NuBean.com software company. Deepak is a Sun Certified Java Programmer and Web Component Developer, and has worked in the fields of XML and Java programming, and J2EE for over five years.

Deepak is the co-author of the Apress book *Pro XML Development with Java Technology* and was the technical reviewer for the O'Reilly book *WebLogic: The Definitive Guide*. Deepak was also the technical reviewer for the Course Technology PTR book *Ruby Programming for the Absolute Beginner*, and the technical editor for the Manning Publications book *Prototype and Scriptaculous in Action*.

Deepak is also the author of the Packt Publishing books *JDBC 4.0 and Oracle JDeveloper for J2EE Development, Processing XML documents with Oracle JDeveloper 11g*, and *EJB 3.0 Database Persistence with Oracle Fusion Middleware 11g*.

www.PacktPub.com

Support files, eBooks, discount offers and more

You might want to visit www.PacktPub.com for support files and downloads related to your book.

Did you know that Packt offers eBook versions of every book published, with PDF and ePub files available? You can upgrade to the eBook version at www.PacktPub.com and as a print book customer, you are entitled to a discount on the eBook copy. Get in touch with us at service@packtpub.com for more details.

At www.PacktPub.com, you can also read a collection of free technical articles, sign up for a range of free newsletters and receive exclusive discounts and offers on Packt books and eBooks.

http://PacktLib.PacktPub.com

Do you need instant solutions to your IT questions? PacktLib is Packt's online digital book library. Here, you can access, read and search across Packt's entire library of books.

Why Subscribe?

- Fully searchable across every book published by Packt
- Copy and paste, print and bookmark content
- On demand and accessible via web browser

Free Access for Packt account holders

If you have an account with Packt at www.PacktPub.com, you can use this to access PacktLib today and view nine entirely free books. Simply use your login credentials for immediate access.

Instant Updates on New Packt Books

Get notified! Find out when new books are published by following @PacktEnterprise on Twitter, or the *Packt Enterprise* Facebook page.

Table of Contents

Preface

Java Platform, Enterprise Edition is a widely used platform for enterprise server programming in the Java programming language.

This book covers exciting recipes on securing, tuning, and extending Enterprise Applications using a Java EE 6 implementation.

The book starts with the essential changes in Java EE 6. Then we will dive into the implementation of some of the new features of the JPA 2.0 specification, and look at implementing auditing for relational data stores. There are several additional sections that describe some of the subtle issues encountered, tips, and extension points for starting your own JPA application, or extending an existing application.

We will then look into how we can enable security for our software system using Java EE built-in features as well as using the well-known Spring Security framework. We will then look at recipes on testing various Java EE technologies including JPA, EJB, JSF, and web services.

Next we will explore various ways to extend a Java EE environment with the use of additional dynamic languages as well as frameworks.

The book then covers recipes that touch on the issues, considerations, and options related to extending enterprise development efforts into mobile application development.

At the end of the book, we will cover managing Enterprise Application deployment and configuration, and recipes that will help you debug problems and enhance the performance of your applications.

What this book covers

Chapter 1, Out with the Old, In with the New: This chapter is not a tutorial or primer on the various specifications, but rather aimed at giving a high-level summary of the key changes in the Java EE 6 release. The focus will be directed on how these new features will simplify your development, as well as how to improve your application performance.

Chapter 2, Enterprise Persistence: In this chapter, we will dive into the implementation of some of the new features of the JPA 2.0 specification, and look at implementing auditing for relational data stores. There are also several additional sections that describe some typical issues encountered, further tips, and extension points for starting your own JPA application, or extending an existing application.

Chapter 3, Security: In this chapter, we will look into how we can enable security for our software system using Java EE built-in features as well as using the well-known Spring Security framework, which is a widely accepted framework for more fine-grained security implementation.

Chapter 4, Enterprise Testing Strategies: This chapter covers a wide range of testing techniques to employ in the Enterprise. We cover testing-related recipes for testing various Java EE technologies, including JPA, EJB, JSF, and web services.

Chapter 5, Extending Enterprise Applications: In this chapter, we will explore various ways to extend a Java EE environment with the use of additional dynamic languages as well as frameworks.

We start with a recipe using Groovy as a dynamic language integrating to existing Java code, then move to examples with Scala, followed by a recipe to integrate AspectJ aspect weaving into an existing application.

We will then end this chapter with two standard Java EE 6 extensions, the Decorator and Interceptor. These are new CDI features that have similar capability and extensibility as we might get from Aspects.

Chapter 6, Enterprise Mobile Device Integration: This chapter will cover recipes that touch on the issues, considerations, and options related to extending Enterprise development efforts into mobile application development.

Chapter 7, Deployment and Configuration: In this chapter, we will cover issues and solutions to application configuration. The solutions described will cover the use of standard Java EE APIs to access external properties files, as well as Groovy-based configuration scripts.

Advanced configuration topics will be covered using the Java Management Extensions (JMX) including detailed configuration and recipes explaining the use of tools to connect to a JMX service.

This chapter will also cover tools to aid in rapid and hot-deployment of Java EE applications through a development IDE or existing build tool such as Apache Ant or Apache Maven.

Chapter 8, Performance and Debugging: This chapter consists of recipes for solving issues related to the performance and debugging of Java EE applications. The solutions described will help in understanding performance-related issues in a Java EE application and ways to identify the cause. Performance topics that will be covered include profiling application memory, TCP connections, server sockets, and threading-related problems that can face any Java application.

This chapter will also cover how to leverage tools for debugging web service payloads as well as ways to extend the capabilities of those tools. Additionally, we will cover leveraging tools to debug network-related issues, including profiling TCP, HTTP, and HTTPS-based connections. We finish the chapter by leveraging tools for application server monitoring to get a better understanding of the health and performance of a live application and the server it runs on.

What you need for this book

The recipes in this book are of an intermediate to advance nature, so a good understanding of Java is required. All the recipes contain references to the required tools and/or SDKs that are used in each recipe. Many recipes are referencing a specific Java EE 6 container, but any Java EE 6-complient container would suffice.

Who this book is for

This book is aimed at Java developers and programmers who want to secure, tune, and extend their Java EE applications.

Conventions

In this book, you will find a number of styles of text that distinguish between different kinds of information. Here are some examples of these styles, and an explanation of their meaning.

Code words in text are shown as follows: " The `@CollectionTable` annotation can be added to a `Collection<T>` or a `Map<K, V>` entity attribute."

A block of code is set as follows:

```
@ElementCollection
    @CollectionTable(name = Constants.HOBBIES,
        joinColumns = @JoinColumn(name = Constants.CUSTOMER_ID))
    @Column(name = Constants.HOBBY_NAME, nullable = true)
    private Collection<String> hobbies = new HashSet<String>();
```

When we wish to draw your attention to a particular part of a code block, the relevant lines or items are set in bold:

```
@OneToMany(cascade = {CascadeType.ALL},
        fetch = FetchType.EAGER,
        mappedBy = Constants.AUDIT_ENTRY)
private Collection<AuditField> fields;
```

Any command-line input or output is written as follows:

```
classpath group: 'com.yahoo.platform.yui',
    name: 'yuicompressor', version: '2.4.6'
classpath group: 'org.mozilla',
    name: 'rhino', version: '1.7R3
```

New terms and important words are shown in bold. Words that you see on the screen, in menus or dialog boxes for example, appear in the text like this: "You just need to click on the **YourKit** icon."

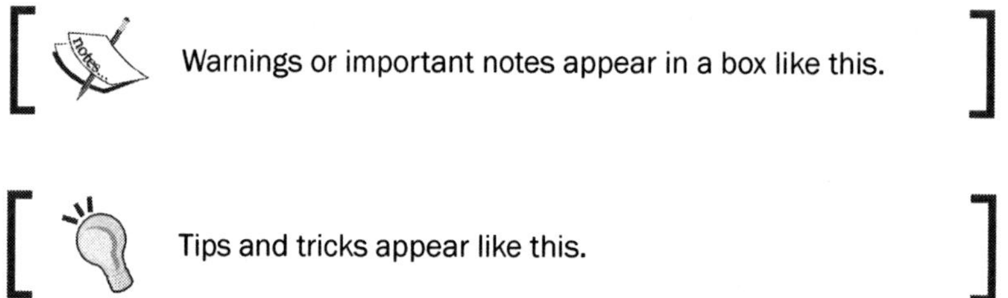

Warnings or important notes appear in a box like this.
Tips and tricks appear like this.

Reader feedback

Feedback from our readers is always welcome. Let us know what you think about this book—what you liked or may have disliked. Reader feedback is important for us to develop titles that you really get the most out of.

To send us general feedback, simply send an e-mail to `feedback@packtpub.com`, and mention the book title through the subject of your message.

If there is a topic that you have expertise in and you are interested in either writing or contributing to a book, see our author guide on `www.packtpub.com/authors`.

Customer support

Now that you are the proud owner of a Packt book, we have a number of things to help you to get the most from your purchase.

Downloading the example code

You can download the example code files for all Packt books you have purchased from your account at `http://www.packtpub.com`. If you purchased this book elsewhere, you can visit `http://www.packtpub.com/support` and register to have the files e-mailed directly to you.

Errata

Although we have taken every care to ensure the accuracy of our content, mistakes do happen. If you find a mistake in one of our books—maybe a mistake in the text or the code—we would be grateful if you would report this to us. By doing so, you can save other readers from frustration and help us improve subsequent versions of this book. If you find any errata, please report them by visiting `http://www.packtpub.com/support`, selecting your book, clicking on the **errata submission form** link, and entering the details of your errata. Once your errata are verified, your submission will be accepted and the errata will be uploaded to our website, or added to any list of existing errata, under the Errata section of that title.

Piracy

Piracy of copyright material on the Internet is an ongoing problem across all media. At Packt, we take the protection of our copyright and licenses very seriously. If you come across any illegal copies of our works, in any form, on the Internet, please provide us with the location address or website name immediately so that we can pursue a remedy.

Please contact us at `copyright@packtpub.com` with a link to the suspected pirated material.

We appreciate your help in protecting our authors, and our ability to bring you valuable content.

Questions

You can contact us at `questions@packtpub.com` if you are having a problem with any aspect of the book, and we will do our best to address it.

1

Out with the Old, In with the New

In this chapter, we will cover:

- Pruning old APIs
- In with the new
- Implementing Java Context and Dependency Injection (CDI)
- Understanding the EJB 3.1 specification
- Understanding the JPA 2.0 specification
- Understanding the JAX-RS 1.1 specification
- Understanding the Servlet 3.0 specification
- Understanding the WebBeans 1.0 specification
- Understanding the JSF 2.0 specification
- Understanding Bean Validation
- Understanding profiles

Introduction

The goal of this book is to describe recipes for securing, tuning, and extending enterprise applications using a Java EE 6 implementation. First, I want to cover some essential changes in Java EE 6, then later employ some of these changes in recipes that are sure to help you make a more secured and robust application.

This chapter is not a tutorial or primer on the various specifications, but rather aimed at giving a high level summary of the key changes in the Java EE 6 release. The focus will be directed on how these new features will simplify your development, as well as how to improve your application performance. However, if you wish to dive straight in, then feel free to skip this chapter with the ability to return to it for reference.

Pruning old APIs

Before diving into new APIs, we need to understand what has been marked for removal in Java EE 6.

Java EE was first released in 1999 and has had new specifications added to each release. Until Java EE 6, no specifications were removed or marked for removal. Over the years, there have been some features that were not well supported or widely adopted, because they were technologically outdated or other alternatives were made available. Java EE 6 has adopted a pruning process (also known as marked for deletion). This process has already been adopted by the Java SE group. None of the proposed items marked will actually be removed from Java EE 6, but could be removed from Java EE 7.

1. To begin with, let's look at the relationships among the Java EE containers:

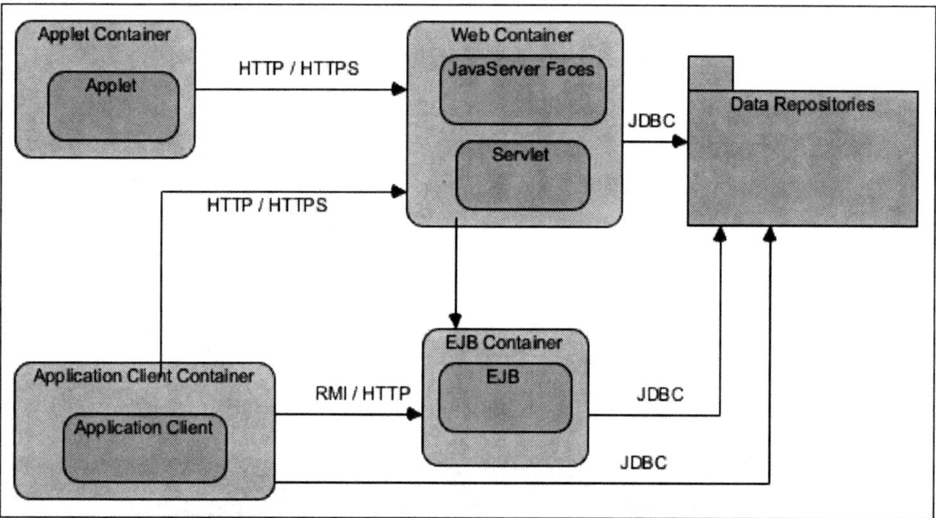

2. Next, we examine the availability of the Java EE 6 APIs in the web container:

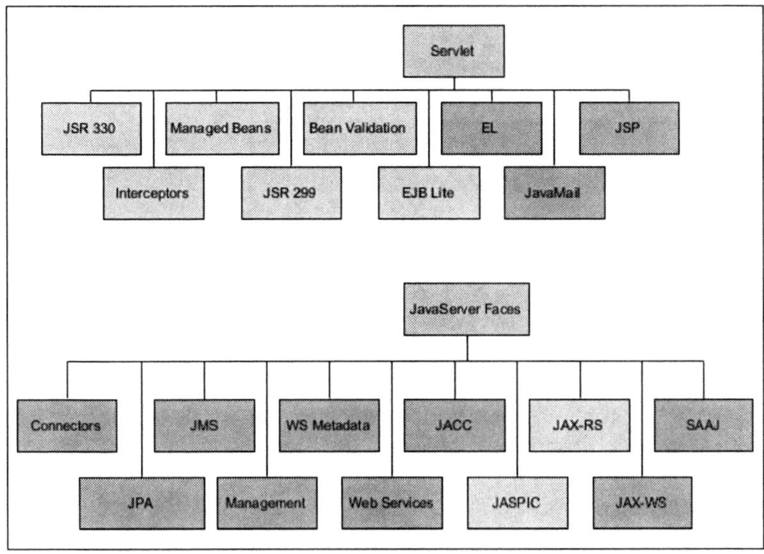

The green boxes denote the new APIs added to Java EE 6.

3. Next, we examine the availability of the Java EE 6 APIs in the EJB container:

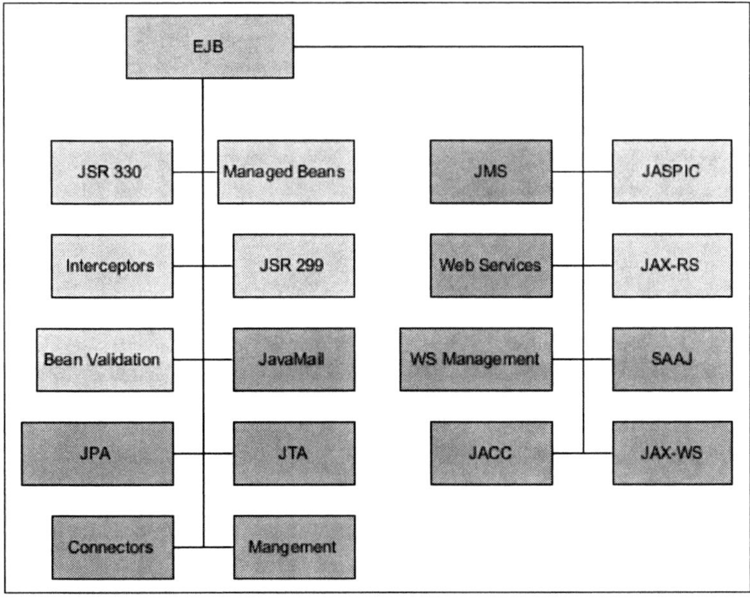

The green boxes denote the new APIs added to Java EE 6.

4. Next, we examine the availability of the Java EE 6 APIs in the application client:

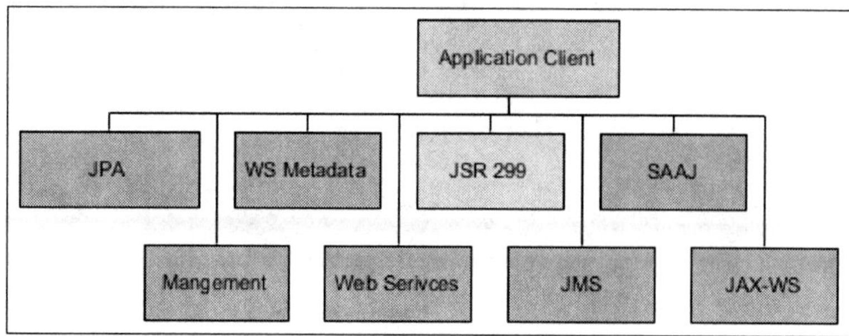

The green box denotes the new API added to Java EE 6.

We will now cover each of the items marked for deletion, why it was marked for deletion, and what will be replacing the pruned specification.

Pruning JAX-RPC

JAX-RPC is an early implementation for web services' interoperability across heterogeneous platforms and languages. JAX-RPC was a great initial implementation, and the JAX-RPC team has done an amazing job of creating this reference implementation. However, when the project started, there were few reference implementations to partner with, such as JAXB. Since the 1.x life span of JAX-RPC, there have been many specifications that have gained momentum, and the JAX-RPC team has used the knowledge learned from 1.x, as well as the widely available and adopted standards, to transform JAX-RPC 1.x into JAX-RPC 2.0.

While this might sound like a major release, it is much more than that. With the advent of JAX-RPC, the team, for many reasons, has decided to rename JAX-RPC 2.0 to JAX-WS 1.0. But the really exciting part of the team's efforts is the adoption of JAX-WS by Java EE 6. We will be exploring the JAX-WS specification in more detail later in this chapter, and in later recipes.

Why was it marked for deletion?

JAX-RPC version 1.1 was marked for deletion in Java EE 6. However, JAX-RPC version 2.0 was actually renamed to JAX-WS version 2.0. There are a few reasons for this renaming:

- One reason is that the JAX-RPC name is misleading. Developers assume that all JAX-RPC code is **Remote Procedure Calls** (**RPC**), not Web Services.
- Another important reason is, JAX-RPC 1.x does not use JAXB. The first version of JAX-RPC was completed before JAXB was released. The JAX-RPC writers developed a custom mapping solution instead.
- By maintaining binary compatibility with the JAX-RPC 1.1, APIs would hinder the goal of ease-of-development.

What has replaced this specification?

JAX-RPC 2.0 was renamed JAX-WS 2.0 (Java API for XML Web Services). This is a much more robust, feature-rich, and popular API, effectively superseding the JAX-RPC 1.1 specification.

See also

- *JAX-RPC version 1.1, JSR-101*: `http://jcp.org/en/jsr/detail?id=101`
- *JAX-RPC Overview*: `http://java.sun.com/webservices/jaxrpc/overview.html`
- *JAX-WS version 2.0, JSR-224*: `http://jcp.org/en/jsr/detail?id=224`
- *JAXB*: `http://jaxb.java.net`

Pruning JAXR

The **Java API for XML Registries** (**JAXR**) gives you a uniform way to use business registries that are based on open standards (such as ebXML) or industry consortium-led specifications (such as UDDI). While UDDI and ebXML still have valid use cases in the enterprise, they are not widely supported or used. Thus, the Java EE expert group has chosen not to continue the addition of JAXR in the Java EE 6 specification, and allow this specification to continue to evolve on its own.

Why was it marked for deletion?

Unfortunately, since UDDI is not widely used, JAXR has very limited adoption, deployment, and vendor support.

What has replaced this specification?

There is no replacement for this specification. It will potentially evolve as a separate JSR.

See also

- *JAXR version 1.1, JSR-93*: `http://jcp.org/en/jsr/detail?id=93`
- *JSR-93 Overview*: `http://java.sun.com/webservices/jaxr/overview.html`
- *JAXP*: `http://jaxp.java.net`
- *JAXB*: `http://jaxb.java.net`

Pruning EJB Entity (CMP)

Previous versions of the EJB specification used a type of bean known as **Entity Bean**. These were distributed objects enabling an object-relational, persistent state. Beans in which their container managed the persistent state were said to be using **Container-Managed Persistence** (**CMP**), whereas beans that managed their own state were said to be using **Bean-Managed Persistence** (**BMP**).

Why was it marked for deletion?

The complex, heavyweight, and overkill model of EJB 2.x Entity Beans has been replaced by the popular, lightweight, POJO-based JPA persistence model introduced as a part of EJB 3.0 in Java EE 5. As of EJB 3.1, JPA has been completely separated to its own spec, and EJB will focus only on the core session bean and message-driven bean component models, and their client API.

What has replaced this specification?

JPA 2.0 is the recommended standard for persistence in Java EE 6.

See also

- *EJB version 3.1, JSR-318*: `http://jcp.org/en/jsr/detail?id=318`
- *JPA version 2.0, JSR-317*: `http://jcp.org/en/jsr/detail?id=317`
- Recipes on JPA 2.0 in *Chapter 2, Enterprise Persistence*

Pruning Java EE application deployment

The JSR 88 defines standard application programming interfaces (APIs) to enable deployment of J2EE applications and standalone modules to J2EE product platforms.

Why was it marked for deletion?

JSR 88 was an attempt at developing deployment tools that work across application servers. Unfortunately, this API has never gained much vendor support.

What has replaced this specification?

There is no replacement for this specification. It will potentially evolve as a separate JSR.

See also

- *Java EE Application Deployment version 1.2, JSR-88*: `http://jcp.org/en/jsr/detail?id=88`

Pruning EE Management

The J2EE Management specification (JSR 77) includes standard mappings of the model to **Common Information Model** (**CIM**), **SNMP Management Information Base** (**MIB**), and to the Java object model through a server resident **Enterprise JavaBeans** (**EJB**) component, known as the **J2EE Management EJB Component** (**MEJB**). The MEJB provides interoperable remote access to the model from any standard J2EE application.

Why was it marked for deletion?

Similar to JSR 88, JSR 77 was an attempt at creating application server management tools that work in a cross-vendor manner. This API has not been well supported.

What has replaced this specification?

There is no replacement for this specification. It will potentially evolve as a separate JSR.

See also

- *Java EE Management, JSR-77*: `http://jcp.org/en/jsr/detail?id=77`

In with the new

Now that you've seen what is being marked for removal from the earlier versions of Java EE, you might be wondering what the novelties are in Java EE 6. This section will cover, at a high level, the key new features of Java EE 6. These new features will be employed in the upcoming recipes so you can get a better grasp on these new specifications, and understand how you can use them in your day-to-day problems and solutions.

The main goal of this release is to continue the improved ease of development introduced with Java EE 5. In Java EE 5, EJBs, persistent entities, and web services were remodeled to follow a more object-oriented approach (Java classes implementing Java interfaces), and to use annotations as a new way of defining metadata (XML deployment descriptors becoming optional). Java EE 6 follows this path and applies the same paradigms to the web tier.

Java EE 6 focuses on bringing simplicity to the enterprise by pruning outdated specifications, and introducing new specifications such as Contexts and Dependency Injection (CDI) and profiles. It adds more features to the existing specification (for example, standardizing singleton session beans), while adding new ones such as JAX-RS and JAX-WS.

Lighter

The Java EE 6 expert group had to face an interesting challenge—how to make the platform lighter, while adding more specifications. An application server has to implement 33 specifications in order to be compliant with Java EE 6. To make the platform more lightweight, the group introduced profiles, pruning, and EJB Lite (a subset of the full EJB features focusing on local interfaces, interceptors, transactions, and security only).

The metadata and common annotations

In addition to the various annotations that have been added or modified in Java EE 6, we also have various metadata and common annotations defined in the Java specification, including:

- Annotations related to security, such as `@DeclareRoles` and `@RolesAllowed`
- Annotations to use EJB, such as `@EJB` and `@EJBs`
- Annotations for resource injection, such as `@Resource` and `@Resources`
- Annotations to use JPA, such as `@PersistenceContext`, `@PersistenceContexts`, `@PersistenceUnit`, and `@PersistenceUnits`
- Lifecycle annotations, such as `@PostConstruct` and `@PreDestroy`
- Annotations to provide references to web services, such as `@WebServiceRef` and `@WebServiceRefs`

See also

- *Java Metadata Specification, JSR-175*: `http://jcp.org/en/jsr/detail?id=175`
- *Common Annotations for the Java Platform, JSR-250*: `http://jcp.org/en/jsr/detail?id=250`

Implementing Java Contexts and Dependency Injection (CDI)

Dependency injection is a popular technique in developing enterprise Java applications. In dependency injection, also called **Inversion of Control** (**IoC**), a component specifies the resources that it depends on.

An injector, typically a container, provides the resources to the component. Though dependency injection can be implemented in various ways, many developers implement it with annotations.

The concept of CDI originated in 2002 with Rod Johnson, who released the framework with the publication of his book *Expert One-on-One J2EE Design and Development*. Since then, **Springframework** has become one of the most widely used frameworks in the Java world. Dependency injection is used heavily in Java development frameworks such as Spring and Guice. Unfortunately, there is no standard approach for annotation-based dependency injection. In particular, a framework such as Spring takes a different approach to annotation-based dependency injection, than that of a framework such as Guice.

These services allow Java EE components, including EJB session beans and **JavaServer Faces** (**JSF**) managed beans, to be bound to lifecycle contexts, to be injected, and to interact in a loosely coupled way by firing and observing events. CDI unifies and simplifies the EJB and JSF programming models and allows enterprise beans to replace JSF managed beans in a JSF application.

JSR 299 can be broken down to these main packages:

- Scopes and contexts: `javax.context`
- Dependency injection service: `javax.inject`
- Framework integration SPI: `javax.inject.manager`
- Event notification service: `javax.event`

JSR 299 relies heavily on Java annotations for the Context and Dependency Injection specification, JSR 330. JSR 330 contains a set of annotations for use on injectable classes. The annotations are as follows:

- `@Qualifier`: Identifies qualifier annotations. Qualifiers are strongly-typed keys that help distinguish different uses of objects of the same type.
- `@Inject`: Identifies injectable constructors, methods, and fields.
- `@Named`: Is a String-based qualifier.
- `@Scope`: Identifies scope annotations.
- `@Singleton`: Identifies a type that the injector only instantiates for a single instance.

@Qualifier

The JSR 330 `@Qualifier` annotation identifies a specific implementation of a Java class or interface to be injected:

```
@Target({ TYPE, METHOD, PARAMETER, FIELD })
@Retention(RUNTIME)
@Documented
@Qualifier
public @interface InjectableType {...}
```

@Inject

The JSR 330 `@Inject` annotation identifies a point in which a dependency on Java class or interface can be injected into a target class. This injection not only creates a new instance, or prototype object by default, but can also inject a singleton object as well:

```
@Stateful
@SessionScoped
@Model
public class ServiceWithInjectedType {
    @Inject InjectableType injectable;
...
```

The container will find the injectable type specified by `@Qualifier` and automatically inject the reference.

@Named

The JSR 330 `@Named` annotation allows for the String-based versus type-based qualification of injectable assets. An example would be:

`http://download.oracle.com/javaee/6/api/javax/inject/Named.html.`

```
@Named
public class NamedBusinessType
  implements InjectableType {...}
```

@Scope

Within a web application, a bean needs to be able to hold the state of duration of the client's interaction with the application. The following table details the available bean scopes:

Scope	Annotation	Duration
Request	`@RequestScoped`	Clients' interaction for a single HTTP Request.
Session	`@SessionScoped`	Clients' interaction across multiple HTTP Requests.
Application	`@ApplicationScoped`	Shared state across all clients' interactions.
Dependent	`@Dependent`	Default scope if none is specified. Means an Object exists to serve exactly one client (bean), and has the same lifecycle as that client (bean).
Conversation	`@ConversationScoped`	Clients' interaction with JSF application within developer-controlled boundaries that extend across multiple invocations of the JSF lifecycle.

The Scoped class-based annotation would look like:

```
@Stateful
@SessionScoped
@Model
public class ServiceWithInjectedType {
    @Inject InjectableType injectableType;
```

You can also create your own custom scope handling by using the `@Scope` annotation:

```
@java.lang.annotation.Documented
@java.lang.annotation.Retention(RUNTIME)
@javax.inject.Scope
public @interface CustomScoped {}
```

See also

- *Contexts and Dependency Injection for the Java EE Platform (CDI), JSR-299*: `http://jcp.org/en/jsr/detail?id=299`
- *Dependency Injection for Java, JSR-330*: `http://jcp.org/en/jsr/detail?id=330`
- *Springframework*: `http://springframework.org`
- *Google Guice*: `http://code.google.com/p/google-guice/`

Understanding the EJB 3.1 specification

Enterprise JavaBeans (**EJB**) is a managed, server-side component architecture for modular construction of enterprise applications. EJB was originally introduced in 1998, which included Session Beans and Entity Beans; Java EE 6 now focuses only on Session Beans. Entity Beans (CMP) have been replaced with the newly adopted JPA specification.

The EJB 3.1 specification simplifies the development and deployment by leveraging new annotations, and making XML descriptors optional.

@Stateless

The EJB 3.0 local client view is based on a **Plain Old Java Interface** (**POJI**) called a local business interface. A local interface defines the business methods that are exposed to the client and that are implemented on the bean class. Having a separate interface from the implementation is sometimes unnecessary and cumbersome. In these situations, to further ease the use of EJBs locally, you can simply annotate a class (POJO). There is no interface required to create a simple stateless EJB. EJBs can also be deployed directly in a WAR file without being previously packaged in a JAR file:

```
@Stateless
public class CustomerEJB {
  @PersistenceContext(unitName = "businessData")
  private EntityManager em;

  public Customer findCustomerById(Long id) {
    return em.find(Customer.class, id);
  }
  public Customer createCustomer(Customer customer) {
    em.persist(customer);
    return customer;
  }
}
```

@EJB

The ease of use for the new EJB annotations extends to the client side as well. Invoking a method on EJB requires only annotating a reference using dependency injection.

Dependency injection allows a container (client, web, or EJB container) to automatically inject a reference on EJB with the help of the `@EJB` annotation:

```
@EJB
private CustomerEJB customerEJB;

    ...

    Customer customer =
      customerEJB.findCustomerById(123L);
```

Even though there is no interface, the client cannot instantiate the bean class using the `new()` operator explicitly. That's because all bean invocations are made through a special EJB reference or proxy provided by the container, which allows the container to provide all the additional bean services, such as pooling, container-managed transactions, and concurrency management.

@Remote

If EJB needs to be invoked remotely, then it needs to implement a remote interface. The only difference between a normal Java interface and a remote interface is the presence of the `@Remote` annotation, as shown in the following code example:

```
@Remote
public interface CustomerEJBRemote {
  public List<Customer> findCustomers();
  public Customer findCustomerById(Long id);
  public Customer createBook(Customer customer);
  public void deleteCustomer(Customer customer);
  public Customer updateCustomer(Customer customer);
}
```

@Singleton

A singleton bean, also known as a singleton, is a new kind of session bean that is guaranteed to instantiate a single instance for an application JVM.

You define a singleton with the `@Singleton` annotation, as shown in the following code example:

```
@Singleton
public class ServiceBean {
    ...
}
```

@Asynchronous

By default, session bean invocations through remote, local, and no-interface views are synchronous:

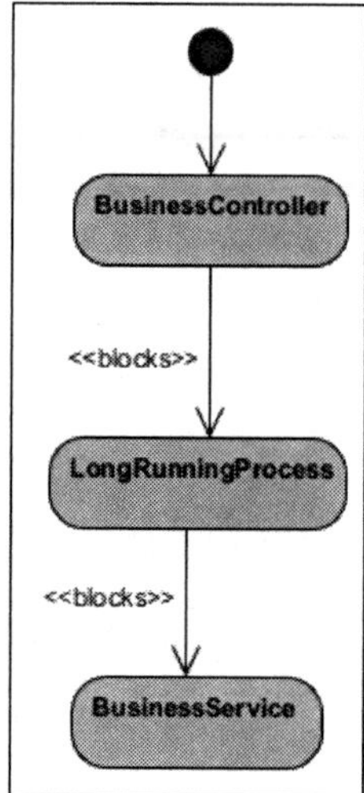

A client invokes a method, and it gets blocked for the duration of the invocation until the processing has completed; the result is returned, and the client can carry on with their work.

But asynchronous processing is a common requirement in many applications handling long-running tasks, or for tasks that are fire-and-forget, where you might be able to increase response time:

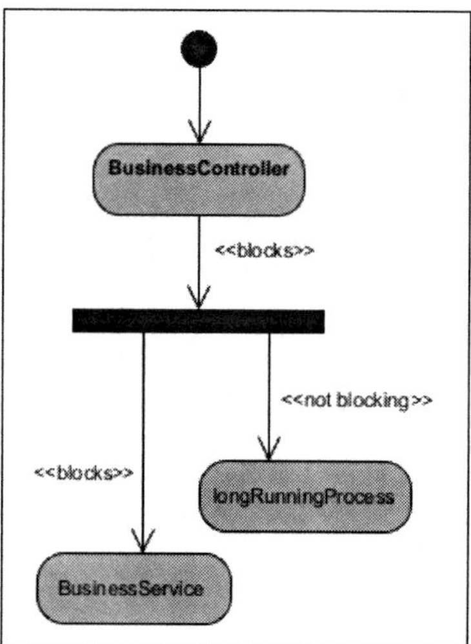

Since EJB 3.1, you can call methods asynchronously simply by annotating a session bean method with `@Asynchronous`.

Asynchronous methods can return a `java.util.concurrent.Future<V>` object or `void`. A `Future<V>` object holds the result of an asynchronous operation. You can access the `Future<V>` object to retrieve a result value, check for exceptions, or cancel an in-progress invocation. The `Future<V>` interface provides a `get()` method to retrieve the value:

```
public class AppointmentBeanImpl
  implements AppointmentService{
    public Future<XMLGregorianCalendar>
      getAppointment (String accountNumber){
      ...
      XMLGregorianCalendar result = ...;
      return new AsyncResult
        <XMLGregorianCalendar>(result);
    }
}
```

The call to the `getAppointment` method will return a pointer to `FUTURE` and the call will not block until you make the request for the represented type in the `Future<V>` by calling `get()` in the `Future<V>`:

```
public Object getFromFuture(Future future)
    throws Exception {
      Object t;
      try {
          t = future.get
            (EXECUTION_TIMEOUT_IN_SECONDS, TimeUnit.SECONDS);
      }
      ...
      return t;
    }
```

See also

- *EJB specification, JSR-318*: `http://jcp.org/en/jsr/detail?id=318`
- *Singleton Pattern*: `http://en.wikipedia.org/wiki/Singleton_pattern`

Understanding the JPA 2.0 specification

The **Java Persistence** API is the standard for persisting Java objects to a relational database. This specification includes metadata definition mappings and configuration. It also includes a standard **Service Provider Interface** (**SPI**) that allows applications to easily plug-in different JPA providers, such as Hibernate, or iBatis, just to name a few.

@ElementCollection

Another useful new mapping type in JPA 2.0 is the element collection, which allows an entity to reference a collection of objects that are of a basic type (such as String or Integer). The `@ElementCollection` annotation is used to indicate the mapping. The objects are stored in a separate table called a collection table, which is by default named as `<entityName>_<attributeName>`:

```
@Entity
public class Customer {
    ...
    @ElementCollection
    @Column(name="SNAME")
    Collection<String> screennames;
    ...
}
```

@CollectionTable

If you want to override the default mapping name convention of the `@ElementCollection` annotation, it can be overridden with the `@CollectionTable` annotation:

```
@Entity
public class Customer {
    ...
    @ElementCollection
    @CollectionTable(name="SCREENNAMES")
    @Column(name="SNAME")
    Collection<String> screennames;
    ...
}
```

Pessimistic locking

In the JPA 2.0 specification, pessimistic locking has been a needed improvement, especially in high data concurrency systems.

In order to enable this functionality, the entity manager, `find()` and `refresh()` methods take a lock mode at the operational level.

Criteria API

An exciting new feature is the Criteria API. This allows you to leverage the Criteria API to add nodes programmatically to the criteria tree, and then pass to a criteria wrapper for evaluation. The two types are String-based and Strongly-typed criteria.

String-based criteria

With string-based criteria, you specify attribute names as strings similar to many of the existing criteria APIs, as well as expression frameworks such as Hibernate:

```
CriteriaBuilder cb =
  em.getCriteriaBuilder();
CriteriaQuery c =
  cb.createQuery(Customer.class);
Root cust = c.from(Customer.class);
c.select(cust).
  where(cb.equal(cust.get("name"), "BASE Logic"));
List result =
  em.createQuery(c).getResultList();
```

Strongly-typed criteria

A string-based criterion seems familiar, but can lead to difficulties in finding defects if attributes are mistyped or a wrong attribute is used. The compiler will not catch these errors, and the exception manifests itself only at runtime such as searching for a Customer's name with `cust.get("name")`. Using strongly-typed criteria will bind the criteria to the attribute of the Customer Object as seen in the following listing:

```
CriteriaBuilder cb = em.getCriteriaBuilder();
CriteriaQuery<Customer> c =
  cb.createQuery(Customer.class);

Root<Customer> cust = c.from(Customer.class);
c.select(cust) where (cb.equal
  (cust.get(Customer_.name), "BASE Logic"));
List<Customer> result =
  em.createQuery(c).getResultList();
```

Additional JPQL

There are several additional JPQL features worth noting. The following listing details the key addition, a description, and a given example on how this might be used:

Feature	Description	Example
CASE statement	CASE { WHEN conditional THEN [expr]+ ELSE [expr] END	UPDATE Customer c SET c.creditLimit = CASE WHEN c. creditScore = 600 THEN c. creditLimit * 2.0 ELSE c. creditLimit * 1.5 END
Collection input parameters	Allow parameter arguments to be collections	SELECT c FROM Customer c WHERE c.lastName IN :names
Date, time, and timestamp literals	JDBC syntax was adopted: {d 'yyyy-mm-dd'} {t 'hh-mm-ss'} {ts 'yyyy-mm-dd hh-mm- ss'}	SELECT c FROM Customer c WHERE c.lastupdate < {d '2011-01-08'}
INDEX in a List	Refer to an item's position index in a list	SELECT c FROM Appointment a JOIN a.waitingList c WHERE a.num = 454 AND INDEX(c) = 0
Map support - KEY, VALUE, ENTRY	Allow comparison and selection of keys and values and selection of entries	SELECT c.name, KEY(p), VALUE(p) FROM Customer c JOIN c.phones p WHERE KEY(p) IN ('Work', 'Cell')
Non-polymorphic queries - TYPE	Can query across specific subclasses of a superclass	SELECT p FROM Division d WHERE TYPE(p) = SouthernDivision OR TYPE(p) = NorthernDivision
NULLIF, COALESCE	Additional CASE variants: COALESCE([expr], [expr]+)	SELECT COALESCE (d.name, d.id) FROM Department d
Scalar expressions in the SELECT clause	Return the result of performing a scalar operation on a selected term	SELECT LENGTH(c.name) FROM Customer c

Feature	Description	Example
Variables in SELECT constructors	Constructors in SELECT clause can contain identification variables	`SELECT new CustInfo (c.name, a) FROM Customer c JOIN c.address a`

See also

- *JPA 2.0 specification, JSR-317*: http://jcp.org/en/jsr/detail?id=317
- *Hibernate*: http://www.hibernate.org/
- *iBatis*: http://ibatis.apache.org/

Understanding the JAX-RS 1.1 specification

A long-awaited feature for Java EE 6 is the advent of RESTful Web Services. **Representational State Transfer** (**REST**) attempts to describe architectures that use HTTP or similar protocols by constraining the interface to a set of well-known, standard operations (such as GET, POST, PUT, DELETE for HTTP). Here, the focus is on interacting with stateful resources, rather than messages or operations.

The term Representational State Transfer was introduced and defined in 2000 by Roy Fielding in his doctoral dissertation.

JAX-RS enables you to rapidly build lightweight web services that conform to the REST style of software architecture. An important concept in REST is the existence of resources, each of which can be referred to with a global identifier, that is, a URI. In particular, data and functionality are considered resources that can be identified and accessed through URIs.

JAX-RS furnishes a standardized API for building RESTful web services in Java. The API contributes a set of annotations and associated classes and interfaces. Applying the annotations to POJOs enables you to expose web resources. This approach makes it simple to create RESTful web services in Java.

@Path

The @Path annotation sets the relative URI path. While this feature is quite powerful, this annotation becomes even more important with the concept of URI Templates. A URI Template allows you to embed variables within your URI syntax. These variables are substituted at runtime in order for a resource to respond to a request based on the substituted URI. Variables are denoted by curly braces:

```
@Path("/customers/{name}")
public class CustomerController {
```

```
        @GET
        @Produces("text/xml")
        public String getCustomer
          (@PathParam("name") String name) {
            ...
        }
    }
```

HTTP Methods

Several HTTP Method resource designator annotations, such as `@Get`, `@Put`, `@Post`, `@Delete`, and `@Head` are supported; they correspond to the similarly named HTTP methods.

@Produces

The `@Produces` annotation is used to specify the MIME types, which a resource can produce and return to a client. Common MIME types include `PLAIN_TEXT`, `TEXT_XML`, `APPLICATION_XML`, and `APPLICATION_JSON`:

```
    @Path("/order")
    public class OrderController {
            // Return JSON
            @GET
            @Produces({ MediaType.APPLICATION_XML,
            MediaType.APPLICATION_JSON })
            public Order getJSONOrXML() {
                ...
        }

        // Return Text/Xml
        @GET
        @Produces({ MediaType.TEXT_XML })
        public Order getHTML() {
                ...
        }

        // Return plain text
        @GET
        @Produces({ MediaType.TEXT_PLAIN })
        public Order getText() {
                ...
        }
    }
```

@Consumes

The @Consumes annotation is used to specify the MIME types that a resource can consume, which were sent from a client. Common MIME types include PLAIN_TEXT, TEXT_XML, APPLICATION_XML, and APPLICATION_JSON.

See also

- *JAX-RS 1.1 specification, JSR-311*: http://jcp.org/en/jsr/detail?id=311

Understanding the Servlet 3.0 specification

Unlike some previous releases of the Servlet specification, the Servlet 3.0 specification is packed with lots of exciting features, facilitating annotation-based configuration. Some of the key additions include:

- Ease of development with annotations
- Optional deployment descriptors
- Asynchronous support
- Security enhancements
- Other miscellaneous changes

@WebServlet

To define a Servlet component in a web application, you use @WebServlet. The @WebServlet annotation has many attributes, such as name, urlPatterns, and initParams, which you use to define the Servlet's behavior. At least, name and urlPatterns are required:

```
@WebServlet(name="HealthMonitorServlet",
  urlPatterns="/health")
public class
  ServletHealthMonitor extends HttpServlet {
    ...
}
```

@WebFilter

You use the `@WebFilter` annotation to define a filter. You can use `@WebFilter` on any class that implements the `javax.servlet.Filter` interface. Just like the `@WebServlet` annotation, you must specify the `urlPatterns` on this annotation as well:

```
@WebFilter(filterName = "AuthenticateFilter",
  urlPatterns = {"/customer", "/getOrders"})
public class AuthenticateFilter implements Filter {
    ...
}
```

@WebInitParam

You use the `@WebInitParam` annotation to specify the init parameters to a Servlet or Filter. This annotation is especially helpful for configuration, and as we will see in later recipes, it can allow us greater control over application configuration:

```
@WebServlet
  (name="HealthMonitorServlet", urlPatterns="/health")
@WebInitParam
  (name = "serverId", value = "XYZ:8080")
public class
  ServletHealthMonitor extends HttpServlet {
    ...
}
```

@WebListener

You use the `@WebListener` annotation on a class that acts as a listener to events in a given web application context. You can use `@WebListener` to annotate a class that implements `ServletContextListener`, `ServletContextAttributeListener`, `ServletRequestListener`, `ServletRequestAttributeListener`, `HttpSessionListener`, and `HttpSessionAttributeListener`.

Here is an example with `ServletContextListener`:

```
@WebListener
public class AuditServletContextListener
  implements ServletContextListener {
    ...
}
```

Web fragments

One of Servlet 3.0's most significant concepts is the idea of **web fragments** or **modular** web.xml. The idea is to be able to create modular and reusable web components. These components would typically be packed inside of a JAR and contain a descriptor such as this web-fragement.xml packaged into the JAR's META-INF directory:

```
<web-fragment>
    <servlet>
        <servlet-name>
            myReusableServlet
        </servlet-name>
        <servlet-class>
            ch01.myReusableServlet
        </servlet-class>
    </servlet>

    <listener>
        <listener-class>
            ch01.myReusableListener
        </listener-class>
    </listener>
</web-fragment>
```

This reusable JAR is placed into the WEB-INF/lib directory of the web applications in which you want to use this reusable component. During the application startup, it is the responsibility of the Container to scan the information that is found in the /META-INF/web-fragment.xml file available in the application's classpath.

Asynchronous servlet processing

Along the same lines as the @Asynchronous annotation we have seen earlier, the Servlet 3.0 specification now has support for asynchronous servlet processing:

```
public void doGet
  (HttpServletRequest request,
  HttpServletResponse response) {
    AsyncContext context =
      request.startAsync(request, response);
    ServletContext scope =
      request.getServletContext();
    ((Queue<AsyncContext>)
      scope.getAttribute("jobQueue")).add(context);
..
```

This new feature is especially useful for AJAX-based interaction with Web 2.0 designs. We will investigate several asynchronous recipes to demonstrate how this can be a great performance enhancement to the user experience.

See also

- *Servlet 3.0 specification, JSR-315*: `http://jcp.org/en/jsr/detail?id=315`

Understanding the WebBeans 1.0 specification

The name of the JSR was changed from **WebBeans** to **Contexts and Dependency Injection** for Java.

See also

- *Contexts and Dependency Injection for the Java EE Platform (CDI), JSR-299*: `http://jcp.org/en/jsr/detail?id=299`
- *Dependency Injection for Java, JSR-330*: `http://jcp.org/en/jsr/detail?id=330`

Understanding the JSF 2.0 specification

Java Server Faces (**JSF**) was initially released in 2004, and has been met with both criticism and embrace, as with many specifications. But time has tested and revealed that JSF is a solid framework, and Java EE embraces the new JSF 2.0 specification. With the advent of the new JSF 2.0 model, several new annotations are now available to simplify development and configuration.

@ManagedBean

The `@ManagedBean` annotation is used for defining a POJO as a JSF Managed Bean. This will be especially helpful for applications not using `@EJBs`.

@ResourceDependency

The `@ResourceDependency` annotation allows you to define resources to be used in your pages. This is a more elegant way to include resources such as styles and scripts:

```
@ResourceDependency(library="corp_en", name="css_english.css")
```

@ListenerFor

The `@ListenerFor` annotation allows a component to subscribe to a particular event as a listener:

```
@ListenerFor(systemEventClass=
  AfterAddToParentEvent.class, sourceClass=UIOutput.class)
public class CustomRenderer
  extends Renderer
  implements ComponentSystemEventListener {
    ...
    public void processEvent
      (ComponentSystemEvent event)
      throws AbortProcessingException {
      ...
```

@FacesConverter

The `@FacesConverter` annotation allows you to register a class as a runtime `Converter`:

```
@FacesConverter(value = "callConverter")
public class CallConverter
  implements Converter {
  @Override
  public Object getAsObject
      (FacesContext ctx, UIComponent component,
      String value) {
    return value;
  }

  @Override
  public String getAsString
      (FacesContext ctx, UIComponent component,
      Object value) {

  }
}
```

@FacesValidator

The `@FacesValidator` annotation allows you to register a class as a runtime `Validator`:

```
@FacesValidator(value = "accountValidator")
public class AccountValidator implements Validator {

@Override
public void validate(FacesContext context, UIComponent component,
Object value) throws ValidatorException {
...
```

See also

- *JSF 2.0 specification, JSR-314*: `http://jcp.org/en/jsr/detail?id=314`

Understanding Bean Validation

The Java API for JavaBeans Validation (Bean Validation) provides a mechanism for validating application data. Bean Validation is integrated into the Java EE containers, allowing the same validation logic to be used in any of the tiers of an enterprise application. This allows for a simplified and more readable application when utilizing Bean Validation in JSF, JAX-RS, or your JPA services.

Getting ready

The Bean Validation is built into the Java EE 6 compliant containers, so there is no preparation that you need to employ for these techniques.

How to do it...

Bean Validation can be as simple as null and size checks on your domain objects such as:

```
public class Customer {
    @NotNull
    @Size(min=2, max=16)
    private String firstname;
```

In addition to standard validation annotations, the new `@Pattern` annotation allows complex, property-type validation based on regular expressions. The following depicts the validation of a phone number:

```
@Pattern(regexp="^\\(?(\\d{3})\\)?[- ]?(\\d{3})[- ]?(\\d{4})$",
         message="{invalid.phonenumber}")
protected String officePhone;
```

The `@Pattern` annotation has an optional message property associated with the validation failure.

There's more...

The built-in Bean Validation constraints are shown in the following table:

Feature	Description	Example
`@AssertFalse`	Match the field or property against Boolean false.	`@AssertFalse boolean isComplete;`
`@AssertTrue`	Match the field or property against Boolean true.	`@AssertTrue boolean isEnabled;`
`@DecimalMax`	Match the field or property against a decimal value lower than or equal to the element value.	`@DecimalMax("8.75") BigDecimal taxRate;`
`@DecimalMin`	Match the field or property against a decimal value higher than or equal to the element value.	`@DecimalMax("4.20") BigDecimal taxRate;`
`@Digits`	Match the field or property against a number in a specific range.	`@Digits(integer=6, fraction=2) BigDecimal cost;`
`@Future`	Match the field or property against a future date.	`@Future Date endDate;`
`@Max`	Match the field or property against an integer value less than or equal to the element value.	`@Max(3) int attempts;`
`@Min`	Match the field or property against an integer value greater than or equal to the element value.	`@Min(1) int quantity;`
`@NotNull`	Match the field or property to be not null value.	`@NotNull String username;`
`@Null`	Match the field or property to be a null value.	`@Null String errors;`
`@Past`	Match the field or property against a past date.	`@Past Date startDate;`
`@Pattern`	Match the field or property against the given regular expression.	

Feature	Description	Example
`@Size`	Match the field or property against specific size boundaries. If the field or property is a `String`, the size of the string is evaluated. If the field or property is a `Collection`, the size of the `Collection` is evaluated. If the field or property is a `Map`, the size of the `Map` is evaluated. If the field or property is an array, the size of the array is evaluated.	`@Size(min=2,max=240) String briefMessage;`

Do not confuse `@Future` with `Future<V>` in the concurrency package.

Timezone and locale

An important note about `@Future` and `@Past` is that each validator uses the current time-zone and current locale for the constraint. If you are validating in varying timezones, then you will need to create a custom constraint to accomplish the task. We will create custom constraints in later chapters, to demonstrate how to solve these frequent occurrences.

See also

- *Bean Validation 1.0 specification, JSR-303*: `http://jcp.org/en/jsr/detail?id=303`
- *@Past*: `http://docs.oracle.com/javaee/6/api/javax/validation/constraints/Past.html`
- *Regular Expressions*: `http://en.wikipedia.org/wiki/Regex`

Understanding profiles

Profiles are a major new feature in the Java EE 6 environment. Their main goal is to allow developers to pick-and-choose the specifications from the Java EE stack they need, and allow for smaller footprints for projects that do not need certain specifications from the 33 different ones included in Java EE 6. Many people have complained that Java EE was too large. Servlet containers such as Tomcat have allowed many developers to use a small subset Java EE, such as Servlets, JSF, and JSPs, but have forced developers to add other frameworks, such as **Spring** or **Guice** to accomplish even medium complex solutions to everyday problems.

We will utilize various aspects of these profiles as we work through the proceeding chapters.

See also

- *Web Profiles 6.0 specification, JSR-316*: `http://jcp.org/en/jsr/detail?id=316`
- *Contexts and Dependency Injection for the Java EE Platform (CDI), JSR-299*: `http://jcp.org/en/jsr/detail?id=299`
- *Dependency Injection for Java, JSR-330*: `http://jcp.org/en/jsr/detail?id=330`
- *EJB Lite specification, JSR-318*: `http://jcp.org/en/jsr/detail?id=318`
- *JPA 2.0 specification, JSR-317*: `http://jcp.org/en/jsr/detail?id=317`
- *JTA specification, JSR-907*: `http://jcp.org/en/jsr/detail?id=907`
- *Servlet 3.0 specification, JSR-315*: `http://jcp.org/en/jsr/detail?id=315`
- *JSF 2.0 specification, JSR-314*: `http://jcp.org/en/jsr/detail?id=314`
- *Bean Validation 1.0 specification, JSR-303*: `http://jcp.org/en/jsr/detail?id=303`

2
Enterprise Persistence

In this chapter, we will cover:

- Understanding @CollectionTable
- Auditing previous JPA Operations
- Auditing historical JPA Operations
- Profiling and testing JPA Operations

Introduction

In this chapter, we will dive into the implementation of some of the new features of the JPA 2.0 specification. We will then look at implementing auditing for relational data stores. There are also several additional sections that describe some typical issues encountered, further tips, and extension points for starting your own JPA application, or extending an existing application.

Understanding @CollectionTable

The new @CollectionTable annotation specifies the table that is used for the mapping of collections of basic or embeddable types. This can be applied to the collection-valued field or property in an Entity Class. The embeddable objects are not stored in the embedded source object's table, but stored in a separate collection table. This is similar to a OneToMany, except the target object is an embeddable object instead of an @Entity. This allows collections of simple objects to be easily defined, without requiring the simple objects to define an ID or ManyToOne inverse mapping.

There are limitations to the ElementCollection instead of a OneToMany relationship. The target collection object cannot be queried, persisted, or merged independently of their parent object. ElementCollection are strictly privately-owned (dependent) objects, the same as an Embedded mapping. ElementCollection have no option to cascade and these target objects are always persisted, merged, or removed with their parent. ElementCollection can use a fetch type and defaults to LAZY the same as other collection mappings.

Getting ready

In order to use the @CollectionTable annotation, you first need to understand why they have been added to the JPA specification. While I feel this is a powerful new feature, it is important not to overuse this feature for mapping.

How to do it...

The @CollectionTable annotation can be added to a Collection<T> or a Map<K, V> entity attribute. This allows for some interesting mappings to store related entities.

In the case of a Collection<V>, you can choose a String or Integer as your collection element such as Collection<String>. You might also choose to have a custom collection of Objects such as List<Phone>. You might even find a usage for implementing a Map<K, V> Collection table. In these cases, you will still use a String or Integer as a key, and a custom object as your value such as Map<String, Address> to define your custom mapping:

1. To start with a simple example, we can start by mapping a collection of Strings to our Entity:

```
@ElementCollection
@CollectionTable(name = Constants.HOBBIES,
    joinColumns = @JoinColumn(name = Constants.CUSTOMER_ID))
@Column(name = Constants.HOBBY_NAME, nullable = true)
private Collection<String> hobbies = new HashSet<String>();
```

2. We need to annotate this collection with `@ElementCollection` to denote that this is a basic attribute type, and that it is not acting as a container. We then define `@CollectTable` annotation where we can specify the table name used for the hobbies and the respective joinColumn, or foreignKey referring back to our customer. When we generate a `<dataset>` for testing this mapping, we end up with the following code:

   ```
   <CUSTOMER id='103' USERNAME="user3"
       FIRSTNAME="Foo" LASTNAME="UserTwo"/>
   <HOBBIES CUST_ID="102" HOBBY_NAME="BASE-Jumping"/>
   ```

3. The same mapping will work when trying to map a collection of custom objects such as `List<Phone>`. Our `@JoinColumn` still allows JPA to map the Phone back to the Customer to whom this phone belongs. When we generate a `<dataset>` for testing this mapping, we end up with the following code:

   ```
   <CUSTOMER id='103' USERNAME="user3"
       FIRSTNAME="Foo" LASTNAME="UserTwo"/>
   <HOBBIES CUST_ID="102" HOBBY_NAME="BASE-Jumping"/>

   <PHONES AREACODE="415" PHONE_NUMBER="5551212"
       TYPE="WORK" CUST_ID="102"/>
   ```

4. When we start getting a little more complex by mapping a `Map<K,V>` into our Entity, we need to be more specific on how JPA will map our custom object.

   In this case, we still define our `@ElementCollection`, and our `@CollectionTable` just as mapping a collection, List, or Set:

   ```
   @ElementCollection
   @CollectionTable(name = Constants.CUSTOMER_ADDRESSES,
         joinColumns = @JoinColumn(name =
             Constants.CUSTOMER_ID))
   @MapKeyColumn(name = Constants.ADDRESS_KEY)
   private Map<String, Address> addresses =
       new HashMap<String, Address>();
   ```

5. We now add an additional annotation, `@MapKeyColumn`, to denote the key in our Address that we want to map back to our Customer. When we look at the `<dataset>` used for testing this Entity, we can see that our `ADDRESS_KEY` and `CUST_ID` are merged into one table:

   ```
   <CUST_ADDRESSES ADDRESS_KEY="Primary" CITY="Exton"
                   POSTCODE=""
                   PROVINCE="91335"
                   STATE="PA" STREET="555 Boot Road"
                   STREET2="b101" TYPE="RESIDENTIAL"
                   CUST_ID="102"/>
   ```

6. The `ADDRESS_KEY` denotes the Key used in the `Map<K,V>`, for our Address Object. Then we have a reference `CUST_ID` back to our Customer Table.

How it works...

Whether collection tables are easy, or hard to conceive, the **Entity Relationship Diagram** (**ERD**) is fairly simple to understand:

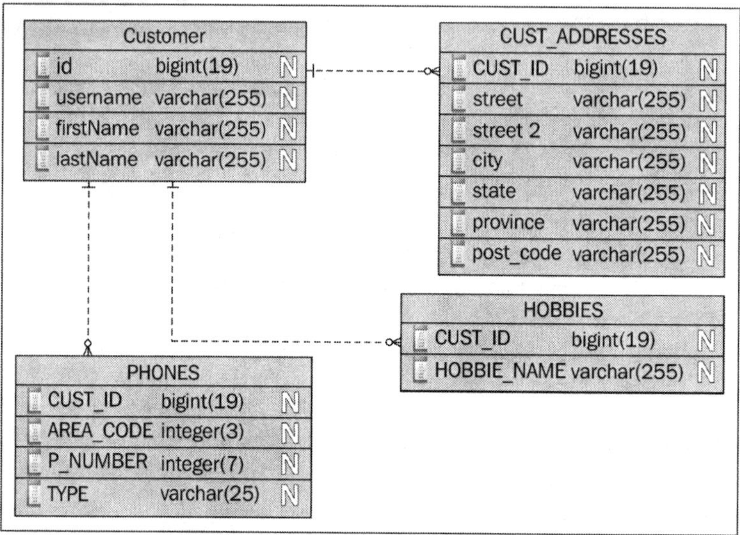

In this listing, we see that a customer has hobbies, phones, and addresses. Each of these relationships is bound by a foreign key to the customer's ID.

However, when we look at the Class model for the related entities, we see a slightly different view:

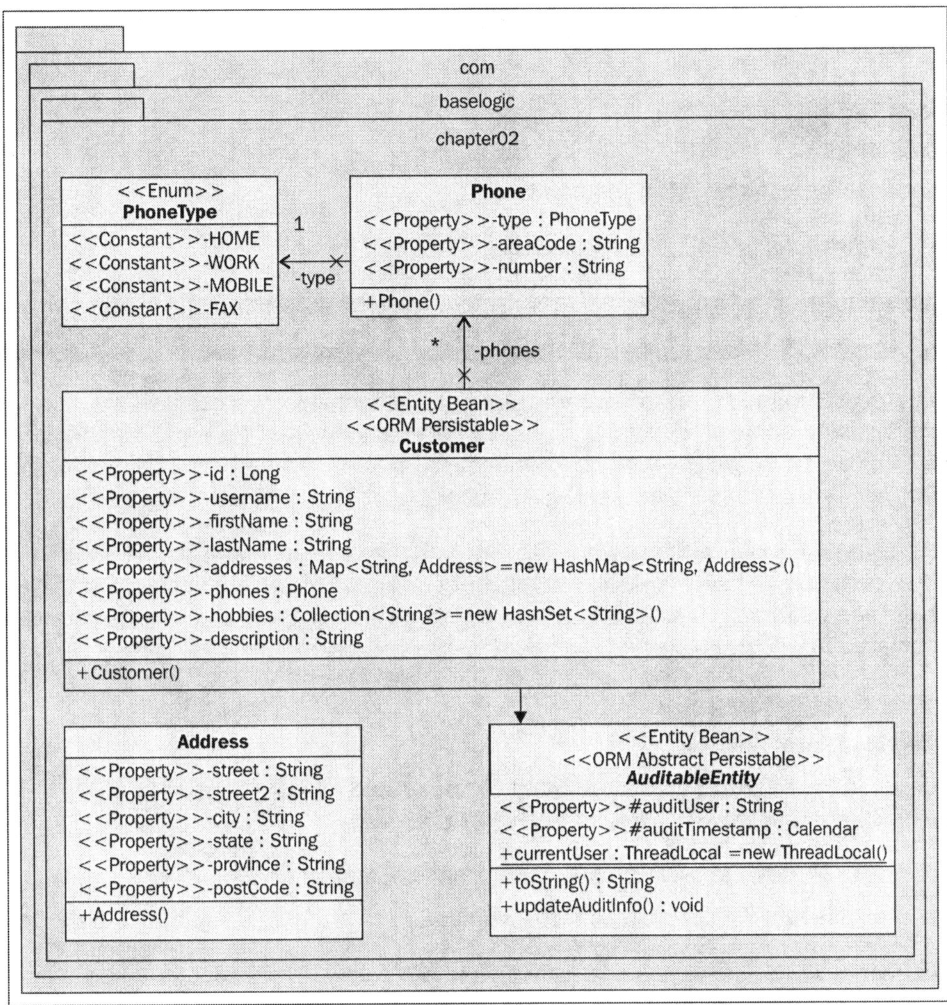

Here we see the relationship a customer has with a phone, but there is no direct relationship a customer has with an address. Furthermore, we do not see where hobbies might get mapped to in the underlying datastore just by looking at the Class model.

Aggregate mappings

There are some nuances that you need to take care with when taking a test-driven approach to JPA and the `@CollectionTable`. If you create an element with a default constructor and try to persist the entity, you are likely to get an error similar to the following:

```
Exception Description: No subclass matches this class [class com.
baselogic.test.CustomerFixture$2$1] for this Aggregate mapping with
inheritance.
```

This is due to not being allowed to add an `object [{0}]` aggregate object as per ECLIPSELINK-00068.

See also

In *Chapter 1, Out with the Old, In with the New:*

- *Understanding JPA 2.0 specification*

Auditing previous JPA Operations

The next recipe I wanted to cover concerns security and auditing. For sensitive data, it is important to keep an audit trail of the various CRUD operations that are performed. This recipe can have many design variations that need to be considered when implementing this solution. This recipe will focus on creating the most recent update in the entity table itself.

This recipe uses a synchronous operation to intercept the various database operations. This can be of particular concern in a high volume application, which can lead to database latency affecting the performance of your application. If we were to explore read and write databases, and master to slave replication, we could even further reduce our database latency.

Getting ready

Building upon the first recipe, we start with a customer, and we want to audit all CRUD operations that occur. We can achieve this in two basic ways:

- Using `@PrePersist` and `@PreUpdate` annotations
- Implement a JPA Lifecycle Change Listener

Using `@PrePersist` and `@PreUpdate` are simple and easy to implement. However, they are only going to allow for one revision to be saved. This might suffice for minimal auditing:

```
public static ThreadLocal currentUser = new ThreadLocal();

@Column(name = Constants.AUDIT_USER)
protected String auditUser;


@Temporal(TemporalType.TIMESTAMP)
@Column(name = Constants.AUDIT_TIMESTAMP)
protected Calendar auditTimestamp;
```

We need to add a property to our entity for holding the user that made the last update, and when the last update occurred. This gives us the managed properties we need in order to add our audit information.

How to do it...

To implement a single audit record implementation, we can simply add a service method to our Entity, which is annotated with `@PrePersist` or `@PreUpdate` respectively to be initiated during the respective lifecycle:

```
@PrePersist
@PreUpdate
public void updateAuditInfo() {
    setAuditUser((String) currentUser.get());
    setAuditTimestamp(Calendar.getInstance());
}
```

Usually you would create a super class that contains the properties you want to share with children. In this case, we have an `AuditableEntity` that is extended by customer. In this recipe, we have created an `AuditableEntity` that our customer extends.

How it works...

The `@PrePersist` or `@PreUpdate` respectively, are JPA hooks that will process the annotated method before persisting or updating any entity.

There's more...

You could choose to have a separate service method for each annotation, which would give you more fine grained control over how and what was stored based on each operation.

Pre- and post-lifecycle hooks

We have shown how hooking into the pre-lifecycle phase can allow you to audit information before the operation completes. Sometimes it can be helpful to also audit information after the operation completes. Using `@PostPersist`, `@PostUpdate`, and `@PostLoad` can help to achieve these hooks.

See also

In this chapter:

- *Auditing historical JPA Operations*

Auditing historical JPA Operations

This recipe will extend the previous initial audit pattern to allow for historical audit recording. This allows for more detailed logs of who made the change, when the change occurred, and the change itself. This recipe implements a **JPA Lifecycle Change Listener** in order to log all CRUD operations.

Getting ready

Building upon the previous recipe, we start with a customer, and we want to audit all CRUD operations that occur. In addition to using `@PrePersist` and `@PreUpdate` annotations, we need to create two new entities to implement a JPA Lifecycle Change Listener.

Using a JPA Lifecycle Change Listener is more in depth, but allows for a more historical audit report to be kept. If you need more than just the most recent operation recorded, then you will need to use a Lifecycle Change Listener. Another advantage with using a Lifecycle Change Listener is that it does not require you to modify your entity to add specific audit properties and operations, which is a far cleaner approach.

To achieve this recipe, we only have two additional tables to store our audit data as depicted in this ERD:

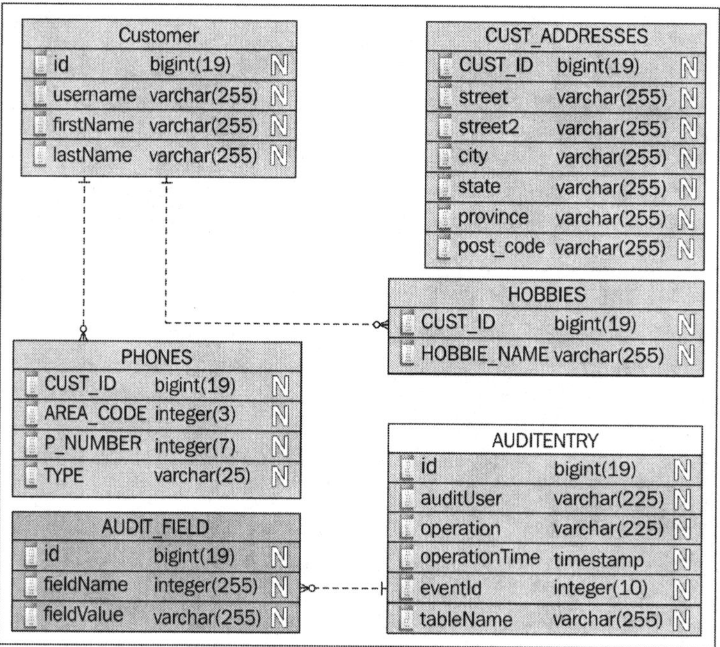

In addition to the two entities we need for the storage of audit data, we also need a Lifecycle Listener as depicted in this class diagram:

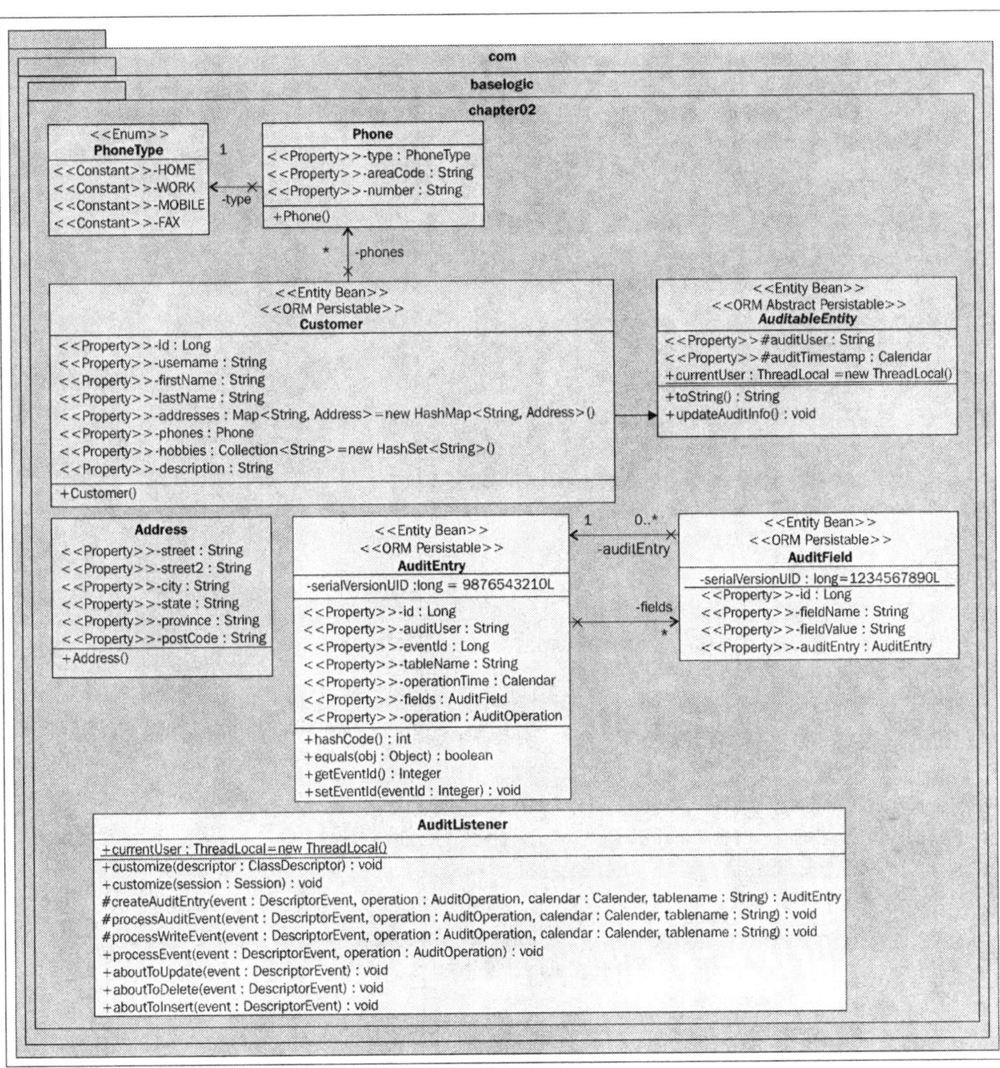

This is a fairly non-intrusive existing entity model, and requires very little editing of existing code to implement. The only hook we need to add is an annotation on our entity for our `AuditListener`:

```
@EntityListeners({AuditListener.class})
@MappedSuperclass
public abstract class AuditableEntity implements Serializable {
```

That is the only addition that is needed for existing code.

How to do it...

Now that our auditable entity object has been annotated, the next steps will be to create the audit logic to store the data for the audit:

1. First we can create two entities to store our audit data. The main Entity will be an `AuditEntry`:

```
@Entity
public class AuditEntry implements Serializable {

    private static final long serialVersionUID = 2L;

    @Id
    @GeneratedValue
    private Long id;

    @Column(name = Constants.AUDIT_USER)
    private String auditUser;

    @Column
    private Long eventId;
    private String tableName;

    @Enumerated(EnumType.STRING)
    private AuditOperation operation;

    @Temporal(TemporalType.TIMESTAMP)
    @Column(name = Constants.AUDIT_TIMESTAMP)
    private Calendar operationTime;

    @OneToMany(cascade = {CascadeType.ALL},
            fetch = FetchType.EAGER,
            mappedBy = Constants.AUDIT_ENTRY)
    private Collection<AuditField> fields;
```

2. In the previous step we are concerned with recording the user, table name, operation, timestamp, and possibly a Collection of AuditFields in the event we change field level attributes of an entity, as seen in our `<dataset>`:

   ```
   <AUDITENTRY ID="2" EVENTID="26869725" OPERATION="INSERT_OPERATION"
   AUDIT_TIMESTAMP="2011-02-06 11:10:51.785" TABLENAME="CUSTOMER"/>
   ```

3. The `AuditField` is basically going to store a field name and field value to be updated:

   ```
   @Entity
   public class AuditField implements Serializable {

       private static final long serialVersionUID = 1L;

       @Id
       @GeneratedValue
       private Long id;

       @Column
       private String fieldName;

       @Lob
       private String fieldValue;

       @ManyToOne
       @JoinColumn(name = Constants.AUDIT_ENTRY_ID)
       private AuditEntry auditEntry;
   ```

4. Our `<dataset>` shows the field name that is to be modified, as well as the new value for the field:

   ```
   <AUDITFIELD ID="10" FIELDNAME="username" FIELDVALUE="newUsername1"
   AUDIT_ENTRY_ID="8"/>
   ```

5. Most updates will be fairly standard and small in terms of data length. But in some cases, it is not enough to have a standard `@Column` attribute to define the changed value. Note that our fieldValue is not a standard `@Column`. The reason for this is because `@Column` will create a database column that is a `VARCHAR(255)`, which limits the column size to 255 characters and some auditable fields, such as Calendar timestamps, will be over 700 characters long. Using `@Lob` will store this field as a large object to a database-supported large object type.

For example, in our <dataset> for an `auditField` where we have updated the auditTimestamp of an entity, the field value becomes the entire object, not just the timestamp value:

```
<AUDITFIELD ID="9" FIELDNAME="auditTimestamp" FIELDVALUE="java.
util.GregorianCalendar[time=1297008654457,areFieldsSet=true
,areAllFieldsSet=true,lenient=true,zone=sun.util.calendar.
ZoneInfo[id=&quot;America/New_York&quot;,offset=-18000000,dstSav
ings=3600000,useDaylight=true,transitions=235,lastRule=java.util.
SimpleTimeZone[id=America/New_York,offset=-18000000,dstSavings=3
600000,useDaylight=true,startYear=0,startMode=3,startMonth=2,sta
rtDay=8,startDayOfWeek=1,startTime=7200000,startTimeMode=0,endMo
de=3,endMonth=10,endDay=1,endDayOfWeek=1,endTime=7200000,endTime
Mode=0]],firstDayOfWeek=1,minimalDaysInFirstWeek=1,ERA=1,YEAR=20
11,MONTH=1,WEEK_OF_YEAR=7,WEEK_OF_MONTH=2,DAY_OF_MONTH=6,DAY_OF_
YEAR=37,DAY_OF_WEEK=1,DAY_OF_WEEK_IN_MONTH=1,AM_PM=0,HOUR=11,HOUR_
OF_DAY=11,MINUTE=10,SECOND=54,MILLISECOND=457,ZONE_OFFSET=-
18000000,DST_OFFSET=0]" AUDIT_ENTRY_ID="8"/>
```

So making the fieldValue a `@Lob` allows us to store these large object graphs for auditing.

6. Next, we need to create our Listener implementation:

```
public class AuditListener extends DescriptorEventAdapter
```

   By extending `DescriptorEventAdapter.class`, we can now override the lifecycle hooks such as `aboutToInsert(DescriptorEvent)`, `aboutToUpdate(DescriptorEvent)`, and `aboutToDelete(DescriptorEvent)` for each respective CRUD operation. This is more explicit, about the nature of the hook you are implementing, and gives you more fine grained control over the lifecycle operations.

7. We now can override the operational methods we are interested in auditing:

```
    public static ThreadLocal currentUser = new ThreadLocal();

    /** this will audit a specific class. */
    @Override
    public void customize(ClassDescriptor descriptor) {
        descriptor.getEventManager().addListener(this);
    }

    /** this will audit all classes. */
    @Override
    public void customize(Session session) {
        for (ClassDescriptor descriptor :
            session.getDescriptors().values()) {
                customize(descriptor);
        }
```

```
    }

    @Override
    public void aboutToInsert (DescriptorEvent event) {
        processEvent(event, AuditOperation.INSERT_OPERATION);
    }

    @Override
    public void aboutToUpdate (DescriptorEvent event) {
        processEvent(event, AuditOperation.UPDATE_OPERATION);
    }

    @Override
    public void aboutToDelete (DescriptorEvent event) {
        processEvent(event, AuditOperation.DELETE_OPERATION);
    }
```

8. Named differently than `@Pre` and `@Post`, the `DescriptorEventAdapter.class` has defined `aboutTo*(*)` methods respectively.

How it works...

Each lifecycle hook calls a service method called `processEvent(DescriptorEvent)` that takes the `DescriptorEvent` and a given `AuditOperation`. The `DescriptorEvent` has access to the TableNames that are being modified, as well as the Record of the changes occurring:

```
@SuppressWarnings("unchecked")
protected void processEvent(DescriptorEvent event,
    AuditOperation operation) {
    Calendar calendar = Calendar.getInstance();
    for (String table : (List<String>)
        event.getDescriptor().getTableNames()) {
        event.getRecord().put(table + "." +
        Constants.AUDIT_USER, (String)
        AuditListener.currentUser.get());
        event.getRecord().put(table + "." +
            Constants.AUDIT_TIMESTAMP, calendar);
        if (operation == AuditOperation.UPDATE_OPERATION) {
                processWriteEvent(event, operation, calendar,
                table);
        } else {
            processAuditEvent(event, operation, calendar, table);
        }
    }
}
```

We have further abstracted this operation to call either a WriteEvent or a standard AuditEvent. The main difference is a WriteEvent involves editing of field level attributes, whereas an AuditEvent only pertains to inserts and deletes. A given event can have many tables that are intended to be modified in some way. We want to audit each of these events individually.

Let's start with a simple audit event to see what we plan to audit and how. First we are interested in processing this audit event, by creating an AuditEvent entity, then saving that entity in the same session we are auditing:

```
protected void processAuditEvent(DescriptorEvent event,
    AuditOperation operation, Calendar calendar,
    String tableName) {
    AuditEntry entry = createAuditEntry(event, operation,
    calendar, tableName);
    InsertObjectQuery insertQuery = new InsertObjectQuery(entry);
    event.getSession().executeQuery(insertQuery);
}
```

The given event for this operation has the Session context, and within this transaction, we are able to save our `AuditEntry`. When we look at creating the AuditEntry entity, we are only setting the operation user, operation type, timestamp, and table name:

```
protected AuditEntry createAuditEntry(DescriptorEvent event,
    AuditOperation operation, Calendar calendar, String tableName)
{
    AuditEntry entry = new AuditEntry();
    entry.setAuditUser((String) AuditListener.currentUser.get());
    entry.setOperation(operation);
    entry.setOperationTime(calendar);entry.setEventId(Long.
valueOf(event.getSource().hashCode()));
    entry.setTableName(tableName);
    return entry;
}
```

This creates an `AuditEntry` for every table that is inserted into, or deleted from the event in question. For each `AuditEntry`, we create a new `InsertObjectQuery` to save our newly created `AuditEntry` to our database with the same session as the event where the modification is occurring.

When we get an Update event, we need to record more information about the operation. We still need to create an `AuditEntry` container, but now we need to create `AuditField` entries for every `ChangeRecord` that occurs in the given table. We are interested in `DirectToFieldChangeRecord`s specifically, not just generic `ChangeRecord`s:

```
    protected void processWriteEvent(DescriptorEvent event,
        AuditOperation operation, Calendar calendar, String tableName)
{
        AuditEntry entry = createAuditEntry(event, operation,
calendar,
        tableName);

        Collection<AuditField> fields = new LinkedList<AuditField>();
        WriteObjectQuery query = (WriteObjectQuery) event.getQuery();
        List<ChangeRecord> changes =
        query.getObjectChangeSet().getChanges();

        for (ChangeRecord change : changes) {
            if (change instanceof DirectToFieldChangeRecord) {
                DirectToFieldChangeRecord fieldChange =
                (DirectToFieldChangeRecord) change;
                AuditField field = new AuditField();
                field.setAuditEntry(entry);
                field.setFieldName(fieldChange.getAttribute());
                field.setFieldValue(fieldChange.getNewValue().
toString());
                fields.add(field);
            }
        }

        entry.setFields(fields);

        InsertObjectQuery insertQuery = new InsertObjectQuery(entry);
        event.getSession().executeQuery(insertQuery);

        for (AuditField field : fields) {
            insertQuery = new InsertObjectQuery(field);
            event.getSession().executeQuery(insertQuery);
        }
    }
```

Before we can process each individual `AuditField`, we need to save our `AuditEntry` to our database. This way as we save each `AuditField`, we have an `AuditEntry` in our database to associate the `AuditField` to. Specifically, we have our entity mapping from our `AuditEntry`:

```
@OneToMany(cascade = {CascadeType.ALL},
        fetch = FetchType.EAGER,
        mappedBy = Constants.AUDIT_ENTRY)
private Collection<AuditField> fields;
```

And we have our reference from our `AuditField` back to `AuditEntry`:

```
@ManyToOne
@JoinColumn(name = Constants.AUDIT_ENTRY_ID)
private AuditEntry auditEntry;
```

EclipseLink Customizers

You can implement various Customizers such as SessionCustomizer and DescriptorCustomizer if you need to customize dynamically or specify configuration values not available through annotations or XML.

Caching and security

This recipe has some security concerns that need to be considered. The examples in this recipe use EclipseLink as the JPA provider implementation, and each provider will have different security implementations. EclipseLink, by default, maintains a shared (L2) object cache. If the user-based security is used to prevent the reading of certain tables/classes, then cache may need to be disabled for these secure classes. It is recommended that a thorough review of the security and caching design be reviewed carefully to avoid vulnerabilities.

aboutTo*(*) versus pre*(*) and post*(*)

An issue that I ran into while extending DescriptorEventAdapter is the difference between `aboutTo*(*)` versus `pre*(*)`. While it seems natural to want to use `preInsert(*)`, taking from the `@PrePersist` annotation, note that the DescriptorEvent which is passed to these methods does not contain valid event records:

```
public void preInsert(DescriptorEvent event) {...}
```

To remedy this, we can use the more phonetic implementation:

```
public void aboutToInsert(DescriptorEvent event) {...}
```

The lifecycle hook method now contains the event record for the given operation, which is associated with given events.

Common database user ID, and managing auditing and security in the application

In this recipe, auditing is managed by having an application user, and a single shared database user. The implementation adds an `AUDIT_USER` and `AUDIT_TIMESTAMP` column to all of the audited tables and `auditUser` and `auditTimestamp` field to all of the audited objects. When the application inserts or updates an object, it will set these fields and they will be stored in the database. These events are used to record the audit information, or to write to a separate audit table. EclipseLink also support full history support, which allows a complete history of all changes made to the database to be tracked in a mirror history table.

See also

Eclipselink API: `http://www.eclipse.org/eclipselink/api/latest/index.html`

Profiling and testing JPA Operations

Rather than profiling when you have integrated your application, or worse, being forced to profile an application running in production due to various performance issues, it is best to start profiling your application during development. This has several different positive effects on your application, and your overall knowledge of running your application.

By profiling during development, you will first start getting familiar with the call hierarchy of your code. This is especially helpful in Java EE applications and other technologies such as AspectJ where services or aspects might be calling your application unbeknown to you. The more you know about who and how your code is interacting with, the more prepared you are for troubleshooting issues.

Another positive outcome from profiling your application while developing is that you can find any issues with your application early in the development cycle. Many of these issues appear minimal at first, but can cause bigger issues if you later realize they cause performance issues.

Getting ready

Getting started with profiling during development starts with getting a profiling tool integrated with your IDE, and for this I started with **IntelliJ IDE** and **YourKit** profilers.

The first thing we need to do is install IntelliJ and YourKit on your development environment. Once each has been installed, we must ensure that Intellij is not running. Then we want to start YourKit and look for the **Integrate with IDE...** option:

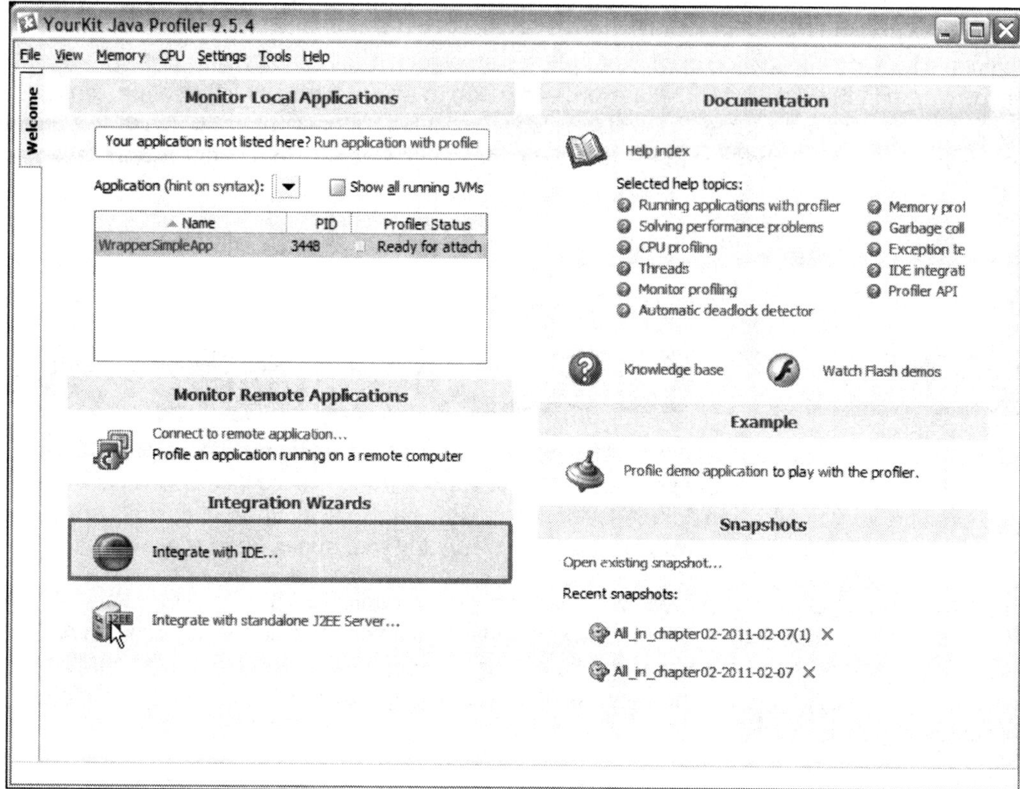

After you click on the **Integrate with IDE...** link, you will get an option to select your Development Environment, and for the case of Intellij, we are going to select **IntelliJ X (10)** and use the default **plugins directory**:

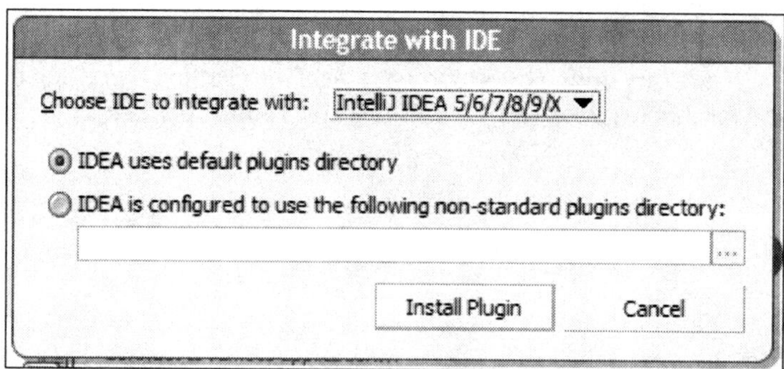

YourKit is going to install the Intellij integration as a plugin, so you will be prompted to close Intellij before installing:

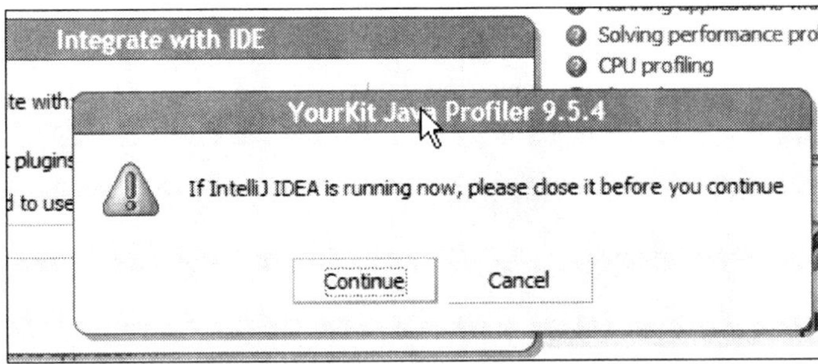

Once the installation is successfully completed, you can close YourKit:

The next time you open Intellij, you will notice a new **YourKit** icon in the toolbar:

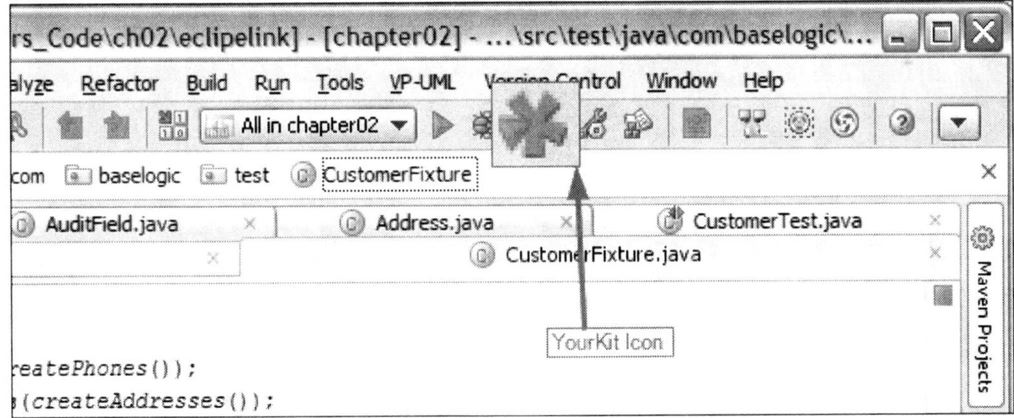

At this point you are ready to use YourKit to profile your run configurations within your integrated development environment.

How to do it...

One of the easiest ways to start profiling your application is to profile an existing run configuration. For this recipe I created a run configuration to execute all unit tests in this project:

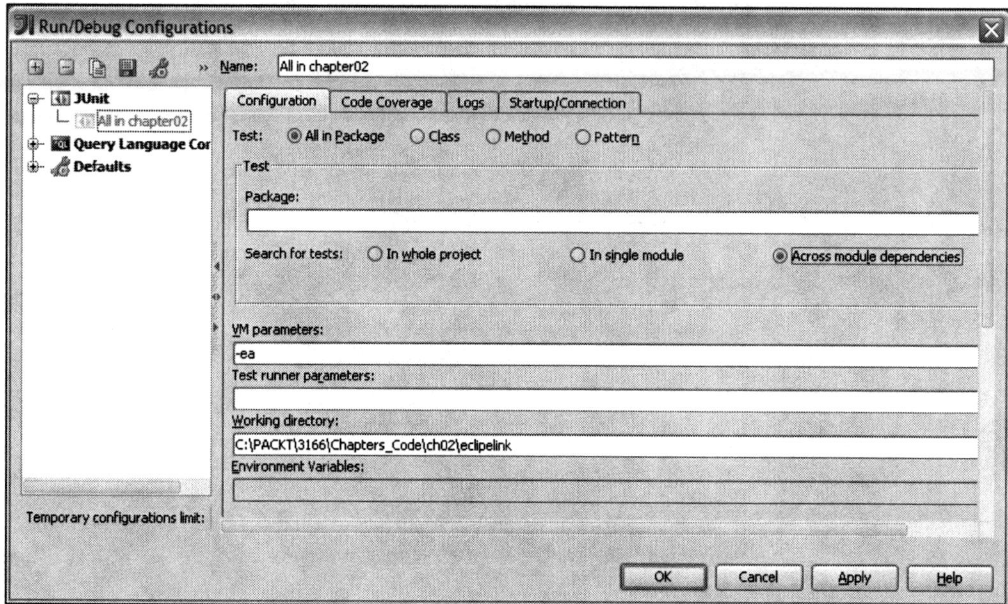

Next we will run this run/debug configuration to ensure the execution performs as expected and does not contain any failures. This will isolate any issue you might have before adding the profiler to the matrix:

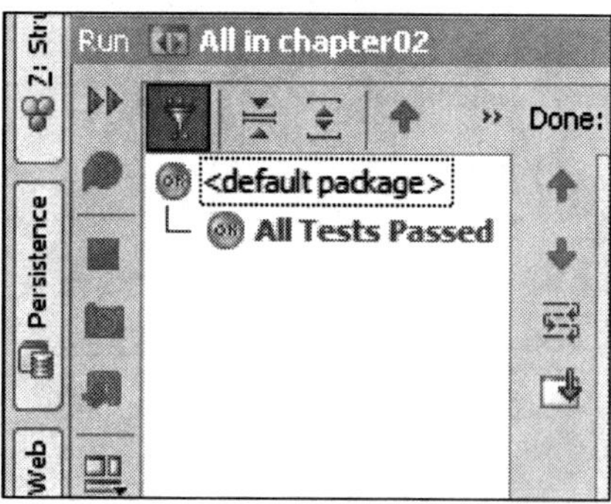

In order to execute the run configuration as Profile execution, you just need to click on the **YourKit** icon. Then your run configuration will begin to execute, and YourKit will also start profiling the running execution. This session window will give you real-time results of the application being executed:

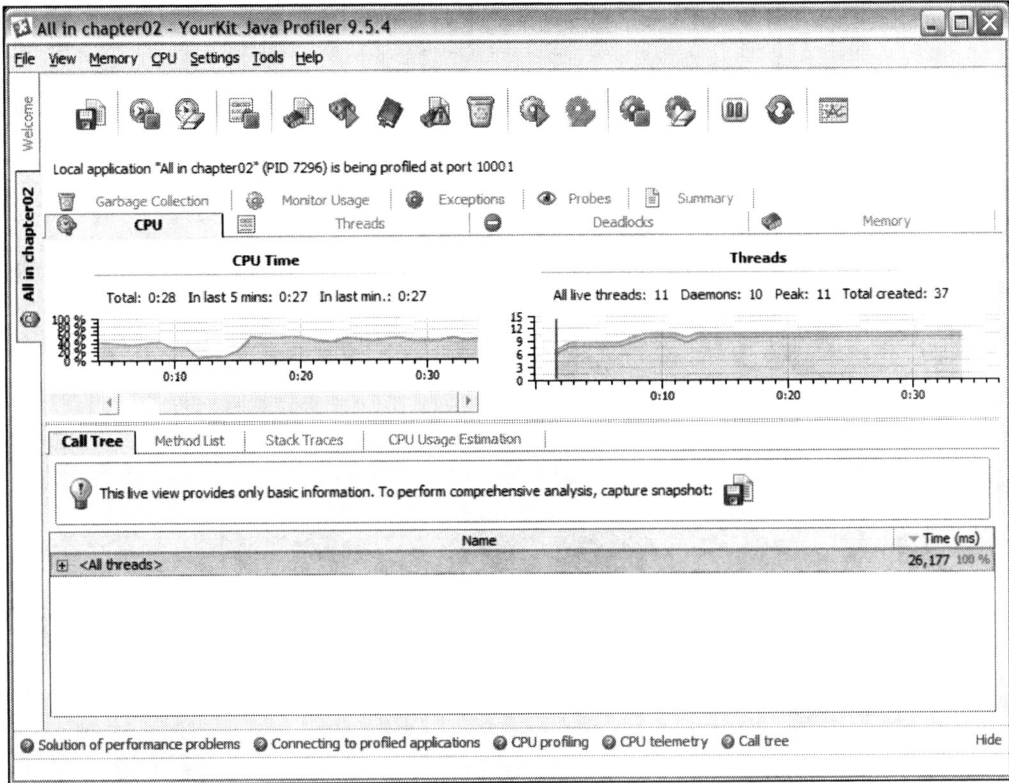

How it works...

At this point we have a profile session from the execution of the last run configuration. This can be helpful to look at some statistics such as:

- CPU
- Garbage Collection
- Memory
- Probes
- Threads

There might be valuable information in this data, but if you want to take a deep dive into the execution, you need to save the session as a snapshot:

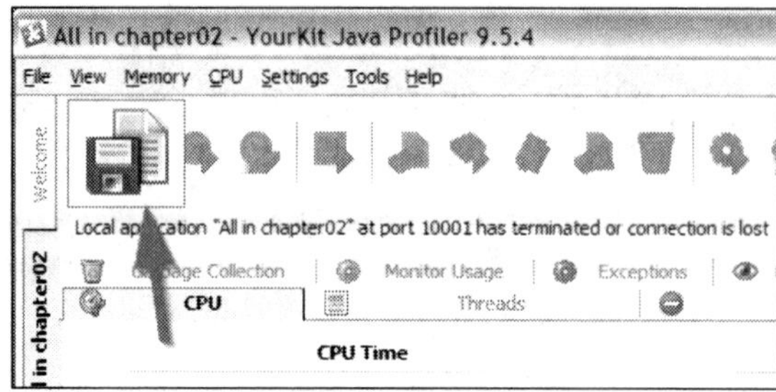

This snapshot will allow you to dig deep into the execution, and can also allow you to compare snapshots between run executions. This is valuable when you are refactoring and want to compare the performance differences between two executions:

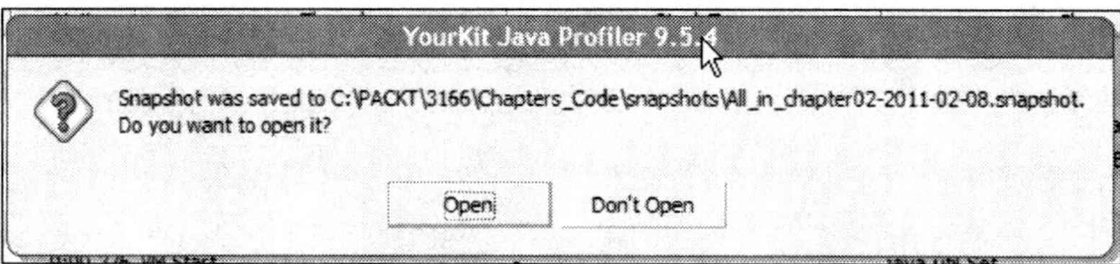

After you have saved the snapshot, you can choose to open the snapshot for immediate review:

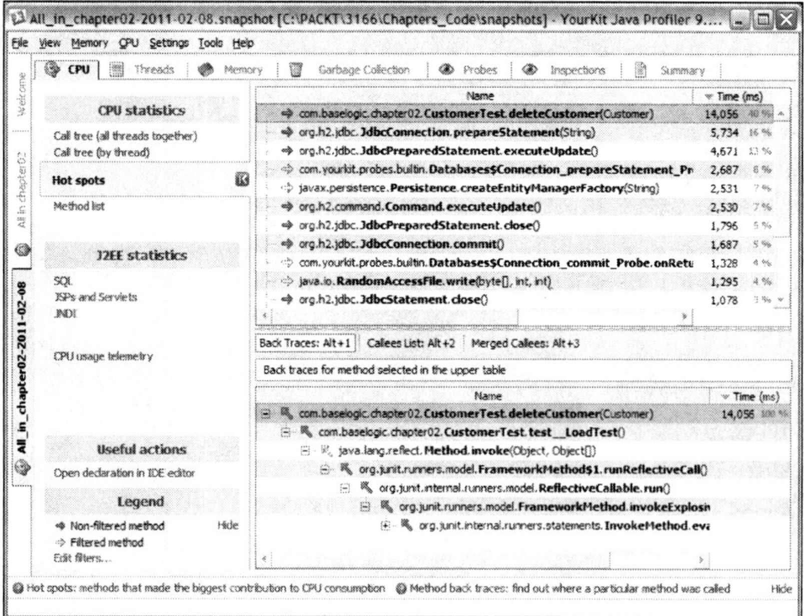

When we open the snapshot, the interface is similar, but some things we notice immediately; you will see more data available such as **Call Tree**, **Hot Spots**, and **Method List** from the session. It is easiest to look at hot spots initially, because this will give you a list of methods that took the longest to finish executing before returning back to their respective caller accumulated for the length of the execution:

Name	Time (ms)
com.baselogic.chapter02.**CustomerTest.deleteCustomer**(Customer)	14,056 40 %
org.h2.jdbc.**JdbcConnection.prepareStatement**(String)	5,734 16 %

The top hot spot for this session was for an accumulated execution of deleting a customer that used 14 seconds. This excessive accumulation was caused by a unit test that was excessively creating and deleting customer objects:

```
@Test
public void test__LoadTest() throws Exception {
    // You can turn the number of operations up to larger
    numbers to
    // be able to detect issue.
    for(int i =0; i < 10000; i++){
        Customer customer = createCustomer();
        assertNotNull("ID should not be null", customer.getId());

        deleteCustomer(customer);
    }
}
```

By removing this unit test, we are able to reduce the largest execution hot spot from 14 seconds, down to a little over two seconds:

Name	Time (ms)
javax.persistence.**Persistence.createEntityManagerFactory**(String)	2,359 37 %
java.lang.**ClassLoader.loadClass**(String)	953 15 %
org.h2.**Driver.connect**(String, Properties)	625 10 %

Simple reviews like this can really give you a head start on identifying execution and memory issues before they get out of hand, or become too costly.

There's more...

Reviewing the **Probes** section of your snapshots is also a great place to find execution issues. Under the **Timeline** tab, you can see each execution and the time range. When scanning through these, you may notice some taking longer than others. During one execution, there were two entries for the processing of `orm.xml` that took over two seconds combined:

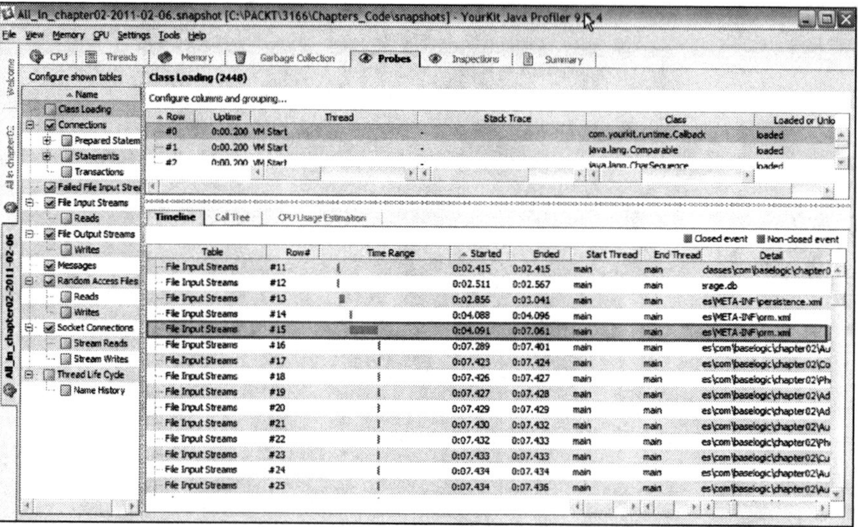

On further investigation, it turns out that `orm.xml` was created at some point, but was empty and JPA was still attempting to process this file even though it was not being used, and contained zero mappings:

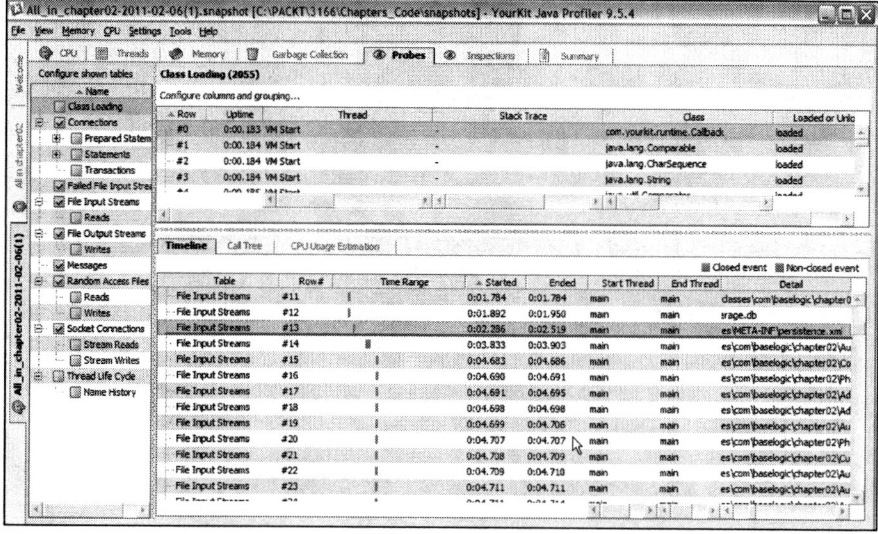

After removing `orm.xml` we are able to witness JPA only processing the `persistence.xml` and saving over two seconds of processing time.

Inspections tab

Another important section to review is the **Inspections** tab, which traces common issue patterns in the session execution. When running all inspections from the previous session, there where several *file closed in finalizer* issues raised:

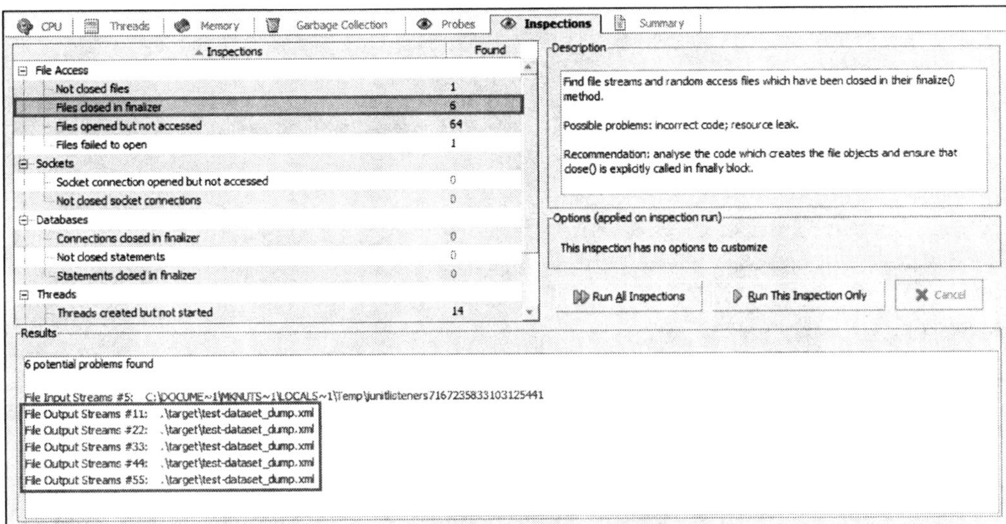

When looking at the inspection results, there were five occurrences of `\target\test-dataset-dump.xml` that where causing these issues.

It might seem right to create an anonymous `FileOutputStream` object to write to, however this puts the burden of closing the file until the `finize()` method is called, if ever, which is no guarantee:

```
// If we use this method, the stream is closed in the
finalizer.
FlatXmlDataSet.write
  (dataSet, new FileOutputStream(dataSetOutputFile));
```

We only have to make a subtle change to explicitly create a `FileOutputStream` then explicitly close that stream:

```
// Explicitly closes the Stream:
FileOutputStream fos =
    new FileOutputStream(dataSetOutputFile);
FlatXmlDataSet.write(dataSet, fos);
fos.close();
```

Now by re-running the execution and viewing our new **Inspections**, we have removed this potential issue:

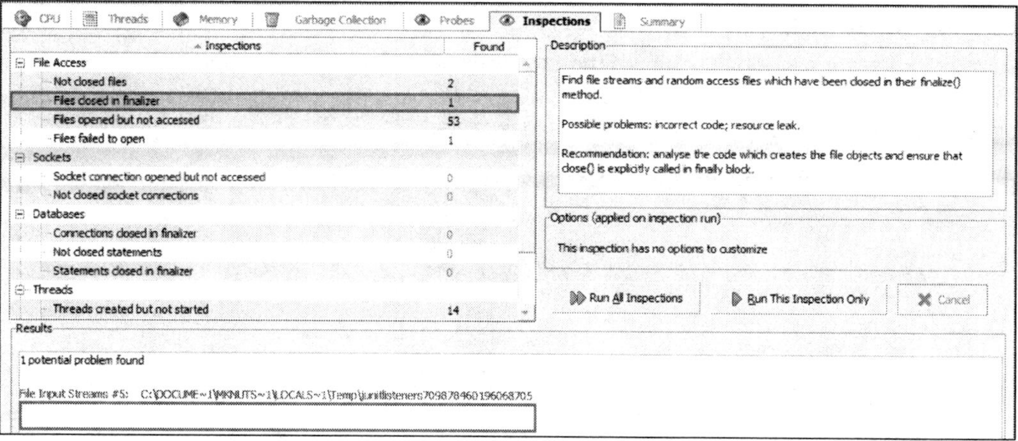

Note about unit testing

Just to note some observations about unit testing this JPA recipe. If you review your unit tests, and the code you are testing continuously as you are developing, you can start to see patterns of unused code in both unit tests, as well as application code.

Looking at the `AuditListener` class, you can see that our Class customizer and Session customizer do not get called in our unit test:

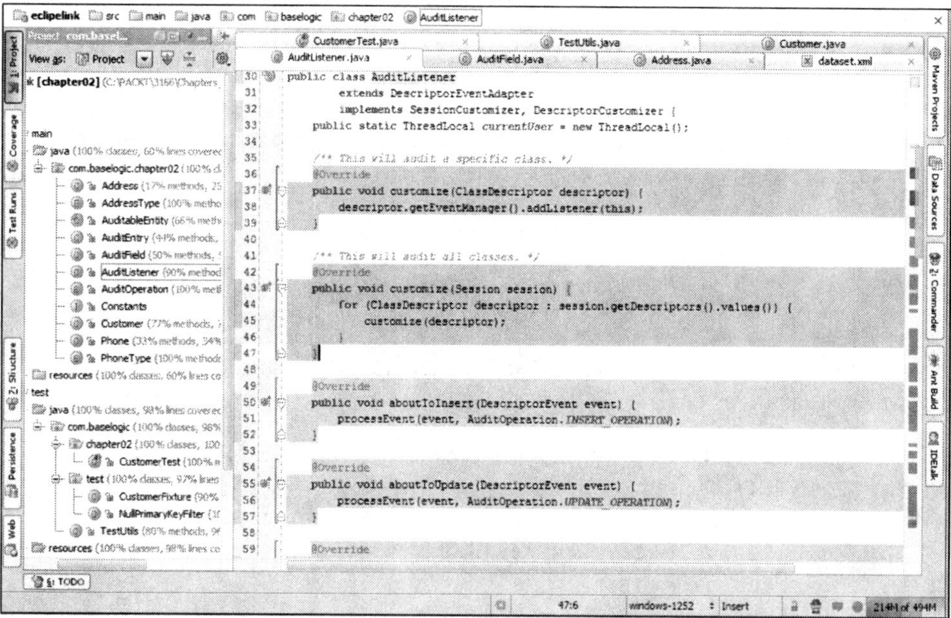

Inspecting unused code and removing if not necessary is always a good practice to employ every chance you get. You would expect to measure code coverage on blocks that are directly executed, but as you can see from the previous code coverage image, there are methods that usually get called indirectly that may or may not get executed during our testing:

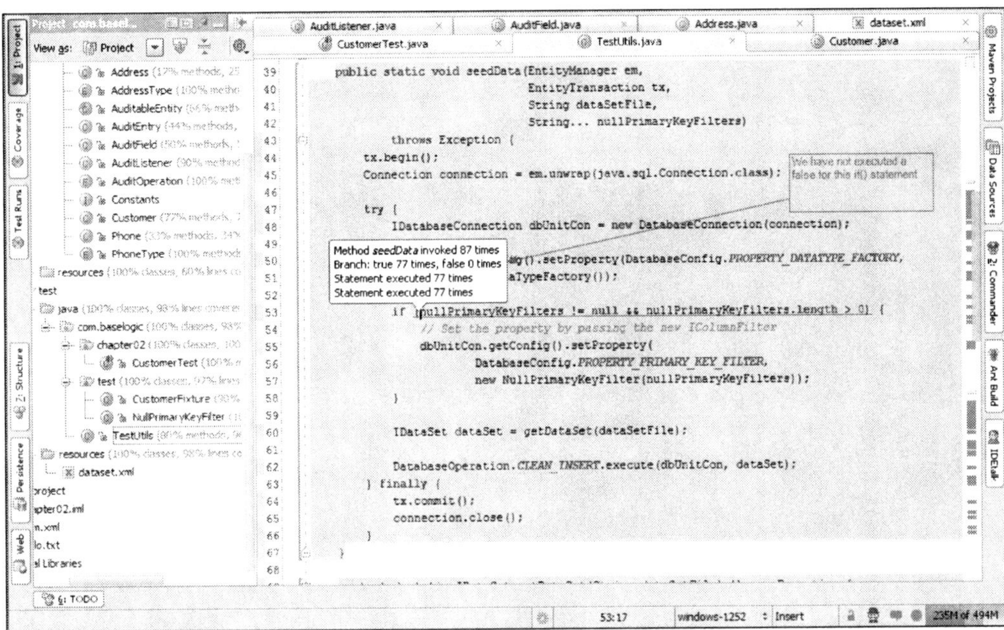

Another point of interest that should be considered is the code in your unit test. Many times throughout the process of refactoring during your test-driven development lifecycle, you can accumulate code blocks and entire tests that are not used or executed. Over time, you can also accumulate redundant unit tests. This redundancy does not provide any benefit, but merely adds to the unit test time cycle, slowing development down. The earlier you can start this practice, the better you can control your testing and code creations. Ultimately, we should not create code that is not used or executed as per the application requirements.

See also

Chapter 4, Enterprise Testing Strategies

In Chapter 8, Performance and Debugging

- *Profiling memory with jVisualVM*
- *Using jstatd to enable VisualGC*

IntelliJ: `http://www.jetbrains.com`

YourKit: `http://www.yourkit.com`

3 Security

In this chapter, we will cover:

- Performing authentication in Java EE
- Authorization in Java EE
- Enforcing security in Enterprise Applications
- Programmatic security and annotations in Java EE
- Securely signing JAR artefacts
- Configuring Linux firewall rules
- Securely obfuscating Java byte-code
- Minification and obfuscation of web resources

Introduction

In this chapter, we will look into how we can enable security for our software system using Java EE built-in features as well as using the well-known Spring Security framework, which is a widely accepted framework for more fine-grained security implementation.

Before diving into the recipes and learning how to implement different aspects of the system security, let's spend some time on learning the common terms and expressions we will deal with in the security domain.

A **user** is the entity that wants to access a resource in our system. The user can either be another program or it can be a human user. A user is usually a member of one or more groups. A user may have an anonymous principal assigned by default, and can also have a unique security principal.

A **group** is an abstract name for an arbitrary number of users with common characteristics, which usually leads them to have a common set of access permissions.

A **security realm** is the abstraction on top of the storage that our users and groups are stored in. For example, we can have a JDBC security realm or an LDAP security realm, in which the first one is the abstraction on top of the tables and columns in the database holding our users' information, whereas, in the second one we are referring to the abstraction over the LDAP directory server containing our users, and their group associations.

A **role** is an application level concept that we use, to design the application security levels and permissions. A role in the application can map one or more groups in the security realm. This is how the application security is independent of where the users are stored, or how the users and groups are associated together in the environment in which we will deploy our application.

A **principal** is an identity that can be authenticated using one or more credentials, which are part of the principal.

A **credential** contains or references information used to authenticate a principal. The combination of a username and password is a sample of credentials.

Security and Java EE containers

When a user is authenticated in one container, for example, the Web container, and there is a call from the Web container to the EJB container, the user's principal will propagate to the EJB container, and the EJB container will use the same principal for access control.

The same identity propagation happens when we are using the Application Client container, hosting an application client that interacts with the EJB container. The authentication happens in the Application Client container, and the identity is propagated to the EJB container when an invocation is performed.

Java EE deployment descriptors

Some of the Java EE development and deployment configurations are common between all vendors, and it is mandatory for all vendors to adhere and comply with them. Some other configurations are open for the vendors to decide how to include them in the application server and how to expose the configuration elements to the users. In the security area, some of the security configurations are made in the standard deployment descriptors and are the same for all vendors, and some are open for the vendors to specify how administrators and developers should use them.

The following figure shows the deployment descriptor names and their locations in the enterprise application archive:

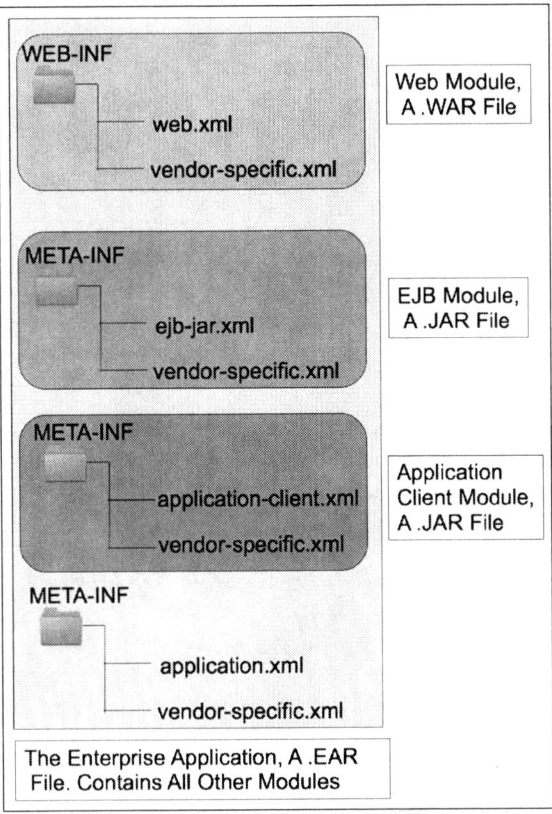

For the security configurations required for Java EE, defining authentication and access control is done in the standard deployment descriptors, while mapping the application roles to security realm groups and principals are done in the vendor-specific way.

Defining the security realm itself is something that each vendor manages in its own specific way.

For example, the GlassFish application server requires an additional `sun-web.xml` deployment descriptor to map `<security-role>` elements in an application's `web.xml` file:

```
<web-app version="3.0"
        xmlns="http://java.sun.com/xml/ns/javaee"
        xmlns:xsi="http://www.w3.org/2001/XMLSchema-instance"
        xsi:schemaLocation="http://java.sun.com/xml/ns/javaee
        http://java.sun.com/xml/ns/javaee/web-app_3_0.xsd">
    ...
    <security-role>
```

```
        <description>Patients</description>
        <role-name>patients</role-name>
    </security-role>
    ...
</web-app>
```

Mapping a `<security-role-mapping>` element for GlassFish:

```
<!DOCTYPE sun-web-app
        PUBLIC "-//Sun Microsystems, Inc.//DTD GlassFish Application
Server 3.0 Servlet 3.0//EN"
        "http://www.sun.com/software/appserver/dtds/sun-web-app_3_0-0.
dtd">
<sun-web-app error-url="/error.xhtml">
    <context-root>/ch03</context-root>

    <security-role-mapping>
        <role-name>patients</role-name>
        <group-name>patients</group-name>
    </security-role-mapping>
    ...
</sun-web-app>
```

See also

GlassFish Security: `http://www.packtpub.com/glassfish-security/book`

GlassFish Administration: `https://www.packtpub.com/glassfish-administration/book`

Performing authentication in Java EE

In this recipe, we will learn how we can use Java EE built-in functionalities to enforce authentication in our web applications.

Getting ready

Authentication is one of those areas in which both vendor-specific configurations and Java EE standard configurations come into play. In this recipe, we will be using the GlassFish application server.

GlassFish is a complete Java EE application server, in contrast to a Servlet container that would provide the Java EE web profile capabilities. GlassFish has an open source and supported version, and is described by the java.net project as:

> *An open source, production-ready, Java EE-compatible application server.*
>
> *GlassFish version 3 provides a small footprint, fully-featured implementation of Java EE 6.*
>
> *The Java EE 6 platform significantly improves developer productivity, introduces the lightweight Web Profile for Web-centric applications, and includes the latest versions of technologies such as JAX-RS 1.1, JavaServer Faces (JSF) 2.0, Enterprise JavaBeans (EJB) 3.1, Java Persistence (JPA) 2.0, Context and Dependency Injection (CDI) 1.0, and more. GlassFish is a Java EE open source application server.*

Apache Tomcat is maintained by the Apache foundation and described as:

> *Apache Tomcat is an open source software implementation of the Java Servlet and JavaServer Pages technologies. The Java Servlet and JavaServer Pages specifications are developed under the Java Community Process.*

Tomcat is an excellent choice for projects that do not require enterprise services from Java EE.

How to do it...

When we talk about authentication, we want to make sure that not everyone can access some resources that we only share with a specific group of our users.

A web application can use one of the five different methods of authentication provided by the Java EE, which are as follows:

HTTP BASIC Authentication (`BASIC`): This is the most basic way of implementing authentication for a web application and is suitable when we are accessing the application using both browser and other software such as scripts and so on. In this mode, when accessed by a browser, the browser will use its standard dialog to collect the credentials.

It is easy to implement, but the credentials will be transmitted as plain text and anyone can collect them if we do not have SSL or some network-level encryption in place. Before transmitting the username and password entered by the user, the two are concatenated with a colon separating the two values; the resulting string is Base64 encoded. For example, given a username `mick` and password `secret key`, the string "`mick:secret key`" will be encoded with the Base64 algorithm resulting in `bWljazpzZWNyZXQga2V5`. The Base64-encoded string is transmitted in the HTTP header and decoded by the receiver, resulting in the decoded, colon-separated username and password string.

Encoding the username and password with the Base64 makes them unreadable visually, but they are easily decoded. Confidentiality is not the intent of the encoding step. Rather, the intent is to encode non-HTTP-compatible characters that a username or password may contain, into those that are HTTP-compatible.

If you use the `@ServletSecurity` annotation, you do not need to specify security settings in the deployment descriptor such as a `<auth-method>BASIC</auth-method>` entry in `web.xml`. Use the deployment descriptor to specify settings for non-default authentication mechanisms, for which you cannot use the `@ServletSecurity` annotation.

HTTPS Client Authentication (`CLIENT-CERT`): In this method, the server or client or both of them will identify themselves using a digital certificate acceptable for the other end. The server should be able to validate the client digital certification for successful authentication, and the client should be able to successfully verify the server certificate for the authentication to complete. This method is very secure, but hard to implement and administer.

Transport Security (SSL `HTTPS`): Additionally, transport security constraints can be defined to be `CONFIDENTIAL`, `INTEGRAL` or `NONE`. This can be defined in the applications `web.xml`, such as the following listing:

```
<security-constraint>
    <web-resource-collection>
        <web-resource-name>customer</web-resource-name>
        <url-pattern>/customers/*</url-pattern>
    </web-resource-collection>
    <auth-constraint>
        <role-name>customer</role-name>
    </auth-constraint>
    <user-data-constraint>
        <transport-guarantee>CONFIDENTIAL</transport-guarantee>
    </user-data-constraint>
</security-constraint>
```

Digest Authentication (`DIGEST`): This method is similar to the BASIC Authentication method, but instead of the password, a digest of the password is transmitted.

Digest communication starts with a client that requests a resource from a web server. If the resource is secured with Digest Authentication, the server will respond with the HTTP status code 401, which means the client is unauthorized to access this resource.

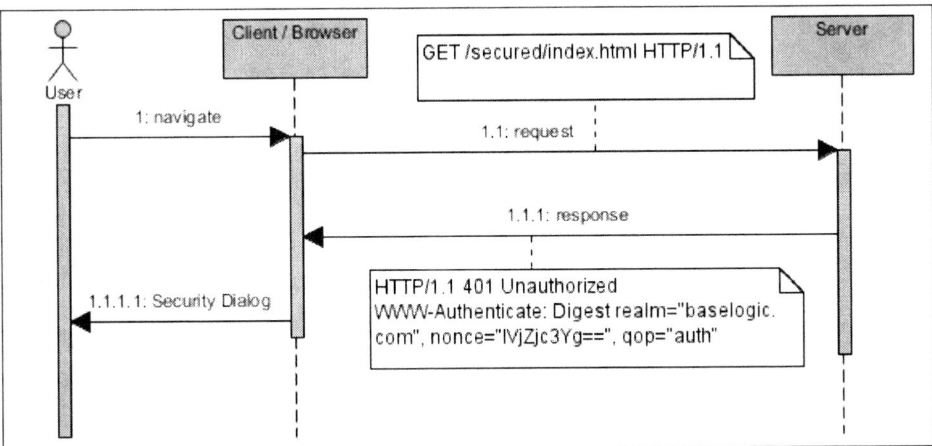

In the response from the initial request, the server indicates in the HTTP header with which mechanism the resource is secured. The HTTP header contains the following:

WWW-Authenticate: Digest realm="baselogic.com", nonce="lVjZjc3Yg", qop="auth".

You should notice the term **Digest** in the response, which indicates that the resource requested by the client is secured using Digest Authentication.

The server also indicates the type of Digest Authentication algorithm used by the client with **Quality Of Protection** (**QOP**) and the nonce string, which is a Base64-encoded timestamp and private hash generated by the server:

```
String nonce = Base64.encode(new Timestamp() : "Private MD5 Hash")
```

The private hash is created by the server, and the Base64 encoding allows for decoding of the timestamp and private hash, even though the private MD5 hash is a one-way encryption.

An Internet browser responds to this by presenting the user with a dialog; in this dialog the user is able to enter a username and password for credentials. The dialog does not show the warning about transmitting the credentials in clear text as with a Basic Authentication secured site:

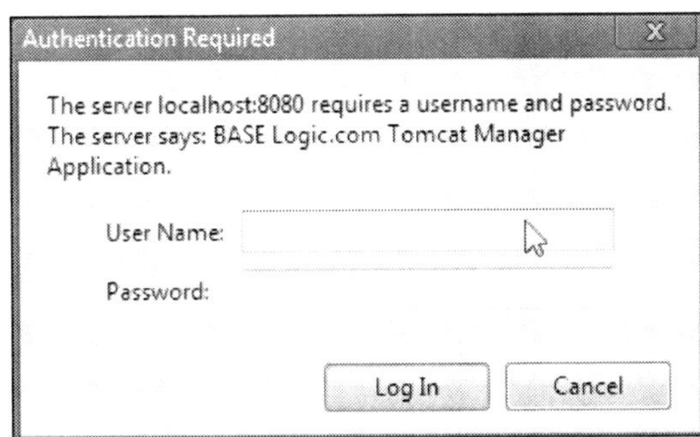

When the user enters the credentials in this dialog, the browser requests the resource from the server again. This time, the client adds additional information to the HTTP header regarding Digest Authentication:

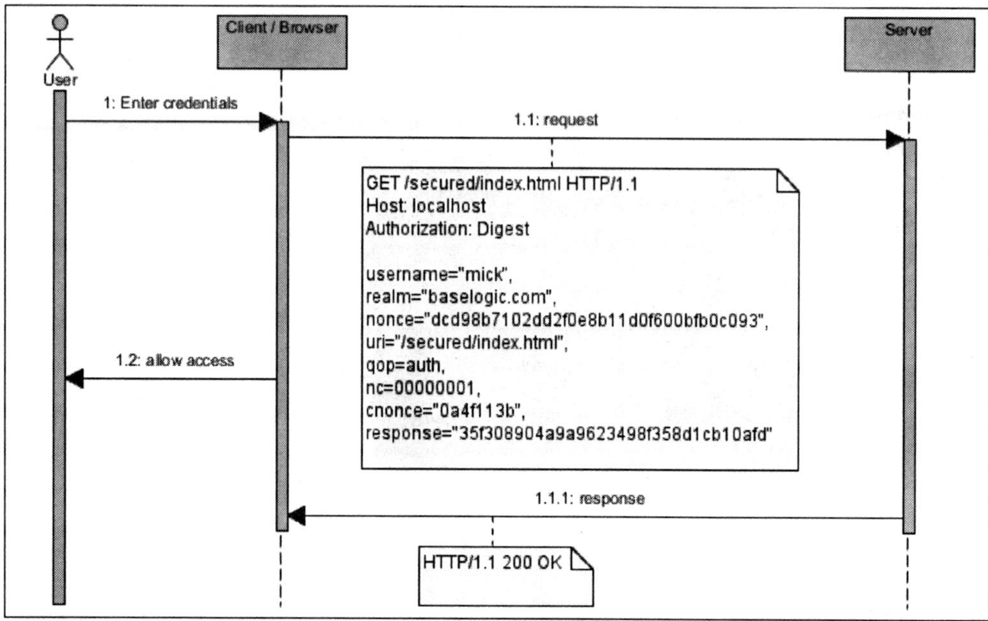

The server validates the information and returns the requested resource to the client. Looking at the headers between these requests, we will see that the initial client request will look like:

```
GET /secured/index.html HTTP/1.0
Host: localhost
```

Then the server sends a response stating the request is not authorized, and includes the required digest information to proceed with the authentication handshake:

```
HTTP/1.0 401 Unauthorized
Server: HTTPd/0.9
Date: Sun, 10 Apr 2005 20:26:47 GMT
WWW-Authenticate: Digest realm="baselogic.com",
         qop="auth",
                        nonce="dcd98b7102dd2f0e8b11d0f600bfb0c093",
          opaque="5ccc069c403ebaf9f0171e9517f40e41"
Content-Type: text/html
Content-Length: 311

<!DOCTYPE HTML PUBLIC "-//W3C//DTD HTML 4.01 Transitional//EN"
 "http://www.w3.org/TR/1999/REC-html401-19991224/loose.dtd">
```

```
<HTML>
  <HEAD>
    <TITLE>Error</TITLE>
    <META HTTP-EQUIV="Content-Type" CONTENT="text/html;
charset=ISO-8859-1">
  </HEAD>
  <BODY><H1>401 Unauthorized.</H1></BODY>
</HTML>
```

Now, the user can enter the credentials using `mick` as the username and `secret key` as the password:

```
GET /secured/index.html HTTP/1.1
Host: localhost
Authorization: Digest username="mick",
                      realm="baselogic.com",
                      nonce="dcd98b7102dd2f0e8b11d0f600bfb0c093",
                      uri="/secured/index.html",
                      qop=auth,
                      nc=00000001,
                      cnonce="0a4f113b",
                      response="35f308904a9a9623498f358d1cb10afd"
```

The response is generated by several digest properties sent from the client, with the addition to an `HA1` and `HA2` value concatenated together, then MD5 hash encrypted. The algorithm is the following:

```
Response = MD5( "HA1:\
                 nonce:\
                 nc:\
                 cnonce:\
                 qop:\
                 HA2" )
```

The `HA1` hash is the username, realm, and password separated by colons:

```
HA1 = MD5( "mick:baselogic.com:secret key")
```

The `MD5` hash for the `HA1` is: `935f1e7b1582ffd6e05e7dc8e949ac6f`.

The `HA2` hash is the initial `HTTP GET` request made to the server:

```
HA2 = MD5( "GET:/secured/index.html" )
```

The `MD5` hash for the `HA2` is: `cc21ab6caf04c32228f0250c9eb48705`.

The final response MD5 hash algorithm would look like this:

```
Response = MD5( "935f1e7b1582ffd6e05e7dc8e949ac6f:\
                 dcd98b7102dd2f0e8b11d0f600bfb0c093:\
                 00000001:0a4f113b:auth:\
                 cc21ab6caf04c32228f0250c9eb48705")
```

This would result in `35f308904a9a9623498f358d1cb10afd`, which is the value for the response to the client sent to the server for authentication.

Digest Authentication is supported by most Java EE containers. In order to use Digest Authentication in a web application, we need to configure a login `<auth-method>` to instruct the container that DIGEST should be used as seen in the following listing:

```
<login-config>
  <auth-method>DIGEST</auth-method>
  <realm-name>
    BASE Logic.com Tomcat Manager Application
  </realm-name>
</login-config>
```

Form-based Authentication (`FORM`): In this mode, we can use our own form to collect the username and password. It is very flexible in terms of implementation and how we ask for the username and password, but requires extra work for implementing the forms.

This method suffers from the same security risk as the BASIC method because the credentials are transmitted as plain text.

This is still, however, the most user-friendly type of authentication as it allows site owners to control the look-and-feel of the user experience during site navigation.

To add authentication to our web application, we only need to include the required configuration in our web application deployment descriptor. The following code snippet shows the required elements, which we can add to `web.xml` to enforce authentication where required. The `web.xml` file is located in the `WEB-INF` directory of the web application:

```
<login-config>
   <auth-method>FORM</auth-method>
   <realm-name>file</realm-name>
   <form-login-config>
      <form-login-page>
        /auth/login.html</form-login-page>
      <form-error-page>/auth/loginError.html</form-error-page>
   </form-login-config>
</login-config>
```

This code snippet tells the application server to initiate authentication using the FORM Authentication method and use the file to check the user credentials with the storage.

The FORM authentication method gives us the flexibility to implement our credentials collecting mechanism ourselves, so we need to implement the form that will collect the username and password. That means any kind of web page, such as HTML or a JSP page, is required to collect the username and password. The following listing shows the `login.html` page source code:

```
<html>
  <head>
    <title></title>
    <meta http-equiv="Content-Type" content="text/html; charset=UTF-8
  </head>
  <body>
 <form method="POST" action="j_security_check">
  Username: <input type="text"     name="j_username"><br />
  Password: <input type="password" name="j_password"><br />
  <br />
  <input type="submit" value="Login">
  <input type="reset" value="Reset">
</form>
  </body>
</html>
```

As you can see, we are posting the form to a service called `j_security_check` that all Java EE containers must support, which is the default action for authentication, for which we should deliver the username and password. The Java EE standard specifies the action as well as the field names for the username and password, in which we should deliver the username and the password to the server for authentication.

We now have the authentication in place. The next step is to specify when the authentication should kick in. The authentication is supposed to protect some restricted resources when a user tries to access them. So we need to specify the restricted resources we want the user to authenticate, before accessing them:

```
<security-constraint>
        <display-name>
          Login page Protection
        </display-name>
        <web-resource-collection>
            <web-resource-name>
              Authentication
            </web-resource-name>
            <description/>
            <url-pattern>/auth/*</url-pattern>
            <http-method>GET</http-method>
            <http-method>POST</http-method>
        </web-resource-collection>
```

```
        <user-data-constraint>
            <description/>
            <transport-guarantee>
              CONFIDENTIAL
            </transport-guarantee>
        </user-data-constraint>
</security-constraint>
```

By using the `security-constraint` element, we can define a set of resources we want to protect, from unauthorized access. With the preceding snippet, we are instructing the application server to enforce authentication when a request wants to reach any URL pattern matching `/auth/*`. This means a request to `http://127.0.0.1:8080/index.html` would not have authentication enforced, but a request to `http://127.0.0.1:8080/auth/index.html` would have authentication enforced.

The next step in adding authentication to a web application is configuring the security realm in the application server level.

In our case, we will use the GlassFish application server, and the following steps can be used to add some users to the file realm we are using:

1. Start the application server using the following command:

   `%GLASSFISH_HOME%\bin\asadmin.bat start-domain domain1`

2. Open the administration console at `http://127.0.0.1:4848`, if you did not change the default settings.
3. In the navigation tree at the right, open **Configurations | server-config | Security | Realms | file**.
4. Click on the **Manage Users** button.
5. Add two new users with the following details:

Username	Password	Group
employee	employee	employee_group
manager	manager	manager_group

Now we are done with setting up the authentication for our application. The sample code provided for this chapter shows the complete application with authentication, access control, and transport security implemented.

How it works...

When we specify the authentication method and login forms, we are telling the server to kick in when a user tries to access a constrained resource. The server then asks for the user's credentials, and compares those credentials with the user information storage specified using the `realm-name` element.

The `login-config` element by itself does not affect the way the application works, as long as we do not add any constraint over the application resources to cause `login-config` to take effect.

See also

The next three recipes are about authentication and enforcing access control in the web application. Reviewing the source code for the sample application included in the download bundle is also highly recommended, as you will be able to see complete source codes instead of snippets.

Detailed instructions for adding new users to the file realm can be found at `http://download.oracle.com/docs/cd/E19798-01/821-1841/bnbxs/index.html`.

Detailed instructions on starting and stopping the application server can be found at `http://download.oracle.com/docs/cd/E18930_01/html/821-2416/gitwj.html`.

GlassFish: `http://glassfish.java.net/`.

Tomcat: `http://tomcat.apache.org/`.

Grizzly: `http://grizzly.java.net/`.

Digest Authentication: `http://en.wikipedia.org/wiki/Digest_access_authentication`.

Authorization in Java EE

In this recipe, we will look into how we can use Java EE built-in features to enable authorization or access control. It basically means we specify which roles are allowed to access a resource or set of resources, and how these roles can be mapped to actual users in the security realm.

Getting ready

In this recipe, we will continue working on the same sample application we worked on in the previous recipe. In case you skipped the previous step, it may be helpful to review the previous recipe to familiarize yourself with the application structure.

How to do it...

Enabling authorization has two steps: the first step is to specify the restricted resources and the roles that are able to access these resources, and the second step entails mapping these roles to actual user groups in the security realm.

The first step is application server neutral and will be the same in all application servers. The second step involves vendor-specific deployment descriptors.

The following snippet shows how we can define security constraint over a collection of web resources. We can have as many `security-constraint` elements as we need, to properly configure the access control in the application:

```
<security-constraint>
      <display-name>You should be a manager</display-name>
      <web-resource-collection>
          <web-resource-name>Inch</web-resource-name>
          <description/>
          <url-pattern>/jsp/toInch.jsp</url-pattern>
          <http-method>GET</http-method>
          <http-method>POST</http-method>
      </web-resource-collection>
      <auth-constraint>
          <description/>
          <role-name>manager_role</role-name>
      </auth-constraint>
  </security-constraint>
```

The following table explains each element and its options:

Element	Description
`security-constraint`	The top element we use to define a restriction over a set of resources for specified HTTP methods in our web applications.
`web-resource-collection`	The element used to specify the resource URLs or URL patterns as well as the set of HTTP methods we want to protect the URL patterns from.
`url-pattern`	Specifies the URLs or the URL patterns we want to put under protection of this constraint. We can have as many `url-pattern` elements for `web-resource-collection` as we need.
`http-method`	The HTTP methods we want the resource collection to be protected from. If no http-method elements are defined, the collection will be protected from all methods. It is recommended that we protect the resource from all methods unless we don't need to.

Element	Description
auth-constraint	This element specifies the list of roles that are allowed to access the resource collection.
role-name	Name of the roles we want to grant access to the collection. We can have as many role-name elements as we need.

Each role that we use in the security constraint configuration needs to be declared in the deployment descriptor using the security-role element. For example, the manager_role element we used in the previous snippet needs to have a corresponding role declaration as follows:

```
<security-role>
        <description/>
        <role-name>manager_role</role-name>
</security-role>
```

With declaring the roles, we have all that we require for the standard deployment descriptor. Now we need to map the roles to the application server's security realm groups and principals.

Different application servers use different ways to map the roles to groups and principals. Here, we will show how it can be done in the GlassFish application server. For the GlassFish application server, we have glassfish-web.xml for GlassFish 3.1 and above, or the sun-web.xml file for older versions, to use for the vendor-specific configurations. The file is located in the same directory as the web.xml file, which is WEB-INF/:

```
<security-role-mapping>
    <role-name>manager_role</role-name>
    <group-name>manager_group</group-name>
    <principal-name>tom</principal-name>
</security-role-mapping>
```

This snippet simply instructs the application server that any user in the manager group of the security realm is granted manager_role , that we used in our application. In addition to all members of manager_group, a user identified as tom is granted manager_role as well.

How it works...

When we add a security-constraint element to the web.xml file, we are instructing the application server to protect the resources we define in that resource from the methods specified, and allow only authenticated users with the specified roles to access that resource.

So, when an authenticated user tries to access that resource, its set of roles will be examined to check whether it has any of the authorized roles. If so, the user's request will reach the resource, otherwise the user will encounter the HTTP Error 401. I will explain the HTTP errors in detail in the *Programmatic security and annotations in Java EE* recipe of this chapter.

If the user is not already authenticated, then the container will try to collect its username and password or other types of credentials and proceed with authentication, and after successful authentication the authorization process will commence.

See also

To learn more about enabling Java EE security in other application servers and the Java EE security itself, review the following documents:

- Review the Java EE security refcardz available at `http://refcardz.dzone.com/refcardz/getting-started-java-ee`
- Review the Java EE tutorial's security section available at: `http://download.oracle.com/javaee/6/tutorial/doc/bnbwj.html`

Enforcing security in Enterprise Applications

In this recipe, we will look at how to enforce access control for the EJB module, as well as discuss how we can unify the role declaration and the role mapping for both EJB and web modules in the application deployment descriptors.

Getting ready

Understanding the sample application we discussed in the previous recipe will help you get more from this recipe.

How to do it...

In the *Introduction* section, we discussed the identity propagation from the frontend container to the EJB container. The frontend container can be an application client container or a Web container, which is our case.

Because of the authentication delegation, we do not need to specify any authentication for the EJB modules, and the only part we need to take care of is enforcing access control or authorization for the EJBs.

Between the EJBs, we don't need any security measure for the Message Driven Beans or MDBs as they are not invoked by a user, and rather, are completely managed by the container itself.

A **Message Drive Bean** (**MDB**) is an enterprise bean that can process requests asynchronously by acting as a JMS listener for messages. These messages can be sent by Java EE components, other enterprise beans, web components, a JMS application, or other messaging system that does not use Java EE technology.

Now, let's take a look at all the descriptor elements we can use to enforce access control on EJBs, and then review how we can use these elements. The following snippet shows how to restrict access to a method named `Employee#updateSalary` to users with `manager_role`:

```
<assembly-descriptor>

  <method-permission>
    <role-name>manager_role</role-name>
    <role-name>hr_role</role-name>
    <method>
        <ejb-name>Employee</ejb-name>
        <method-name>updateSalary</method-name>
    </method>
     <method>
        <ejb-name>Employee</ejb-name>
        <method-name>getSalary</method-name>
    </method>
  </method-permission>

</assembly-descriptor>
```

The following table shows the elements along with their description:

Element	Description
`method-permission`	The parent node, which contains permissions for one or more methods. Methods will have the same access level.
`role-name`	We can have as many roles for each method permission as we require.
`method`	Parent node, which contains the method we want to define its permission. We can have as many method elements as we require.
`ejb-name`	Name of the EJB.
`method-name`	Method name.

The `assembly-descriptor` is a direct child of the `ejb-jar` element in the `ejb-jar.xml` file.

We need to declare the roles that we used using the `security-role` elements similar to the `web.xml` syntax we saw in the previous recipe. For example, to declare `manager_role`, we need to add the following snippet to the `ejb-jar.xml` file:

```
<assembly-descriptor>

  <description/>
  <role-name>manager_role</role-name>

</assembly-descriptor>
```

Now that we have declared the access control, we need to map the roles to the application server security domain groups and principals. To do this, we can use the vendor-specific deployment descriptor file for EJB modules. The syntax is the same as what we had for the web module, so I will just briefly mention them here. For the GlassFish application server, the file name is `glassfish-ejb-jar.xml` for GlassFish 3.1, and `sun-ejb-jar.xml` for older versions. The following snippet shows how to define the mapping between the roles and groups:

```
<security-role-mapping>
        <role-name>manager_role</role-name>
        <group-name>manager_group</group-name>
        <principal-name>tom</principal-name>
</security-role-mapping>
<security-role-mapping>
        <role-name>hr_role</role-name>
        <group-name>hr_group</group-name>
</security-role-mapping>
```

Now the security enforcement for the EJBs is in place, and any users who want to access the `getSalary` or `updateSalary` in the `Employee` bean need to have the right role.

An enterprise application is usually a combination of more than just one module. In fact, it is quite likely that it is several Web and EJB modules all packaged as one enterprise application. When this is the case, we can move all of the common descriptions and declarations to the application level deployment descriptors, to facilitate the management and administration of the application.

Each enterprise application has two deployment descriptors:

- The standard deployment descriptor, which is named `application.xml` and can hold security role declarations shared between all modules.

- The vendor-specific deployment descriptors, which can be used to define the role mappings shared between all child modules. In the case of GlassFish, it is called `glassfish-application.xml` for GlassFish 3.1, and `sun-application.xml` for older versions.

The syntax will be the same as the module-specific deployment descriptors that we already discussed.

In the next recipe, we will look at how we can use annotations to enforce access control in EJBs, as in the web layer.

How it works...

The application server intercepts all invocations of the EJB methods, and when security constraint is defined it will enforce access control, and only the users with specified roles will be able to invoke the methods.

There's more...

Sometimes, we have internal roles in our application that are not to be assigned to any user. These roles will be used for outgoing calls of an EJB, for example, calls to another EJB, a process server, and so on. We use these internal roles to ensure that the outgoing calls from our EJB have the proper role assigned, independent of the roles that are assigned to the current user.

In such cases, we can use the `security-identity` element to specify the internal role, or instruct the application server to use the current identity for outgoing calls. The `security-identity` element is a child element of the EJB description. For example:

```
<enterprise-beans>
        <session>
            <ejb-name>ConversionBean</ejb-name>
                <security-identity>
                    <!--<use-caller-identity/>-->
                 <run-as>internal_role</run-as>
                </security-identity>
            </session>
</enterprise-beans>
```

This snippet instructs the application server to use `internal_role` when the EJB is making any external call.

See also

To learn more about enabling Java EE security in other application servers and the Java EE security itself, review the following documents.

- Review the Java EE security refcardz available at: `http://refcardz.dzone.com/refcardz/getting-started-java-ee`
- Review the *Security* section of *The Java EE tutorial* available at: `http://download.oracle.com/javaee/6/tutorial/doc/bnbwj.html`

Programmatic security and annotations in Java EE

In Java EE 5, and then in Java EE 6, annotations were introduced to define the security constraints for different Java EE components such as Servlets and EJBs. In Java EE 6, a new set of APIs was introduced to facilitate the programmatic security functions, including programmatic authentication and login.

In this recipe, we will look into annotations as well as the programmatic security in both EJB and Web modules.

Getting ready

Before using the security annotations, we should review the available annotations and their functions. The following table lists all available security-related annotations:

Annotation	Description
`@ServletSecurity`	This is used to enforce security over a Servlet. This annotation causes the container to apply the security enforcement on the URL pattern defined for this Servlet. It can optionally get `@HttpMethodConstraint` and `@HttpConstraint` as its parameters. The `@HttpMethodConstraint` element is an array specifying the HTTP methods' specific constraint, while `@HttpConstraint` specifies the protection for all HTTP methods that are not specified in the `@HttpMethodConstraint`.
`@DeclareRoles`	This annotation declares the roles that we want to use in our application. It is similar to the `security-role` element in the deployment descriptor.
`@RolesAllowed`	An array of roles allowed to access the annotated target. For example, if the target is an EJB, then all of the EJB methods will be available to the list of roles unless they are marked with `@RolesAllowed` with a different set of roles.

Annotation	Description
@PermitAll	Permits all roles to access the annotated target.
@DenyAll	If placed on a method, no one can access that method. In the case of class level annotation, all methods of annotated EJB are inaccessible to all roles, unless a method is annotated with a @RolesAllowed annotation with an array or roles.
@RunAs	Works similar to run-as or security-identity elements discussed in previous recipes.

Now that we know the security-related annotations, the following list shows the security-related annotations along with their target components and the target level that can be a method or the class:

Annotation	Target kind	Target level
@ServletSecurity	Servlet	Class
@DeclareRoles	Servlet, EJB	Class
@RolesAllowed	EJB	Class, Method
@PermitAll	EJB	Class, Method
@DenyAll	EJB	Method
@RunAs	Servlet, EJB	Class

Now that we have a clear picture of the annotations, let's put them to some use.

How to do it...

We will use each one of those annotations in the order they appear in the preceding tables.

The @ServletSecurity annotation is the only web module-specific security annotation, and we can use it to define all security configuration elements for a servlet and its mapped URL.

For example, placing the following annotation on a servlet will result in enforcing the listed security constrained for its mapped URL:

```
@ServletSecurity(@HttpConstraint
  (rolesAllowed = {" employee", " manager"}))
```

The previous listing enforces authentication for all HTTP types, and only users with either the manager or employee role are authorized access to the Servlet.

The previous `@ServletSecurity` annotation will enforce authorization based on the `<security-role-name>` constraints defined in the following application's `web.xml` `<security-constraint>` descriptor:

```
<security-constraint>
      <web-resource-collection>
             <url-pattern>/mappedURL</url-pattern>
      </web-resource-collection>
      <auth-constraint>
             <security-role-name>manager</security-role-name>
      <security-role-name>employee</security-role-name>
      </auth-constraint>
</security-constraint>
```

To study the shared and EJB-specific annotations, we can use the following EJB and examine how the annotations affect the security enforcement on the entity:

```
@Entity
@DeclareRoles(
  {"employee", "manager ", "hr_mananger "})
@RolesAllowed("hr_mananger_role")
public class Employee implements Serializable {

    @PermitAll
    public String getName() {
        return "name";
    }

    @RolesAllowed("manager ")
    public List<EvalRecords>
      getEvaluationRecords(Date from, Date to) {
        List<EvalRecords> evalRecord = null;
        //return a list containing all
        // EvalRecords of
        //this employee
        return evalRecord;
    }
    @Id
    private Integer id;

    public Employee() {
    }
}
```

First, we declare the roles we want to use, using `@DeclareRoles`.

Next, we use `@RolesAllowed` at the class level, to make all the entity methods available to `hr_management`.

Next, we use `@PermitAll` to allow users with any role to invoke the `getName` method.

Next, we use `@RolesAllowed` to make the `getEvaluationRecords` method available to `manager` as well as to `hr_manager`.

The introduction of a new programmatic security enhancement in Java EE 6 makes programmatic security more viable in context of Java EE applications. The following table shows the available programmatic security methods of the `HTTPServletRequest`:

Method	**Description**
`void login(String username, String password)`	Authenticates the given username and password with the configured security realm for the application, and if successful, logs in the user. It is similar to the `BASIC` or `FORM` methods, but with the developer completely in control of the process.
`Void logout()`	Resets the current return value of `getUserPrincipal`, `getRemoteUser`, and `getAuthType` to null.
`boolean isUserInRole(String role)`	Checks whether the current user has the given role or not.
`String getAuthType()`	Returns the authentication type configured for the application.
`String getRemoteUser()`	If the user is authenticated, it returns the username otherwise it returns null.
`Principal getUserPrincipal()`	Returns a `java.security.Principal` object corresponding to the current user.
`String getScheme()`	Returns the URL schema, `HTTP` or `HTTPS`.

The following sample code shows how we can use the programmatic login to authenticate a user. We should have the security realm already configured for the application:

```
String user =
  request.getParameter("user");
String password =
  request.getParameter("password");

try {
    request.login(user, password);
    if (request.isUserInRole("manager "))
        response.sendRedirect("/mgr/index.jsp");
        else response.sendRedirect
          ("/emp/index.jsp");
}catch(ServletException ex) {
//Handling Exception
    return;
}
```

In this sample code, we are collecting the username and the password from a form, and then using the collected username and password to perform the authentication and log in the user. If the authentication is successful and `ServletException` is not thrown, then we check for the user's role and redirect the user to its appropriate home page depending on its role.

How it works...

The container will use the annotations to form the security constraint schema of the application and use that schema to enforce authentication or access control, when required.

There's more...

We can use `@RunAs(value="ROLE_NAME")` to specify a different role for the outgoing calls that the component is making. For example, if placed on a servlet, independent of what the current principal role is, the container will assign this role to the current security identity to make any call to any external resource or component. This annotation is the metadata twin of `run-as` in `web.xml` or `security-identity` in the `ejb-jar` file that we can use in the deployment descriptor.

Using annotation and deployment descriptors together

When we use both the deployment descriptor files and the annotations, the deployment descriptor content will override the annotations of the same purpose. For example, if we specify the role permissions for an EJB method in both the deployment descriptor and in using annotations, the deployment descriptor content will override the annotations.

The point behind overriding the annotations is that we can easily edit the descriptor files in the deployment time, while the annotations are easier to use during development.

See also

To learn more about enabling Java EE security in other application servers and the Java EE security itself, review the following documents:

- Review the *Java EE security refcardz* available at: `http://refcardz.dzone.com/refcardz/getting-started-java-ee`
- Review the *web module security* section of *The Java EE Tutorial* available at: `http://download.oracle.com/javaee/6/tutorial/doc/bncas.html`
- Review the *EJB security* section of *The Java EE Tutorial* available at: `http://download.oracle.com/javaee/6/tutorial/doc/bnbyk.html`

Securely signing JAR artefacts

Signing an archive will place a digital signature into the `META-INF` folder of that archive. A digital signature is generated based on the exact set of data in the archive, using an entity's private key.

There are many potential reasons to sign an archive:

- Used in the runtime environment to support assertions of who signed the code
- Used in the runtime environment to ensure that the byte-code being executed and other resources being used match what existed at the time of the signature generation
- Used in a download situation to ensure that the downloaded archive contains what was signed by an expected party
- Used in a diagnostic or forensic process to ensure that the deployed code matches what was signed at the time of being released for production

The entire contents of an archive are processed, including media and class files. It is worth noting that the original purpose of signing an archive was to support processing them as applets in remote environments. This meant that the signing and verification infrastructure needed to be consistent across Java platforms. The processing had to encompass both the class files, and any resources associated with the graphically oriented applet. There were strong considerations given to bandwidth and to the impact when the signing was not going to be used:

- There will be two files generated as a result of the signing process. They will be placed into the `META-INF` folder.
- These files are relatively small in size, having minimal impact on storage and transmission.
- If the archive is being used in an environment that is not performing some type of verification, the only impact is adding a small overhead to the initial processing of the archive itself. For JAR files, this would impact the class loading process. For JEE archives, this would impact the deployment process that explores the archive and sets up the server's file structure.

The advantages of signing an archive include:

- It has minimal impact on the development processes and runtime environment.
- Once generated, it is small, in a consistent location, and persists for the life of the archive.

- The Java runtime and scripting environments have the infrastructure in place to generate and process a signed archive.
- The signature artifacts are contained inside the archive, meaning that they are an integral part of what they sign. This facilitates seamless distribution of the signature.

The disadvantages of signing an archive include:

- Signing an archive will impact the process of packaging the code and preparing it for distribution or deployment
- There is always a cost associated with managing the private key and certificates that are needed to support signing

The challenges to effectively using signed archives are:

- The signing entity's certificate must be available in the environment where the verification is taking place
- There is always a cost associated with managing the certificates that are needed to support verification
- Only Java environments can process the signature

Getting ready

In order to sign an archive, several items must be in place:

- The signing entity must have a public-private key combination, and at least one certificate associated with the public key.
- The signing entity must have the private key in a keystore in the runtime context when the signature is generated. The following is an example of generating a key and placing it into a keystore:

  ```
  keytool \
    -genkey \
    -alias 3166_javaee \
    -keyalg RSA \
    -keystore src/main/keystore/signing-jar.keystore \
    -storepass 3166_javaee \
    -keypass 3166_javaee \
    -dname "CN=domain"
  ```

  The generated key will have an alias `3166_javaee`, and can only be accessed using the combination of `storepass` and `keypass`. The keystore will be created, if it does not already exist. Best practices dictate that there be passwords for the keystore, as well as for each key in the keystore. In addition, a given keystore should only be used for a specific set of operations or security domain.

- The certificate must be distributed in some fashion to any environment that needs to verify the signature. The private key must, of course, always be kept close to the vest and handled with great care. You can use the keytool to self-generate a certificate (not recommended), or you can generate a request for a certificate from a certifying authority.
- The certificate that is used must be within its valid life (past its initial valid date and before its end date).
- The archive that needs to be signed must exist.

How to do it...

Signing an archive is typically done within the context of a Maven or Ant script, since it can be performed using the jarsigner tool. The following Maven example illustrates how this can be done:

```
<plugin>
  <groupId>org.apache.maven.plugins</groupId>
    <artifactId>
        maven-jar-plugin
    </artifactId>
    <version>${plugin.jar.version}</version>
    <executions>
      <execution>
        <goals>
          <goal>sign</goal>
        </goals>
      </execution>
    </executions>
    <configuration>
      <keystore>
        src/main/keystore/signing-jar.keystore
      </keystore>
      <alias>3166_javaee</alias>
      <storepass>3166_javaee</storepass>
      <signedjar>
        ${project.build.directory}/
        signed/${project.build.finalName}.jar
      </signedjar>
      <verify>true</verify>
    </configuration>
</plugin>
```

How it works...

As a result of signing an archive, there will be up to three new files added to the `META-INF` folder inside the archive. The three files are:

- The manifest file, which may already exist in the archive and is always named `MANIFEST.MF`. Additional information will be added to the manifest file. Each file in the archive will have a two-part entry in the manifest file. The first part of the entry lists the path and filename. The second part of the entry is a digest generated from the contents of the file:

  ```
  Name: com/domain/Driver.class
  SHA1-Digest: iWzc6BiiDgA2m+zaGRkH2PrQOJ8=
  ```

- The signature file, which has an extension of "`.SF`". By default, its name will be based on the first eight characters of the key's alias name in the signer's keystore. This can be overridden. The signature file will include specifics on how the digests were generated (subsequently used to process the signatures). Each file in the archive will have a two-part entry in the signature file. The first part of the entry lists the path and file name. The second part of the entry is a digest generated from the lines in the manifest file, for the file:

  ```
  Signature-Version: 1.0
  SHA1-Digest-Manifest-Main-Attributes: ZYD4IlVUAPkXHqO/L6w0h/GmlIw=
  Created-By: 1.6.0_25 (Sun Microsystems Inc.)
  SHA1-Digest-Manifest: NoXchAXCWB//vucaIrbBX69K9R4=

  Name: com/domain/Driver.class
  SHA1-Digest: ejjdaZn6f3sCmI71XMFUQacHf08=
  ```

- The third file is the signature block, which will have an extension of either `DSA` or `RSA` depending on the source of keys being used. It follows the same naming convention as the signature file, and contains the encrypted certificate corresponding to the private key that was used in signing.

There's more...

There can be multiple signatures associated with an archive. The jarsigner tool must be run multiple times with a different key being specified (as the alias).

Programmatically signing an archive is not supported in the Java platform, although there are solutions available through other sources for performing the signing from within Java.

The OSGi framework places some criteria on signature validity that are more restrictive than what the Java criteria specifies. For more details on this, please refer to the following articles:

- https://www.owasp.org/index.php/Signing_jar_files_with_jarsigner
- http://www.rzo.free.fr/bundle_signature.php

There are various options for processing the signature or signatures in an archive. In all cases, a certificate with the signer's public key must be in an accessible keystore. The options include:

- Using the jarsigner tool from the JDK. This is a command line or scripting option that can be used to verify that the archive is valid to the signature.
- Programmatically checking an archive using the `java.util.jar.JarFile` class.
- Using Java 2 Security; setting up permissions that are based on who signed the code. The following example illustrates such a permission:

```
keystore " src/main/keystore/signing-jar.keystore ";

grant codebase "file: project.build.finalName.jar"
  signedBy "3166_javaee " {
    permission java.io.FilePermission
      "com/domain/Driver.class",
      "read,write";
    permission java.util.PropertyPermission
      "*", "read";
};
```

See also

- *JAR*: http://en.wikipedia.org/wiki/JAR_(file_format)

Configuring Linux firewall rules

I felt a personal attachment to writing a recipe on setting up firewall rules on the Linux server, because several years ago I fell victim to an invasion on a Linux server that cost almost $10,000 in bandwidth charges in five days. Basically, I was hacked because I allowed several standard ports to be opened, even though they were not being actively used.

The `iptables` project (`netfilter.org`) is a user command-line program that allows a system administrator to configure the Linux IPv4 packet filtering rules to create very simple, to incredibly complex firewalls.

Getting ready

Since `iptables` is included with pretty much every modern Linux distribution, there should be no need to install anything. The only caveat would be if there were some esoteric module needed, that wasn't included by default. For the purposes of this recipe, we'll ignore anything outside of the packages installed by default.

NOTE: You can potentially lock yourself out of your server if you're not careful. Please make sure you have a backup plan for getting into your server, should you find your terminal unresponsive after typing in a command or running a script. You have been warned!

How to do it...

First log into your server, either over SSH or local console if you have access. It is assumed you have root access or at least sudo rights, as you'll need escalated privileges in order to run these commands:

1. At the command prompt, type the following to list your current `iptables` rules:

   ```
   /sbin/iptables -L
   ```

2. You may see output similar to the following:

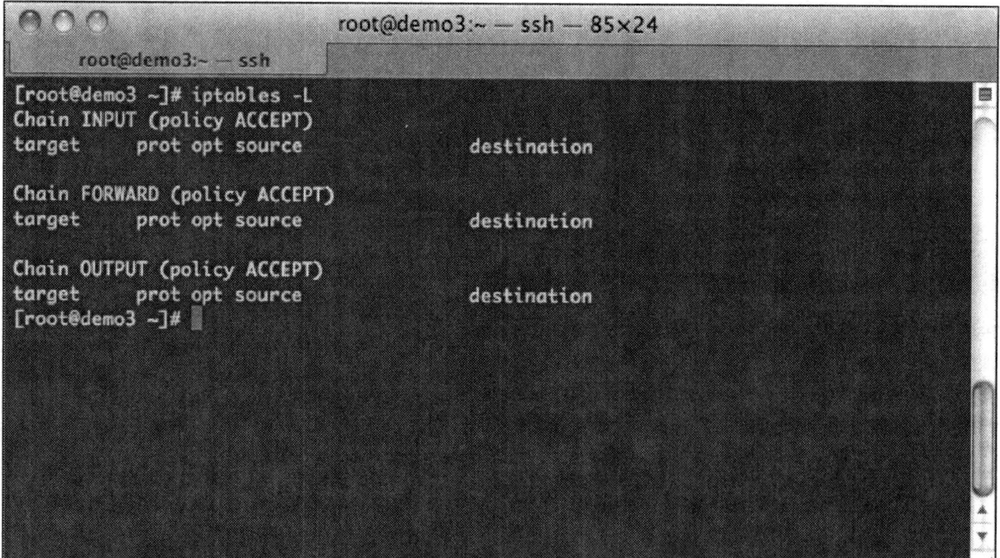

3. Next, we'll work on building up our ruleset. Let's start by flushing the current ruleset, and then creating a rule to allow `ICMP` (`ping`). We'll need to create a rule allowing SSH traffic to keep us from getting disconnected. We'll also add a rule to allow all `ESTABLISHED` and `RELATED` traffic using the state module with the `-m` flag:

```
root@demo3:~ — ssh — 85×24
root@demo3:~ — ssh
[root@demo3 ~]# iptables -F
[root@demo3 ~]# iptables -A INPUT -p icmp -m icmp --icmp-type 8 -j ACCEPT
[root@demo3 ~]# iptables -A INPUT -i eth0 -p tcp -m tcp --dport 22 -j ACCEPT
[root@demo3 ~]# iptables -A INPUT -m state --state ESTABLISHED,RELATED -j ACCEPT
[root@demo3 ~]#
```

4. Now, block all the incoming and forwarding traffic, and allow all outgoing and loopback traffic. Let's also add a rule in the `INPUT` chain that drops all traffic to the loopback IP, which doesn't originate from the loopback device:

```
root@demo3:~ — ssh — 85×24
root@demo3:~ — ssh
[root@demo3 ~]# iptables -A INPUT -j REJECT
[root@demo3 ~]# iptables -A FORWARD -j REJECT
[root@demo3 ~]# iptables -A OUTPUT -j ACCEPT
[root@demo3 ~]# iptables -I INPUT -i lo -j ACCEPT
[root@demo3 ~]# iptables -I INPUT ! -i lo -d 127.0.0.0/8 -j REJECT
[root@demo3 ~]#
```

So now we have a very basic firewall that will let us ping our server (for simple monitoring purposes) and allow us to SSH to it. You can view the rules as shown:

```
Iptables -L --line-numbers
```

```
root@demo3:~ — ssh — 85×24
root@demo3:~ — ssh
[root@demo3 ~]# iptables -L --line-numbers
Chain INPUT (policy ACCEPT)
num  target     prot opt source               destination
1    REJECT     all  --  anywhere             loopback/8          reject-with icmp-po
rt-unreachable
2    ACCEPT     all  --  anywhere             anywhere
3    ACCEPT     icmp --  anywhere             anywhere            icmp echo-request
4    ACCEPT     tcp  --  anywhere             anywhere            tcp dpt:ssh
5    ACCEPT     all  --  anywhere             anywhere            state RELATED,ESTAB
LISHED
6    REJECT     all  --  anywhere             anywhere            reject-with icmp-po
rt-unreachable

Chain FORWARD (policy ACCEPT)
num  target     prot opt source               destination
1    REJECT     all  --  anywhere             anywhere            reject-with icmp-po
rt-unreachable

Chain OUTPUT (policy ACCEPT)
num  target     prot opt source               destination
1    ACCEPT     all  --  anywhere             anywhere
[root@demo3 ~]#
```

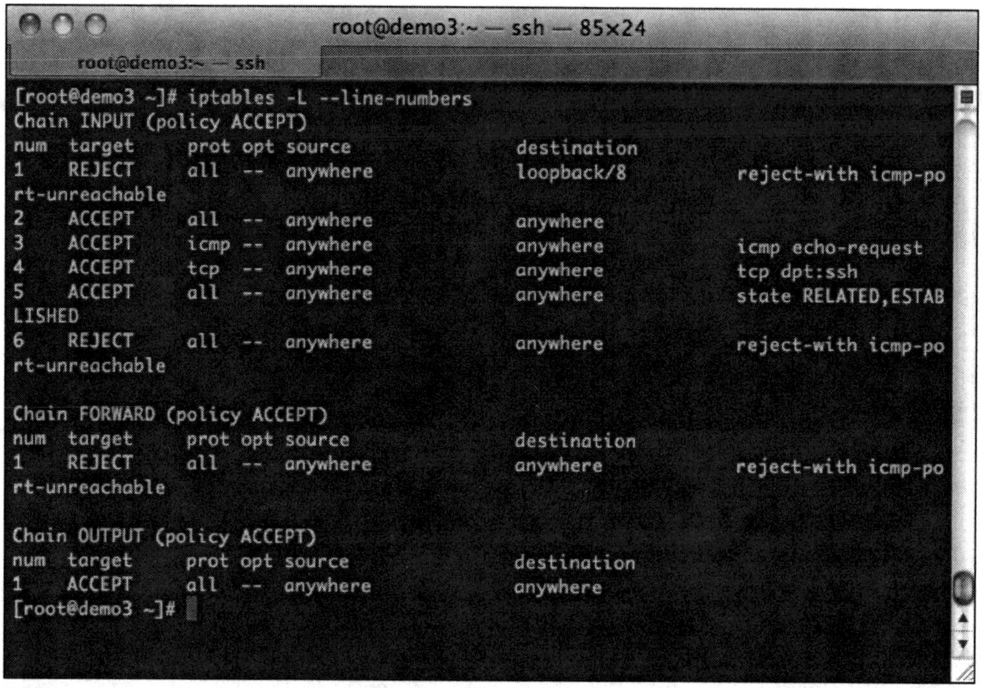

Precautions during testing

To prevent accidentally getting locked out of a remote server while testing firewall configurations, create a script that resets the firewall rules. Create a file called `/tmp/resetFirewallRules.sh` containing the following commands:

```
/sbin/iptables -F
/sbin/iptables -X
/sbin/iptables -t nat -F
/sbin/iptables -t nat -X
/sbin/iptables -t mangle -F
/sbin/iptables -t mangle -X
/sbin/iptables -P INPUT ACCEPT
/sbin/iptables -P FORWARD ACCEPT
/sbin/iptables -P OUTPUT ACCEPT
```

Then, create a `crontab` entry to run the new script every 15 minutes as depicted:

```
*/15 * * * * /tmp/resetFirewallRules.sh
```

This will reset the `iptables` rules every 15 minutes. When the `iptables` rules have been validated to perform as expected, this `crontab` and script should be removed from the server.

Web server configuration

As we're running a web server, it doesn't make much sense to block access to it. Let's open up port 80 and 443 so we can get to it. We're going to insert these rules a bit higher in the chain, rather than just appending:

```
root@demo3:~ — ssh — 85×24
root@demo3:~ — ssh
[root@demo3 ~]# iptables -I INPUT 5 -p tcp --dport 80 -j ACCEPT
[root@demo3 ~]# iptables -I INPUT 5 -p tcp --dport 443 -j ACCEPT
[root@demo3 ~]#
```

As each rule was added, it was inserted (using the `-I` flag) into the chain at line 5. If you view the rules again using `iptables -L`, you can see our new rules where we had placed them:

```
root@demo3:~ — ssh — 85×24
root@demo3:~ — ssh
[root@demo3 ~]# iptables -L --line-numbers
Chain INPUT (policy ACCEPT)
num  target     prot opt source               destination
1    REJECT     all  --  anywhere             loopback/8          reject-with icmp-po
rt-unreachable
2    ACCEPT     all  --  anywhere             anywhere
3    ACCEPT     icmp --  anywhere             anywhere            icmp echo-request
4    ACCEPT     tcp  --  anywhere             anywhere            tcp dpt:ssh
5    ACCEPT     tcp  --  anywhere             anywhere            tcp dpt:https
6    ACCEPT     tcp  --  anywhere             anywhere            tcp dpt:http
7    ACCEPT     all  --  anywhere             anywhere            state RELATED,ESTAB
LISHED
8    REJECT     all  --  anywhere             anywhere            reject-with icmp-po
rt-unreachable

Chain FORWARD (policy ACCEPT)
num  target     prot opt source               destination
1    REJECT     all  --  anywhere             anywhere            reject-with icmp-po
rt-unreachable

Chain OUTPUT (policy ACCEPT)
num  target     prot opt source               destination
1    ACCEPT     all  --  anywhere             anywhere
[root@demo3 ~]#
```

After adding the rules, you should now be able to view any page served by your web server (both http and https).

Back-up and Restore rules

You can save a copy of your firewall by using the `iptables-save` command, and redirect the output into a file as shown here:

```
iptables-save > my.firewall
```

This will create a file called `my.firewall` with all your rules in their current running order that you can use as a backup, or copy over to other servers to use. Run the following command to restore the backup:

```
iptables-restore < my.firewall
```

Application server configuration

For our Java EE server, we will use Tomcat for this section; the process is the same, we're just changing the port number when adding our firewall rule. The default port for Tomcat is 8080, so let's add our rule in the same place that we added the rule for port 80:

```
root@demo3:~ — ssh — 85×24
root@demo3:~ — ssh
[root@demo3 ~]# iptables -I INPUT 5 -p tcp --dport 8080 -j ACCEPT
[root@demo3 ~]#
```

Let's take a look at our rules so far:

```
root@demo3:~ — ssh — 85×25
root@demo3:~ — ssh
[root@demo3 ~]# iptables -L -n --line-numbers
Chain INPUT (policy ACCEPT)
num  target     prot opt source               destination
1    REJECT     all  --  0.0.0.0/0            127.0.0.0/8         reject-with icmp-po
rt-unreachable
2    ACCEPT     all  --  0.0.0.0/0            0.0.0.0/0
3    ACCEPT     icmp --  0.0.0.0/0            0.0.0.0/0           icmp type 8
4    ACCEPT     tcp  --  0.0.0.0/0            0.0.0.0/0           tcp dpt:22
5    ACCEPT     tcp  --  0.0.0.0/0            0.0.0.0/0           tcp dpt:8080
6    ACCEPT     tcp  --  0.0.0.0/0            0.0.0.0/0           tcp dpt:443
7    ACCEPT     tcp  --  0.0.0.0/0            0.0.0.0/0           tcp dpt:80
8    ACCEPT     all  --  0.0.0.0/0            0.0.0.0/0           state RELATED,ESTAB
LISHED
9    REJECT     all  --  0.0.0.0/0            0.0.0.0/0           reject-with icmp-po
rt-unreachable

Chain FORWARD (policy ACCEPT)
num  target     prot opt source               destination
1    REJECT     all  --  0.0.0.0/0            0.0.0.0/0           reject-with icmp-po
rt-unreachable

Chain OUTPUT (policy ACCEPT)
num  target     prot opt source               destination
1    ACCEPT     all  --  0.0.0.0/0            0.0.0.0/0
[root@demo3 ~]#
```

We should be able to see our rule for port 8080 on line 5, and anything running on that port should now be viewable.

Redirecting traffic

By default, Tomcat runs on port 8080. Getting it to answer requests on port 80 (http) by default, can be done in a number of ways. However, the method we're going to use here, is to redirect traffic using `iptables`. This will allow you to run a standalone Tomcat server as a non-privileged user and have it answer requests on port 80 as if it were any other http server.

As we've already got our firewall rules in place to allow access to a web server (port 80) and our Tomcat server (port 8080), all we need now is a rule to accept traffic on one port and pass it on to the other.

The following line should do the trick:

```
iptables -A PREROUTING -t nat -i eth0 -p
  tcp --dport 80 -j REDIRECT --to-port 8080
```

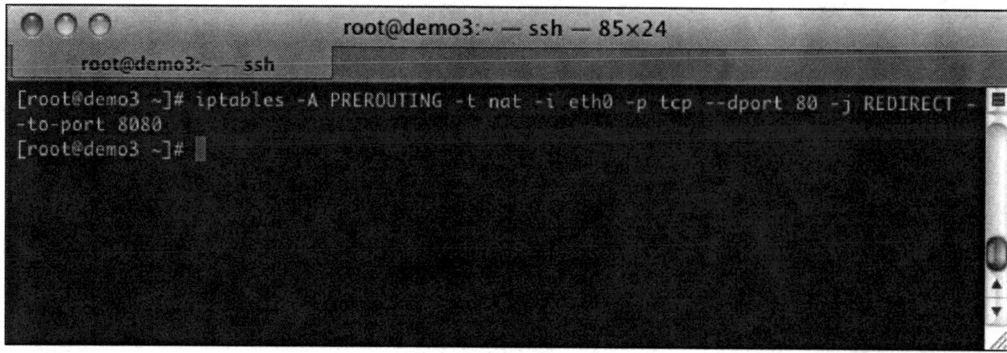

To show the NAT rules, run the following command:

```
iptables -t nat -L
```

You should then see some output similar to the following screenshot:

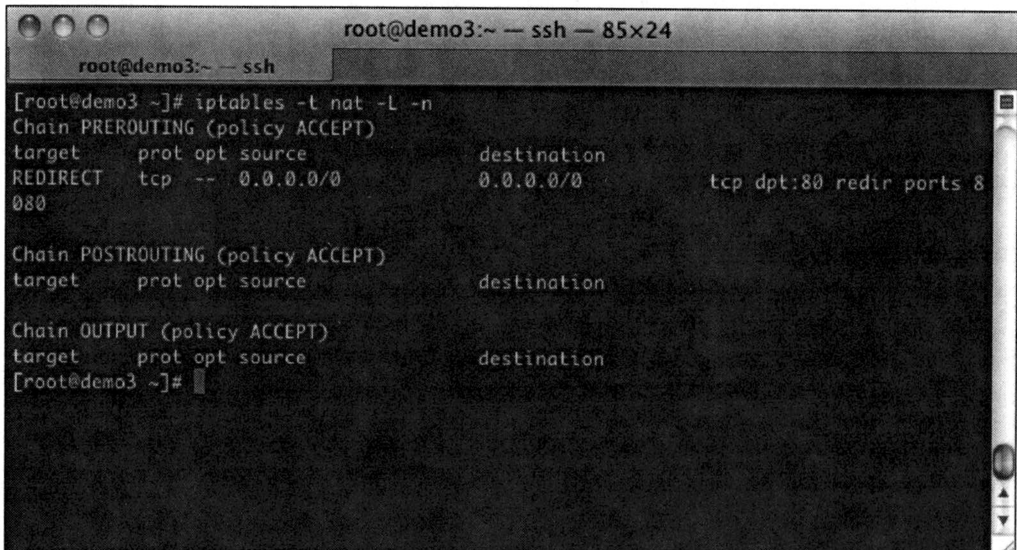

See also

- *IPtables*: `http://wiki.centos.org/HowTos/Network/IPTables`
- *IPtables Ubuntu*: `https://help.ubuntu.com/community/IptablesHowTo`

Securely obfuscating Java byte-code

Java and other byte-code languages are written in somewhat intuitive phonetic language, which makes the readability for development and maintenance easy. This poses a significant issue for intellectual property and other information that needs to be maintained in confidence.

If there is potential access to compiled resources such as JAR libraries, there are several decompilers on the market that can decompile these class files into readable code.

For developers of Java, Android-based applications for Google Android, Blackberry Playbook or similar applications based on an APK compilation containing `.dex` and other resources, there is a tool called **dex2jar**, which can decompile `.dex` compiled files back to `.class` files and put into a `.jar` file, which can then be decompiled by standard bytecode decompilers.

So all-in-all, both `.class` and `.dex` compiled resources are fairly easy to decompile and view.

Obfuscation is the act of scrambling and minifying a code to make it difficult to read by humans. Obfuscating code is a deterrent, and just makes the act of viewing source code more difficult. If a person puts enough effort into the task, they can also piece together the information they require. Obfuscating will make that task as difficult as possible.

Getting ready

To begin obfuscating an artefact, we need to first choose the library to use for obfuscation. There are several on the market, both open source and commercially available.

For this recipe, we will be using yGuard, which is not available in a Maven repository. So, we will need to manually download the latest `yguard.jar` file from `http://www.yworks.com/en/downloads.html#yGuard` and add it to the `build` classpath, so it can be referenced by the Ant task.

How to do it...

I have used Groovy language running under Gradle in order to use a standard Ant task to rename and shrink the compiled `.class` from the original project JAR, which was designed to create a new obfuscated JAR:

```
ant.taskdef(name: 'yguard',
  classname: 'com.yworks.yguard.YGuardTask',
  classpath: taskJar)

ant.yguard {
    inoutpair
      (in: originalJar, out: targetJar)

    externalclasses {
        pathelement(path: externalClasses)
    }
```

```
        shrink (logfile: "${shrinkLog}"){
            keep {
                'class'(classes: "protected",
                  methods: "protected",
                  fields: "protected"
                  ){
                    patternset{
                      include(name:
                        "com.baselogic.javaee6.*")
                      exclude(name:
                      "com.baselogic.javaee6.dao.*")
                    }
                }
            }
        }

        rename (logfile: renameLog) {
          property(name: "error-checking",
            value: "pedantic")
        }
    }
```

The same task can be run through Ant's XML syntax as depicted in the following listing:

```
<target depends="jar" name="yguard">
  <taskdef name="yguard"
    classname="com.yworks.yguard.YGuardTask"
    classpath="../libs/yguard.jar"/>
  <yguard>

    <inoutpair in="${originalJar}"
      out="${targetJar}"/>

    <shrink logfile="${shrinklog}">

      <keep>
        <class classes="protected"
          methods="protected" fields="protected">
          <patternset>
            <include name="com.baselogic.javaee6.**.*"/>
            <exclude name="com.baselogic.javaee6.dao.*"/>
          </patternset>
        </class>
      </keep>
    </shrink>

    <rename logfile="${renamelog}">
        <property name="error-checking"
          value="pedantic"/>
    </rename>

  </yguard>
</target>
```

The obfuscation process is fairly easy and can be done from the command line, or any build technology that will allow a Java class to be executed. The difficulty comes with configuring the code to be obfuscated, and including dependent libraries as external classes on the `yGuard` classpath so it can reference external classes when shrinking and renaming.

After we run the precious task, we should end up with the following files if we run this against the *Chapter 02, Enterprise Persistence*, code-base:

- `ch02-1.0.2.jar` (21kb)
- `ch02-1.0.2-obf.jar` (16kb)
- `ch02-1.0.2-obf.jar.renamelog.xml`
- `ch02-1.0.2-obf.jar.shrinklog.xml`

At this point, `ch02-1.0.2-obf.jar` had its classes obfuscated by renaming, and its overall size shrunk to create a smaller JAR file. The obfuscation process reduced the overall artefact size by 24 percent.

How it works...

Let's look at the resulting obfuscation artefact and logs to see how this process worked:

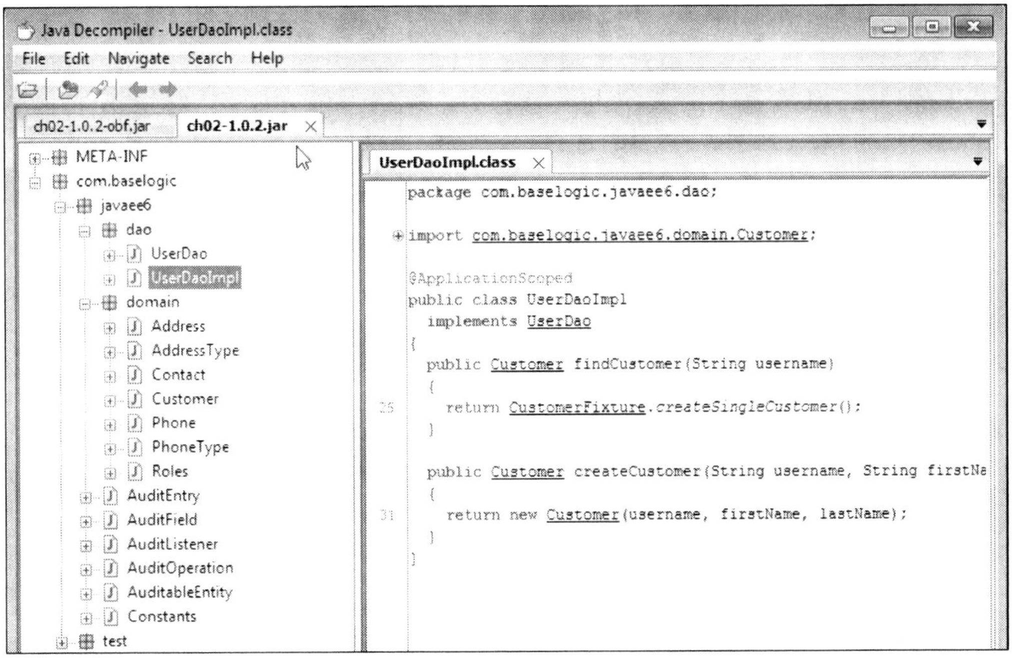

If we open our non-obfuscated JAR, `ch02-1.0.2.jar`, to inspect the contents, we will see phonetic packages and classnames such as `com\baselogic\javaee6\dao\` and `UserDao.class` respectively.

When we open the obfuscated JAR file, `ch02-1.0.2-obf.jar` to view its contents, we now see very different contents as we see a package structure such as `A\A\A\A\` and classnames such as `A.class`:

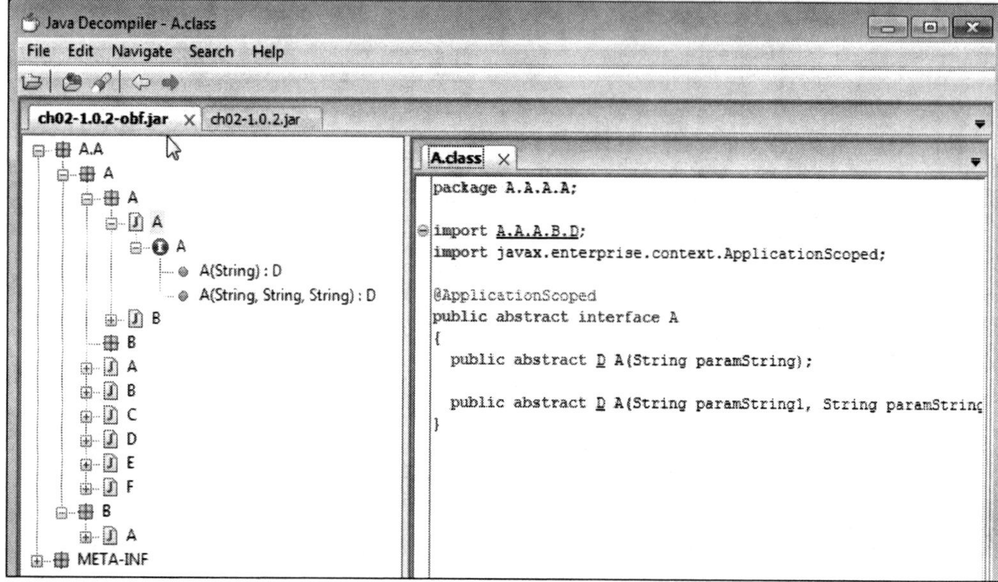

This renaming makes introspecting into the compiled code far more difficult. You can also see that external classes are still referenced unobfuscated.

There's more...

When we obfuscate an artefact, most tools create logs that allow for proper de-obfuscation. For yGuard, we have a `ch02-1.0.2-obf.jar.renamelog.xml` file that details how package and respective classes were renamed so yGuard could de-obfuscate the artefact:

```
<map>
  <package
    name="com"
    map="A"/>
  <package
    name="com.baselogic"
    map="A"/>
  <package
    name="com.baselogic.javaee6"
```

```
      map="A"/>
    <package
      name="com.baselogic.javaee6.dao"
      map="A"/>
    <class
      name="com.baselogic.javaee6.dao.UserDao"
      map="A"/>
    <method
      class="com.baselogic.javaee6.dao.UserDao"
      name="com.baselogic.javaee6.domain.Customer
      findCustomer(java.lang.String)"
      map="A"/>
    <method
      class="com.baselogic.javaee6.dao.UserDao"
      name="com.baselogic.javaee6.domain.Customer
      createCustomer(java.lang.String, java.lang.String, java.lang.
String)"
      map="A"/>
    <class
      name="com.baselogic.javaee6.dao.UserDaoImpl"
      map="B"/>
    <method
      class="com.baselogic.javaee6.dao.UserDaoImpl"
      name="com.baselogic.javaee6.domain.Customer
      findCustomer(java.lang.String)"
      map="A"/>
    <method
      class="com.baselogic.javaee6.dao.UserDaoImpl"
      name="com.baselogic.javaee6.domain.Customer
      createCustomer(java.lang.String, java.lang.String, java.lang.
String)"
      map="A"/>
```

Next, we look into `ch02-1.0.2-obf.jar.shrinklog.xml` to view how yGuard shrank the artefact by 24%:

```
<removed-code>
  <field name="serialVersionUID"
      class="com.baselogic.javaee6.AuditEntry" />
  <field name="serialVersionUID"
      class="com.baselogic.javaee6.AuditField" />
  <method signature="void &lt;init&gt;()"
      class="com.baselogic.javaee6.domain.Address" />
     <method signature="java.lang.String getStreet()"
      class="com.baselogic.javaee6.domain.Address" />
  ...
     <class name="com.baselogic.javaee6.domain.Contact" />
  <removed-resources>
  </removed-resources>
```

You can see that shrinking involves removing fields, methods, classes, and potentially, resources that are not used in the current artefact. This is where it sometimes gets tricky—knowing what to remove and what to keep. Most tools, including yGuard, allow you to define what elements to keep:

```
<keep>
    <class classes="protected"
      methods="protected"
      fields="protected">
        <patternset>
          <include name=
            "com.baselogic.javaee6.**.*"/>
          <exclude name=
            "com.baselogic.javaee6.private.*"/>
          <include name=
            "com.baselogic.javaee6.reflection.**.*"/>
        </patternset>
    </class>
</keep>
```

This way, you can tailor the obfuscation process to suit the needs of the intended artefact.

Deobfuscating artefacts

yGuard comes with a simple GUI tool, which allows the obfuscating party to deobfuscate stack traces that have been obfuscated using yGuard. As seen previously, yGuard creates an XML log file for shrinking and renaming.

In order to run the yGuard deobfuscation tool, run the following command:

```
java -jar ../../../libs/yguard.jar ch02-1.0.2-obf.jar.renamelog.xml
```

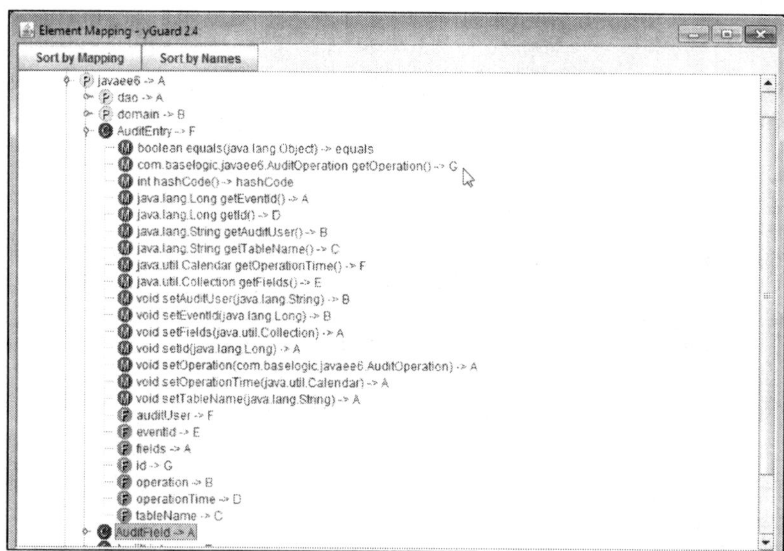

As you can see, this is a great debugging tool, which enables you to track down obfuscated names with the original corresponding names.

As you might have noticed, there is no information for a shrink log. If you run the following command, you will see that the tool displays no mapping information for anything that was removed:

```
java -jar ../../../libs/yguard.jar ch02-1.0.2-obf.jar.shrinklog.xml
```

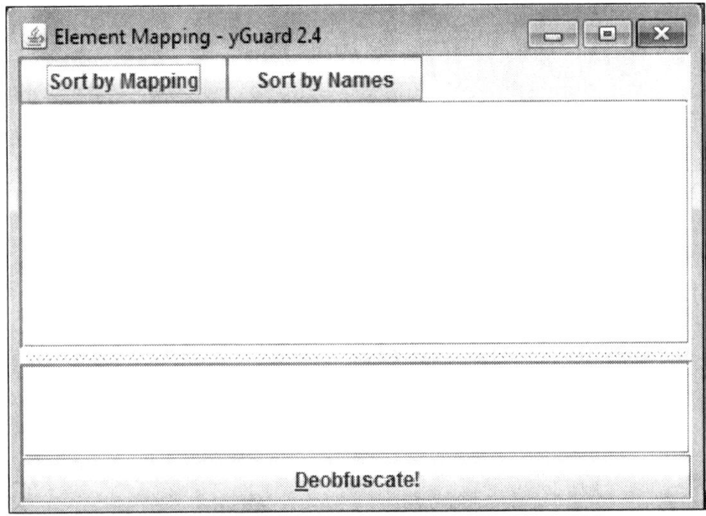

GZipping log files

If you name the output log files to `*.gz`, they will automatically get GZipped, which will save space and allow for easier archiving.

SHA-1, MD5 MANFEST.mf for all artefact entries

A somewhat undocumented feature of yGuard is that it, by default, creates `SHA-1` and `MD5` digest entries for every class obfuscated. This is used by some Java EE containers to validate the classes that are loaded, for added security:

```
Name: A/A/A/E.class
SHA-1-Digest: Jh+MbQn4MFvacpD50AKkXL8KFBg=
Digest-Algorithms: SHA-1, MD5
MD5-Digest: +f4IM8E8Hp4kqxPgaeTDig==
```

This technique is similar to JAR signing, but does not use a public-private keystore to digitally sign the JAR.

See also

- *JAR*: `http://en.wikipedia.org/wiki/JAR_(file_format)`
- *APK*: `http://en.wikipedia.org/wiki/APK_(file_format)`
- *Dex*: `http://en.wikipedia.org/wiki/Dex_format`
- *jReverse Pro*: `https://github.com/akkumar/jreversepro`
- *Jode*: `http://jode.sourceforge.net/`
- *JD Decompiler*: `http://java.decompiler.free.fr`
- *Bytecode Obfuscation*: `https://www.owasp.org/index.php/Bytecode_obfuscation`
- *Code Obfuscation*: `http://en.wikipedia.org/wiki/Code_obfuscation`
- *yGuard*: `http://www.yworks.com/en/products_yguard_about.html`
- *ProGaurd*: `http://proguard.sourceforge.net/`
- *ZKM Klassmaster*: `http://www.zelix.com/klassmaster/featuresZKMScript.html`
- *Manifest*: `http://java.sun.com/developer/Books/javaprogramming/JAR/basics/manifest.html`

Minification and obfuscation of web resources

Minification (also minimisation or minimization) is a technique used to reduce the size, and partially obfuscate web resources, such as cascading stylesheets (`.css`) and JavaScript (`.js`) files. This is done by removing all the unnecessary characters from source code, without changing its functionality. This unnecessary code usually includes whitespace characters, newline characters, comments, and sometimes block delimiters, which are used to add readability to the code but are not required for it to execute. This minified source code is especially useful for interpreted languages deployed and transmitted on the Internet (such as JavaScript), because it reduces the amount of data that needs to be transferred. Minified source code is also very useful for HTML code, but the act of pre-minifying code does not work especially well for JSP, JSF and Servlet based UI components because they are typically not pre-processed, but rather compiled, or can be pre-compiled at runtime.

There are several resource minification libraries on the market, but we are going use a compression library from Yahoo! called YUI compressor.

YUI about...

YUI compressor is a compression and minification tool developed and maintained by Yahoo!. The project home page is located at `http://developer.yahoo.com/yui/compressor/` and contains good information about the tool itself, but does not exhaustively cover build and automation integrations, which we will cover here in this recipe.

Getting ready

The usage and requirements of `yuicompressor` will vary slightly, depending upon the build system and use-case you plan to implement.

In this recipe, we will first focus on using the Gradle build system and create a custom task to aid in the processing of resources.

You need to import Yahoo's YUI Compressor and Mozilla Rhino libraries into your build as depicted in the following listing:

```
classpath group: 'com.yahoo.platform.yui',
    name: 'yuicompressor', version: '2.4.6'
classpath group: 'org.mozilla',
    name: 'rhino', version: '1.7R3
```

Gradle needs the YUI compressor package and Mozilla's JavaScript package as Groovy needs access to `JavaScriptCompressor`, `CssCompressor`, and `SystemOutErrorReporter` respectively. So, we need to add the following imports:

```
import com.yahoo.platform.yui.compressor.*
import org.mozilla.javascript.*
```

How to do it...

The task work itself is fairly straightforward. We are basically going to pull files from a target directory matching the type of file we want to process (`*.js` or `*.css`), then in a move process, we will use a new compressor object to compress each file, and then move it to a destination directory. One feature of this process is that YUI is going to combine.

Here, we merely create a new `JavaScriptCompressor` object, which allows us to compress and combine all the JavaScript (`*.js`) files in our input directory and create the final JavaScript file in the defined output directory:

```
class CatPack extends DefaultTask {
    @InputDirectory
    File inputFolder =
      file("src/main/webapp/resources/js");
```

```
@OutputFile
File outputFile =
  file("$buildDir/jsmin/modules.min.js");

@TaskAction
public void doCatPack() {
    def fw = new FileWriter(outputFile)
    inputFolder.eachFileMatch(~/.*\.js/) { File file ->
      def c = new JavaScriptCompressor
        (file.newReader(), new SystemOutErrorReporter())
        c.compress(fw, -1, false, false, false, false)
    }
    fw.flush()
    fw.close()
}
```

We can first examine the original JavaScript file, which has comments and whitespace intact:

```
        // Global declarations - assignment
        var hdrMainvar = null;
        var contentMainVar = null;
        var ftrMainVar = null;
        var contentTransitionVar = null;
        var stateLabelVar = null;
        var whatLabelVar = null;
        var stateVar = null;
        var whatVar = null;
        var form1var = null;
        var confirmationVar = null;
        var contentDialogVar = null;
        var hdrConfirmationVar = null;
        var contentConfirmationVar = null;
        var ftrConfirmationVar = null;
        var inputMapVar = null;
```

Then, if we examine the processed JavaScript file, we no longer have comments or whitespace, thus reducing the size of the script:

```
var hdrMainvar=null;var contentMainVar=null;var ft
contentTransitionVar=null;var stateLabelVar=null;v
stateVar=null;var whatVar=null;var form1var=null;v
contentDialogVar=null;var hdrConfirmationVar=null;
contentConfirmationVar=null;var ftrConfirmationVar
MISSING="missing";var EMPTY="";var NO_VOLUME="0oz"
NO_ABV="0%";
```

We can now create another task that will create a `CssCompressor` object, which allows us to compress and combine all the JavaScript (`*.js`) files in our input directory and creates the final JavaScript file in the defined output directory:

```
class CssPack extends DefaultTask {
    @InputDirectory
    File inputFolder;
    @OutputFile
    File outputFile;
    @TaskAction
    public void doCssPack() {
        def fw = new FileWriter(outputFile)
        inputFolder.eachFileMatch(~/.*\.css/) {
            File file ->
            def c = new CssCompressor(file.newReader())
            c.compress(fw, -1)
        }
        fw.flush()
        fw.close()
    }
}
```

We can first examine the original CSS file that has comments and whitespace intact:

```
body {
    background: #333;
    margin:0;
    padding:0;
    font-family: Verdana, Geneva, sans-serif;
    font-size: 13px;
    color: #666;
}

* {
    margin:0;
    padding:0;
}

/** element defaults **/
table {
    width: 100%;
    text-align: left;
}
```

Then, if we examine the processed CSS file, we no longer have comments or whitespace, thus reducing the size of the script:

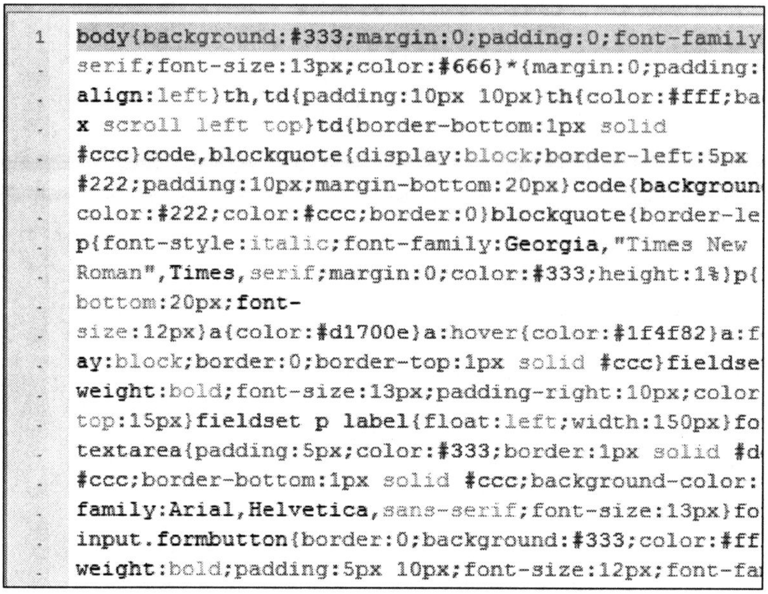

```
body{background:#333;margin:0;padding:0;font-family
serif;font-size:13px;color:#666}*{margin:0;padding:
align:left}th,td{padding:10px 10px}th{color:#fff;ba
x scroll left top}td{border-bottom:1px solid
#ccc}code,blockquote{display:block;border-left:5px
#222;padding:10px;margin-bottom:20px}code{backgroun
color:#222;color:#ccc;border:0}blockquote{border-le
p{font-style:italic;font-family:Georgia,"Times New
Roman",Times,serif;margin:0;color:#333;height:1%}p{
bottom:20px;font-
size:12px}a{color:#d1700e}a:hover{color:#1f4f82}a:f
ay:block;border:0;border-top:1px solid #ccc}fieldse
weight:bold;font-size:13px;padding-right:10px;color
top:15px}fieldset p label{float:left;width:150px}fo
textarea{padding:5px;color:#333;border:1px solid #d
#ccc;border-bottom:1px solid #ccc;background-color:
family:Arial,Helvetica,sans-serif;font-size:13px}fo
input.formbutton{border:0;background:#333;color:#ff
weight:bold;padding:5px 10px;font-size:12px;font-fa
```

As you can see, compressing and minifying JavaScript and CSS resources are fairly simple to run in Java or Groovy code by leveraging the classes provided.

There's more...

The processing of resources can easily be added to an existing build lifecycle by hooking into the artefact creation phase, depending upon your build system, and the artefact you are creating.

During the JAR creation process, we can then minify all resources:

```
jar {
    exclude '**/*js*/*'
    exclude '**/*styles*/*'
    from (jsMini) {
        into("resources/js")
    }
    from (cssMini) {
        into("resources/styles")
    }
}
```

During the WAR creation process, we can minify all resources:

```
war {
    exclude '**/*js*/*'
    exclude '**/*styles*/*'
    from (jsMini) {
        into("resources/js")
    }
    from (cssMini) {
        into("resources/styles")
    }
}
```

Running by the command line

This utility can be run on the command line with the following simple command:

java -jar yuicompressor-[version].jar myScripts.js -o myScripts-min.js

The [version] should be replaced by the exact version of yuicompressor that you plan to use.

Running by means of Ant Java task

We can also run this utility as a Java executable from an Ant build with the same options as the command-line execution:

```
<java jar="yuicompressor-[version].jar">
    <arg value="myScripts.js" />
    <arg value="-o myScripts-min.js"/>
    <classpath>
        <pathelement location=
          "yuicompressor-[version].jar"/>
    </classpath>
</java>
```

The [version] should be replaced by the exact version of yuicompressor that you plan to use.

This will allow for more control and automation for this compression task. By using Ant, we can now use this tool in Maven, and other build tools.

See also

- *Yahoo YUI Library*: `http://en.wikipedia.org/wiki/YUI_Library`
- *Minification*: `http://en.wikipedia.org/wiki/Minification_(programming)`
- *Code Obfuscation*: `http://en.wikipedia.org/wiki/Code_obfuscation`
- *YUI Compressor*: `http://developer.yahoo.com/yui/compressor/`

4

Enterprise Testing Strategies

In this chapter, we will cover:

- Remote debugging of Java EE applications
- Testing JPA with DBUnit
- Using Mock objects for testing
- Testing HTTP endpoints with Selenium
- Testing JAX-WS and JAX-RS with soapUI

Introduction

This chapter is going to cover a wide range of testing techniques to employ in the enterprise. We cover testing-related recipes for testing various Java EE technologies, including JPA, EJB, JSF, and web services.

Remote debugging of Java EE applications

Most Integrated Development Environments have the ability to debug Java applications. Most debugging is done locally while the application is being developed and while unit testing. This is a useful practice, but sometime issues arise when running applications on servers outside the development sandbox. These issues can be caused for various reasons and are usually not reproducible on a local development machine. In these cases, having the ability to debug through an application running on a target remote machine is the only way to deduce application issues.

In this recipe we are going to learn how to attach a remote debugger process to a Maven build running outside of the IDE.

Getting ready

Maven has debugging capabilities built into it as of version 2.0.8. The easiest way to start Maven in debug mode is to set the `surefire debug` option parameter and run your tests:

```
mvn -Dmaven.surefire.debug test
```

The default port will be 5005, and any IDE can attach to it.

Another option is to explicitly set the debug properties. This is especially helpful if you want to change the debug ports the IDE needs to attach to:

```
mvn -Dmaven.surefire.debug="-Xdebug
  -Xrunjdwp:transport=dt_socket,
  server=y,
  suspend=y,
  address=8000
  -Xnoagent -Djava.compiler=NONE" test
```

After executing Maven with the debug flag enabled, the Maven process opens a debug port. it will appear as though the Maven build has paused, waiting for something to attach to that debug port. The build will not continue unless a debug process connects to the opened debug port. In the following case you see that port 5005 is the socket that Maven is listening to for debug connections to:

```
[INFO] --- maven-surefire-plugin:2.7.1:test (default-test) @ ch03 ---
[INFO] Surefire report directory: C:\usr\SYNCH\PACKT\3166\Chapters_
Code\ch03\target\surefire-reports
Listening for transport dt_socket at address: 5005
```

At this point, we will open our IDE and create a new, remote-run configuration which will attach to the port that Maven is listening on:

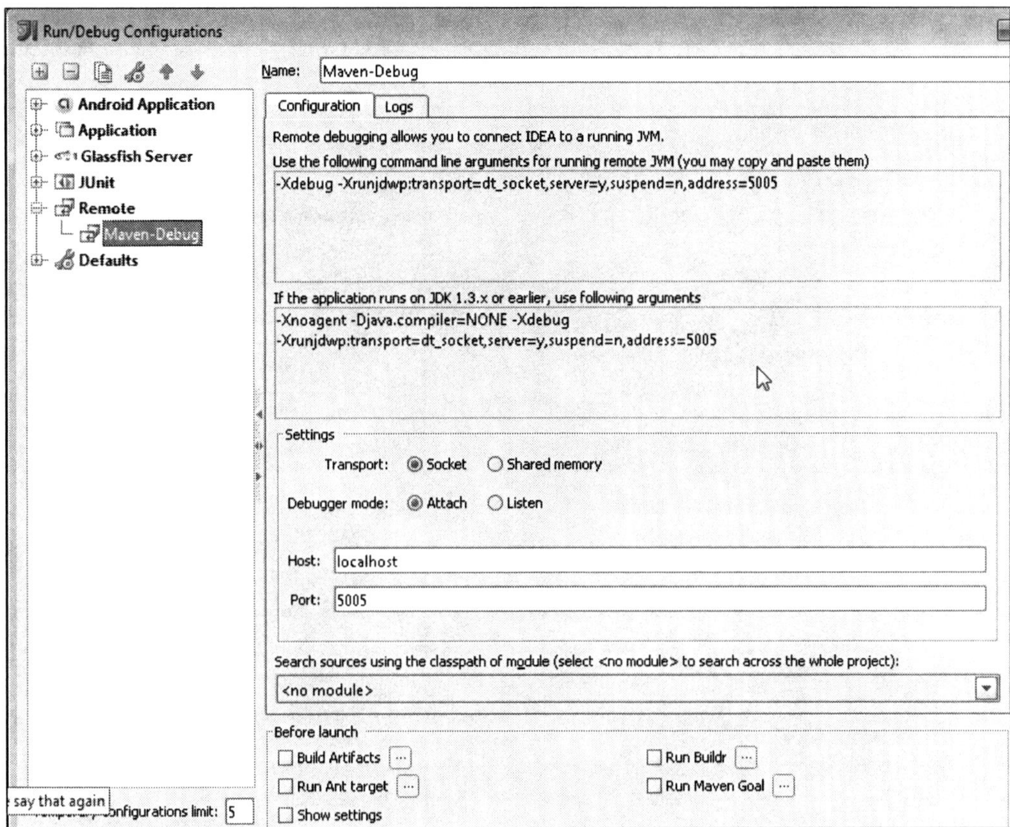

How to do it...

Now that we have created a remote-run configuration, we can debug that configuration. As soon as the IDE attaches to the port that Maven is listening on, Maven will continue the build process.

As Maven continues the build process and gets to the portion of code that you have set as a breakpoint, you will notice that Maven will stop and your breakpoint will be active for the session you're running currently:

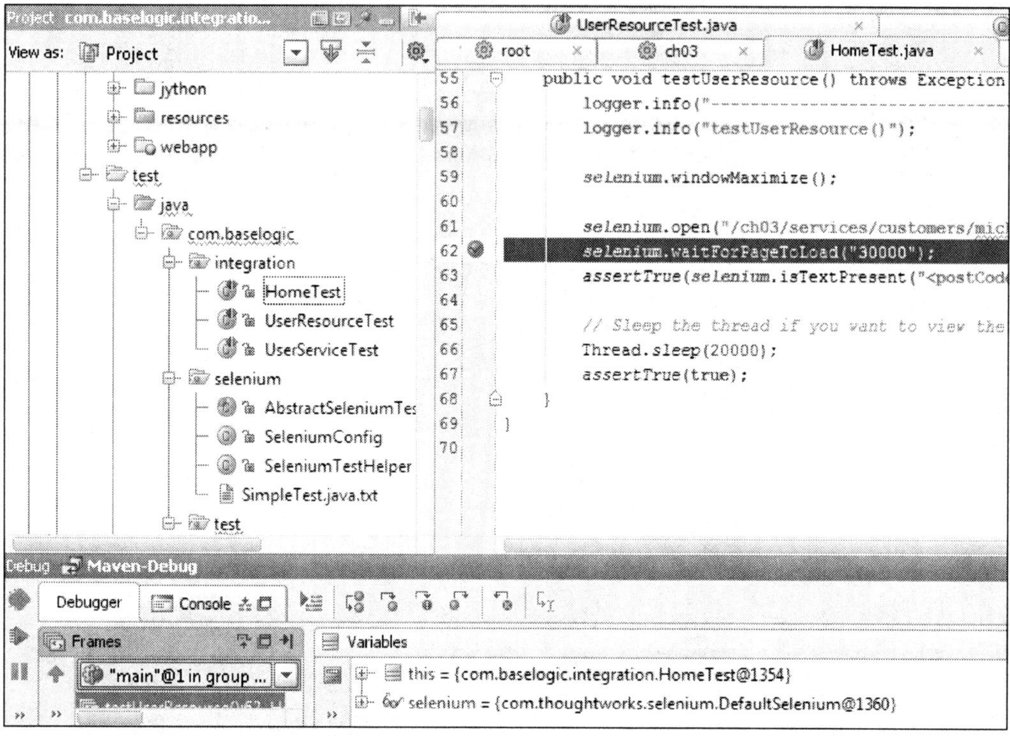

Remote debugging not only works through the Maven test phase, as done in this section, but also works through the entire Maven build lifecycle. This method is extremely helpful when deploying a web application to an embedded container, so that you can debug a running web page within a local build.

How it works...

Remote debugging uses the **Java Platform Debugger Architecture** (**JPDA**) in order to broker information from a running **virtual machine** (**VM**) and a debugging tool, usually an IDE capable of interacting with the **Java Debug Wire Protocol** (**JDWP**).

Adding JVM debug options with Ant

When using Ant to build and run an application, you can add JVM arguments to the `<java>` Ant task to add debugging settings to the running JVM as seen in the following listing:

```
<java fork="on"
      failonerror="true"
      classpath="com.baselogic"
      classname="SomeClass">
   <jvmarg line="-Xdebug
      -Xrunjdwp:transport=dt_socket,
      server=y,
      suspend=y,
      address=4000
      -Xnoagent -Djava.compiler=NONE" />
    <arg line="--arg1 arg2 --arg3 arg4"/>
</java>
```

Starting Gradle in debug mode

Gradle is a build system that uses Groovy to script the build that feels very intuitive for Java developers.

If you are running Linux, you can simply export `GRADLE_OPTS`, as shown in the following code:

```
export GRADLE_OPTS="-Xdebug
    -Xrunjdwp:transport=dt_socket,
    server=y,
    suspend=y,
    address=8000
    -Xnoagent -Djava.compiler=NONE"
```

If you are running Windows, you can simply export `GRADLE_OPTS`, as shown here:

```
set GRADLE_OPTS="-Xdebug
    -Xrunjdwp:transport=dt_socket,
    server=y,
    suspend=y,
    address=8000
    -Xnoagent -Djava.compiler=NONE"
```

Adding debug options to JAVA_OPTS

Besides running in a build system that is starting the Java processes for you, there are instances when you may want to add debugging options to all the running processes that might take advantage of remote debugging.

If you are running Linux, you can simply export `GRADLE_OPTS`, as shown here:

```
export JAVA_OPTS="-Xdebug
    -Xrunjdwp:transport=dt_socket,
    server=y,
    suspend=y,
    address=4000
    -Xnoagent -Djava.compiler=NONE"
```

If you are running Windows, you can simply export `JAVA_OPTS`, as shown in the following code snippet:

```
set JAVA_OPTS="-Xdebug
    -Xrunjdwp:transport=dt_socket,
    server=y,
    suspend=y,
    address=4000
    -Xnoagent -Djava.compiler=NONE"
```

See Also

- *IDEA Debugging*: `http://www.jetbrains.com/idea/documentation/howto_02.html`
- *Jetty Debugging*: `http://docs.codehaus.org/display/JETTY/Debugging+Jetty+with+IntelliJ+IDEA`
- *Maven Debugging*: `http://maven.apache.org/plugins/maven-surefire-plugin/examples/debugging.html`
- *Java Platform Debugger Architecture (JPDA)*: `http://java.sun.com/javase/technologies/core/toolsapis/jpda/index.jsp`
- *JPDA Architecture*: `http://java.sun.com/javase/technologies/core/toolsapis/jpda/index.jsp`

Testing JPA with DBUnit

In *Chapter 2, Enterprise Persistence*, we touched on some examples where we were testing our JPA examples. In this recipe, we will take a step-by-step approach on how to use JUnit and DBUnit in your Java EE application. First, I want to review each tool, and the benefits it will provide for this recipe.

The JUnit lifecyle is a fixed series of method calls to ensure consistency when running unit tests. In the following screenshot, we can see the lifecycle that BDUnit and any other unit tests will follow:

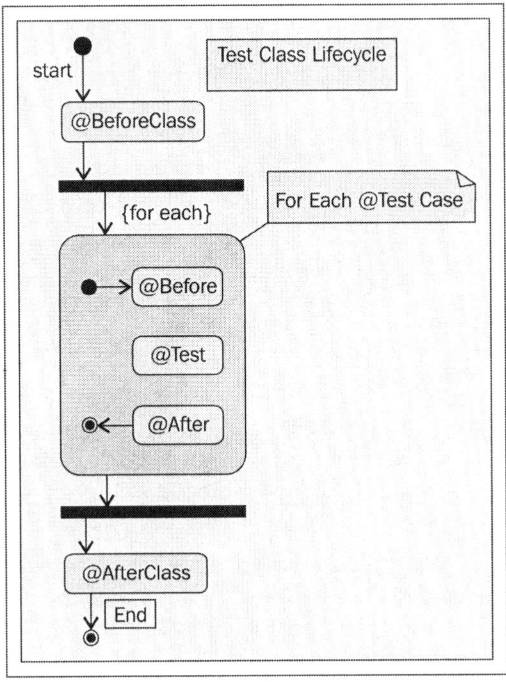

The lifecycle of all unit test classes is exactly the same. You can perform processing before and after the class is created, with additional processing before and after each and every test case:

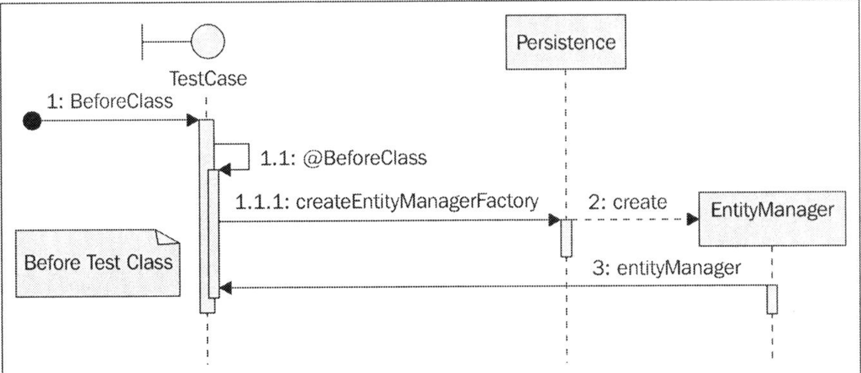

This allows you to instantiate costly objects such as entity managers and database connections once, and share them for all tests cases:

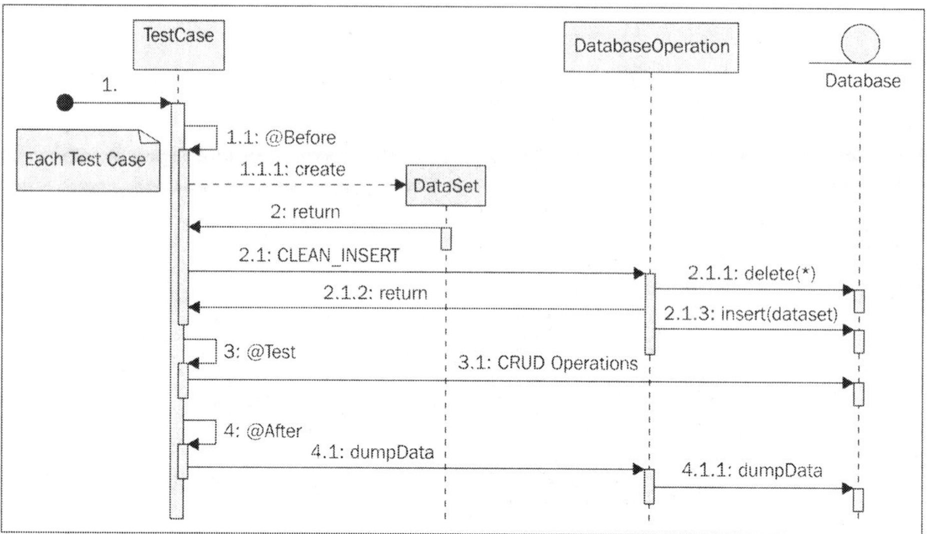

For each test case that is run, you must ensure you have the same starting point as all the other tests. This means that your tests will always be repeatable, no matter what order they are run in. Before we run a test, we are going to clean the database, and re-insert a test dataset. This way we know what we are testing against. After we have performed pre-processing operations, we can run our test. Then, when the test is complete, we can dump the finished data into an SQL file for later review. This can be quite helpful in order to debug issues wherein your data is not what you expected. I usually write this SQL file into the build's output directory, so it is created each time I run my unit tests, and is also deleted every time I run a clean; this way it is not accidentally checked into source control:

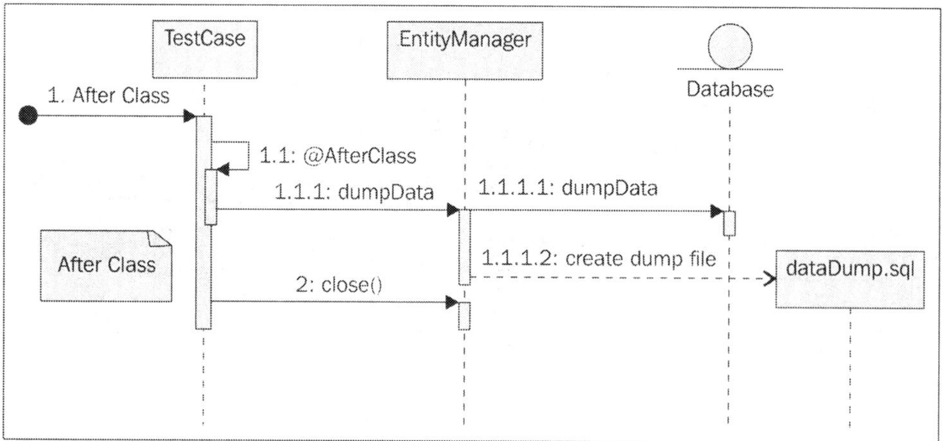

After all the tests have run, you can perform post-processing operations to clean up loose ends. This can include closing entity manager and database connections, creating or deleting SQL dump files, or removing other objects you are finished with.

Getting ready

Getting ready to create a JUnit test and seeding a test database with DBUnit, we need to first import `junit.jar` and `dbunit.jar` into our project. In the case of this recipe, we are going to use the Maven build system:

```
<dependency>
    <groupId>junit</groupId>
    <artifactId>junit</artifactId>
    <version>${junit.version}</version>
    <scope>test</scope>
</dependency>
<dependency>
    <groupId>org.dbunit</groupId>
    <artifactId>dbunit</artifactId>
    <version>${dbunit.version}</version>
    <scope>test</scope>
</dependency>
```

Once we have defined the two dependencies in our `pom.xml` file to ensure we have the JUnit and DBUnit libraries, we only need to add our Surefire plugin which will run all tests:

```
<plugin>
    <groupId>org.apache.maven.plugins</groupId>
    <artifactId>maven-surefire-plugin</artifactId>
    <version>${plugin.surefire.version}</version>
    <inherited>true</inherited>
</plugin>
```

This simple Surefire plugin will run all tests under:

`[project_root]/src/test/java/**`

This is quite simple in Maven by using just the defaults, but if needed, further configuration can be made to do very complex testing patterns.

This recipe builds upon the work done in *Chapter 2, Enterprise Persistence*, so we are assuming we already have our domain objects created, and are basically able to create a Customer entity using EclipseLink. If you need help, the source code for *Chapter 2, Enterprise Persistence*, actually has the Entities, as well as the test selections for this recipe.

A key feature of EclipseLink from *Chapter 2, Enterprise Persistence*, is how it processes the `persistence.xml` file:

```
<property name="eclipselink.ddl-generation" value="drop-and-create-
tables"/>
```

This entry will create your database schema on startup, and drop that database on application shutdown.

DDL generation

In *Chapter 2, Enterprise Persistence*, and in this chapter, examples use drop-and-create tables for the DDL generation mechanism. This is only designed to be used for testing and should not be used in production environments, unless you have a specific use case to do so, because all the existing table structures and the data contained in all tables will be lost.

How to do it...

Assuming we have a valid JPA domain object created, and EclipseLink has been properly configured as per *Chapter 2, Enterprise Persistence*, we are now ready to start this testing recipe.

To begin, we need to create a Java class called `CustomerTest` and because we are using Maven to compile, build, and run our unit tests, we will put these calls in `src/test/java`. This is going to be a common JUnit test class, and uses annotations and signatures you are already familiar with, if you are writing JUnit test cases in your current project.

Step 1: Imports

With the advent of JUnit 4.x, and specifically 4.5+, there are several imports I like to add to each of my tests to import static references, which will make unit tests easier to read and understand the tests intentions.

The following import allows a shorter version of assertions to be used such as `assertNotNull(obj)` versus the longer version `Assert. assertNotNull(obj)`:

```
import static junit.framework.Assert.*;
```

These two imports will allow for a more readable assertion such as `assertThat( someString, is( "Success"))`.

```
import static org.junit.Assert.assertThat;
import static org.hamcrest.CoreMatchers.is;
```

Look at `org.hamcrest.CoreMatchers` for the various methods available for matching.

Step 2: Attributes

There are several attributes that are used by each test case:

```
private static EntityManagerFactory emf;
private static EntityManager em;
public static final String dataSetFile =
      "./src/test/resources/dataset.xml";
public static final String dataSetOutputFile =
      "./target/test-dataset_dump.xml";
public static final String[] nullPrimaryKeyFilters =
      {"ID", "ADDRESS_KEY", "P_NUMBER", "HOBBY_NAME"};
```

Null Primary Key Filter

An important note for using DBUnit is knowing that, when seeding data for your tests, DBUnit does not work well with tables that do not have explicit primary keys such as new `CollectionTables`. This is easily remedied by adding explicit filters to allow for null primary keys in such cases. We will use these filters in our lifecycle methods later in this chapter.

Lifecycle methods

Next, we will create our lifecycle methods that include all before and after lifecycles. These methods are run before and after every Class instantiation, or test run, which ensures consistent test conditions.

The `@BeforeClass` is called when the class is instantiated before anything else occurs:

```
@BeforeClass
public static void initEntityManager() throws Exception {
      emf = Persistence.createEntityManagerFactory
            (Constants. PERSISTENCEUNIT);
      em = emf.createEntityManager();
}
```

At this stage in the lifecycle, we can create the entity manager, which will be used for all the tests in this class. The creation of the entity manager is based on `PERSISTENCEUNIT`. This means that EclipseLink is going to create an instance of our database without any data and it will now be available to all tests.

When all the tests are complete, we need to clean up the `EntityManager` and any other objects we might have created:

```
@AfterClass
public static void closeEntityManager()
    throws SQLException {
      if (em != null) {
          em.close();
      }
```

```
        if (emf != null) {
            emf.close();
        }
}
```

Before each and every unit test, we need to ensure we have consistent data. So, we need to start by seeding our database:

```
@Before
public void initTransaction()
  throws Exception {
      TestUtils.seedData(em,
              dataSetFile,
              nullPrimaryKeyFilters);
}
```

To keep the unit test classes clean, I re-factored most of the DBUnit helper utilities into a separate TestUtils class:

```
public static void seedData(EntityManager em,
                            String dataSetFile,
                            String... nullPrimaryKeyFilters)
        throws Exception {
1   em.getTransaction().begin();
2   Connection connection = em.unwrap(java.sql.Connection.class);

    try {
3       IDatabaseConnection dbUnitCon = new DatabaseConnection(connection);

4       dbUnitCon.getConfig().setProperty(DatabaseConfig.PROPERTY_DATATYPE_FACTORY,
                new H2DataTypeFactory());

        if (nullPrimaryKeyFilters != null && nullPrimaryKeyFilters.length > 0) {
            // Set the property by passing the new IColumnFilter
5           dbUnitCon.getConfig().setProperty(
                    DatabaseConfig.PROPERTY_PRIMARY_KEY_FILTER,
                    new NullPrimaryKeyFilter(nullPrimaryKeyFilters));
        }

        IDataSet dataSet = getDataSet(dataSetFile);
6
        DatabaseOperation.CLEAN_INSERT.execute(dbUnitCon, dataSet);
    } catch (Exception exc) {
        exc.printStackTrace();
    } finally {
7       em.getTransaction().commit();
        connection.close();
    }
}
```

Let's go through this utility to describe in detail the important operation that is initiated:

1. Before we start any database operations, we need to begin a new database transaction.
2. DBUnit requires a `java.sql.Connection`, and we need to get a valid instance from the `EntityManager`.
3. We now create a DBUnit `IDatabaseConnection`, wrapping the `java.sql.Connection`.
4. Based on the database type you are using, we need to create a database type factory for our DBUnit operations. This allows for proper data type conversion for the database you are using.
5. If there are any DBUnit-specific properties that need to be set before the DBUnit start, we need to add them now. In this case, the addition of any Primary Key Filters is needed.
6. Based on the test data file, we need to create an `IDataSet`, and then perform `CLEAN_INSERT`.
7. At the end of seeding our database, we need to commit the transaction and close the `java.sql.Connection` we created.

<dataset>

Now we can start creating a test data to test against:

```
<?xml version='1.0' encoding='UTF-8'?>
<dataset>
    <CUSTOMER id='100100' USERNAME="user1" FIRSTNAME="Mick"
LASTNAME="Knutson"/>

    <HOBBIES CUST_ID="100200" HOBBY_NAME="BASE-Jumping"/>
    <HOBBIES CUST_ID="100200" HOBBY_NAME="Skydiving"/>

    <PHONES AREACODE="415" PHONE_NUMBER="5551212" TYPE="WORK" CUST_
ID="100200"/>

    <CUST_ADDRESSES ADDRESS_KEY="PRIMARY" CITY="Exton"
                    POSTCODE="91335"
                    PROVINCE=""
                    STATE="PA" STREET="555 Main Street"
                    STREET2="Suite 101" TYPE="RESIDENTIAL"
                    CUST_ID="100200"/>
</dataset>
```

To create a test data to be inserted by DBUnit, we can start by creating an XML tag per domain object. In this case, there is a single `CUSTOMER` tag with all the fields we want this domain to possess. You can add additional domain objects, and have those additional objects reference parent domain objects. In this way, testing relationships can be quite easy.

<dataset> ordering

It is worth noting that the `<dataset>` domain object ordering is very important, as DBUnit processes this file from top to bottom. Thus, you must define parent objects first, and followed by child objects. The aforementioned code creates a `CUSTOMER` first, then creates the customer address object, which references `CUSTOMER` via `CUST_ID`.

Step 3: Unit testing

We now have everything in place to create unit tests that can create, read, update, and delete data from our database.

To begin database operations, a transaction must begin the initiation CRUD operations, and then commit the transaction:

```
em.getTransaction().begin();

// Creates an instance of Customer
Customer customer = CustomerFixture.createSingleCustomer();

// Persists the Customer to the database
em.persist(customer);
em.getTransaction().commit();

assertNotNull("ID should not be null", customer.getId());
```

From a testing perspective, this gives the tester ability to begin a transaction, perform some database interactions, then commit the changes that should be durable during the scope of this unit test.

There's more...

Similar to seeding data into a database for testing, you can also dump data after a unit test for review and validation:

```
IDataSet dataSet = dbUnitCon.createDataSet();

FileOutputStream fos =
     new FileOutputStream(dataSetOutputFile);
FlatXmlDataSet.write(dataSet, fos);
fos.close();
```

This is especially helpful with operations such as update timestamps, and other insert and update operations, where manual validation can be useful for debugging purposes.

Multiple databases

Sometimes, with testing, it can be useful to test against more than one database:

```
<persistence-unit name="DERBY_PU" ...>
    ...
    <properties>
        <property
            name="eclipselink.target-database"
            value="DERBY"/>
        ...
        <property
            name="javax.persistence.jdbc.driver"
            value="org.apache.derby.jdbc.EmbeddedDriver"/>
        <property
            name="javax.persistence.jdbc.url"
            value="jdbc:derby:memory:chapter02DB;create=true"/>
        <property
            name="javax.persistence.jdbc.user" value="APP"/>
        <property
            name="javax.persistence.jdbc.password" value="APP"/>
    </properties>
</persistence-unit>
```

It is easiest to create another unit test class, and then use `Persistence.createEntityManagerFactory("DERBY_UNIT")` in the `@BeforeClass` initialize, to use this alternative persistence unit.

See also

- *Chapter 2, Enterprise Persistence*
- *Apache Maven*: `http://maven.apache.org`
- *DBUnit*: `http://dbunit.org`
- *DBUnit Primary Key Filter*: `http://www.dbunit.org/apidocs/org/dbunit/database/PrimaryKeyFilter.html`

Using Mock objects for testing

In order to properly execute a unit test, you must be able to create an isolated unit of work that can be measured in isolation. When you are attempting to isolate portions of a Java EE application, you quickly find there are many supporting services and external systems that a Java EE application requires, but which can interfere with isolation. In order to enforce test isolation, you can introduce Stubs and Mocks into your tests. In the recipe for DBUnit testing, we saw how there can be many complexities in seeding data for external systems such as databases, to ensure consistent and reliable tests. Introducing Mock objects can aid in reducing the complexity of testing, and help foster isolated testing.

This recipe is going to focus on a pattern to utilize Mock object, or 'Mocks' in order to facilitate test isolation. There are many popular Mock frameworks such as EasyMock, JMock, and many others, but this recipe is going to focus on a framework called Mockito (`http://mockito.org`) as well as Powermock (`http://code.google.com/p/powermock/`) to add support for static and private method testing.

Getting ready

To begin this recipe, you first need to include the Mockito and Powermock JARs into your Maven project's `pom.xml` file, similar to this:

```
<dependency>
    <groupId>org.mockito</groupId>
    <artifactId>mockito-all</artifactId>
    <version>${mockito.version}</version>
    <scope>test</scope>
</dependency>

<dependency>
    <groupId>org.powermock</groupId>
    <artifactId>powermock-api-mockito</artifactId>
    <version>${powermock.version}</version>
    <scope>test</scope>
</dependency>

<dependency>
    <groupId>org.powermock</groupId>
    <artifactId>powermock-module-junit4</artifactId>
    <version>${powermock.version}</version>
    <scope>test</scope>
</dependency>
```

We are now ready to start writing Mock test cases.

How to do it...

To start from the beginning, create a test class to run our first Mockito JUnit test such as the following:

```
public class OrderMockServiceTests {}
```

The next thing we need to do is add some imports to allow easy use and readability of our tests, as shown here:

```
// Hamcrest_____
import static org.hamcrest.Matchers.*;
import static org.hamcrest.MatcherAssert.assertThat;

// JUnit_____
// use MatcherAssert.assertThat instead
//import static org.junit.Assert.*;
import org.junit.After;
import org.junit.Before;
import org.junit.Test;
import org.junit.runner.RunWith;

// Mockito_____
import static org.mockito.Matchers.any;
import static org.mockito.Mockito.*;
import org.mockito.runners.MockitoJUnitRunner;
import org.mockito.stubbing.Answer;
import org.mockito.InjectMocks;
import org.mockito.Mock;
import org.mockito.MockitoAnnotations;
import org.mockito.invocation.InvocationOnMock;
import org.mockito.stubbing.Answer;

// PowerMock_____
import org.powermock.api.mockito.PowerMockito;
import org.powermock.core.classloader.annotations.PrepareForTest;
import org.powermock.core.classloader.annotations.
SuppressStaticInitializationFor;
import org.powermock.modules.junit4.PowerMockRunner;
```

Adding static reference to Hamcrest matchers, JUnit assertions, Mockito, and Powermock methods will allow for more legible unit tests.

First we are going to use Mockito as the JUnit runner for this test:

```
@RunWith(MockitoJUnitRunner.class)
public class OrderMockServiceTests {}
```

Next, we need to create an instance of our Mock object; creating a global instance and recreating the Mock for each test ensures our test will always have a fresh Mock:

```
@InjectMocks private OrderServiceImpl classUnderTest;

@Mock private OrderDAO supportingDao;
```

Here, we create a member variable for our class under test `OrderServiceImpl` and annotate it with `@InjectMocks` which tells Mockito that this class will need to have one or more supporting Mock objects injected into it at the beginning of the unit test.

Then, we create a member variable, annotated by `@Mock`, for the Mock that we are using for this unit test, to tell Mockito that this variable is eligible for injection into the `@InjectMocks` class under test.

We then need to tell Mockito to create an instance of the class under test, and inject all Mock objects into it before each unit test by initializing Mocks:

```
@Before
public void setup() {
    MockitoAnnotations.initMocks(this);
}
```

Now that we have set up the class under test and Mock objects, we can begin writing individual test cases.

Let's go through how we will create a simple Mock interaction between our class under test and our Mock.

First, let's understand the role of the Mock by looking at the method we want to isolate and test, in our class under test:

```
public Order placeOrder(Order order){
    return orderDao.placeOrder(order);
}
```

Here, we have a method inside our `OrderServiceImpl` class, which takes an order as a parameter, then calls `OrderDao` with that order, to place the order. The main point is that in isolation, we don't care what actually happens in `OrderDao`, all that we are concerned with is the type—if `OrderDao` accepts any, and what `orderDao` returns. With that information, we can begin to simulate the inputs and expected outputs for the Mock `OrderDao`.

Step 1:

Create an `Order` object which we expect `OrderDao` to receive when it is called:

```
// Control input
Order orderInput = new Order();
orderInput.setDescription("Mick's Order");
```

Step 2:

Create an `Order` object which we expect `OrderDao` to return when it is called:

```
// Control Sample
Order orderOutput = new Order();
orderOutput.setDescription("Someone Else's Order");
```

Step 3:

Define expected behavior for the Mock when the class under test interacts with it. We want to instruct the Mock that it should expect to be called with `Order.class`, then we expect it to return the `orderOutput` object we created as a return control sample:

```
// Create Mock Behavior
when(supportingDao.placeOrder(any(Order.class)))
    .thenReturn(orderOutput);
```

Step 4:

Now we will execute the class under test's place order method, using the `orderInput` object we created as a return control sample:

```
// execute class under test
Order resultOrder =
    classUnderTest.placeOrder(orderInput);
```

Step 5:

We can now perform assertions on the returned object to determine whether the object returned was the expected object:

```
assertThat(resultOrder.getDescription(),
    is("Someone Else's Order"));
```

We expect `orderOutput` to be the order object that was returned.

Step 6:

We need to verify the Mock `OrderDao` object was actually called in the manner you expected:

```
// Verify behavior for supporting were executed
verify(supportingDao).placeOrder(any(Order.class));
```

At this point we have successfully written our first Mock test case.

How it works...

What is really happening under the covers? Mockito is creating an instance of the dependent class you want to Mock, and based on the instructions on how the mock should behave, Mockito will play back the instructions you have defined:

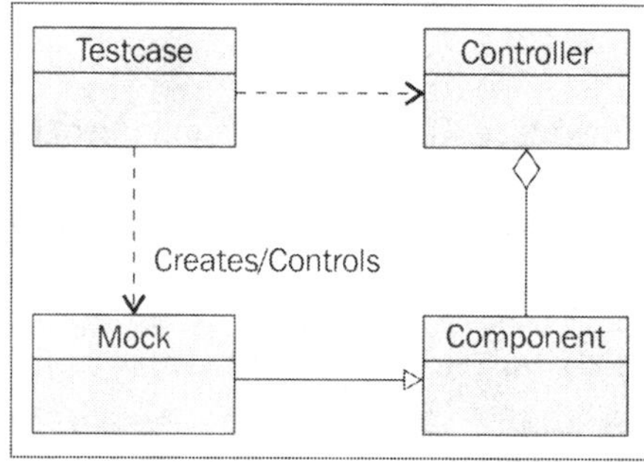

Testing successful scenarios is usually the first task for developers; you must also be diligent about testing, this should include testing failure scenarios.

There's more...

As seen above, mocking of custom objects and objects that are not available can simplify testing, and in some cases is the only way testing in isolation is possible.

Mocking a custom object is not the only use case for Mocking and any non-final class or interface can be mocked.

Mocking all object types

Mockito is not limited to just the custom objects that you have created. You can mock any type of object, including Java EE components as shown in the following listing:

```
@Mock HttpServletRequest servletRequest;
@Mock HttpSession httpSession;
when(servletRequest.getSession())
    .thenReturn(httpSession);
```

Here we mock `HttpServletRequest` to send back a mocked HttpSession when called. This is an important concept because many Java EE objects are interfaces, and Mockito will create an implementation of the interface for you.

Simulating service delays

Another common scenario is to simulate the service that delays longer than a given period of time. You can achieve this by adding a custom answer to be returned during the mock interaction with a call to the `thenAnswer()` method:

```
when(mockService.lookupAppointment
    (any(AppointmentRequest.class)))
    .thenAnswer(delayedAnswerWithObject(response, 10000));


Future<Object> future =
    controller.queryAppointment
    ("12345", new Request());
```

You can externalize the creation of a custom `Answer` with a simple static utility:

```
public static Answer delayedAnswerWithObject
  (final Object o, final long delay) {
      return new Answer() {
          @Override
          public Object answer(InvocationOnMock invocation)
            throws Throwable {
                Thread.sleep(delay);
                return o;
            }
      };
}
```

This will simply put the current thread to sleep for a given delay.

```
@Override
public Object answer(InvocationOnMock invocation) throws Throwable {
    try {
          Thread.sleep(delay);
    }
    catch (InterruptedException e) {
          if (throwExceptions) {
```

```
                throw e;
            }
        }
        return o;
}
```

The mock answer that is created might need to catch various exceptions and, as shown in the previous code listing, are re-thrown. It is also possible to consume, or ignore these exceptions in certain situations, and because this answer is a mock, we can control object attributes without changing the class under test.

Partial Mocking

In a scenario wherein a class under test has a supporting method it calls, which you want to isolate from the test, a partial Mock that will only Mock the method described in behavior can be created.

Step 1:

Create a new instance of the class under test, using the Spy feature of Mockito, to allow Mockito to spy into an object and add custom behavior:

```
OrderServiceImpl partialMock = spy(classUnderTest);
```

Step 2:

Define the expected behavior for the partial mock:

```
when(partialMock.getMessage())
    .thenReturn("partially mocked message");
```

Again, we want to control the returned value from a Mock method call with a customer String.

Step 3:

Now we will execute the class under test's place order method using the `orderInput` object we created as a return control sample:

```
String partialResult = partialMock.getProxiedMessage();
```

Step 4:

We can now perform assertions on the returned object to determine whether the object returned was the expected object or not:

```
assertThat(partialResult, is("partially mocked message"));
```

Step 5:

We need to verify the Mock was actually called in the manner you expected:

```
verify(partialMock).getMessage();
```

Mocking exception scenarios

Instructing a Mock to throw an exception is just a matter of instructing the behavior of the Mock to throw an exception instead of returning a value type:

```
when(supportingUtils.nestedFunction())
    .thenThrow(new RuntimeException("mock Exception"));
```

Mocking methods returning void

When a method to be mocked does not return a value it is denoted as returning void, which is `Void.class`. In order to mock this type of method, you can define the Mock behavior to do nothing when it is called:

```
doNothing()
    .when(supportingUtils)
    .voidMethod();
```

You can also add behavior to have a void method throw an exception:

```
doThrow(new RuntimeException
  ("void stubbed method exception"))
     .when(supportingUtils)
     .voidMethod();
```

Multiple interactions with a Mock

Sometimes you have a Mock that will be called multiple times, and each time the Mock is called, we want the Mock to return a different value. This behavior is going to have three different values returned for three subsequent calls to the Mock:

```
when(supportingUtils.nestedFunction())
    .thenReturn("1st mocked message")
    .thenReturn("2nd mocked message")
    .thenReturn("nth mocked message");
```

The first time the Mock is called, it returns "1st mocked message", the second time it is called, it returns "2nd mocked message", and the third and subsequent time this mock is called, it returns "nth mocked message".

Ensuring Mocks called in order

Another common situation involves testing a method which makes multiple, different Mock calls and we want to ensure the Mocks get called in the correct order.

To accomplish this, we set up the Mock behavior as we normally would for our test:

```
when(supportingUtils.nestedFunction())
    .thenReturn("1st mocked message");

when(supportingUtils.nestedFunctionTwo())
    .thenReturn("Another mock being called");
```

Next, we need to create an ordered container, so Mockito can keep track of the ordered calls to the Mock:

```
InOrder inOrder = inOrder(supportingUtils);
```

Then execute the class under test:

```
String result = classUnderTest.callsFunctionInOrder();
```

Now, assert which Mocks should be called in what order:

```
// nestedFunction() should have been called first
    inOrder.verify(supportingUtils).nestedFunction();

// nestedFunctionTwo() should have been called first
    inOrder.verify(supportingUtils).nestedFunctionTwo();
```

Mocking static methods

Another tricky situation is isolating the static method calls in a method under test. Take the following listing for example:

```
public Object staticFunctions(){
    Object object;
    try {

      Object result =
        ExampleUtils.staticFunction(); // Static Call

    } catch (Exception e){
```

```
        logger.error( e.getMessage() );
    }

    return object;
}
```

We see that there is a static call which returns an object, and can also throw an Exception when called.

To mock a static method call, we need to use Powermock to provide the functionality.

It is recommended to keep all tests that require static mocks separate from the ones that only require Mockito. This is because Powermock requires more memory to process static classes than Mockito needs for mocking instance classes. This allows you to easily isolate the types of tests, and manage the test lifecycle in your build.

In order to begin, we need to decorate the unit test with `PowerMockRunner.class` instead of `MockitoJUnitRunner.class`:

```
@RunWith(PowerMockRunner.class)
@PrepareForTest(
  { ExampleUtils.class, OrderServiceImpl.class })
public class OrderPowerMockServiceTests {
...
```

The previous listing tells JUnit to use `PowerMockRunner.class` to run the entire test class of tests. Then the `@PrepareForTest` annotation tells the `PowerMockRunner.class` to prepare a list of classes to have the behavioral instructions for testing added to them. This is different than using the `@Mock` annotation because we will not have an instance of the class available for testing, so the `@PrepareForTest` annotation can be thought of as creating the Mock placeholder.

We then continue to set up Mockito Mock objects in the same way, as in the previous examples.

Let's go step-by-step to see how to mock a static call, and then look at the complete unit test:

Step 1:

We begin with a standard JUnit `@Test` method, afterwhich we need to instruct Powermock to mock the static methods present in the class we want to mock:

```
@Test
 public void staticMock() throws Exception {

PowerMockito.mockStatic(ExampleUtils.class);
```

Step 2:

Create the behavior expected when the Mock is called during the test:

```
when(ExampleUtils.staticFunction())
    .thenReturn("some static mocked value");
```

Step 3:

Execute the class under test:

```
String result = classUnderTest.staticFunctions();
```

Step 4:

Perform any assertions on the values that the class under test returns:

```
assertThat(result, is
    ("OrderServiceImpl:
    function():
    some static mocked value:
    staticFunction"));
```

Step 5:

Lastly, and most importantly, you must have Powermock verify each mocked static call before you can execute another mocked static call:

```
PowerMockito.verifyStatic();
```

This might seem like a limitation if you are confronting a method that has more than one static call in it. In such a situation, we can refactor the method under test into a more cohesive design and avoid this problem altogether.

This is what our final test method would look like:

```
@Test
public void staticMock() throws Exception {

  PowerMockito.mockStatic(ExampleUtils.class);

  when(ExampleUtils.staticFunction())
 .thenReturn("some static mocked value");

  String result =
 classUnderTest.staticFunctions();

  assertThat(result, is
 ("OrderServiceImpl:
 function():
 some static mocked value: staticFunction"));

  PowerMockito.verifyStatic();
}
```

Mocking private methods

One of the most difficult mock testing patterns is isolating private methods. Let's look at a method we want to test, which calls two different private methods:

```
public String executeInternalPrivate(){
  String result = "OrderServiceImpl: executeInternalPrivate()";
  result += ": " + privateFunction();
  result += ": " + privateFunction("privateFunction");
  return result;
}

private String privateFunction() {
  return "OrderServiceImpl: privateFunction";
}

private String privateFunction(String privateString) {
  return "OrderServiceImpl: privateFunction: " + privateString;
}
```

In our test, we want to isolate the following two private method calls:

- `private String privateFunction();`
- `private String privateFunction(String privateString);`

Using the same test class as the previous example, we already have Powermock set up and ready to run our tests. Let's go step-by-step to see how to mock the two private calls, and then look at the complete unit test:

Step 1:

We are going to create a partial mock of the class under test, which we will be mocking:

```
OrderServiceImpl classUnderTest =
  PowerMockito.spy(new OrderServiceImpl());
```

Step 2:

We will then add the expected behavior to a private class called `privateFunction`, which does not take any arguments:

```
PowerMockito.doReturn
  ("private string with no params")
  .when(classUnderTest, "privateFunction");
```

Powermock uses this String-based name for the method we intend to mock, because Powermock will use reflection at runtime to see this private method, and then add the desired behavior.

We also add behavior to a private method which takes any String as an argument:

```
PowerMockito.doReturn
  ("some altered private string")
  .when(classUnderTest, "privateFunction", anyString());
```

Step 3:

Execute the class under test:

```
String result =
  classUnderTest.executeInternalPrivate();
```

Step 4:

Perform any assertions on the values that the class under test returns:

```
assertThat(result, is
  ("OrderServiceImpl:
  executeInternalPrivate():
  private string with no params:
  some altered private string"));
```

Step 5:

Unlike verifying static calls, where we are required to verify one call at a time, mocking a private method is the same as mocking an instance method where we can ask Powermock to verify whether the private method was called:

```
PowerMockito.verifyPrivate
  (classUnderTest, times(1))
  .invoke("privateFunction");
```

We also can verify whether private methods were called with different arguments:

```
PowerMockito.verifyPrivate
  (classUnderTest, times(1))
  .invoke("privateFunction", anyString());
```

The following is what our final test method would look like:

```
@Test
public void privatePartialMock()
  throws Exception {

     OrderServiceImpl classUnderTest =
    PowerMockito.spy(new OrderServiceImpl());

      // use PowerMockito to set up your expectation
```

```
        PowerMockito.doReturn
          ("private string with no params")
          .when(classUnderTest, "privateFunction");

        PowerMockito.doReturn
          ("some altered private string")
          .when(classUnderTest, "privateFunction", anyString());

        // execute your test
        String result =
          classUnderTest.executeInternalPrivate();

        assertThat(result, is
          ("OrderServiceImpl:
          executeInternalPrivate():
          private string with no params:
          some altered private string"));

        // Use PowerMockito.verify() to verify result
        PowerMockito.verifyPrivate
          (classUnderTest, times(1))
          .invoke("privateFunction");

        PowerMockito.verifyPrivate
          (classUnderTest, times(1))
          .invoke("privateFunction", anyString());
    }
```

As you can see, using Mocks can be a powerful tool to help increase test code coverage and isolate components.

See also

- *EasyMock*: `http://easymock.org`
- *Mockito*: `http://mockito.org`
- *Powermock*: `http://code.google.com/p/powermock/`

Testing HTTP endpoints with Selenium

In order to test web application services, such as JSP and JSF pages that are dynamically generated, you need to deploy those artefacts to a Java EE or Servlet container in order to test them. While manual testing of page content is possible, automating this task will greatly increase the development lifecycle, and it will also reduce errors in validating repeated test cycles to ensure consistent test results.

In order to automate web-based testing, you need to employ a mechanism in which a test will simulate web navigation, and input and result validation for given scenarios. The Selenium test runner comes to the rescue. Selenium allows a serial set of web integration instructions to be executed on a given URL, and asserts rules to determine the expected outcomes for a scenario or a functional path defined.

Selenium can also test HTTP endpoints, such as REST services that are local or remote. It is possible to create a suite of tests that perform deployment validation of applications for QA as well as production environment, so you have quite a bit of flexibility.

Getting ready

There are a few steps involved to integrate Selenium into your build. There are several different ways you can run Selenium. Some of the alternative possibilities are to run either an embedded application server within the build process, or have a local or remote application server running with the application under test, and then run the Selenium tests. In this recipe, we will be using an embedded application server running the application under test.

Dependencies

There are several dependencies that will be required in order to run Selenium tests. You will need JUnit for running your tests. Also, you will need `selenium-server`, which creates your remote control test server, and lastly, you will need a Selenium Java client driver, which will specifically allow you to run JUnit-based test cases.

We first start by adding the following dependencies to your Maven `pom.xml` file:

```
<dependency>
    <groupId>junit</groupId>
    <artifactId>junit</artifactId>
    <version>${junit.version}</version>
    <scope>test</scope>
</dependency>
<dependency>
    <groupId>org.hamcrest</groupId>
    <artifactId>hamcrest-all</artifactId>
    <version>${hamcrest.version}</version>
    <scope>test</scope>
</dependency>
<dependency>
    <groupId>org.seleniumhq.selenium.server</groupId>
    <artifactId>selenium-server</artifactId>
    <version>${selenium.server.version}</version>
    <scope>test</scope>
</dependency>
```

```
<dependency>
    <groupId>org.seleniumhq.selenium.client-drivers</groupId>
    <artifactId>selenium-java-client-driver</artifactId>
    <version>${selenium.client.version}</version>
    <scope>test</scope>
    <exclusions>
        <exclusion>
            <groupId>org.openqa.selenium.server</groupId>
            <artifactId>selenium-server</artifactId>
        </exclusion>
    </exclusions>
</dependency>
```

This is all that's required to run Selenium.

Application server

In order for Selenium to test a web application, the application must be running in a web container; Selenium will interact with live pages in order to perform testing. To do this, we can use an embedded application server, which we will start before our integration test phase, and deploy our application to that server. Once the integration test phase is complete, we will underfloor the application and stop the server:

```
<plugin>
    <groupId>org.glassfish</groupId>
    <artifactId>
        maven-embedded-glassfish-plugin
    </artifactId>
    <version>
        ${glassfish.embedded.plugin.version}
    </version>
    <configuration>
        <app>
            ${project.build.directory}/
              ${project.build.finalName}.war
        </app>
        <port>
            ${glassfish.domain.port}
        </port>
        <contextRoot>
            ${project.build.finalName}
        </contextRoot>
        <autoDelete>true</autoDelete>
    </configuration>
    <executions>
```

```
            <execution>
                <id>start-glassfish</id>
                <phase>pre-integration-test</phase>
                <goals>
                    <goal>start</goal>
                    <goal>deploy</goal>
                </goals>
            </execution>
            <execution>
                <id>glassfish-undeploy</id>
                <phase>post-integration-test</phase>
                <goals>
                    <goal>undeploy</goal>
                    <goal>stop</goal>
                </goals>
            </execution>
        </executions>
    </plugin>
```

JUnit

We need to configure Surefire to run Selenium tests only during the integration test phase, so we can ensure our application is ready:

```
    <plugin>
        <groupId>
            org.apache.maven.plugins
        </groupId>
        <artifactId>
            maven-surefire-plugin
        </artifactId>
        <version>
            ${plugin.surefire.version}
        </version>
        <configuration>
            <argLine>
                -Xmx256m -DuseSystemClassLoader=true
            </argLine>
            <testFailureIgnore>
                True
            </testFailureIgnore>
            <excludes>
                <exclude>**/selenium/*</exclude>
            </excludes>
        </configuration>
        <executions>
```

```
        <execution>
            <id>integration-tests</id>
            <phase>integration-test</phase>
            <goals>
                <goal>test</goal>
            </goals>
            <configuration>
                <includes>
                    <include>**/selenium/*</include>
                </includes>
            </configuration>
        </execution>
    </executions>
</plugin>
```

Selenium

Selenium has a great plugin to run your tests within a defined Maven build lifecycle. The goal of the plugin is to define the execution phase in which you want to run a Selenium server:

```
<plugin>
    <groupId>org.codehaus.mojo</groupId>
    <artifactId>selenium-maven-plugin</artifactId>
    <version>${plugin-selenium-version}</version>
    <executions>
        <execution>
            <phase>pre-integration-test</phase>
            <goals>
                <goal>start-server</goal>
            </goals>
            <configuration>
                <background>true</background>
                <logOutput>true</logOutput>
            </configuration>
        </execution>
        <execution>
            <id>stop</id>
            <phase>post-integration-test</phase>
            <goals>
                <goal>stop-server</goal>
            </goals>
        </execution>
    </executions>
</plugin>
```

At this point, we have our dependencies and an application server, a Selenium server, and Surefire configured to run in a pre- and post-integration test, and during the integration test phase of a Maven build:

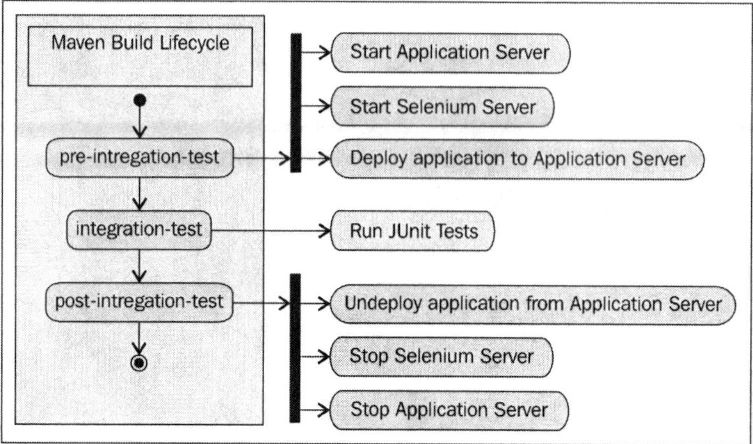

We can now start writing our first Selenium test cases.

How to do it...

To begin with, we need to create a Java Selenium controller which will interact with the Selenium server that needs to be started. In the following listing, we will create a helper method that will initialize the Selenium server and start the controller, making it available for remote controlling:

```
public static DefaultSelenium init() {
    logger.info("*** Starting selenium client driver ...");

    DefaultSelenium defaultSelenium =
      new DefaultSelenium
      (SeleniumConfig.getSeleniumServerHostName(),
      SeleniumConfig.getSeleniumServerPort(),
      "*" + SeleniumConfig.getTargetBrowser(),
      http://
      + SeleniumConfig.getApplicationServerHostName()
      + ":"
      + SeleniumConfig.getApplicationServerPort()
      + "/");
    defaultSelenium.start();
    return defaultSelenium;
}

public static void destroy(Selenium selenium){
    selenium.stop();
}
```

In order to create a Selenium client driver, we need to know the Selenium server hostname, port, and the target browser to be used for the testing. The Selenium client controls the target application based on the test scenarios. In the previous example, the Selenium configuration is externalized, which will allow more flexibility with configuring the Selenium client driver at runtime. Here is what the Selenium configuration looks like:

```
public class SeleniumConfig {
    private static String seleniumServerHostName = "localhost";
    private static int seleniumServerPort = 4444;
    private static String applicationServerHostName = "localhost";
    private static int applicationServerPort = 8888;
    private static String targetBrowser = "firefox";
```

For each test class, you can create one Selenium client driver and reuse it for every test you are running. To do this, we initialize the client driver in `@BeforeClass` and stop the server in the `@AfterClass` method:

```
protected Selenium selenium;

@BeforeClass
public static void beforeClass() throws Exception{
    selenium = SeleniumTestHelper.init();
}

@AfterClass
public static void destroy(){
    SeleniumTestHelper.destroy(selenium);
}
```

Now, writing the unit test becomes very straightforward. In the following code snippet, we will open an HTTP resource or page, wait for the page to load, then assert a response containing the desired content:

```
@Test
public void testUserResource() throws Exception {
    selenium.open("/ch03/services/customers/mickknutson");
    selenium.waitForPageToLoad("3000");
    assertTrue(selenium.isTextPresent
      ("<postCode>94110</postCode>"));
}
```

In the previous listing, we call `selenium.open()` to the application context to open the page under test. Next we call `selenium.waitForPageToLoad()` and wait 300 milliseconds to ensure the page loads completely before continuing with the test. At this point, there are a multitude of different options for validating the responses for each page, as well as controlling the next interaction.

When Selenium runs, it will open up one browser which is the test overview screen:

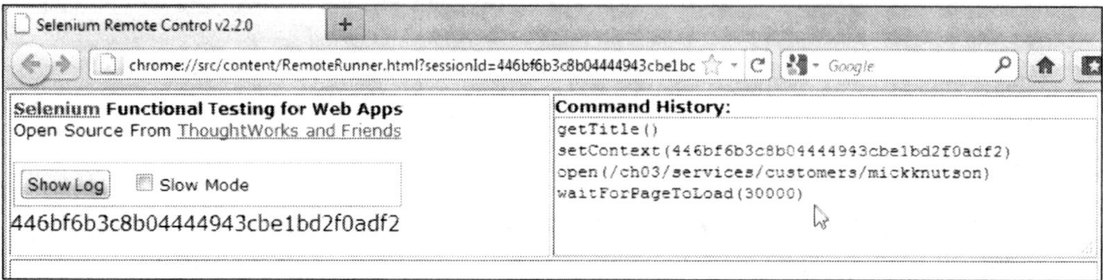

Selenium will open another browser window to execute the commands of your test:

http://localhost:88...stomers/mickknutson
http://localhost:8888/ch03/services/customers/mickknutson
This XML file does not appear to have any style information associated with it. The document tree is shown belo
- <Customer>
- <addresses>
- <entry>
<key>359</key>
- <value>
<city>359.1193162112837</city>
<postCode>94114</postCode>
<state>CA</state>
<street>359.95312199704114</street>
<type>RESIDENTIAL</type>
</value>
</entry>
</addresses>

How it works...

In order to run a Selenium test, you need to have a Selenium server running which launches and kills browsers, interprets and runs test commands from your tests, and acts as a proxy to verify the interaction between your tests and your browser commands that are executed. The following diagram shows the interaction between the unit test, the Selenium server, the web application under test, and the web browser that interacts with the test web application:

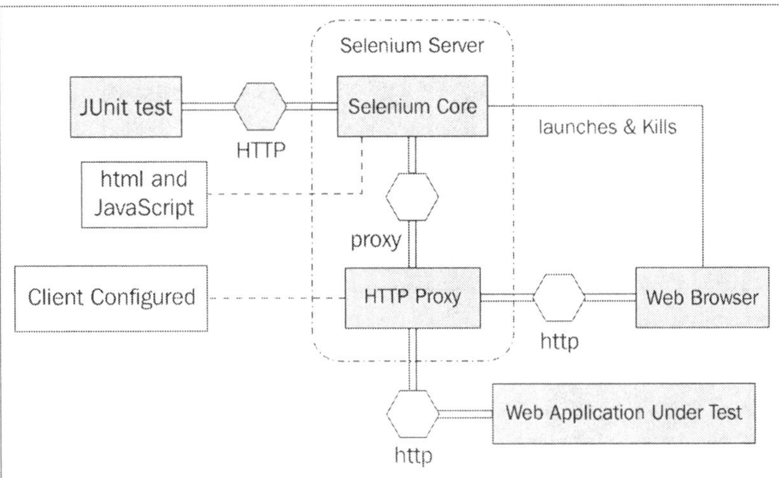

There's more...

If your goal is to test web-based applications with Selenium, Selenium IDE is a Firefox plugin that will allow you to navigate your page while recording the steps. You can then export those recordings as a Selenium test case. This can be a huge timesaver.

WebDriver integration

Selenium now supports integration with WebDriver, which is a compact tool that allows easier integration with browser-based applications. You can review migration tips and other differences at `http://seleniumhq.org/docs/appendix_migrating_from_rc_to_webdriver.html`.

There are some issues trying to validate XML passed to pages, so this will be more for HTML-based pages.

See also

- *Selenium*: `http://seleniumhq.org/`
- *Documentation*: `http://seleniumhq.org/docs/03_webdriver.html`
- *Javadocs*: `http://selenium.googlecode.com/svn/trunk/docs/api/java/index.html`
- *Selenium IDE*: `http://seleniumhq.org/docs/02_selenium_ide.html`

Testing JAX-WS and JAX-RS with soapUI

soapUI is a cross-platform function testing solution for SOAP, REST, Web, JDBC, and much more. soapUI also has the capability to test for security vulnerabilities such as XML Bomb, SQL Injection, Malformed XML-testing, and many other types of scans. soapUI allows you to create and execute any functional, regression, and loads tests in minutes.

There is an open source edition named "soapUI", and a professional edition named "soapUI Pro". The professional edition has additional wizard forms for the interface, provides test data integration, and extended reporting capabilities.

This recipe will focus on how to use soapUI as a functional testing tool. It will cover testing REST and SOAP services. This recipe will also cover creating test cases and integrating Mocks into tests. Finally, the recipe will cover extending soapUI with Groovy scripting for added functionality and logging.

Getting ready

soapUI is a Java-based application and is available with or without a **Java Runtime Engine** (**JRE**). This recipe assumes the target machine has soapUI or soapUI Pro installed and running.

soapUI works similarly to the Eclipse IDE, where the application has a workspace that can consist of one or more projects. When soapUI is started, choose a workspace location that will be used for the projects in this recipe.

How to do it...

Open soapUI with a new workspace, then we will explore creating a RESTful service first, and continue with a SOAP service next:

Testing RESTful services

soapUI comes with an extensive support for testing WADL-based RESTFul services. We will begin with testing a REST-based service.

1. First, we create a new project from the context menu located at **File | New soapUI Project**.
2. On the **New soapUI Project** dialog box, enter a unique project name and select the **Add REST Service** option as shown in the following listing:

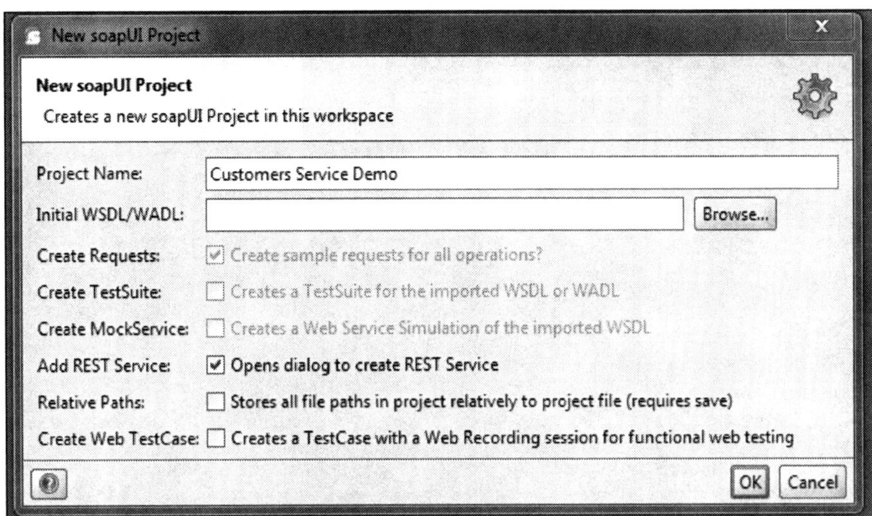

3. Click on the **OK** button to create the new project.
4. After creating the project, a dialog window will appear; it requires input for the REST service this project will be interacting with.
5. Enter a unique service name, and for the service endpoint, we need to enter the fully qualified URI for the REST service; include any optional query parameters inside curly braces.

   The following screenshot depicts a **Customers Service Demo** service, with a **username** query parameter:

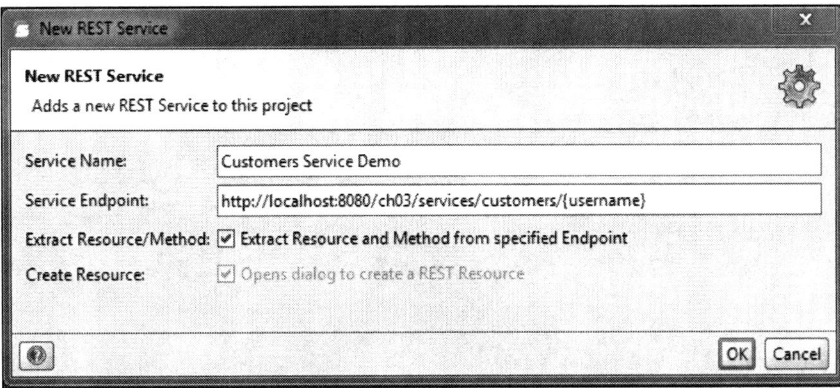

6. Clicking the **OK** button will automatically extract the **username** query argument from the endpoint and display a dialog with the new REST resource for this service:

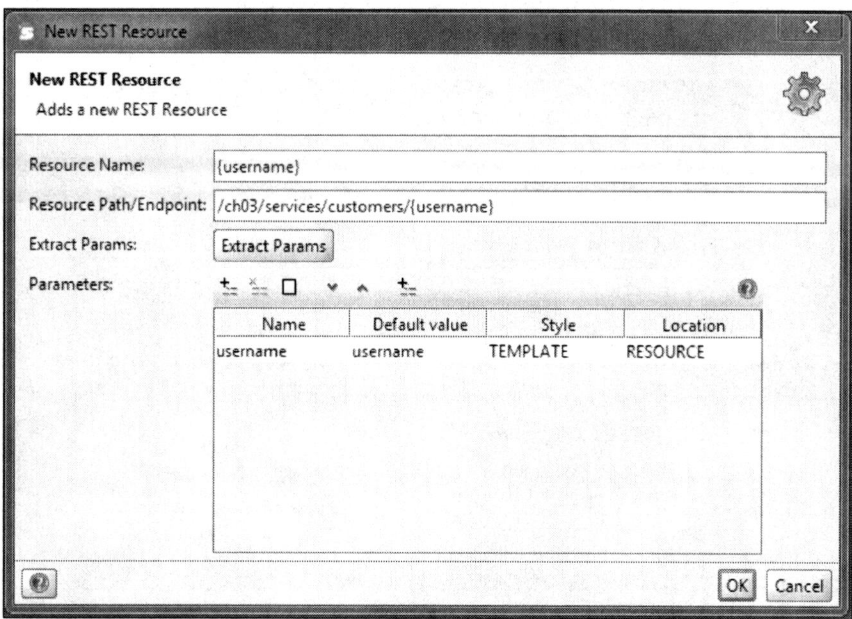

In this example, there are no additional parameters, but if one were required, it can be added.

7. Press the **OK** button to create the initial request to the new REST service and open a request editor form, as shown in the following screenshot:

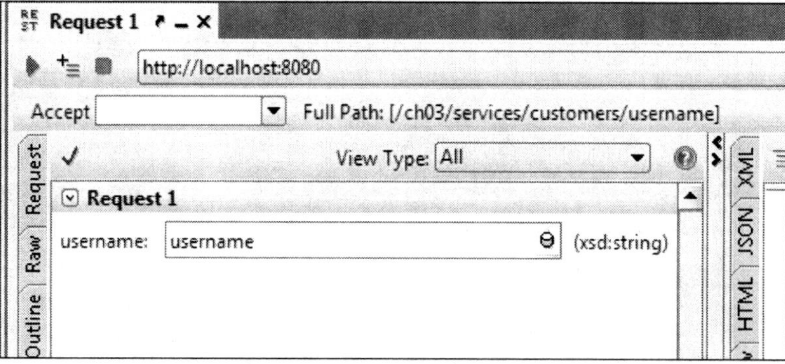

This request form has one parameter for a username which is expecting a String value. In the actual request, type `mickknutson` in the **username** text field and press the **green arrow** at the top-left side of the page, and you can see the XML output returned by the service, as shown in the following screenshot:

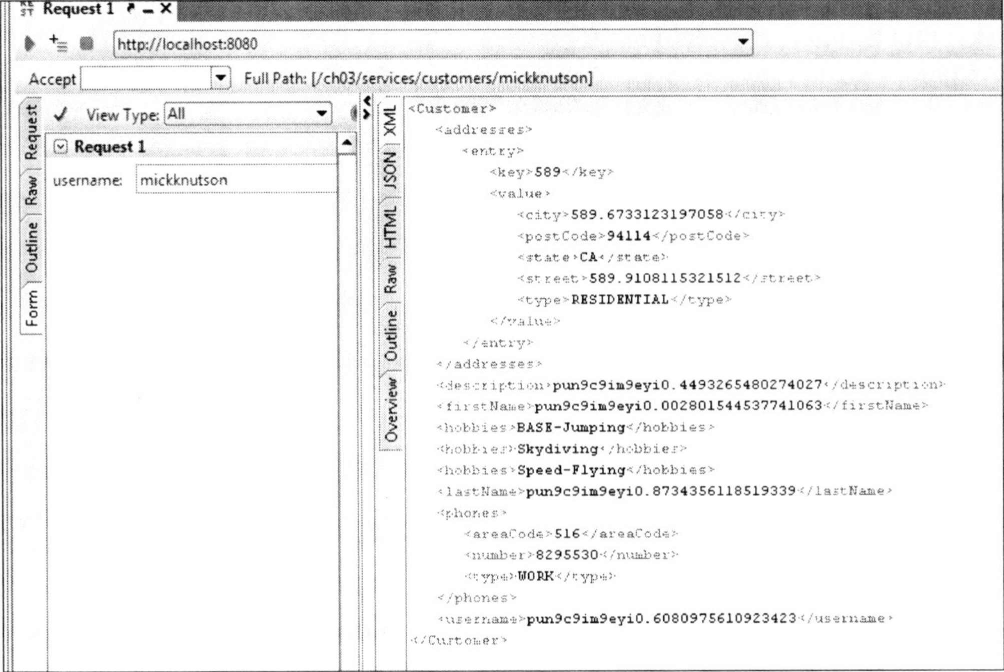

8. At this point we have used soapUI as a client to a published REST service. Next, create a new Test Suite by right-clicking on the **Customers Service Demo** project.
9. When prompted, enter **Customers Service Test Suite** for the **TestSuite** name.
10. Next, right-click on **Customers Service Test Suite** and select **New TestCase**.
11. Next, enter a name for the **TestCase** and click the **OK** button.
12. Now you can see the **Customers Service Test Suite** on the left-hand side. Double-click on the test suite and then press the **green arrow** button at the top-left to run test cases of this test suite.

13. The test should complete successfully as depicted in the following screenshot:

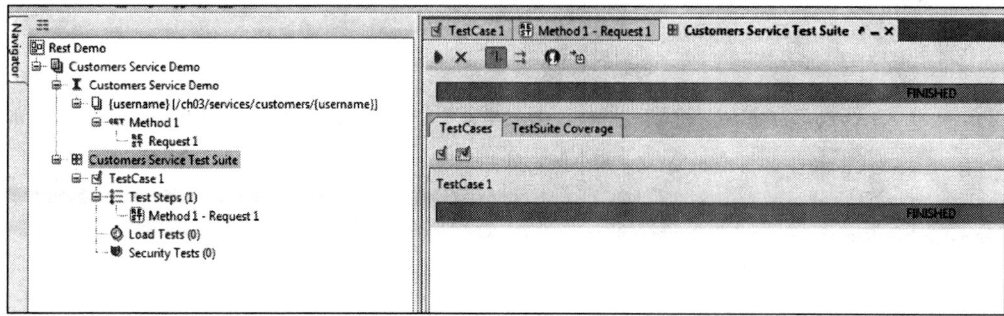

Testing in soapUI is all about the assertions. Assertions are the checks to validate the message received by a TestStep, usually by comparing the parts of the response or the entire response to the expected response. soapUI offers many different built-in assertions. The most common assertions are *contains* (checks for presence of a specified string), *not contains* (checks for the non-existence of a specified string), *XPath* or *XQuery match* (compares the result of an XPath expression to an expected value) and *Scripts* (validates the response using script). Any number of assertions can be added to validate different aspects or content of the response.

We will add an actual assertion to validate the content of the response. In our first assertion, we are just going to check that we get three hobbies back from the service for username `mickknutson`. The response is listed in the right-hand side of the window.

Now select the **Outline** view and right-click on the first **hobbies** item, in the generated XML:

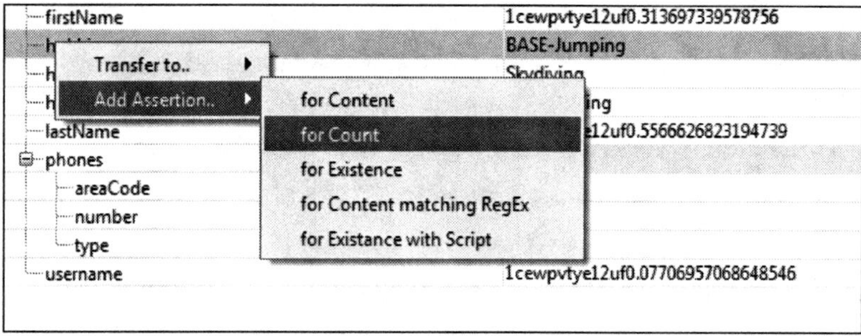

In the second example, we can add another XPath assertion to verify the content of the phone number, as shown in the following screenshot:

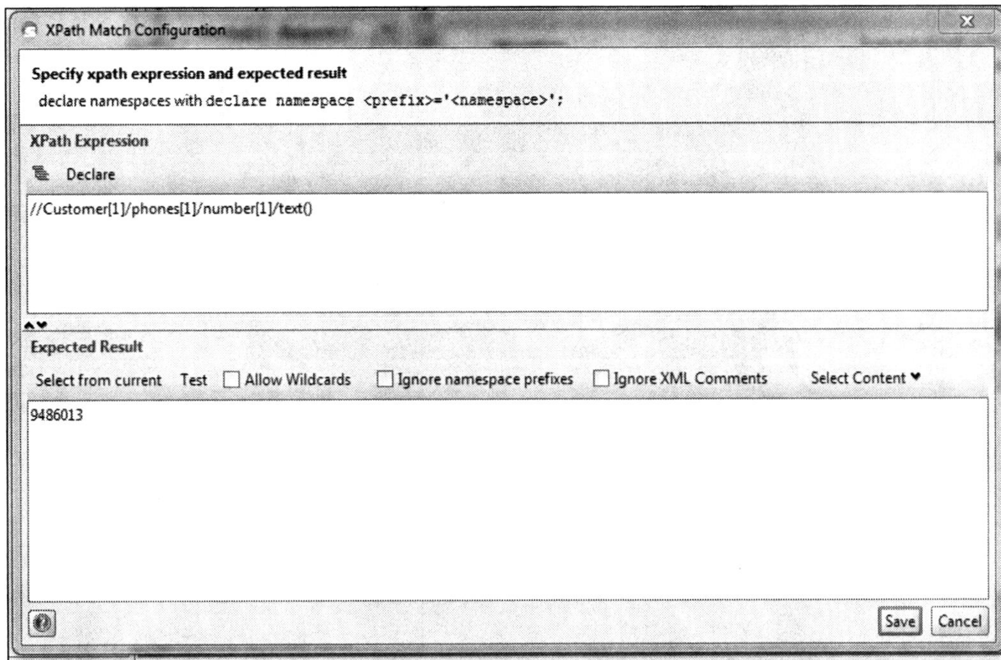

Similarly, we can add two more assertions to check the existence of customer address, and the response will be of valid HTTP status code.

Run the TestCase with the **green arrow** at the top-left side of the window. This will result in the aforementioned output, in the log at the bottom as shown in the following screenshot:

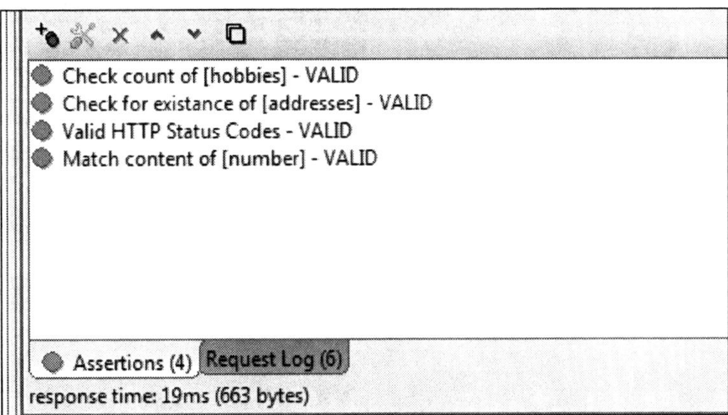

Testing SOAP services

soapUI comes with a very extensive support for testing WSDL and SOAP-based services. The WSDL files are central to testing SOAP-based services. They define the actual contract a service exposes and are required by soapUI to generate and validate tests.

Create another new project in the existing workspace by importing stockQuote public service WSDL as shown in the following screenshot:

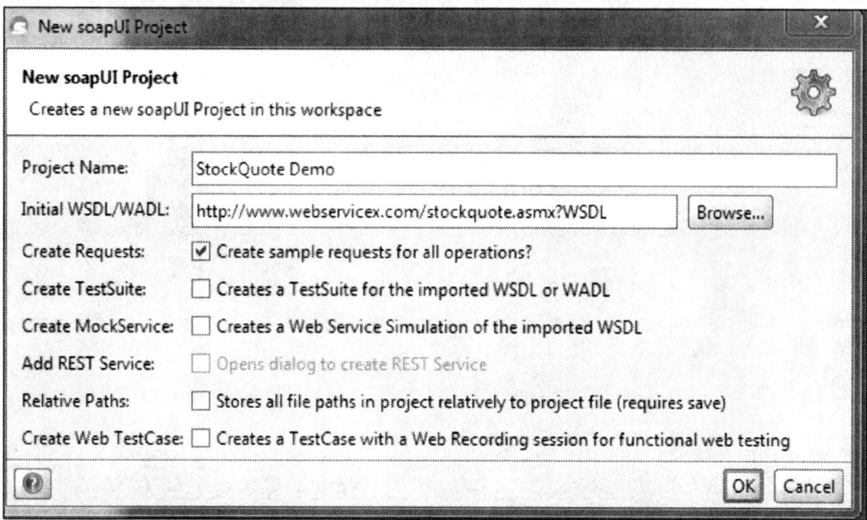

After clicking on the **OK** button, soapUI will load the stockQuote WSDL and parse its contents.

The following screenshot depicts the **GetQuote** service being executed with a valid symbol parameter and the SOAP response being returned:

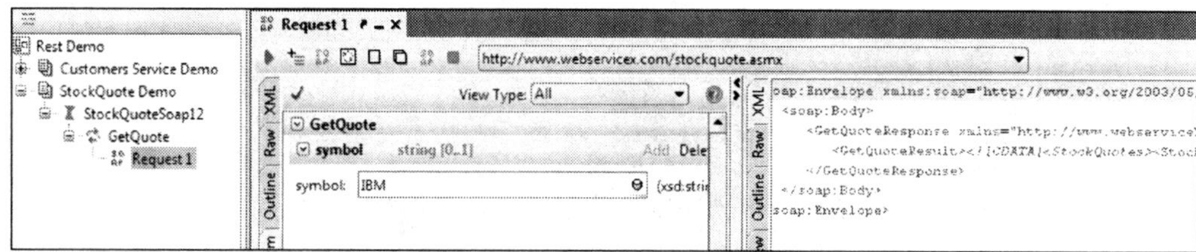

There's more...

soapUI can also help to automate functional tests using the command line tools bundled with soapUI, and can also be run using a Maven build system. In order to have soapUI run during a build process, you will need to first save the soapUI project file in your source tree, such as `/src/soapui/3166_soapui_project.xml`; then add the following Maven plugin to be run during the test phase of the build:

```
<plugin
    <groupId>eviware</groupId
    <artifactId>maven-soapui-plugin</artifactId
    <version>${soapui.plugin.version}</version
    <configuration
        <outputFolder>
          ${project.basedir}/target/soapui/output
        </outputFolder>
        <junitReport>true</junitReport>
    </configuration>
    <executions>
        <execution>
            <id>Customer Service Test Suite</id>
            <phase>test</phase>
            <goals>
                <goal>test</goal>
            </goals>
            <configuration>
                <projectFile>
                  ${project.basedir}/src/test/resources/soapui/3166-
soapui-project.xml
                </projectFile>
            </configuration>
        </execution>
    </executions>
</plugin>
```

The previous listing will instruct Maven to execute the `maven-soapui-plugin` with the `3166-soapui-project.xml` project file during the test lifecycle phase of the build.

Testing with Mock services

Testing with mock objects using Mockito or EasyMock are commonly used in unit testing. Mock objects simulate real objects, and they can be configured to match the behavior of real objects that are not available or cannot be incorporated into unit tests.

soapUI is capable of mocking any external service that is not available, or that cannot be incorporated into a given test case. The only thing required is the WSDL of the external service to be mocked.

In order to begin, right-click on the project and select **Generate MockService** from the context menu as depicted in the following screenshot:

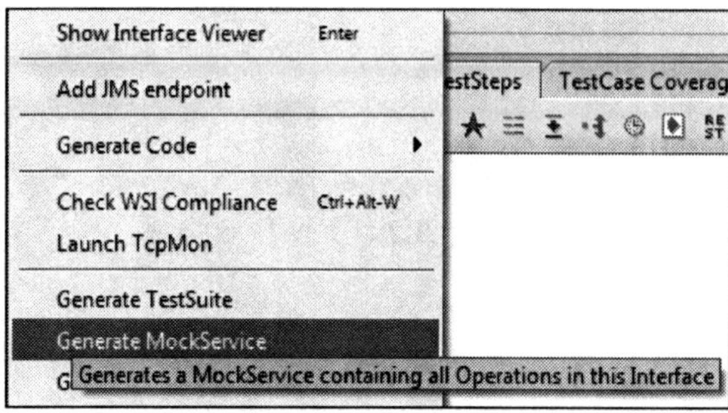

The next dialog window allows configuration of the services, operations, and URI for the new Mock. The following dialog window depicts the imported WSDL for the stockQuote service:

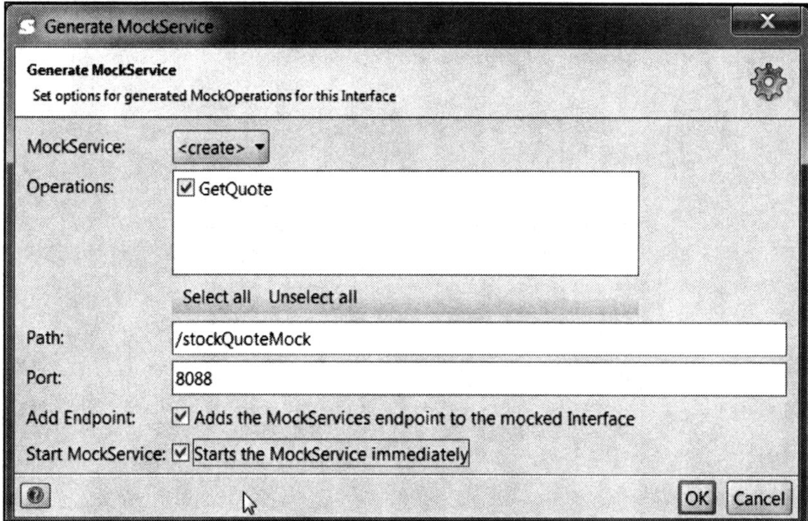

After clicking on **OK**, you will see new **StockQuoteSoap MockService** created with a new Mock response. The SOAP message response can be modified to simulate the response needed for the given test. As depicted in the following screenshot, the response for the **GetQuote** operation for **StockQuoteSoap MockService** will return a valid SOAP response:

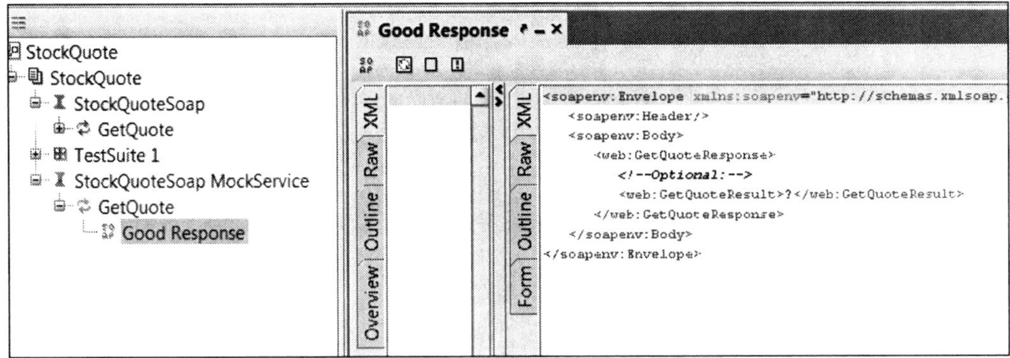

The previous mock SOAP response for the **GetQuote** operation returns a result as an XML String, such as the following listing:

```
<web:GetQuoteResult>1000</web:GetQuoteResult>
```

The **StockQuoteSoap MockService** is now ready to handle incoming SOAP requests on the configured endpoint `http://localhost:8088/stockQuoteMock` as shown in the following screenshot:

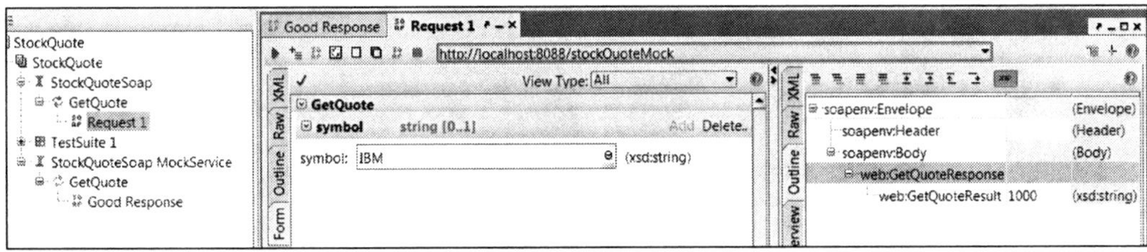

Numerous Mock response messages can be created for a given Mock service; they can be tailored to return various values for various test outcomes. This can include different quote amounts and various fault scenarios. Creating mock responses can help with code coverage for web services.

Extending soapUI capabilities with Groovy

soapUI provides extensive and powerful options for scripting using the Groovy language that is accessible from within all soapUI projects.

In this recipe, we will explore extending the capabilities of soapUI with Groovy scripting for testing and debugging.

Getting ready

We will begin with the previous soapUI project, named **Customers Service Demo**, which was created earlier in this chapter. The following screenshot depicts the project, and the TestSuite and TestCase for the project:

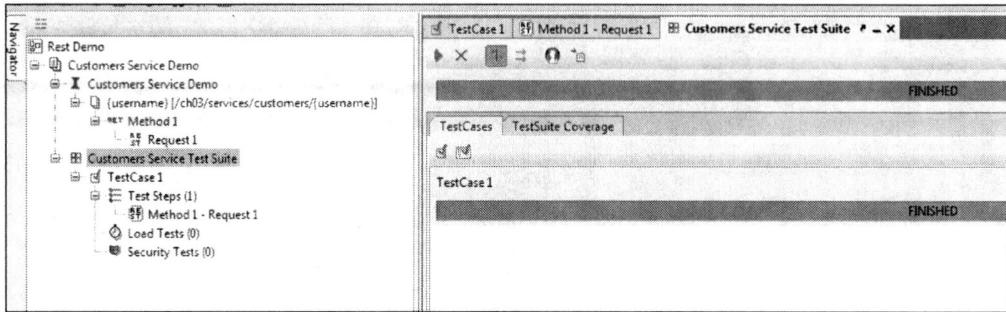

In a soapUI TestCase, a **Manual TestStep** can be created; we will use this as an assertion placeholder. Later, this manual step will be referenced by our Groovy script. The following screenshot depicts how to add a manual step by right-clicking the **Test Steps** and selecting **Manual TestStep**, which is located in the context menu at **Add Step | Manual TestStep**:

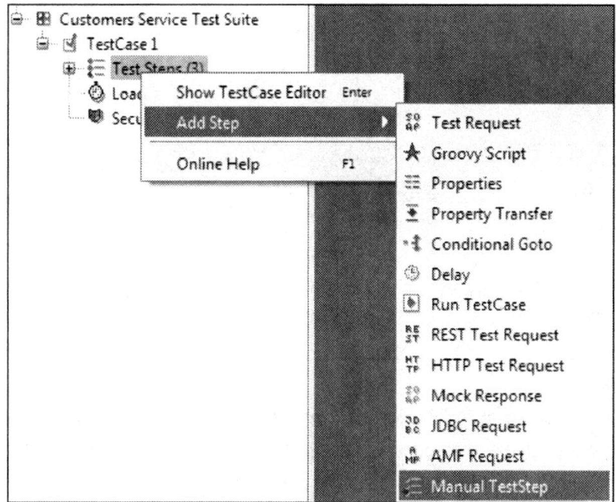

Next, we need to add the expected response for the **Manual TestStep**, which will be the valid Customer as depicted in the following screenshot:

```
<Customer>
   <addresses>
      <entry>
         <key>589</key>
         <value>
            <city>589.6733123197058</city>
            <postCode>94114</postCode>
            <state>CA</state>
            <street>589.9108115321512</street>
            <type>RESIDENTIAL</type>
         </value>
      </entry>
   </addresses>
   <description>pun9c9im9eyi0.4493265480274027</description>
   <firstName>pun9c9im9eyi0.002801544537741063</firstName>
   <hobbies>BASE-Jumping</hobbies>
   <hobbies>Skydiving</hobbies>
   <hobbies>Speed-Flying</hobbies>
   <lastName>pun9c9im9eyi0.8734356118519339</lastName>
   <phones>
      <areaCode>516</areaCode>
      <number>8295530</number>
      <type>WORK</type>
   </phones>
   <username>pun9c9im9eyi0.6080975610923423</username>
</Customer>
```

The manual step uses the expected result for assertions. The Groovy script that is created, is going to use the expected result as though it was the actual response. This can be thought of as a mock response to the Groovy script.

How to do it...

At this point the project has everything required to run a successful test, now we want to add a Groovy script to the test step:

1. To begin with, add a new **Groovy Script** step by right-clicking on **Test Step**, and navigating to **Add Step | Groovy Script**, as depicted in the following screenshot:

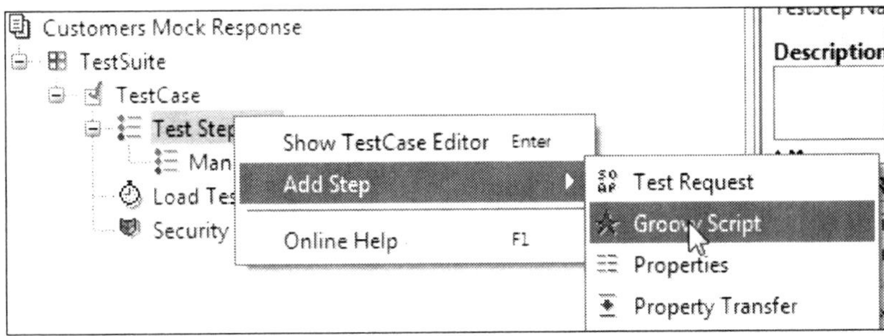

   This will create a Groovy script under **Test Step**.

2. Double-click the **Groovy Script** to open the file with the embedded Groovy editor in soapUI. In this editor, we will write the Groovy script to parse the Customers service response.

Groovy makes it very easy to inspect or parse anything from the response. The Groovy editor has access to all the context-related variables and log objects. We can retrieve any property from the response using the context variable by right-clicking in the editor and selecting **Get Data** from the menu, as depicted in the following screenshot:

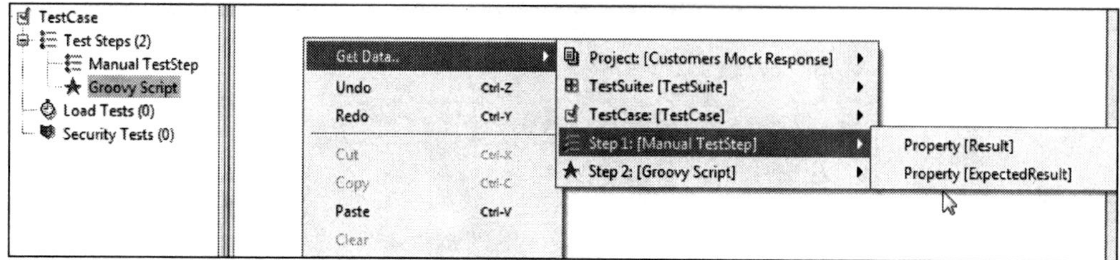

Earlier in this recipe, the **Manual TestStep** was configured with an **ExpectedResult**. The previous screenshot depicts the ExpectedResult property from the Manual TestStep being added to the Groovy script.

Within the editor, we will retrieve **postCode** from the **ExpectedResult** property, with XPath, and add the result to a new variable as shown in the following listing:

```
def zipCode = context.expand(
  '${Manual TestStep#ExpectedResult#//Customer[1]/
  addresses[1]/entry[1]/value[1]/postCode[1]}' )
```

When the test case is run, this code listing will result in the following **Information** dialog window:

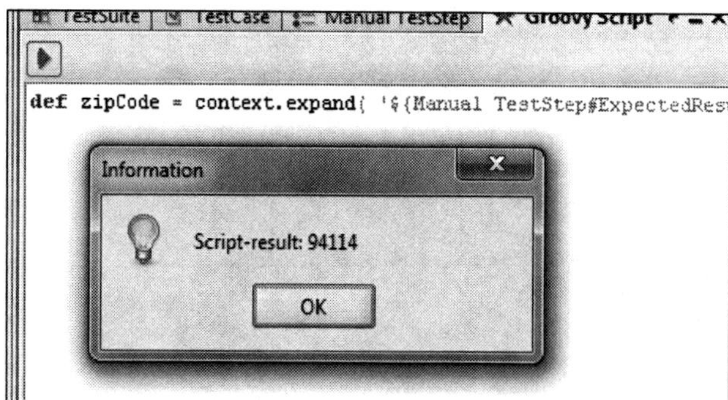

We can also parse the response by using soapUI Groovy utilities. The `GroovyUtils` class is used to create an `XMLHolder` to retrieve properties from the response object. The following sample code demonstrates how to create an `XmlHolder` from the soapUI `GroovyUtils` wrapper object, then `XmlHolder` is used to parse the XML and retrieve **postCode** from the **ExpectedResult** with XPath:

```
def groovyUtils =
  new com.eviware.soapui.support.GroovyUtils( context )
def holder =
  groovyUtils.getXmlHolder( "Manual TestStep#ExpectedResult" )
holder["//Customer[1]/addresses[1]/entry[1]/value[1]/postCode[1]"]
```

When the test case is run, this code listing will result in the following **Information** dialog window:

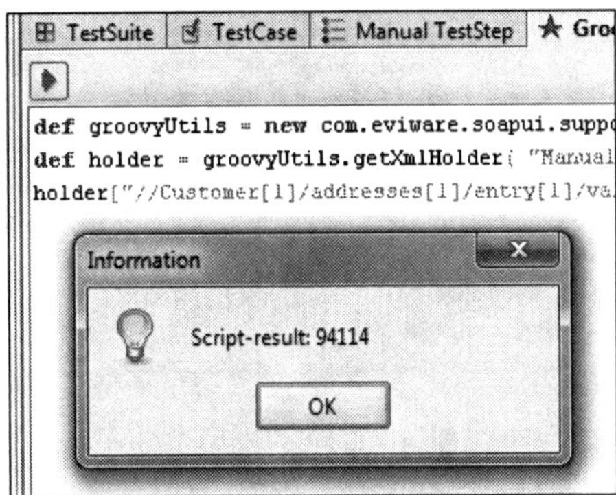

The `XMLHolder` can be used for a variety of other XML-related activities, such as a count on the response properties:

```
def groovyUtils =
  new com.eviware.soapui.support.GroovyUtils( context )
def holder =
  groovyUtils.getXmlHolder( "Manual TestStep#ExpectedResult" )
def numberOfCustomers = holder["count(//Customer)"]
assert numberOfCustomers > 0
```

Groovy can write logs from the response, or other information, using the following `log` object:

```
def groovyUtils =
  new com.eviware.soapui.support.GroovyUtils( context )
def holder =
  groovyUtils.getXmlHolder( "Manual TestStep#ExpectedResult" )
log.info "logging Customer Information"
log.info "username - "+ holder["//Customer[1]/username[1]"]
log.info "zipCode - "+ holder["//Customer[1]/addresses[1]/entry[1]/
value[1]/postCode[1]"]
log.info "hobbies - "+ holder["//Customer[1]/hobbies"]
```

When the test case is run with the log statements, the result will be as shown in the following console window for soapUI:

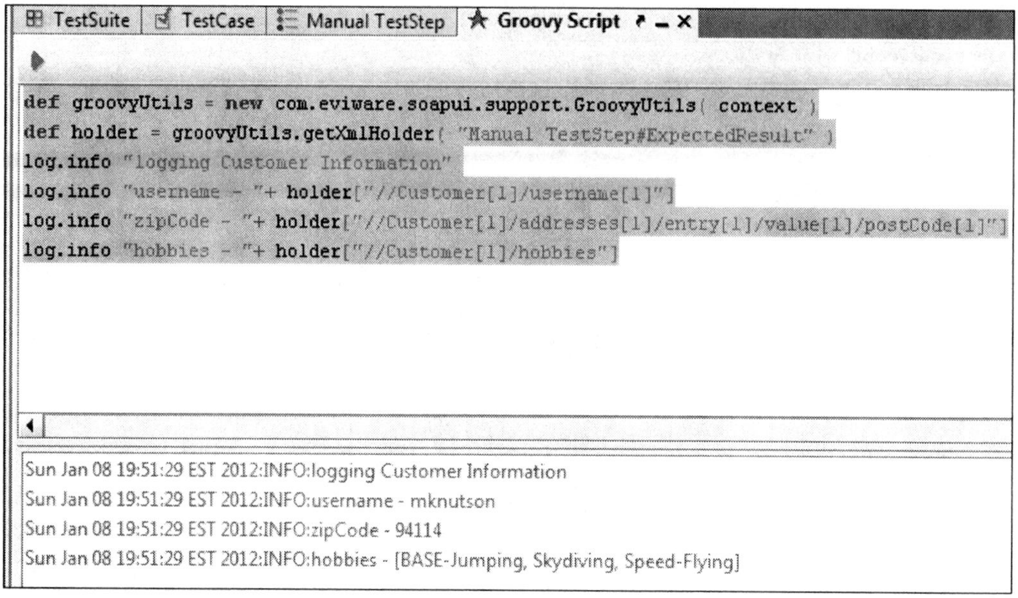

TestSuite | TestCase | Manual TestStep | Groovy Script

```
def groovyUtils = new com.eviware.soapui.support.GroovyUtils( context )
def holder = groovyUtils.getXmlHolder( "Manual TestStep#ExpectedResult" )
log.info "logging Customer Information"
log.info "username - "+ holder["//Customer[1]/username[1]"]
log.info "zipCode - "+ holder["//Customer[1]/addresses[1]/entry[1]/value[1]/postCode[1]"]
log.info "hobbies - "+ holder["//Customer[1]/hobbies"]
```

```
Sun Jan 08 19:51:29 EST 2012:INFO:logging Customer Information
Sun Jan 08 19:51:29 EST 2012:INFO:username - mknutson
Sun Jan 08 19:51:29 EST 2012:INFO:zipCode - 94114
Sun Jan 08 19:51:29 EST 2012:INFO:hobbies - [BASE-Jumping, Skydiving, Speed-Flying]
```

Writing output to file

Response, log, or other information can be written to a file for review and audit. This can be especially helpful if there is a large amount of console data to be captured, or if the project is being executed unattended.

The following listing depicts the creation of a new `File` object, and the addition of data to the file:

```
def groovyUtils =
  new com.eviware.soapui.support.GroovyUtils( context )
def holder =
  groovyUtils.getXmlHolder( "Manual TestStep#ExpectedResult" )
def file = new File( "c:/response.txt" )
file.append "logging Customer Information"
file.append "\nusername - "+ holder["//Customer[1]/username[1]"]
file.append "\nzipCode - "+ holder["//Customer[1]/addresses[1]/
entry[1]/value[1]/postCode[1]"]
file.append "\nhobbies - "+ holder["//Customer[1]/hobbies"]
```

When the test case is run, the output will be written to `C:/response.txt` and the text file can be viewed in a system text editor as seen in the following listing:

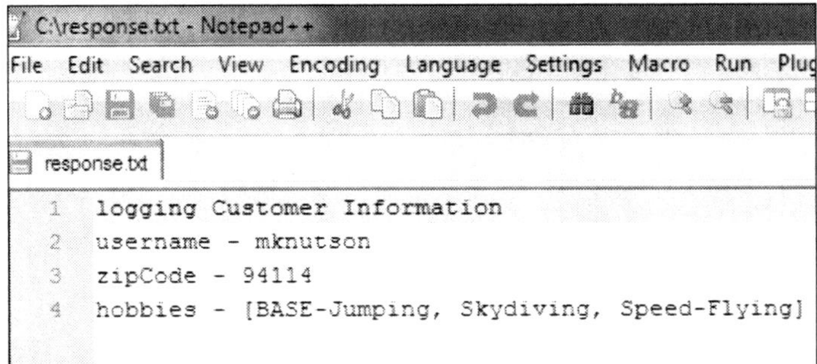

See also

- *SOAP UI*: `http://www.soapui.org/`

5
Extending Enterprise Applications

In this chapter, we will cover:

- Integrating Groovy into Enterprise Applications
- Integrating Jython into Enterprise Applications
- Integrating Scala into Enterprise Applications
- Weaving AspectJ advice into Enterprise Applications
- Weaving AspectJ advice into existing libraries
- Adding advice with CDI Decorators
- Adding advice with CDI Interceptors

Introduction

In this chapter, we will explore various ways to extend a Java EE environment with the use of additional dynamic languages as well as frameworks.

We will start with a recipe using Groovy as a dynamic language integrating to existing Java code, then move to examples with Scala.

The next recipe will be to integrate AspectJ advice weaving into an existing application.

We will then end this chapter with two standard Java EE 6 extensions, the Decorator and Interceptor. These are new CDI features that have similar capability and extensibility as we might get from Aspects.

Integrating Groovy into Enterprise Applications

This recipe is going to cover the use of Groovy as a dynamic language running side-by-side with existing Java code.

Groovy leverages Java's enterprise capabilities but also has many productivity features such as closures, domain specific language (DSL) support, builders, dynamic typing, and meta-programming.

It is hard to create a better introduction to Groovy than on `http://groovy.codehaus.org/`:

Groovy...

- is an agile and dynamic language for the Java Virtual Machine
- builds upon the strengths of Java but has additional power features inspired by languages such as Python, Ruby, and Smalltalk
- makes modern programming features available to Java developers with an almost-zero learning curve
- supports domain specific languages and other compact syntax so your code becomes easy to read and maintain
- makes writing shell and build scripts easy with its powerful processing primitives, OO abilities, and an Ant DSL
- increases developer productivity by reducing scaffolding code when developing web, GUI, database, or console applications
- simplifies testing by supporting unit testing and mocking out of the box
- seamlessly integrates with all existing Java classes and libraries
- compiles straight to Java byte-code so you can use it wherever you can use Java.

In this recipe then, we will not cover all the inner-workings of the Groovy language and all the benefits from this JVM language, but we will cover how to integrate Groovy into a new or existing Enterprise Application and how to use Groovy for unit testing.

Getting ready

In this recipe we are going to use Maven to build our project, and will be using the GMaven plugin by CodeHause. This plugin will generate Java stubs and test stubs from Groovy classes, then compile those Java stubs into `*.class` files. This makes developing Groovy mixed with Java code fairly seamless in many cases.

Though the Groovy syntax has generally stayed consistent, updates to Groovy have meant that the syntax has been amended. The consequence of this is that plugins can be more complicated to configure for. This is important to us because the GMaven plugin only supports Groovy versions 1.5, 1.6, and 1.7. With the current stable version of Groovy being 1.8 (though 2.0 is currently available in BETA) we will first have to configure the GMaven plugin to use the latest version of Groovy (1.8). Using Maven this is what our provider configuration would look like:

```
<plugin>
    <groupId>org.codehaus.gmaven</groupId>
    <artifactId>gmaven-plugin</artifactId>
    <version>1.4</version>
    <configuration>
        <source>${jdk.version}</source>
        <providerSelection>1.7</providerSelection>
    </configuration>
    <dependencies>
        <dependency>
            <groupId>org.codehaus.gmaven.runtime</groupId>
            <artifactId>gmaven-runtime-1.8</artifactId>
            <version>1.4</version>
            <exclusions>
                <exclusion>
                  <groupId>org.codehaus.groovy</groupId>
                  <artifactId>groovy-all</artifactId>
                </exclusion>
            </exclusions>
        </dependency>
        <dependency>
            <groupId>org.codehaus.groovy</groupId>
            <artifactId>groovy-all</artifactId>
            <version>${groovy.version}</version>
        </dependency>
    </dependencies>
    <executions>
        <execution>
            <goals>
              <goal>generateStubs</goal>
              <goal>compile</goal>
              <goal>generateTestStubs</goal>
              <goal>testCompile</goal>
            </goals>
        </execution>
    </executions>
</plugin>
```

Some defined properties that are needed:

```
<properties>
    <jdk.version>1.6</jdk.version>
    <groovy.version>1.8.2</groovy.version>
```

With this plugin configuration we are specifying specific Groovy goals that will be executed during the corresponding Maven build goals. We first want to run (1) `generateStubs`, then (2) `compileour` source files, then (3) `generateTestStubs` for test stubs, then (4) `testCompile` to compile any Groovy test classes that may be present. These goals correspond with standard Maven lifecycles. These lifecycles can be found at `http://maven.apache.org/guides/introduction/introduction-to-the-lifecycle.html`, which covers the theory of a build lifecycle as well as all of the lifecycles and the orders they occur in a Maven build.

The most important thing to consider when using this or any other byte-code generating language is that there is a secondary compilation process involved. This can sometimes cause issues related to the ordering of the compilation process if you have more than one type of compilation such as compiling AspectJ or some additional byte-code compilation such as Scala. The issue results from multiple code generation steps then compilations such as AspectJ or Scala compilation.

With standard Groovy compilation, the Groovy compilation will generate stub `.java` files and the javac compiler will generate `.class` byte-code:

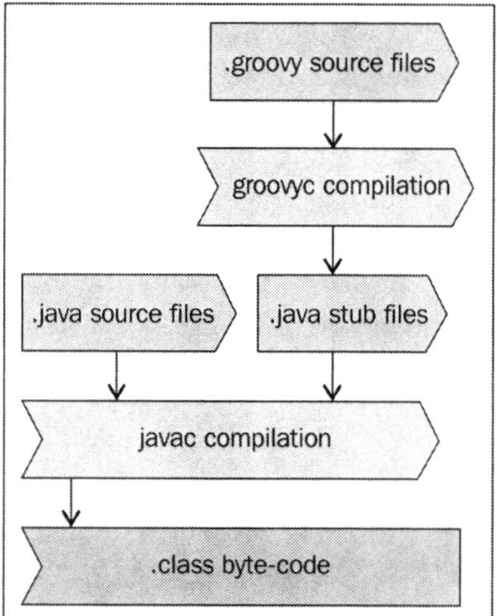

However, when you start adding additional compilation steps such as Scala compilation, you must consider there can be issues with the ordering of the code generation as well as which compiler will be generating the `.class` byte-code:

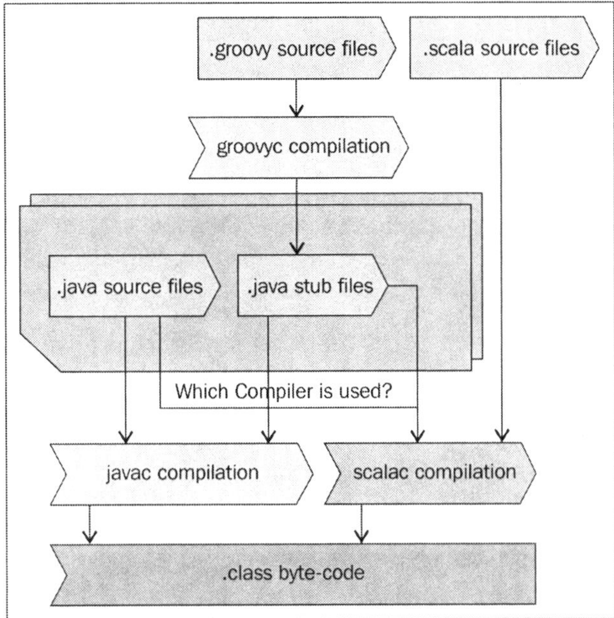

This is just a consideration when adding more than one additional integration language into a given project.

How to do it...

Once we configure the plugin, it will generate Groovy stubs, we then compile those Groovy stubs into byte-code, which we can use to start writing Groovy classes for a Groovy job.

You will need to create a directory specifically for your Groovy files because by default the GMaven plugin looks in `~/src/main/groovy/**` for Groovy source files to be compiled and conversely looks in `~/src/test/groovy/**` for Groovy test files to be compiled and used for testing.

Give Groovy access to any Java library that exists on your classpath interchangeably and you can reference and write Groovy exactly the same as you would with any job such as the following:

```
public static String htmlEncode(String s) {
returnorg.apache.commons.lang.StringEscapeUtils.escapeHtml(s)
    }
```

However, the Groovy magic really comes into picture when you start simplifying the language and utilizing the meta-programming model which Groovy offers such as simplified collection looping:

```
static String getRequestQueryString(Map<String, String> parameters) {
StringBuilder sb = new StringBuilder();
parameters.each() {key, value ->sb.append("${key}=${value}&") };
return sb.toString()
}
```

In the preceding listing, the variable `parameters` are of type Map. Using the `each()` method will iterate over all elements in the Map and assign the key and value of each element to a local variable called `key` and `value` respectively. Iterating over each element, the listing appends the key and value to the `StringBuilder`.

From a simplification point of view, utilizing Groovy versus Java can be an easy transition and can provide a simplified notation that will save time developing your projects. The fact that you can cohabitate Java and Groovy both in files and in syntax eases the burden of this coexistence and allows for quick adaptation as well as the ability to take advantage of the strengths of each of the languages at the same time.

Groovy can also help with file mutilation as well as ant build-related tasks and supports those functions far easier than plain Java code could do.

How it works...

The Groovy magic happens because it allows Java and Groovy source files to coexist in the build system, in our case Maven. When we look at the stub source files Groovy generates from a Groovy class called `StringUtilities.groovy` it results in the corresponding `StringUtilities.Java` file that looks like the following listing:

```
package com.baselogic.chapter05.utils;

...
importjava.util.*;
importgroovy.lang.*;
importgroovy.util.*;

public class StringUtilities
extendsjava.lang.Object  implements
groovy.lang.GroovyObject {

publicStringUtilities
() {}

public  groovy.lang.MetaClassgetMetaClass()
```

```
    { return (groovy.lang.MetaClass)null;}

public  voidsetMetaClass(groovy.lang.MetaClass mc) { }
public  java.lang.ObjectinvokeMethod(java.lang.String method,
    java.lang.Object arguments) { return null;}

public  java.lang.ObjectgetProperty(java.lang.String property)
    { return null;}

public  voidsetProperty(java.lang.String property,
    java.lang.Object value) { }
...
public static  java.lang.StringblankIfNull(java.lang.String s)
    { return (java.lang.String)null;}

public static  java.lang.StringgetRequestQueryString
    (java.util.Map<java.lang.String, java.lang.String>
        parameters) { return (java.lang.String)null;}
```

The refined job-based syntax for a class that implements Groovy Object has several meta-methods at the beginning of the class, which helps the mapping to the Groovy syntax. At this point, the Java compiler has sufficient constructs to compile your Groovy stub source files into byte-code. The standard compilation process is detailed in the following diagram:

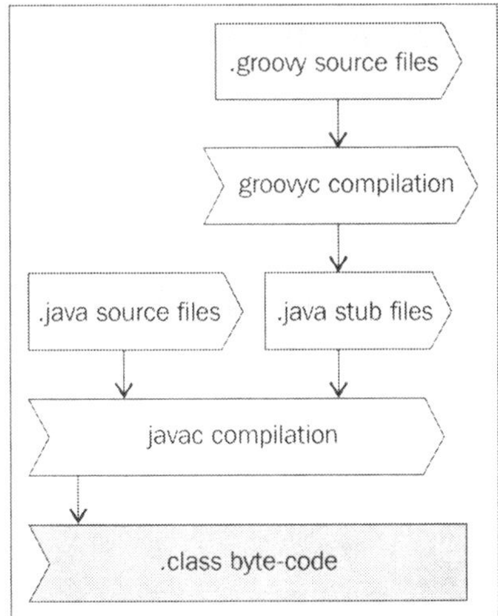

Interchanging Java and Groovy in unit tests

I especially like the ability to utilize many of the Groovy language functions when writing unit tests. Some of those functions include creating sample data sets then corresponding simplified looping constructs enclosures, which allow me to create sample-based tests for many of my utility classes. What would've taken three distinct test methods has now been condensed into one simple method depicted in the following listing:

```
defsampleSets = ["test": "test", "": "", " ": " "] as HashMap

voidtestSampleDataSet() {
sampleSets.each() { testSample, expected ->
    String actual =
        StringUtilities.blankIfNull(testSample);
println("testSample: [" + testSample +"]")
println("expected: [" + expected +"]")
println("actual: [" + actual +"]")
assertEquals(expected, actual)
        };
    }
```

In order to take advantage of Groovy files for unit testing with the Maven plugin as described earlier in this recipe, we only need to add your Groovy classes to `~/src/test/groovy/**` then run your Maven build as you have previously. The third GMaven plugin will compile your test classes combined with your Java test classes during your test phase and execute the Groovy byte-code as unit tests.

As we've seen in these listings, you can harness the power of Groovy meta-programming with the repetitive tasks of unit testing with various samples for various test cases.

In some situations the standard GMaven plugin may not work depending on your configurations. In these cases, there is another Maven plugin that is far more verbose than the GMaven plugin, which is available to you to perform the exact same tasks of compiling your Groovy source and test source code. This listing shows a complete example of using the ant run plugin for Maven:

```
<plugin>
    <artifactId>maven-antrun-plugin</artifactId>
    <executions>
      <execution>
        <id>compile</id>
        <phase>compile</phase>
        <configuration>
          <tasks>
            <taskdef
              name="groovyc"
              classname="org.codehaus.groovy.ant.Groovyc">
```

```
                <classpath refid="maven.compile.classpath"/>
          </taskdef>
          <mkdir dir="${project.build.outputDirectory}"/>
            <groovyc
              destdir="${project.build.outputDirectory}"
              srcdir="${basedir}/src/main/groovy/"
              listfiles="true">
                <classpath refid="maven.compile.classpath"/>
            </groovyc>
        </tasks>
      </configuration>
      <goals>
        <goal>run</goal>
      </goals>
    </execution>
    <execution>
        <id>test-compile</id>
        <phase>test-compile</phase>
          <configuration>
            <tasks>
              <taskdef
                name="groovyc"
                classname="org.codehaus.groovy.ant.Groovyc">
                  <classpath refid="maven.compile.classpath"/>
              </taskdef>
              <mkdir dir="${project.build.testOutputDirectory}"/>
              <groovyc
                destdir="${project.build.testOutputDirectory}"
                srcdir="${basedir}/src/test/groovy/"
                  listfiles="true">
                  <classpath refid="maven.test.classpath"/>
              </groovyc>
            </tasks>
          </configuration>
          <goals>
            <goal>run</goal>
          </goals>
    </execution>
  </executions>
</plugin>
```

The preceding listing is utilizing the Ant build tools along with the Groovy ant tasks that Groovy provides to perform a compilation. The outcome is the same, although by using Ant tasks we do have more control and autonomy over how the process occurs, where the process and the files are found, and where the byte-code output is located.

See also

Groovy Home: `http://groovy.codehaus.org/`

Ant Groovy Compilation: `http://docs.codehaus.org/display/GROOVY/Compiling+With+Maven2`

`http://groovy.codehaus.org/GMaven`

Plugin: `http://docs.codehaus.org/display/GMAVEN/Home`

`http://docs.codehaus.org/display/GROOVY/Compiling+With+Maven2`

Integrating Jython into Enterprise Applications

When considering dynamic Java JVM languages, Jython is a great option for integrating Python scripting support into your applications. Some of the key features are:

- Dynamic and/or Static compilation to Java byte-code
- Ability to extend Java classes
- Easy access to Bean properties
- Fundamentally based on the Python language

In this recipe, we will review using Jython to create a Java Servlet and access Java classes from within the Jython script dynamically.

Getting ready

In order to begin we need to include `jython.jar` into our project:

```
<dependency>
    <groupId>org.python</groupId>
    <artifactId>jython</artifactId>
    <version>2.5.0</version>
</dependency>
```

This includes all the Jython classes required for adding support into a web application.

Next, we need to expose the Python Servlet by adding `PyServlet` into your `web.xml`:

```
<servlet>
    <servlet-name>PyServlet</servlet-name>
    <servlet-class>org.python.util.PyServlet</servlet-class>
    <load-on-startup>1</load-on-startup>
```

```
</servlet>
<servlet-mapping>
    <servlet-name>PyServlet</servlet-name>
    <url-pattern>*.py</url-pattern>
</servlet-mapping>
```

At this point, we need to determine where we are going to store the Python scripts so they will get packaged into your WAR file. There are several possible solutions to this depending upon your build system and projects choice of code organization. This recipe is using Maven to package this WAR file and the Maven-war plugin being used allows specifying additional web resources to be included in the final WAR file:

```
<webResources>
    <webResource>
        <directory>${basedir}/src/main/jython</directory>
        <includes>
            <include>**/*.py</include>
        </includes>
    </webResource>
</webResources>
```

My preference is to separate Python scripts from other resources as well as Java code. If you are not using Maven, or you prefer not to separate the Python source files from other source files, then the build process will need to include these source files into the `target .war` archive.

How to do it...

The only task left is to create Python scripts, and for this recipe, we are going to use Jython to create a Servlet and access existing Java code from that Servlet. We begin by importing Java and custom libraries into a script called `JythonServlet.py` in `/src/main/jython`:

```
import sys
from java.io import *
fromjava.util import Date
fromcom.baselogic.test import CustomerFixture
fromjavax.servlet.http import HttpServlet
```

Now we create a class based on the HttpServlet prototype:

```
classJythonServlet (HttpServlet):
```

Next we just implement handler method for GET and POST operations as needed:

```
defdoGet(self,request,response):
customer = CustomerFixture.createSingleCustomer()

out = response.getWriter()
response.setContentType ("text/html")
out.println ("<html><head><title>Jython Servlet Test</title>" +
    "<body><h1>Jython Servlet Test</h1>")

out.println ("<p><b>Today is:</b>"+Date().toString()+"</p>")
out.println ("<p><b>Java Customer
    :</b>"+customer.toString()+"</p>")
out.println ("</body></html>")
```

As this example shows, you can access any Java classes that are available on the current classpath.

How it works...

This works by configuring the `org.python.util.PyServlet` to process `*.py` scripts dynamically without the need for pre-compilation of Jython scripts into byte-code. When the WAR file is deployed and executed from a web browser at `http://localhost:8080/ch03/JythonServlet.py`, PySevlet renders the Python script into the Servlet:

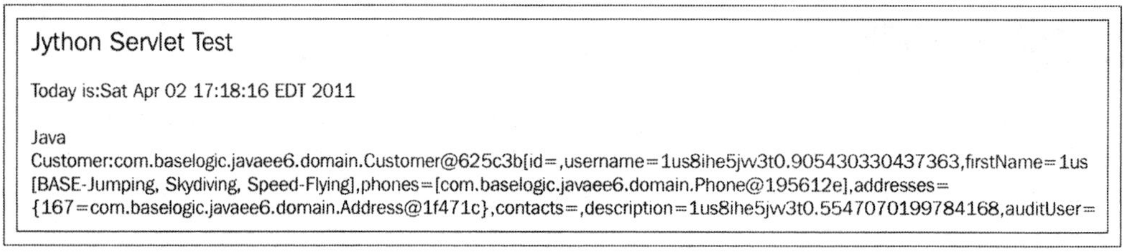

Jython Servlet Test

Today is:Sat Apr 02 17:18:16 EDT 2011

Java
Customer:com.baselogic.javaee6.domain.Customer@625c3b[id=,username=1us8ihe5jw3t0.905430330437363,firstName=1us
[BASE-Jumping, Skydiving, Speed-Flying],phones=[com.baselogic.javaee6.domain.Phone@195612e],addresses=
{167=com.baselogic.javaee6.domain.Address@1f471c},contacts=,description=1us8ihe5jw3t0.5547070199784168,auditUser=

See also

Jython: `http://www.jython.org`

Integrating Scala into Enterprise Applications

Another popular byte-code language called **Scala** was originally released in 2003. Scala has gained great support since its release both for the ability to create Java byte-code classes with a somewhat intuitive and simplified syntax, but also for unit testing. This can be attributed to the natural **behavior-drive design** (**BDD**) support, which allows for very readable code articulation such as:

```
classCustomerSpec extends FlatSpec with ShouldMatchers {

  "A Customer" should "contain a valid e-mail address" in {
  ...
```

The introduction from `scala-lang.org` says it all:

> *Scala is a general purpose programming language designed to express common programming patterns in a concise, elegant, and type-safe way. It smoothly integrates features of object-oriented and functional languages, enabling Java and other programmers to be more productive. Code sizes are typically reduced by a factor of two to three when compared to an equivalent Java application.*

Not only is Scala another resource you can introduce into your existing applications, but it is also a viable solution for new applications.

Getting ready

In order to start compiling Scala source code in your project, you just need to add a simple Scala plugin which requires very little configuration:

```
<plugin>
    <groupId>org.scala-tools</groupId>
    <artifactId>maven-scala-plugin</artifactId>
    <version>2.15.2</version>
    <executions>
        <execution>
            <goals>
                <goal>compile</goal>
                <goal>testCompile</goal>
            </goals>
        </execution>
    </executions>
</plugin>
```

With this plugin configuration, we are specifying specific Scala goals that will be executed during the corresponding Maven build goals. We first want to run `compile` for our Scala source files, then `testCompile` to compile any Scala test classes that may be present. These goals correspond with standard Maven lifecycles. These lifecycles can be found at:

`http://maven.apache.org/guides/introduction/introduction-to-the-lifecycle.html`

`http://maven.apache.org/guides/introduction/introduction-to-the-lifecycle.html`

These cover the theory of a build lifecycle as well as all of the lifecycles and the orders that occur in a Maven build.

The most important thing to consider with using this or any other byte-code generating language is that there is a secondary compilation process involved. This can sometimes cause issues with the ordering of the compilation process if you have more than one type compilation such as compiling AspectJ or some additional byte-code compilation such as Groovy. I have not found any significant issues combining Scala compilation with Java, Groovy or AspectJ.

How to do it...

Once we configure the plugin, the Scala source files will get compiled to byte-code during the defined build lifecycle.

You will need to create a directory specifically for your Scala files. By default the Scala plugin looks in `~/src/main/scala/**` for Scala source files to be compiled and conversely looks in `~/src/test/scala/**` for Scala test files to be compiled and used for testing.

With Scala, you get access to any Java library that exists on your classpath interchangeably and you can reference and write Scala exactly the same way as you would with jobs such as the following listing:

```
package com.baselogic.chapter05.utils;

importjava.util.{Date, Locale}
importjava.text.DateFormat
importjava.text.DateFormat._
importjava.text.SimpleDateFormat
importjava.util.Calendar

objectScalaDateUtilities {
def main(args : Array[String]) : Unit = {
        valmsg = "Hello World";
        print(msg);
```

```
    }

defgetYesterdayDate() : String = {
println("*** SCALA ROCKS ***")
val calendar = Calendar.getInstance();
calendar.add(Calendar.DATE, -1);
val format = new SimpleDateFormat("yyyy-MM-dd");
returnformat.format(calendar.getTime());
    }
}
```

As you might notice, the syntax is easy to read and would allow you to integrate Scala with your Java code or Groovy code.

There's more...

In addition to just using Scala for running custom classes there are several projects and libraries available that aid with behavior-driven development (BDD) such as Cucumber-JVM, EasyB, JBehave, and so on just to name a few. There's also *scalaCheck* and *scalaTest* which are similar BDD style testing frameworks that focus on Scala as the implementing language.

Interchanging Java and Scala in unit tests

You can easily mix Scala and Java to write unit tests. Scala uses a very similar syntax that you may be familiar with using in writing the existing JUnit test cases:

```
object ScalaCheckDataUtilitiesTest extends AssertionsForJUnit {

  @Before def initialize() { }

  @Test def verifyEasy() {
      var calendar: Calendar = Calendar.getInstance
      calendar.add(Calendar.DATE, -1)
      var format: SimpleDateFormat = new SimpleDateFormat("yyyy-MM-
dd")
      var expected: String = format.format(calendar.getTime)
      var result: String = DateUtilities.getYesterdayDate

      assertEquals(expected, result)
  }
}
```

This ease of coexistence with Java allows for easy transition and migration, for those projects will continue Scala and can easily introduce more BDD concepts.

See also

Scala Language home: `http://www.scala-lang.org/`

Maven Scala Plugin: `http://scala-tools.org/mvnsites/maven-scala-plugin/`

ScalaTest: `http://www.scalatest.org`

`http://www.scala-lang.org/http://scala-tools.org/mvnsites/maven-scala-plugin/http://www.scalatest.orgScala`

Check: `http://code.google.com/p/scalacheck/`

Weaving AspectJ advice into Enterprise Applications

Aspect-oriented programming (**AOP**) is a programming paradigm, which aims to increase modularity by allowing the separation of cross-cutting concerns in software design. This leads to a reduction of code scattering for concerns such as security, transactions, logging, and auditing just to name a few.

Cross-cutting concerns

Many parts of an application such as **Data Access Objects** (**DAO**) have a direct concern to perform database operations. However, there are other concerns such as logging, transactions, and security that are also required to perform the execution. These additional concerns such as security and transactions, are not just required by DAOs, but will also be required by other services in your application such as securing a web service. These concerns cut across many application boundaries, thus called cross-cutting concerns.

Advice

Advice is the code you would like to add, or *advice* you would like to give to a target object. Advice can be applied *before*, *after*, *after returning*, *after throwing*, and *around* a target object's execution.

Pointcut

A **pointcut** is a given point of the application execution you wish to have *advice* applied. These pointcuts can occur *before*, *after*, *after returning*, *after throwing*, and *around* a target object's execution.

Aspect

The term **aspect** is the combination of some *advice* and *pointcut*.

The combination of the pointcut and the advice is termed an *aspect*. In the previous example, we add a logging aspect to our application by defining a pointcut and giving the correct advice.

Joinpoint

A **joinpoint** is the point at which *advice* will be applied. The point could be a method being called, an exception being thrown, or a field being modified. The join points are within the normal flow of your application that a joinpoint can define where the *aspect* will be inserted.

Weaving

Aspects are not directly coded into your application, so they must be woven into the byte-code of your application for the *aspect* to work. The weaving process is how you will apply these aspects into your application. This is also the reason for this recipe.

There are three main types of aspect weaving:

- **Compile-time**: Aspects are woven into target classes when they are compiled.
- **Classload time**: Aspects are woven into target classes when they are loaded into the classloader. This requires a special classloader that modifies the byte-code before the class is introduced to the application. This is also known as **Load-time Weaving** (**LTW**) in AspectJ.
- **Runtime**: Aspects can be woven during the execution of the application. This would typically be an AOP container such as a Spring Framework container. This container would dynamically generate proxied objects that have aspects woven in and delegate to the target objects.

AspectJ is the primary library for introducing aspects, or concerns, into new or existing Java based code.

Getting ready

In order to weave aspects at compile-time, we need to introduce the AspectJ compiler to compile your aspects at given build lifecycles, in this case, one of our compile source aspects during the compile lifecycle and compile our test aspects during our test-compile lifecycle:

```
<plugin>
    <groupId>org.codehaus.mojo</groupId>
    <artifactId>aspectj-maven-plugin</artifactId>
    <version>1.3.1</version>
```

```
        <executions>
            <execution>
                <goals>
                    <goal>compile</goal>
                    <goal>test-compile</goal>
                </goals>
            </execution>
        </executions>
        <configuration>
            <complianceLevel>${jdk.version}</complianceLevel>
        </configuration>
    </plugin>
```

Adding AspectJ support into the lifecycle is easy enough but the AspectJ plugin or similar tools use the AJC compiler to compile aspects into byte-code.

How to do it...

Now we can start writing our aspects against code in the existing code base, which does not include external jars, which we talk about in another recipe here in this chapter.

How it works...

Compile-time AspectJ is a compiler replacement that is compiling aspects and Java source files into byte-code as depicted in the following diagram:

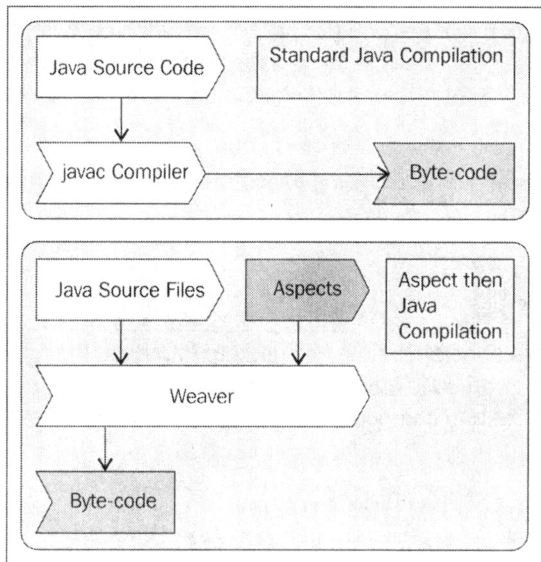

This shows how compile-time weaving can sometimes conflict with other pre and post compiler tools where code generation or byte-code instrumentation is involved. In some of these cases, compile-time weaving will not be possible.

See also

AspectJ: http://www.eclipse.org/aspectj/

Maven AspectJ: http://mojo.codehaus.org/aspectj-maven-plugin/index.html

Weaving AspectJ advice into existing libraries

Applying AspectJ advice to classes allows logic to be indirectly applied to target classes without direct knowledge. This is especially useful when working with libraries that are not directly part of a project, yet advice still needs to be applied.

In this recipe we will cover how to add AspectJ advice to Jar libraries using compile-time weaving.

Getting ready

In order to weave AspectJ advice at compile-time, we need to introduce the AspectJ compiler to compile aspect advice into the target library. Using the `aspectj-maven-plugin`, we can execute this compile task during one of the Maven build lifecycle phases. We compile the source aspects during the compile phase, and then compile the test aspects during the test-compile phase.

In order to weave advice into an existing library, the library or libraries need to be added to the plugin as a `<weaveDependency>` as depicted in the following listing:

```
<plugin>
    <groupId>org.codehaus.mojo</groupId>
    <artifactId>aspectj-maven-plugin</artifactId>
    <version>1.3.1</version>
    <executions>
        <execution>
            <goals>
                <goal>compile</goal>
                <goal>test-compile</goal>
            </goals>
        </execution>
    </executions>
    <configuration>
        <complianceLevel>${jdk.version}</complianceLevel>
```

```
            <weaveDependencies>
                <weaveDependency>
                    <groupId>com.baselogic.javaeecookbook</groupId>
                    <artifactId>ch02</artifactId>
                </weaveDependency>
            </weaveDependencies>
        </configuration>
    </plugin>
```

Weaving AspectJ advice into an existing build lifecycle is easy enough but care must be taken when combining various compilation processes such as Groovy, Scala and JRuby.

How to do it...

At this point you are able to write aspects against the woven libraries.

How it works...

Compile-time AspectJ weaving is accomplished from the AspectJ Compile (AJC). The AJC is a Java JDK compiler replacement that is compiling aspects and Java source files into byte-code as depicted in the following diagram:

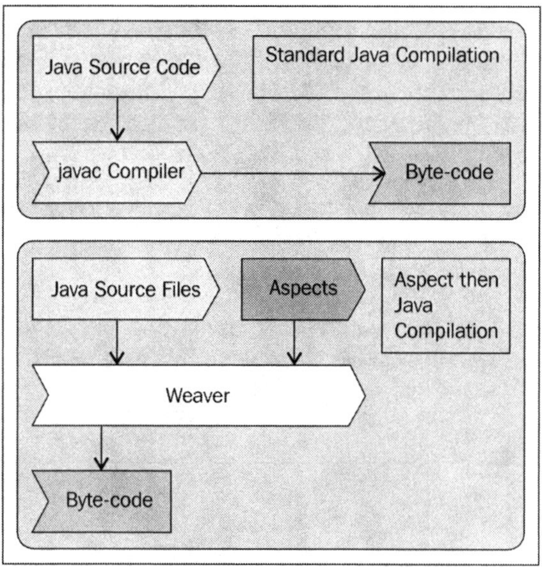

This shows how compile-time weaving can sometimes conflict with other pre and post compiler tools where code generation or byte-code instrumentation is involved. In some of these cases, compile-time weaving will not be possible.

There's more...

Another interesting use for weaving aspects into existing libraries can be to help simulate delays when interacting with those libraries. For example, you may have a library that accesses a remote system and for functional testing you want to simulate a random delay between 0 and 20 seconds per request without actually changing the library itself. This becomes quite easy when you look at creating an around advice aspect that introduces a random number between 0 and 20,000 then initiates a threat sleep before returning control to the legacy class:

```
@Aspect
public class MockDelaySimulationAspect {

@Around("within(com.baselogic.package.to.simulate.delays..*)")
public Object simulateRandomDelays(ProceedingJoinPoint call) throws
Throwable {
        Object point = null;

        Random random = new Random();
finalintrandomSleepTimeInMs = 20000; // 20 seconds

        try {
            Thread.sleep(random.nextInt(randomSleepTimeInMs) + 1);
            point = call.proceed();
            } catch (Throwable t) {
            throw t;
        } finally {
    }
    return point;
    }
}
```

As you can see, aspect-oriented programming can help serve many purposes in your program including working with libraries that you may not even have source code for.

See also

AspectJ: `http://www.eclipse.org/aspectj/`

Maven AspectJ: `http://mojo.codehaus.org/aspectj-maven-plugin/index.html`

Adding advice with CDI Decorators

Interceptors are a powerful solution to capture and separate concerns that are orthogonal to an application. An Interceptor is able to intercept any java-type invocation. Just like aspects, interceptors are perfect for solving technical issues such as transaction management, security, logging, and auditing. By nature, interceptors are not aware of the semantics of the event calls they intercept.

A decorator intercepts invocations only for given Java interface type, and is aware of all the semantics associated with that interface. As decorators directly implement the interface they are decorating with additional business logic, it is more suited for specific business concerns, not cross-cutting concerns such as interceptors. However, this means that decorators will not be as general purpose as interceptors are.

Getting ready

In order to begin we need to assume this code will be run in a CDI-compliant container such as GlassFish. Tomcat does not come with native CDI support.

Before we begin implementing our first decorator, we first want to cover the various elements and how they interact with one another.

Component interface

We first begin with a Java type we want to apply advice to which will be our interface.

Delegate class

Next we need to have a delegate that is a realization of the component interface. This class will be known as our delegate.

Decorator class

The decorator class is an additional implementation as the delegate class, and implements the same component interface, thus sharing the knowledge of the Java-type semantics.

In the following diagram we see the relationship of the three elements:

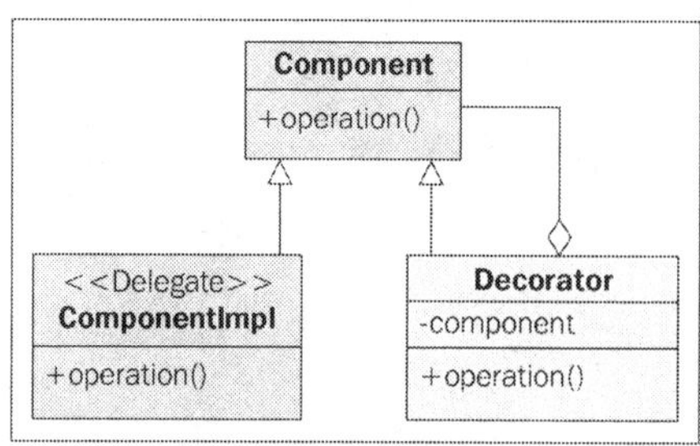

How to do it...

Now that we have an overview, let's begin by creating our first decorator class.

Component interface

We have to have an interface that will define the contracts exposed to callers. We first need to identify a type we want to enrich. Let's start with a `UserService` that will get a customer object from a `@Repository`:

```
public interface Service{

public Customer operation();
}
```

Delegate class

The delegate class is the original implementation of the component interface before the decoration. The implementation of the `UserService` will be unaware of a decorator, or that it is being used as a delegate:

```
@Stateless
public class UserServiceImpl implements UserService {
    @Override
public Customer findCustomer(String username) {
returnuserDao.findCustomer(username);
    }
}
```

Decorator class

The Decorator class is the class that will enrich the existing delegate class by adding additional business logic.

The Decorator is going to implement the typed component, and offer enrichment to the existing delegate in three steps:

1. Perform business logic before calling the delegate.
2. Delegate the request to the target object.
3. Perform additional logic after the delegate returns:

```
@Decorator
public class UserServiceDecorator implements UserService {

    @Inject @Delegate
privateUserServiceuserService;
```

```
    @Override
public Customer findCustomer(String username) {

        // 1. Perform business logic before calling the delegate.

    ...

        // 2. Delegate the request to the target object.
Customer valuedCustomer = userService.findCustomer(username);

        // 3. Perform additional logic after the delegate returns.

    ...

returnvaluedCustomer;
    }
}
```

How it works...

In order for the decorator to work, the container, or reference implementation, must proxy the target delegate type to replace the reference used by any calling object to use the decorator.

When the caller object executes the proxied target, they will actually be executing the decorator class as described in the following diagram:

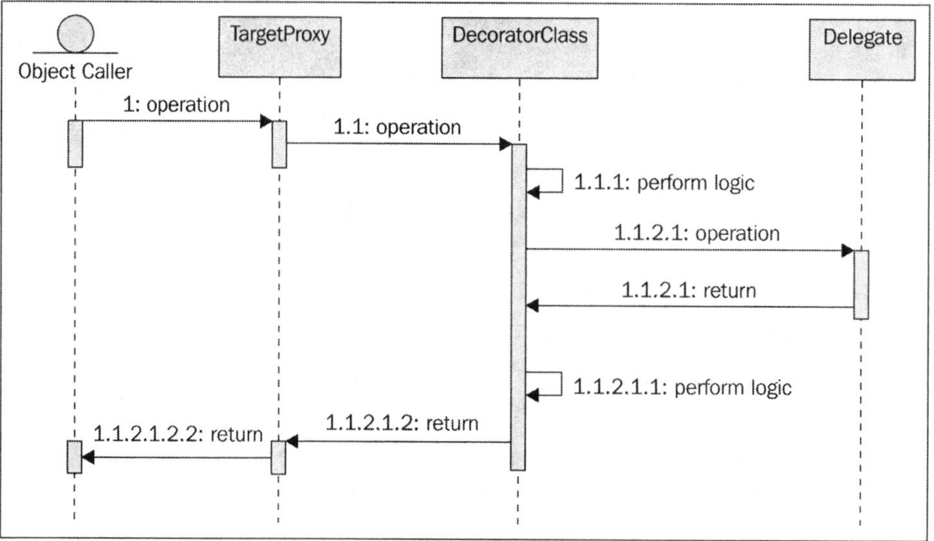

There's more...

Web profiles don't support CDI natively. CDI reference implementations can be added to a container that supports the web profile.

JBoss has released an open source reference implementation of JSR-299 CDI known as Weld that is located on the *seamframework.org* site at `http://www.seamframework.org/Weld`.

Adding CDI support with Weld is fairly simple. First we need to add two libraries to your web application called `weld-core` and `weld-servlet`:

```
<dependency>
    <groupId>org.jboss.weld</groupId>
    <artifactId>weld-core</artifactId>
    <version>1.1.7.Final</version>
</dependency>
<dependency>
    <groupId>org.jboss.weld.servlet</groupId>
    <artifactId>weld-servlet</artifactId>
    <version>1.1.7.Final</version>
</dependency>
```

Next we need to add the Weld Listener to your `web.xml` file:

```
<listener>
    <listener-class>
        org.jboss.weld.environment.servlet.Listener
    </listener-class>
</listener>
```

That is all that is required to add CDI support to a web profile based container.

See also

JSR-299: `http://jcp.org/en/jsr/detail?id=299`

Decorator Pattern: `http://en.wikipedia.org/wiki/Decorator_pattern`

Delegation Pattern: `http://en.wikipedia.org/wiki/Delegation_pattern`

Proxy Pattern: `http://en.wikipedia.org/wiki/Proxy_pattern`

Weld: `http://www.seamframework.org/Weld`

Adding advice with CDI Interceptors

Interceptors are similar to Aspects that allow developers to invoke interceptor methods in conjunction with method invocations or lifecycle events on an associated target class.

Interceptors help eliminate code cluttering and allow implementing of cross-cutting concerns. Interceptors are not as powerful as full AspectJ, but they still provide a great solution for these problem spaces.

Getting ready

To begin we need to assume this code will be run in a CDI-compliant container such as GlassFish. Tomcat does not come with native CDI support.

Before we begin implementing our first interceptor, we first want to cover the various elements and how they interact with one another.

Target class

We first start with an object that we want to apply some advice to. The target class can have one or more interceptor classes associated with it. The order in which the interceptor classes are invoked is determined by the order in which the interceptor classes are defined in the `@Interceptors` annotation.

Annotation marker

We need to create an annotation that will be used as a marker to denote the method on a target class, as well as mark the Interceptor class to be associated with this marker.

Interceptor class

Lastly we can create the interceptor, which will be the advice we want to apply to a target class based on the type of interceptor metadata annotation. Interceptor classes may be designated with the optional `@Interceptor` annotation, but it isn't required to be so annotated. Interceptor classes must have a public, no-argument constructor.

Interceptor classes can also be applied to lifecycle events such as after a target class is fully instantiated (`@PostConstruct`), or before the target object is destroyed (`@PreDestroy`).

In the following diagram we can see the relationship of these objects:

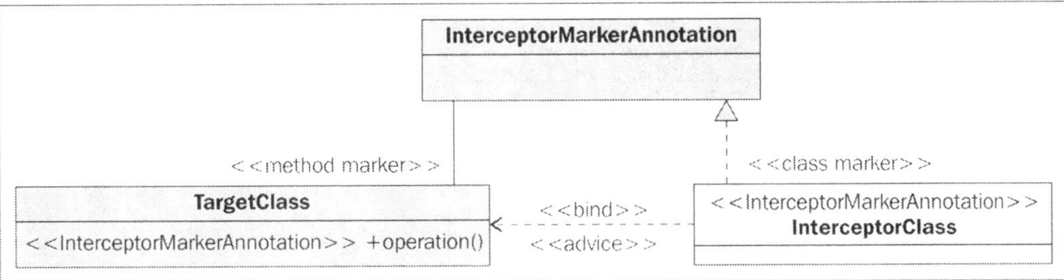

Interceptor metadata annotations

We should now cover the types of interceptor advice that can be applied to target objects:

Interceptor metadata annotation	Description
`@AroundInvoke`	Designates the method as an interceptor method that will apply advice around the target execution
`@AroundTimeout`	Designates the method as a timeout interceptor method that will apply advice around a timeout
`@PostConstruct`	Designates the method as an interceptor method for a post-construct lifecycle event
`@PreDestroy`	Designates the method as an interceptor method for a pre-destroy lifecycle event

How to do it...

Now that we have an overview, let's begin by creating our first interceptor.

Target class

Identify a method on a target class you want to apply interceptor advice:

```
publicObjectinterestingMethod() {
returninterstingDao.performOperation();
}
```

Annotation marker

Now we want to create an annotation that marks both the method on the target class, and interceptor class as well.

We will call with marker *Interceptable* and we need to annotate this interface with `@InterceptorBinding` to tell the container this annotation is going to bind an interceptor to a target class:

```
@InterceptorBinding
@Retention(RUNTIME) @Target({TYPE, METHOD})
public @interface Interceptable {}
```

Interceptor class

Now to create our first interceptor as a plain old java object (POJO) and we can optionally annotate the class with `@Interceptor`, but it isn't required.

We do need to add our marker annotation `@Interceptable` at the class level of our interceptor:

```
@Interceptor
@Interceptable
public class UserServiceInterceptor {

...
}
```

Next we want to add our advice that takes an `InvocationContext` parameter, and optionally returns an object, which we will review shortly:

```
public Object adviceToBeApplied(InvocationContextctx)
throws Exception { ... }
```

Next we want to annotate the advice method with the type of advice to be applied and we are going to cover `@AroundInvoke`, which will allow interception before and after a target method has returned:

```
    @AroundInvoke
public Object adviceToBeApplied(InvocationContextctx)
throws Exception { ... }
```

Now let's look at how we can interact with the around advice. This is going to happen in three steps:

1. Perform logic before target method call.
2. Give control to the target class's method by allowing the target to proceed.

3. Perform additional logic after target method call returns:

```
    @AroundInvoke
public Object adviceToBeApplied(InvocationContextctx)
throws Exception {

// 1. Perform logic before target method call
     ...

     // 2. Give control to the target class's method.

        Object obj = ctx.proceed();

// 3. Perform logic after target method call returns
     ...

returnobj;
    }
```

The magic is in the `proceed()` method where we are essentially telling the call hierarchy to proceed with its execution by executing the target class's method. Then when the target class's method returns, return control back as an object so we can continue to perform logic.

This is what our final interceptor class will look like:

```
@Interceptor
@Interceptable
public class UserServiceInterceptor {

    @AroundInvoke
public Object adviceToBeApplied(InvocationContextctx)
throws Exception {

System.out.println("before call to "
+ ctx.getMethod() + " with args "
+ Arrays.toString(ctx.getParameters()));

        Object obj = ctx.proceed();

System.out.println ("after call to "
+ ctx.getMethod()
+ " returned " + obj);

returnobj;
    }
}
```

There is one last artefact that is required in order for interceptors to work. We need to define the interceptors in `/WEB-INF/beans.xml` so the container can be made aware of their existence and apply them:

```
<?xml version="1.0" encoding="UTF-8"?>
<beans xmlns="http://java.sun.com/xml/ns/javaee"
xmlns:xsi="http://www.w3.org/2001/XMLSchema-instance"
xsi:schemaLocation="http://java.sun.com/xml/ns/javaee http://java.sun.
com/xml/ns/javaee/beans_1_0.xsd">

<interceptors>
<class>com.baselogic.javaee6.service.UserServiceInterceptor</class>
<class>com.baselogic.javaee6.service.TimingInterceptor</class>
<class>com.baselogic.javaee6.service.DebugInterceptor</class>
</interceptors>

</beans>
```

We can have as many interceptor definitions as we want applied at runtime.

How it works...

In order for Interceptors to work, the container or reference implementation must proxy the target class to add the advice based on the marker annotation which we instruct as binding. Then when an object caller executes the target class's method, the target proxy is intercepting the request to apply advice:

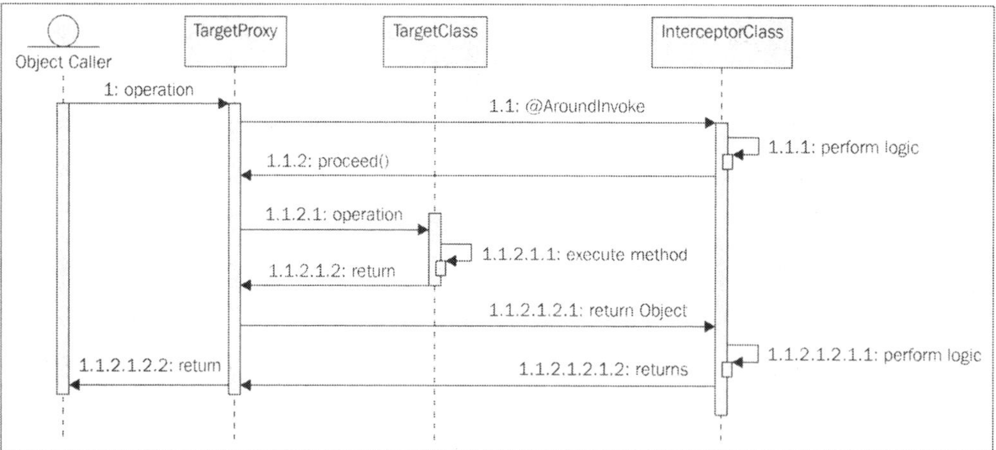

There's more...

Web profiles don't support CDI natively. CDI reference implementations can be added to a container that supports the web profile.

JBoss has released an open source reference implementation of JSR-299 CDI known as Weld that is located on the *seamframework.org* site at `http://www.seamframework.org/Weld`.

Adding CDI support with Weld is fairly simple. First we need to add two libraries to your web application called `weld-core` and `weld-servlet`:

```
<dependency>
    <groupId>org.jboss.weld</groupId>
    <artifactId>weld-core</artifactId>
    <version>1.1.7.Final</version>
</dependency>
<dependency>
    <groupId>org.jboss.weld.servlet</groupId>
    <artifactId>weld-servlet</artifactId>
    <version>1.1.7.Final</version>
</dependency>
```

Next we need to add the Weld Listener to your `web.xml`:

```
<listener>
<listener-class>
org.jboss.weld.environment.servlet.Listener
</listener-class>
</listener>
```

That is all that is required to add CDI support to a web profile-based container.

See also

JSR-299: `http://jcp.org/en/jsr/detail?id=299`

Interceptor Pattern: `http://en.wikipedia.org/wiki/Interceptor_pattern`

Proxy Pattern: `http://en.wikipedia.org/wiki/Proxy_pattern`

Weld: `http://www.seamframework.org/Weld`

6

Enterprise Mobile Device Integration

In this chapter, we will cover:

- Evaluating mobile frameworks
- Native application considerations
- Leveraging mobile design tools
- Testing mobile-web applications with online emulators
- Setting up a local Apache environment
- Native SDK development considerations

Introduction

This chapter will cover recipes that touch on the issues, considerations, and options related to extending enterprise development efforts into mobile application development.

The first thing to consider is the device you plan to target. This might seem simple, but there are many considerations that have various benefits and drawbacks.

There are several device types available to choose from that are widely used. Most people know about the iPhone, iPad, iPod Touch devices produced by Apple, as well as a wide range of devices from several manufacturers that support the Android operating system created by Google. There are several other device types on the market, such as Blackberry, which now has handheld devices as well as the PlayBook™ tablet devices and next-generation handheld devices.

With the mobile device and tool landscape changing daily, it will be difficult to cover certain specific implementations, but we can cover many of the options available and considerations that can be assessed when integrating mobile applications into an enterprise project.

Evaluating mobile framework projects

In this recipe, we are going to look at three different categories of mobile frameworks, how they function, and the implications that must be considered in a project when choosing a framework to be used for an application.

The main reason for deciding to use a mobile framework is to reduce or eliminate the technical challenges and dependencies for creating an application that will run on a variety of platforms. The level of platform expertise varies depending upon the framework and the native services access required by the application being developed.

Mobile-web frameworks

The easiest option to implement a cross-platform application is to leverage a rich-web framework which supports some combination of HTML, CSS, JavaScript, and Flash integration tailored to run on mobile or tablet devices.

This approach is developed as a server-side web application that generates a user interface that will be rendered on a mobile-web browser installed on the target device, and can interact with remote services by HTTP and/or JSONP with AJAX components using JavaScript or similar client-side scripting technology.

Most mobile-web frameworks leverage features of HTML5 which can allow storage of application data locally, with *Web Storage* or *IndexDB*, to the device to reduce the dependency on network connectivity. Several other features are available in the HTML5 specification such as access to *Geolocation*, *multimedia players*, *push notifications*, and *Web Sockets* for bi-directional communication. There is a wide variation of browsers pre-installed on devices by the various manufacturers, so support for specific HTML5 should always be researched to consider how many devices support the feature required by the application:

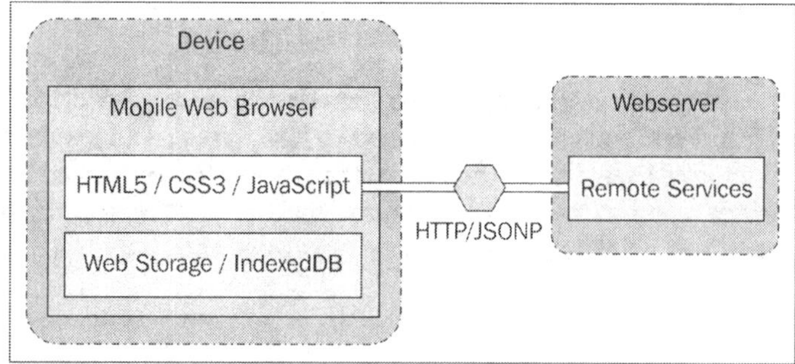

Browser compatibility considerations: The first challenge facing a mobile-web application is mobile web browser support on targeted devices. The device must have a mobile web browser installed and most devices are shipped with a browser pre-installed with the operating system. The mobile framework that is chosen as well as the specific HTML5 feature required might dictate a specific browser be installed in order for the application to render correctly. An example of this would be support for *Notification API* from HTML5 which allows for background alert notifications, which, at the time of writing this book, was supported by the Blackberry browser on tablets and Firefox on Android.

Network connectivity considerations: Devices typically connect to the internet through a cellular network provider if the device has a valid data plan allowing network packet traffic. The main issue with cellular network services is that the network is a "best effort" service where the network does not guarantee the bandwidth or reliability of the data transmission and can vary based on number of users sharing the service currently. Most mobile devices can also access Internet services through wireless connections and do not have or need to be connected to a cellular network provider. The iPod Touch is a perfect example of a device that does not have the ability to connect to a cellular network provider, but can use mobile apps that are connected to a wireless Internet provider. The main issue with wireless network services is that the service connection will not be consistent if the user is travelling outside the coverage range of a given network access point.

Network connectivity imposes two types of issues that must be considered when designing a mobile-web application. An application must consider data transmission between the device and the server, and data storage on a device which will allow use of the application to manipulate data to be used in subsequent server requests.

Data transmission: Mobile-web applications rely heavily on server communications which will require the user to be connected more often than a native application, depending upon the functionality the application needs to provide. Applications must also consider how much data is being transmitted to and from a target device, both in terms of the application content size, as well as user input data. Users connected to a cellular network might have data transfer limitations an application must consider, and the speed of the network can also impede application functionality.

Data storage: Data storage can allow for offline persistence and session storage of the application on the target device. This design consideration can aid in potential network inconsistencies for offline web applications and can give the application experience better perceived performance to the user. Please review *Application Cache* and *Web Storage* specifications from the W3C HTML5 specification.

Mobile-web framework projects

Let's examine a few mobile application frameworks existing today:

1. **jQuery Mobile**: jQuery Mobile is a unified, HTML5-based user interface system for the most popular mobile device platforms, built on the jQuery and jQuery UI foundation.

   jQuery Mobile has broad support for most major desktop, smartphone, tablet, and e-reader platforms, and can boast that it is cross-platform and cross-device.

2. **Sencha Touch**: Sencha Touch is the mobile counterpart to the Sencha project Ext JS framework. Instead of taking an approach of enhancing pre-existing HTML, Sencha Touch generates its own DOM based on objects created in JavaScript.

   Sencha Touch is more extensive than its competitors, with a vast array of UI components, explicit iPad support, storage, and data binding facilities using JSON and HTML5 offline storage, and more. Sencha Touch works hand-in-hand with PhoneGap which will create native applications running as a native web runtime.

   Sencha Touch allows for a **Model-View-Controller** (**MVC**) design which will make your code more reusable and modular.

3. **Modernizer**: Modernizer is a JavaScript library that detects the availability of native implementations for next-generation web technologies such as HTML5 and CSS3 specifications. Mobile and web technologies, in general, are moving fast and browser support on various devices can vary. What Modernizer does is, very simply, tells you whether the current browser has a given feature natively implemented or not.

4. **Other**: Other mobile-web frameworks include xui, jo, and Zepto.JS just to name a few, and there seem to be more frameworks emerging all the time as the mobile device market expands.

Let's examine the PROs and CONs of deciding to use mobile-web frameworks.

PROs

The PROs are as follows:

- **Control over deployment**: Developing a mobile-web application gives the project the ability to control the release cycle of the application, and reduces the dependency on application store both in terms of application preparation as well as delays for the application release approval process, which can take upwards of a few weeks for users to access the new application.
- **Scripting languages**: In a pure mobile-web framework JavaScript, HTML5, and CSS 2/3 are required for building mobile-web applications.
- **Seamless upgrades**: The latest version of your application is centrally located; version control is managed by the project and is not dependent upon the user.

- **Custom event model**: Most JavaScript libraries including jQuery and Sencha Touch provide custom events such as tap and swipe events.
- **Analytics**: Any web application access to various behavioural and user statistics are available immediately.
- **Code generators**: Several different code generators and IDEs are available to help speed up the design and development process.

CONs

The CONs are as follows:

- **Limited access to device hardware and features**: A web application cannot access some resources on the client device because it is not allowed by security constraints.
- **Authentication**: A custom security model must be implemented if user authentication and authorization is required by the application.
- **Heterogeneous browser implementation**: Slight difference between browser implementation, functionality, as well as device capabilities pose unique challenges to make applications consistent across multiple platforms. Browsers might render CSS slightly different than others, and may not support certain HTML5 features.
- **Service versus product**: Monetization differs from web applications as a service offering versus selling an application in stores as a product.

Native code generators

Several frameworks and tools allow projects to create HTML5 pages, potentially with source code such as Java, JavaScript, and C#, which is then generated into a specific native SDK source and is then compiled as a native application for the specific target device:

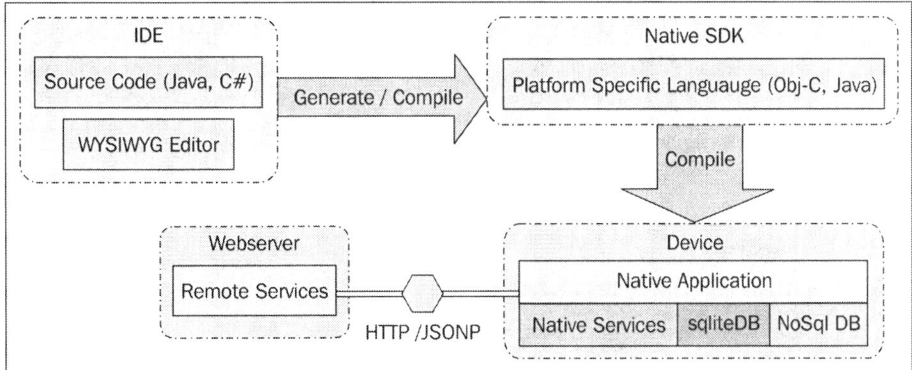

Code generation tools and frameworks are a good solution for projects wanting to develop cross-platform applications while leveraging existing software resources and libraries. This approach can also reduce the technology dependencies for supporting applications in languages other than the team's native language, while still creating cross-platform native applications.

Native code generator projects

Let's examine a few native code generator frameworks and tools:

1. **Appcelerator / Titanium**: Appcelerator allows developers to create a single codebase that can be transformed into desktop applications as well as mobile applications. The Appcelerator / Titanium platform leverages over 5,000 mobile device and operating system APIs to create native iOS, Android, and HTML5 mobile-web applications from a single codebase.
2. **MonoTouch**: MonoTouch is a framework for creating iOS, Android, and Windows Phone applications. MonoTouch boasts the ability for applications to be created with existing C, C#, and .NET while leveraging Visual Studio. MonoTouch can also integrate existing Java libraries into their mobile applications. MonoTouch has an iOS and Android product offering and is not an open source project. The MonoTouch application can directly submit mobile applications to the various app stores.

Let's examine the PROs and CONs of deciding to use native code generator frameworks and tools.

PROs

The PROs are as follows:

- **Performance**: The native code generation approach will allow an application to run faster because it will not be running inside of another application, as is the case with a mobile-web application running inside of a web browser
- **Native components**: A native application will have additional access to services and components on the target device, which may not be available to mobile-web applications through HTML5
- **Cross-platform native code**: A single codebase can generate cross-platform code which runs natively on target devices
- **Code customization**: Developers have the flexibility to customize generated code before compilation

CONs

The CONs are as follows:

- **Multiple code-bases**: Code generators typically create a codebase for each target device which then needs to be compiled for each target language (Objective-C or Java)
- **Code generation**: Code generation customization must typically be executed each time the code is generated
- **Performance**: Code generated applications are most likely slower than truly native applications due to the overhead of wrapper APIs used by the framework
- **Tools**: Code generation tools offer feature-rich editing components, but lack the advanced capabilities of platform-integrated development environments
- **Platform SDKs**: Developers still need platform-specific SDKs to package native binaries for delivery and distribution through app stores

Native web runtime (NWR)

Native Web Runtime Frameworks (**NWRs**) are an effort to offset many of the drawbacks of mobile-web application development. Typically, the device stores a client-side web application locally and an app is built around it to provide native hooks to the device hardware.

A native web runtime, or NWR, is a native mobile application framework that has web technologies that form the core of its implementation. After building an application in HTML5, CSS3, and JavaScript, there is a code generation step for generated native code, followed by a customizations step for plugging into specific device hardware:

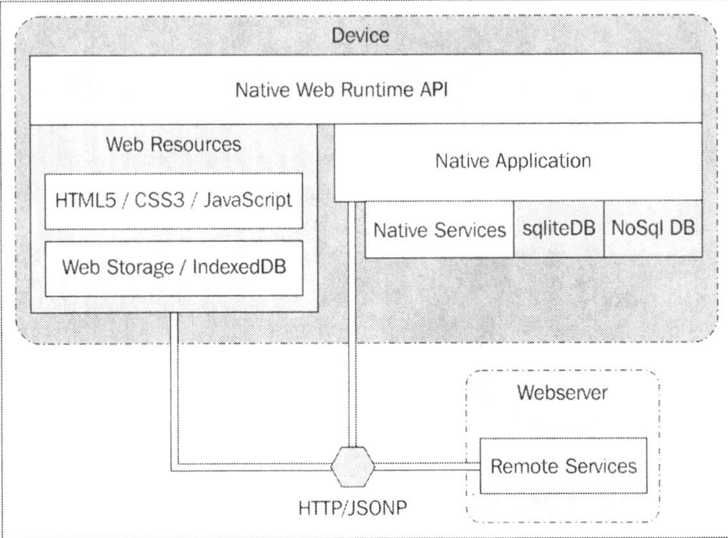

Native web runtime (NWR) projects

Let's examine a few native web runtime frameworks:

1. **PhoneGap**: PhoneGap is an open source framework where applications are written in JavaScript and HTML5 to create native deployable applications for target devices. PhoneGap also works very well with applications generated with using Sencha.
2. **KonyOne**: The KonyOne platform is a paid tool and service offering that encompasses a development environment, code generators, device runtimes, and mobile middleware servers. KonyOne offers a wide range of application options including truly native apps on all native OSs, mobile-web, hybrid, wrapper, and legacy mobile applications. KonyOne supports a wide range of deployment options to offer a feature-rich cross-platform solution.
3. **nimblekit**: nimblekit is a paid framework that integrates with xCode IDE to build applications for iPhone/iPod Touch, iPad, or a universal application to run on both. nimblekit is a good runtime solution for projects that only want to build an application on iOS but want to use HTML and JavaScript instead of Objective-C for creating the application.

PROs

The PROs are as follows:

- **Performance**: The NWR approach will allow an application to run faster because it will not be running inside of another application, as is the case with a mobile-web application running inside of a web browser
- **Native components**: An NWR application will have additional access to services and components on the target device, which may not be available to mobile-web applications through HTML5
- **HTML5 capabilities**: Some NWR frameworks allow developers to leverage HTML5 capabilities
- **Cross-platform native code**: A single code-base can generate cross-platform code which runs natively on target devices

CONs

The CONs are as follows:

- **Native components**: An NWR might not support access to all features of a target device
- **Multiple code-bases**: An NWR typically creates a code-base for each target device which then needs to be compiled for each target language (Objective-C or Java)
- **Platform compilation**: Each time application changes are made, code must be compiled into each target platform

- **Performance**: Code generated applications are most likely slower than truly native applications due to the overhead of wrapper APIs used by the framework
- **Tools**: Code generation tools offer feature-rich editing components, but lack the advanced capabilities of platform-integrated development environments
- **Platform SDKs**: Developers still need platform-specific SDKs to package native binaries for delivery and distribution through app stores

See also

- *JQuery Mobile*: `http://jquerymobile.com/`
- *jQTouch*: `http://jqtouch.com/`
- *Modernizer*: `http://www.modernizr.com/`
- *Sencha*: `http://www.sencha.com/products/touch/`
- *Appcelerator*: `http://www.appcelerator.com/products/`
- *MobiFlex*: `http://viziapps.com/`
- *MonoTouch*: `http://xamarin.com/`
- *KonyOne*: `http://kony.com/konyone`
- *PhoneGap*: `http://phonegap.com/`
- *Nimblekit*: `http://nimblekit.com`
- *HTML5*: `http://www.w3.org/TR/html5/`
- *CSS*: `http://www.w3.org/Style/CSS/`
- *Mobile HTML5*: `http://mobilehtml5.org`
- *HTML5 Test*: `http://html5test.com`
- *CSS3 Test*: `http://css3test.com`
- *W3C Web Storage*: `http://www.w3.org/TR/webstorage/`
- *DOM Storage*: `https://developer.mozilla.org/en/DOM/Storage`

Native application considerations

In this recipe, we will understand the development, deployment, and distribution costs associated with developing on various native application platforms. These restrictions will affect project development in native languages, native code generation tools, as well as projects using native-web runtimes.

We will cover the two main operating system manufacturers on the market, Apple and Google, to better understand the implications of developing native apps.

Development considerations

Let's begin by reviewing the development implications for projects building the various native applications.

iOS

iOS is an Objective-C-based operating system developed by Apple Inc., first introduced in 2007. It incorporates multi-touch gestures, such as a swipe or tap directly on the device screen (branded by Apple as "Cocoa Touch" and derived from the Apple OS X operating system). iOS supports the mobile devices produced by Apple, including the iPhone, iPad, and iPod Touch. Although Objective-C is a "closed" system (Apple controls the source code and therefore the feature set), with over half a billion applications in its app store, iOS has positioned itself as an innovator and early leader in the mobile application marketplace.

Written in Objective-C

Objective-C is an object-oriented programming language, which adds Smalltalk-style messaging to its C-programming language syntax. Objects respond to messages, defined by (and encapsulated in) the object's interface.

The primary platform for iOS development is Mac OS X-based machines. This makes compiling the Objective-C and Cocoa Touch frameworks much easier than developing on Microsoft Windows, since iOS is a direct descendant of OS X. Given Apple's preference for a "closed" system, most find that when in Rome, it's best to do as the Romans, and use the development tools provided by Apple, which in this case includes developing on a Mac. For those whose preference is an open system that allows one to choose the tool for the job, the upside is that Apple has provided a flexible and proficient development environment with its xCode IDE.

IDE

xCode is the primary development IDE and is typically only available for the most recent Apple operating systems (currently OS X 10.7+). It is a free download from the Mac app store. As with many Apple products, xCode is tightly integrated with the hardware and software, allowing for a streamlined development environment with a common interface. The bundled "Instruments" tool set includes invaluable profiling and debugging tools for memory allocation, CPU monitoring and similar metrics.

Other considerations

As with any native application development, one assumes that a decisive decision has been made to benefit from the advantages of developing for the hardware's operating system. Beyond just considerations for specific hardware access, such as a mobile device's camera and GPS, operating system features such as notifications and platform look and feel are important considerations, in addition to how users will access the application. For instance, in the latter case, consider the benefits of a web application in contrast to native development. A user who is using the device's web browser to access the app content will enjoy streamlined access to the content provided by a Web app loaded in the device browser, assuming none of the features specific to native app development are needed, versus having to download a native application to the device. This is just one example to highlight the importance of weighing the pros and cons of native app development. Another critical consideration is which devices need to be supported, as web apps naturally excel in providing access to content across platforms.

Building and deployment of working applications is an essential part of the development and project lifecycle. Let's look as some of the issues a project must consider during the build and deployment lifecycles.

iOS

Both building and deploying an iOS application are a unique experience for those accustomed to command line and/or automated build systems, and as expected, reflect a distinctive Apple methodology. Compiling and linking of the Obj-C codebase is rather straightforward in practice, and is performed in the xCode IDE. Proper configuration of the build for a particular type of distribution license is where the complexity lies, especially when considering targeted device types and operating system levels. Explicitly stating the targeted iOS level and device type is necessary as newer operating features are naturally only available after a particular release and some features are not available for a given device. It is also worth noting that when developing for the iPad, two options are available: An app can be written for both iPhone and iPad in a single installable IPA archive, or a distinct iPad-specific archive can be created. This decision must be made when creating the xCode project.

Build automation

There is no Apple-supported build automation process for iOS application development. Building an iOS application is done, as expected, through xCode. There are third-party efforts to automate building with open source automation environments, such as Jenkins, but these efforts lie outside the scope of this book at present. Apple does provide the "UI Automation" API that uses the Instruments console to execute a custom script written in JavaScript. This method can be useful for automating an application's user interface in the iOS simulator, but given the collection of tools made available by Apple to support iOS development, this particular API extension still leaves a lot to be desired for enterprise-level automation and integration.

Deployment

Within the xCode project, settings are a comprehensive list of property settings that control almost all aspects of the archive file's distribution and deployment. In addition to the vast collection of property options, there are settings for deployment targets, SDK levels, compiler options, and code signing identities, just to name a few. Ultimately, xCode creates an archive bundle with an `.ipa` extension that includes all program assets, and is code-signed for distribution.

Installing an iOS application involves nothing more than downloading the `.ipa` archive file from the device, which iOS will install automatically and make accessible via a desktop icon. The archive can be hosted by Apple's app store, or for enterprise distribution, on an in-house, typically access-controlled intranet server. However, as mentioned previously, the `.ipa` file must be signed appropriately such that the user has appropriate rights to install the archive. When required, iOS will prompt the device user for credentials (for example, when purchasing from the app store).

Android

Building and deploying Android applications is an essential part of the project lifecycle, and is easy to integrate into enterprise teams. The main considerations are integrating the compilation into new or existing build automation ecosystems, and the other is deploying the application for testing and prototyping purposes.

Build automation

Continuous integration and build automation are important facets of Java teams, and Android development can be integrated into these ecosystems with relatively little effort.

Standard build automation tools such as Ant, Maven, and Gradle offer Android compilation, emulation, and packaging that can be automatically run from continuous integration servers such as Jenkins.

Deployment

Applications can be manually copied to a device and installed with the help of file management applications running on the target device, but using the ADB to install applications is a more direct approach for development teams.

Distribution considerations

Let's begin by reviewing the development implications for projects building the various native applications.

iOS

Apple has streamlined the process for end users to purchase and install applications. Convenience for the end user, however, translates to complexity for the application developer. The developer is responsible for proper code signing and distribution of the application distributable. This requires getting familiar with Apple's code-signing and distribution process.

A thorough review of Apple's documentation is required for the proper configuration of a project's build setting and targets in xCode via the aforementioned project property files. This assumes the developer has already requested, downloaded, and installed the appropriate certificates to their system's Keychain. Certificates are used to negotiate the private/public handshake that authenticates the user for a specific domain. Apple users will recognize the Keychain as the location where certificates, keys, passwords, and other security-sensitive data is stored on a Mac.

Certificates

Certificates can be requested and downloaded from the Apple Developer iOS Provisioning Portal, which is accessible online after an Apple Developer account is created. As Apple states, all iOS applications must be signed by a valid certificate in order to be installed on a device. For individual developers needing a testing certificate, be sure to request an iOS Development Certificate. You will also need to set up a Provisioning Profile, which can likewise be configured in the iOS Provisioning Portal. The Provisioning Profile will be tied to various device IDs, known as the UUID (a unique identifier for every Apple device).

Screenshots

The iTunes store requires one splash screen image (512px by 512px) and one to five application screenshots (320px by 480px) in `.png`, `.gif`, or `.jpg` format. iTunes is very specific about the size of the images and will reject images that are not of the exact specified size.

Distribution cost

Apple Developer registration is $99 per year and you can submit multiple applications for distribution per one account. Application submission is not a guarantee the application will be accepted by Apple for inclusion into the iTunes store.

An additional fee of 30% of the app's selling price is charged for paid applications.

Other distribution considerations

A popular distribution platform for testing iOS applications is TestFlight, `http://www.testflightapp.com`. The site is still officially in beta at the time of writing this book but has matured quickly into an impressive team-testing tool used by many companies. TestFlight allows users to register and join teams to support app distribution and testing. There are access controls in place for familiar user roles, such as admin, tester, and so on. Devices must be registered so as to restrict installation only to targeted devices. TestFlight makes available a custom SDK that allows code to be instrumented for fine-grain tracking of test activity and error/crash reporting. TestFlight is definitely worth considering, especially given the cost. It is a free service at the time of writing.

Android

Android applications are fairly easy to distribute but it's a somewhat manual process to add the application to the *Google Play Store* or the little known competitor, *Amazon Appstore*. Both stores have a manual web-based submission process but the process for both can be done in a few pages.

Both stores have an application validation period for new or updated applications and the delay can be anywhere from a few minutes to a few weeks.

In *Chapter 7*, *Deployment and Configuration*, we will cover how to submit an Android application to both Google Play Store, and the Amazon Appstore.

Screenshots

Both Google Play Store and Amazon Appstore require one splash screen image (512px by 512px) and 3 to 10 application screenshots (320px by 480px) in `.png`, `.gif`, or `.jpg` format. Both stores are somewhat lenient on the exact dimensions of the images.

Distribution cost

Google Play: Android Developer registration is a one-time fee of $25 and you can submit multiple applications for distribution per one account.

An additional fee of $20 and 30% of the app's selling price is charged for submitting paid apps.

Amazon Appstore: Amazon Developer registration is $99 per year and you can submit multiple applications for distribution per one account. Application submission can take several weeks before receiving a notification of acceptance or rejection of the application.

Additional fee of 30% of the app's selling price is charged for paid applications.

See also

- *Objective-C*: `http://en.wikipedia.org/wiki/Objective-C`
- *iOS SDK*: `http://www.apple.com/ios/`

- *iOS*: `http://en.wikipedia.org/wiki/IOS`
- *Cocoa Touch*: `http://en.wikipedia.org/wiki/Cocoa_Touch`
- *Apple iOS Dev Center*: `https://developer.apple.com/devcenter/ios/index.action`
- *Android SDK*: `http://developer.android.com/sdk/index.html`
- *Google Developer*: `https://play.google.com/apps/publish/`
- *Amazon Developer*: `http://developer.amazon.com/`

Leveraging mobile design tools

When it comes to designing mobile applications, whether you are going to design a mobile-web or a native application for a specific device, it is very helpful to spend some effort mocking up the proposed design with the business stakeholders as well as team members. These design sessions can help determine initial prototype transitions and layouts. In addition to design and mock-ups, screen captures from prototype applications can be in the project lifecycle and are mandatory for application submissions to stores.

Design and mock-ups

In this recipe we are going to look at tools that can aid a project in mocking screen layouts, transitions wireframes, and create screen captures of the application prototypes.

Android designer

We first want to look at some Android designer tools that allow for mocking of a mobile application and can generate initial layout files that can directly be used in your Android application, and possibly generate a prototype application that can be rendered on a target Android device.

MIT App Inventor

App Inventor was an experimental project created by Google that dropped from the Google line-up in late 2011 and has since been adopted by **Massachusetts Institute of Technology** (**MIT**) and can be found at `http://beta.appinventor.mit.edu`.

The App Inventor interface has decent functionality for an online editor, and has many features including the ability to export a working application that can be installed on an Android device prototyping a design.

In addition, App Inventor offers a desktop application that will allow the application to be directly installed onto a device that is connected to the desktop. This allows for a faster turn-around when prototyping an interface.

DroidDraw

DroidDraw is a Windows desktop application that allows for quick prototyping of user interface components onto an Android emulation. The widgets in this tool are enough to kick-start basic design layouts.

DroidDraw allows for importing and exporting of layout XML files, so once you have a design, you can export the layout and use it in your working Android application. You can also re-import a layout XML file back into DroidDraw after external modification has been made to the layout.

DroidDraw is not a tool for continuous round-trip engineering, but is a valuable tool for starting an Android project:

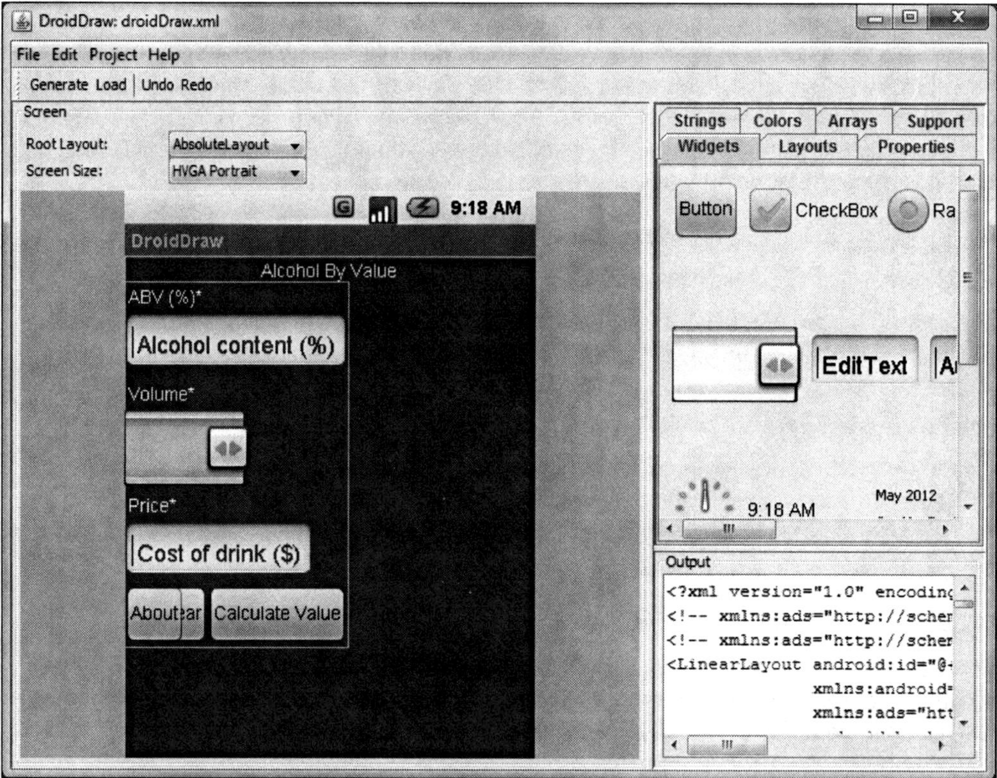

DroidDraw has the ability to generate a deployable application in `*.apk` format which will allow rapid prototyping of designs on target devices.

Another nice feature is a small mobile application called AnDroidDraw which allows you to download and preview your mock-ups on your Android device. AnDroidDraw is a small application that must be installed onto a target device, and then will receive a layout from DroidDraw running on the **Android Debug Bridge** (**ADB**) by a TCP push. This can save you a lot of time during the mock-up and design phase to get your application's look and feel to look exactly the way you need on an actual device.

In order for DroidDraw to connect to a device and push a layout design to AnDroidDraw, there are a few steps you must perform:

1. Start the ADB which will allow the developer to connect a device to a computer for debug control.
2. Next, you need to open a command terminal and tell the ADB to allow DroidDraw, which is communicating on port `6100` to forward the requests to port `7100` which is where the ADB connection to the connected device is running:

   ```
   adb forward tcp:6100 tcp:7100
   ```

3. Start the AnDroidDraw application on the target device.
4. On the DroidDraw GUI, in the **File** menu, select **Project** | **Send GUI to Device**:

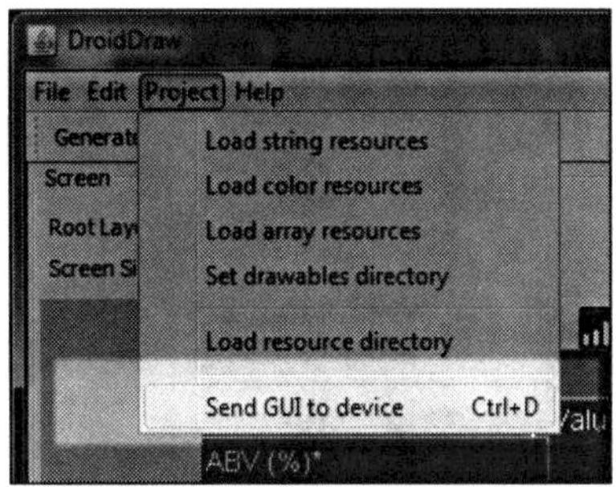

5. AnDroidDraw should now have the layout XML in the form field as seen in the following screenshot:

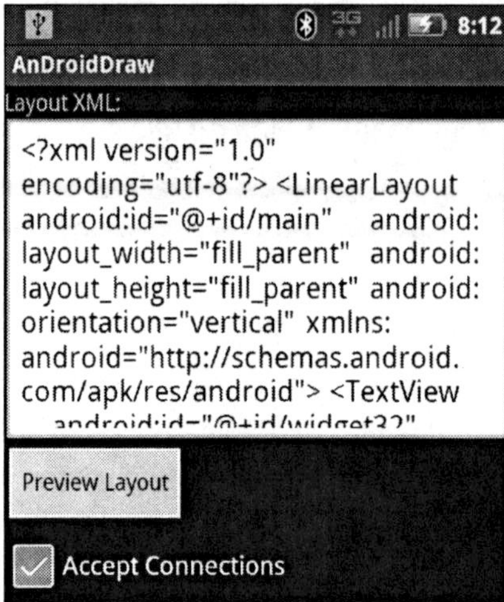

6. Once the layout is loaded into AnDroidDraw, click the **Preview Layout** button to view the layout rendered on the device. Some of the layouts will not render the same as seen in DroidDraw depending upon the device being tested as seen in the following screenshot:

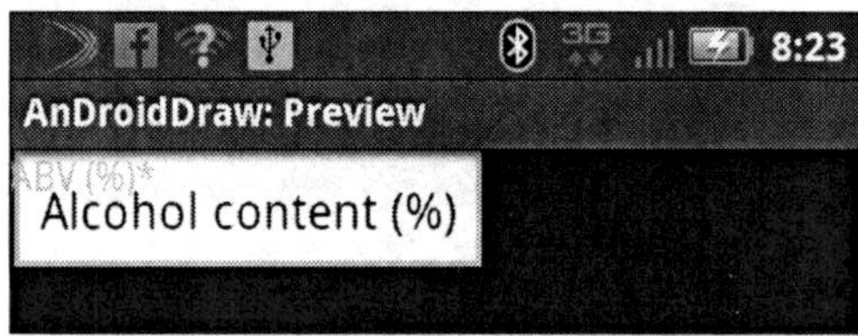

The DroidDraw to AnDroidDraw Bridge works relatively well, but the AnDroidDraw application itself seems to have device-dependent issues running complex layouts built in DroidDraw. These tools can be used for initial prototypes but might not be a strong tool for round-trip engineering of complex Android layouts.

Online designers

Online editors are easy ways to create wire frame mark-ups that don't require specific software installed, in addition to a web browser compatible with the editors implementation, which is usually Adobe Flash.

Online editors have advantages where mark-ups can be edited by several members, and exported for presentation if required for further collaboration. They are typically used for discussion and collaboration and do not typically generate implementable code.

iPlotz

iPlotz is an online wireframe prototyping application which allows you to rapidly create clickable, navigable mock-up wireframes that you can save as projects. They have a free plan with reduced features but also offer monthly or yearly plans with a varying array of additional features.

This is a great tool that is easy to use, so stakeholders and developers can access the projects online and are very easy to create. They even have Android, iPhone, and iPad stencils for cross-device mock-ups.

iPhoneMock-up

iPhoneMock-up is another online mock-up and prototyping application. This gives you the ability to design wireframes with well-formed illustration elements or by creating wireframes with a pencil notation, which gives more of a look of sketching ideas to discuss, versus actual elements by size.

This tool is great during initial collaboration and mind-mapping exercises to delay some of the formality of designing for specific device layouts and just document the ideas to foster further discussion and direction:

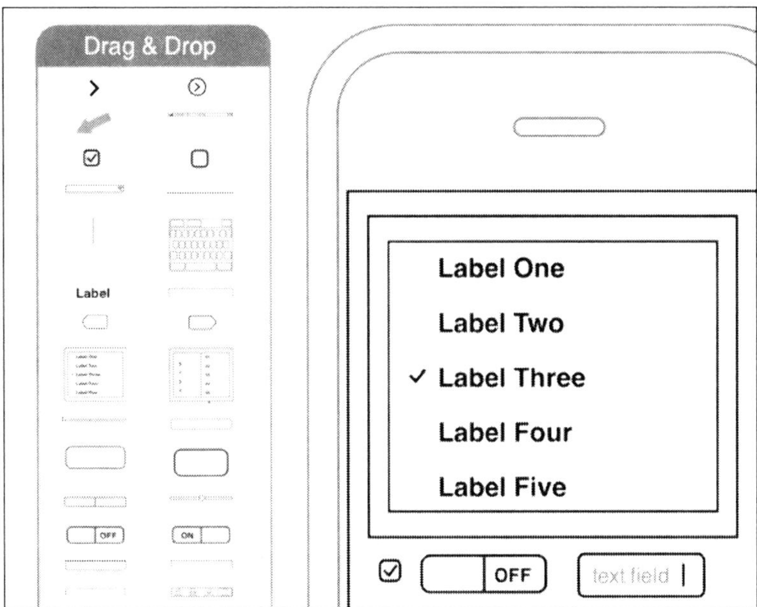

ThemeRoller

ThemeRoller is an online design tool to aid a developer creating a jQuery or jQuery mobile application that wants to preview various theme combinations.

The ThemeRoller mobile tool makes it easy to create custom-designed themes for your mobile site or app. Just pick colors, then share your theme URL, or download the theme and drop it into your site:

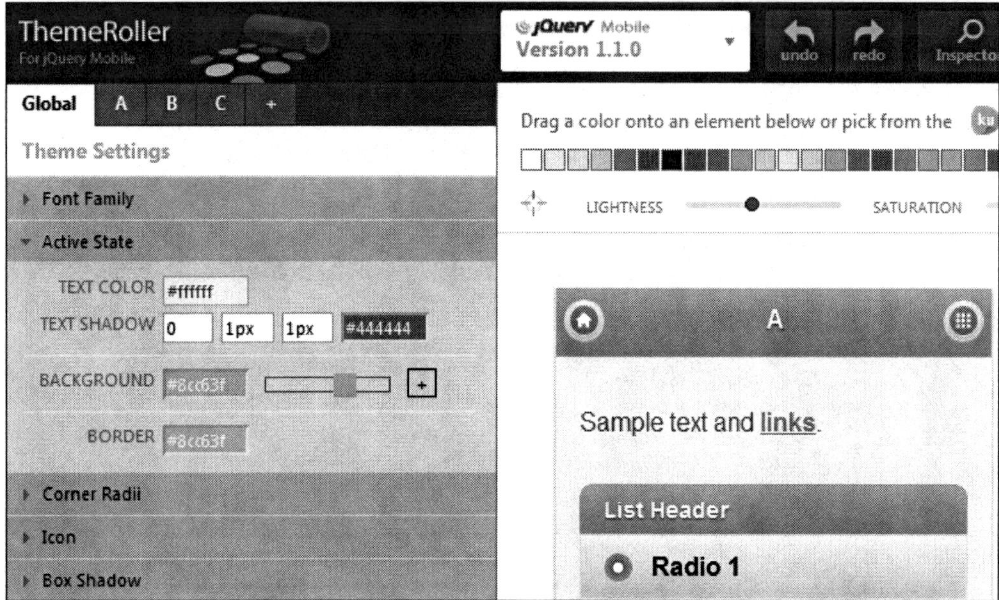

A nice feature of ThemeRoller is the ability to create multiple swatch themes that you can compare just by selecting a new tab.

Additional design resources

There are certainly many more design and wireframe mock-up application stencils and code generation tools for the various types of mobile applications you are planning to build. Many different tools and templates are entering the marketplace every day including Visio, Word, Adobe Photoshop, and many more. The examples in this recipe are only a very small set of the options that are available to teams. I hope this would stress the importance of design preparation for mobile development especially for enterprise developers that are used to designing and developing for backend or MVC2-based applications.

A little planning can help make the transition into mobile device development easier.

There's more...

Any project that plans to release their application to one of the many stores will be required to gather screenshots of the application for the application submission process. Some stores are stricter than others about the resolution and dimensions, but images are what give users the first impression, so having great photos should be an important consideration. Photos can also provide presentation and collaboration material for stakeholders and other team members.

There are several Android applications that assist with taking screen captures, but most of them require a phone to have ROOT access, so device support can be very inconsistent. I have tried several and was not able to have any success running them against Motorola Droid X first generation that did not have ROOT access.

Android Screenshots and Screen Capture

Android Screenshots and Screen Capture (**ASHOT**) worked with little issue getting the application configured. Besides Java, the Android SDK along with the corresponding Google USB drivers is required to be installed for this desktop application to run. The project is hosted on SourceForge at `http://sourceforge.net/projects/ashot/` and the installation instructions are very straightforward.

The things this tool excels at are taking high quality screenshots averaging 250 KB in size and a dimension of 480x854 as shown in the following screenshot:

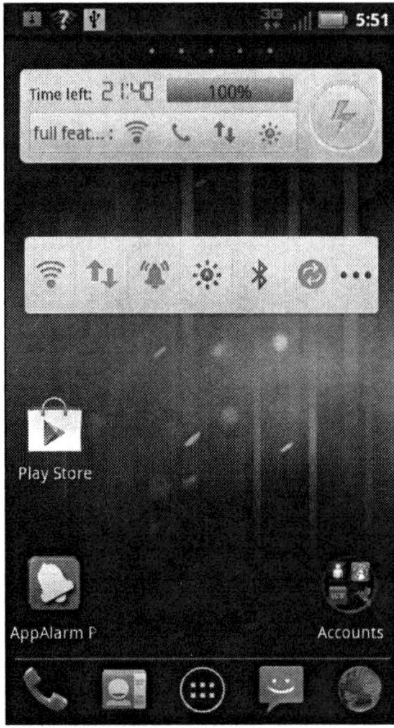

There is also a function to start a capture session where ASHOT will capture a user navigating the device screen-by-screen which can be useful to capture a series of screen transitions.

iPhone screen capture

For taking screen captures on an iPhone device, no additional applications or software is required.

In order to take a screenshot of the current view on your phone, simply press the sleep button on the top of the phone as shown in the following screenshot:

While simultaneously pressing the **Home** button as illustrated here:

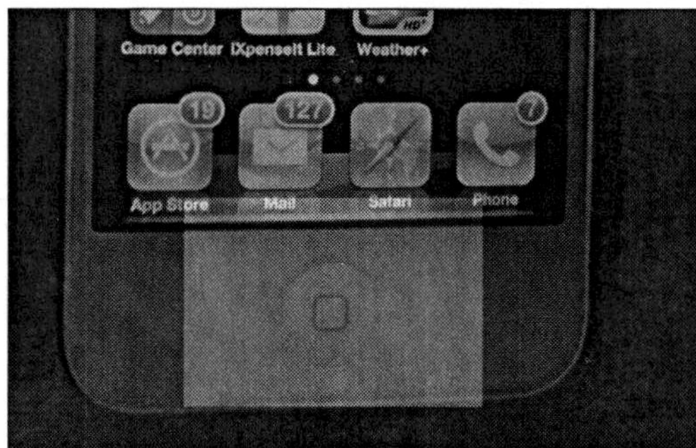

This will capture the current screen and save the image to your iPhone Camera Roll where you can then download or share the image.

It is especially a good idea to view how mobile-web applications render on an iPhone. The example application used in this chapter does not render as large as it did on an Android device, making the interface almost impossible to use.

See also

- *MIT App Inventor*: `http://beta.appinventor.mit.edu`
- *DroidDraw*: `http://www.droiddraw.org/`
- *AnDroidDraw*: `http://www.droiddraw.org/androiddraw.html`

- *Android Screenshots*: `http://sourceforge.net/projects/ashot/`
- *ThemeRoller*: `http://jquerymobile.com/themeroller/`
- *iPlotz*: `http://iplotz.com/index.php`
- *iPhoneMock-up*: `http://iphonemockup.lkmc.ch/`
- *Screenshot UX*: `https://play.google.com/store/apps/details?id=com.liveov.shotux`

Testing mobile-web applications with online emulators

When building a mobile-web application, it is sometimes helpful for emulation of the application without the requirement of installing an emulator just for testing. There are several online options that use Adobe Flash to create an iPhone and Android emulator that will allow for emulation of a mobile-website if the URI is accessible to the emulator.

These online emulators can also be helpful for stakeholders to preview an application, as well as see how the application might look on a device that might not be available to the user.

Getting ready

To begin we first must ensure we have a mobile-web application deployed to a location where the emulators will be able to access. Running an application from a local machine using 127.0.0.1 will not work for remote access and you need to use the IP address designated by the network you are connecting to, such as 192.168.1.101, which can be found by running the `ipconfig` command on a Windows command window or command shell.

Next, you should validate you have a compatible web browser to run the emulator. We will be reviewing several different emulators in this recipe, but they will be essentially from two different providers. The *testiphone.com* emulator requires FireFox 2+, Internet Explorer 7, or Safari 3+ but I have been testing it against the Chrome Dev Channel 20.0.1123.4 and have not found any notable issues.

The **-emulator.org* emulator requires Firefox 3.6+, Chromium 5+, and Opera 10.4+ and I have also been testing it against the Chrome Dev Channel 20.0.1123.4 and did find issues running the application in portrait orientation. I also tested it against Firefox 12 and did not have any success getting a jQuery-Mobile application or mobile.google.com to work.

How to do it...

All you need to do is enter the URL for your mobile-web into the address bar input field and hit the *Enter* key. We will use `http://baselogic.com/abv/abv.html` as the application for this recipe.

The defaults for both emulators are landscape or vertical orientation. The following screenshot shows the application loaded in the iPhone emulator from `testiphone.com`:

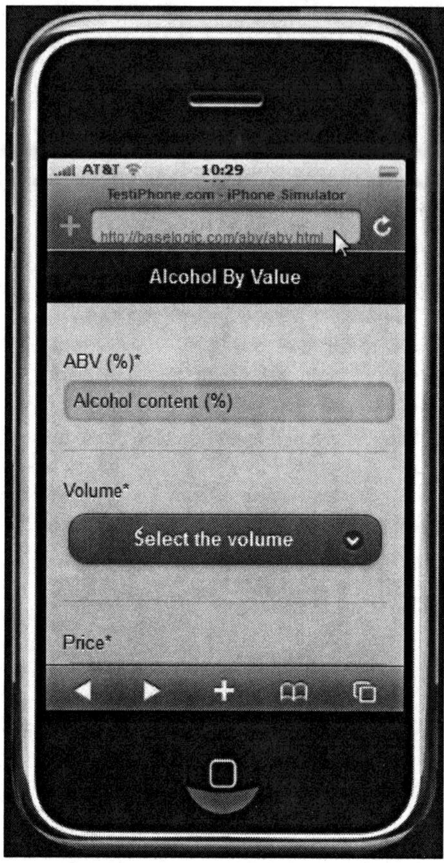

We can also preload the URL to test by passing query string parameters in the browser address bar. For `testiphone.com` we need to send a URL parameter such as:

```
http://testiphone.com/?url=http://baselogic.com/abv/abv.html
```

The emulators on *-emulator.org can also have the URL preloaded by passing a URL parameter such as: `http://android-emulator.org/?url=baselogic.com/abv/abv.html`.

The following screenshot depicts the application on a Motorola Droid device:

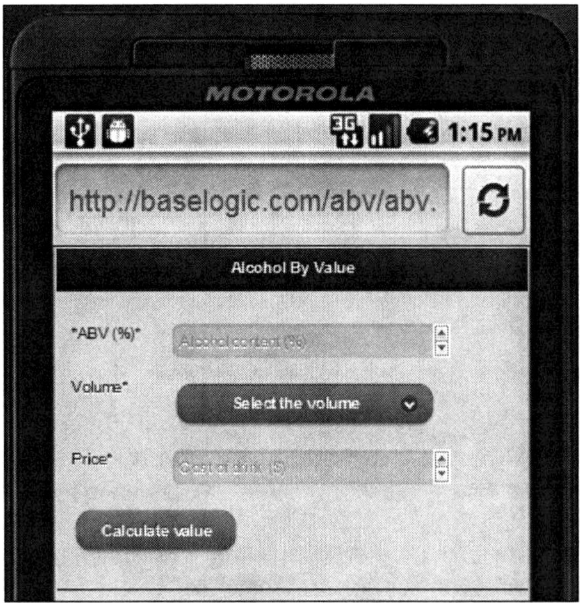

In addition to the Android emulator just depicted, the *-emulator.org series of sites also offers an iPhone emulator (`iphone-emulator.org`), iPad emulator (`ipad-emulator.org`), Blackberry emulator (`blackberry-emulator.org`) and an Android Tablet emulator (`tablet-emulator.org`) which will give a great simulation of various devices.

Unfortunately I was not successful in Chrome or Firefox to simulate horizontal or portrait orientation on *-emulator.org, but the site's notes state it should be possible by appending `&portrait` to the query string as depicted: `http://android-emulator.org/?url=http://baselogic.com/abv/abv.html&portrait`.

I was able to get testiphone.com to work in horizontal mode by adding `view=hor` to the query-string as depicted: `http://testiphone.com/?view=hor&url=http://baselogic.com/abv/abv.html`.

The resulting rendering in the iPhone emulator is depicted in the following screenshot:

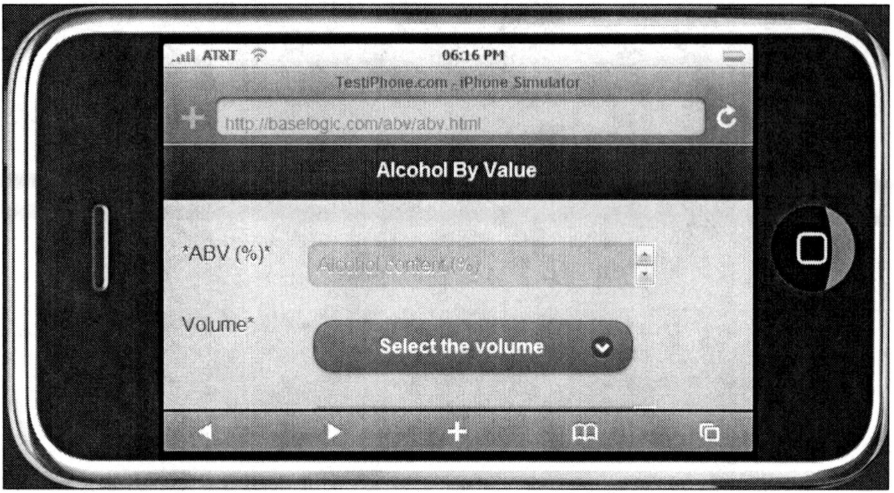

Once the application is running in any of the emulators, you can manipulate the application normally and attain some sense of how the application will look, feel, and operate on the device. The following shows how the emulator will be running the application, and how the results page will be displayed on an iPhone:

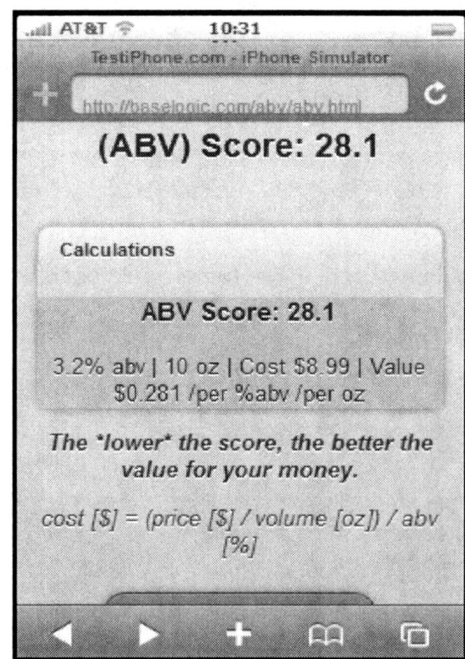

The iPhone emulator can give us a much better perspective of how the application will look on an actual device, in contrast to what you see when you're using a web browser to develop the application as seen here:

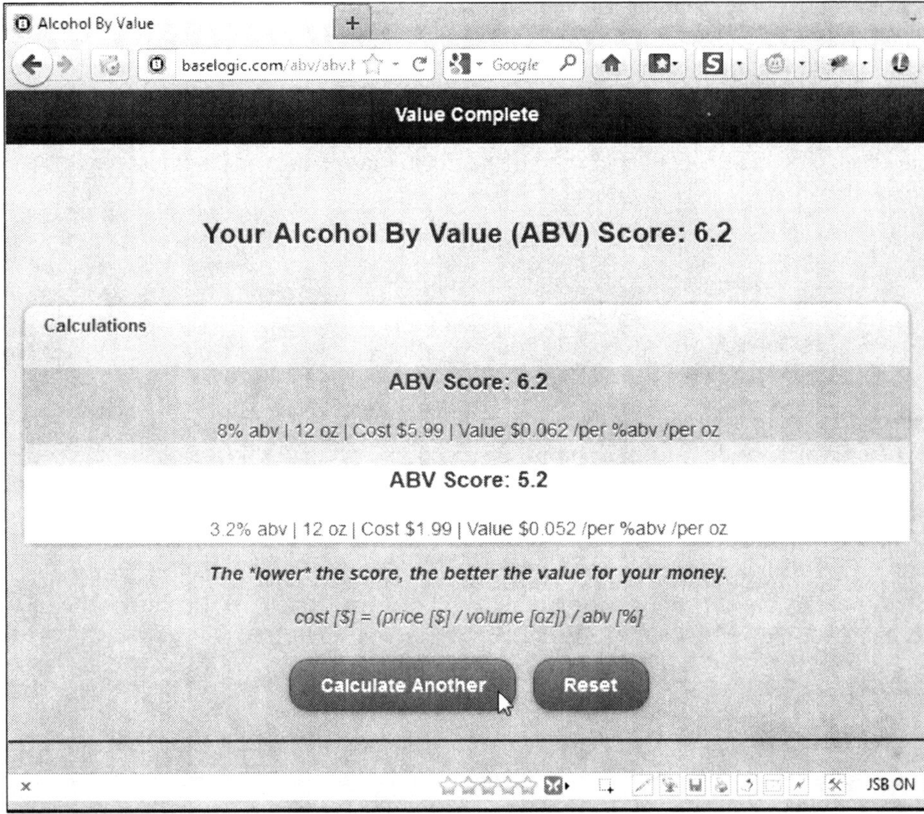

There's a significant difference between the various emulators, but they will still allow us to get a general sense of the look-and-feel early in the development process without too much effort.

See also

- *TestiPhone*: `http://www.testiphone.com/`
- *Android-Emulator*: `http://android-emulator.org`
- *iPhone-Emulator*: `http://iphone-emulator.org`
- *iPad-Emulator*: `http://ipad-emulator.org`
- *Blackberry-Emulator*: `http://blackberry-emulator.org`
- *Tablet-Emulator*: `http://tablet-emulator.org`

Setting up a local Apache environment

XAMPP is an easy to install Apache distribution containing MySQL, PHP, and Perl. XAMPP is really very easy to install and to use: just download, extract, and start. Tomcat 6 is also distributed with XAMPP as of version 1.7.4 but upgrading to Tomcat 7 is fairly simple, and we will cover the upgrade process in this recipe.

This recipe is going to allow us to learn how to leverage Apache and Tomcat locally in a pre-configured distribution which can be useful in many situations, not just for mobile applications.

But for the focus of this chapter on mobile development, we are going to look at how we can deploy and test a mobile-web application such as jQuery-Mobile.

Getting ready

First we need to download the ZIP archive distribution of XAMPP from `http://www.apachefriends.org/en/xampp.html` and, for this recipe, we will cover a Windows installation although Mac OS X, Solaris, and Linux distributions are also available.

"XAMPP Lite" is an extra small XAMPP edition that does come configured with Apache, MySQL, and PHP. To ease the installation of XAMPP configured with relative paths, you can use it on USB devices. However, the standard XAMPP distribution version 1.7.7 contains the new control panel `xampp-control-3-beta` which works well on a USB drive.

How to do it...

Once downloaded, just open in WinZip or other unzip program, then extract the contents to either a physical drive or a USB drive if you plan to re-use this installation on several machines. The extracted contents are approximately 500 MB but if installing on a USB drive, care must be taken to ensure the USB drive has enough capacity for content and web applications to be deployed to the installation.

Once unpacked, open Windows Explorer and navigate to the drive where XAMPP was installed.

Then go into the `E:\xampp` directory and you will see several batch (`*.exe`) files available, specifically `xampp-control-3-beta.exe`, `xampp-control.exe`, `xampp-start.exe`, and `xampp-stop.exe` which are the main applications for running and controlling XAMPP.

How it works...

By executing `xampp-control-3-beta.exe` you will bring up the XAMPP console where you can turn the various components on and off as well as view server status, access logs, and configure the various components.

By default, Apache is running on port 80 and SSL on port 443 and will start automatically. If you want to change which applications get started automatically, you can edit `E:\xampp\xampp-control-3-beta.ini` and edit the servers under the `[Autostart]` section as seen in the following listing:

```
[Autostart]
Apache=1
MySQL=0
FileZilla=0
Mercury=0
Tomcat=1
```

You set the application to one (`1`) to have XAMPP automatically start up when XAMPP starts, and zero (`0`) will require the application to be manually started.

Now at this point you can open a browser to `http://localhost/xampp/index.php` and you should see the following home page:

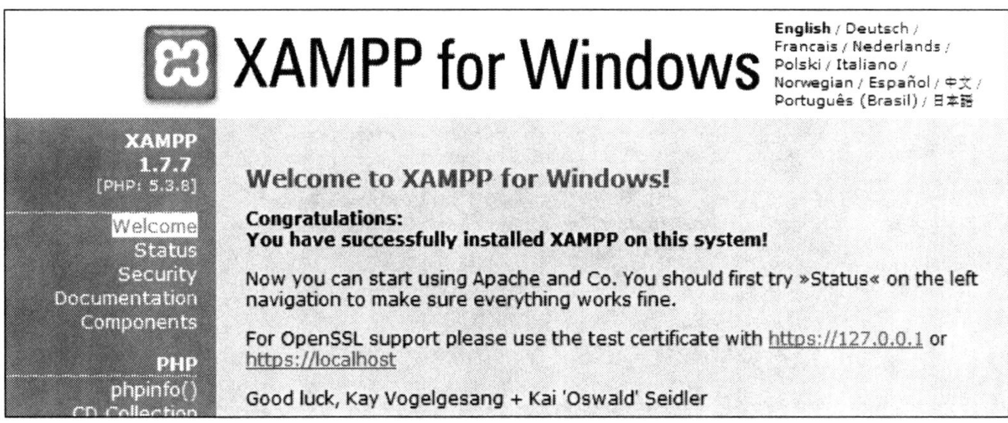

There's more...

At this point we should be able to add content under the Apache folder and have it accessible immediately. The root folder is located at `E:\xampp\htdocs` and, for testing purposes for this recipe, we will navigate to `E:\xampp\htdocs\` in Windows Explorer and create a new directory to place our test files.

This recipe is not intended to cover the creation of web content, but the content used for this example has been added to the public *Github* repository located at `https://github.com/mickknutson/javaeecookbook`.

A JSP was copied to the apache `htdocs` content directory, but Apache does not know how to handle that file type so it will be rendered as plain text. We will cover how to integrate Apache with Tomcat for JSP and Servlet support later in this chapter.

Apache will be able to serve standard HTML content as well as PHP and Perl content out of the box. If we open a page through Apache, we just reference `localhost:80` or `127.0.0.1:80` for non-secured content:

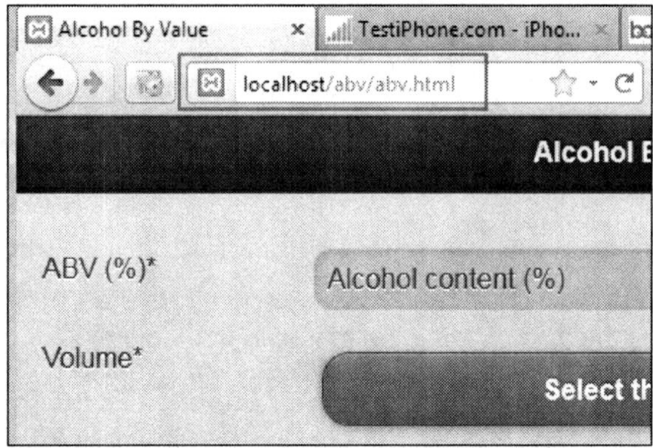

Apache can also serve SSL-secured pages by navigating to `https://localhost` or `https://127.0.0.1` which will most likely result in an SLL error stating the SSL certificate is self-signed and not issued by an Authority:

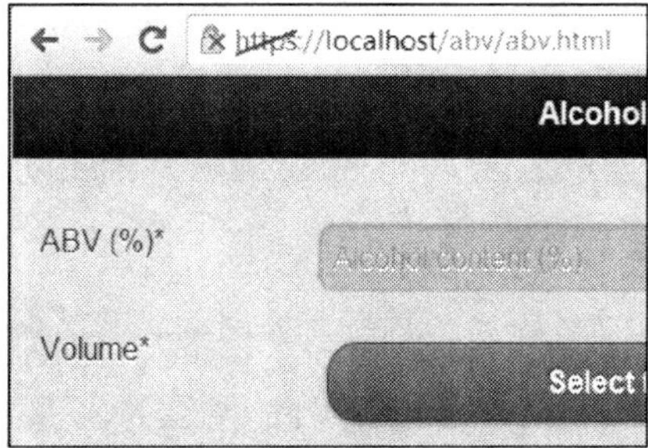

To start, we are going to look at how a local Apache installation can assist in developing mobile-web applications accessing services with JSONP requests. The Remote Service can be any technology that results in HTTP content which will be interpreted by the mobile-web application:

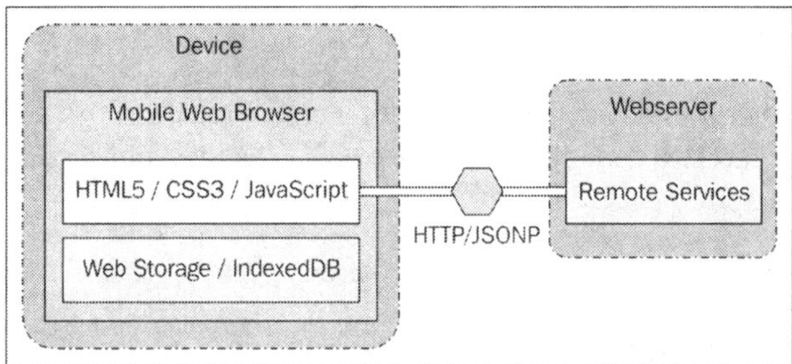

This will give us the ability to create HTML5-based mobile-web applications such as jQuery, deploy and test them in Apache, which will be a faster build cycle, versus creating a WAR and deploying the mobile-web app to Tomcat. This also gives the ability to test and run those applications over non-secured HTTP and secured HTTPS protocols without additional configuration.

Stopping XAMPP

In order to stop the XAMPP control panel, you must click the **Quit** button on the control panel. Clicking the window's close or X icon in the upper-right-hand portion of the window will only minimize, or close the window, but will not stop the control panel and will not stop any of the XAMPP services.

Stopping the XAMPP control panel will not stop the services that were started. In order to stop the services, you need to open the XAMPP control panel and stop the services one at a time, and then quit to the XAMPP control panel to fully exit XAMPP and all of the services.

Upgrading Tomcat 7

XAMPP ships with Tomcat 6 and it is recommended that you upgrade to Tomcat 7.0.27+ to run the example code or to build your own Java EE applications. Tomcat 7 is fairly new as it was released from beta state on January 14th, 2011 and has active development on this project. There have been several issues with some of the early releases, especially related to other frameworks, such as Weld, to provide CDI support to the Web Profile Tomcat supports. A detailed change-log is available on the Tomcat site at `http://tomcat.apache.org/tomcat-7.0-doc/changelog.html`:

1. Stop XAMPP.

   Before we begin, ensure XAMPP is stopped by executing `E:\ xampp_stop.exe` which will stop all services started by XAMPP as well as the XAMPP control panel.

2. Download the Tomcat 7 distribution.

   For this recipe we assumed XAMPP Windows version was used, so when downloading Tomcat 7, download the Windows ZIP version for your system (32-bit or 64-bit). Do not use the Windows installer.

3. Rename existing Tomcat installs.

   Just for safe measure, I recommend renaming the existing Tomcat installation instead of deleting it. Once you have verified that the new installation works as desired, you can delete the old installation.

   Rename `E:\xampp\tomcat\ to E:\xampp\tomcat6\` because XAMPP looks for a directory called Tomcat in order to integrate Tomcat into the control panel.

4. Unpack distribution.

   Unpack the new Tomcat 7 ZIP file into `E:\xampp\` which should result in a directory called `E:\xampp\apache-tomcat-7.0.27\`.

5. Rename the distribution directory.

   In order for XAMPP to find Tomcat, the directory must be renamed from `E:\xampp\apache-tomcat-7.0.27\` to `E:\xampp\tomcat\`. This is hardcoded into the control panel application.

6. Copy start and stop scripts.

   In order for XAMPP to start and stop Tomcat, copy `E:\xampp\tomcat6\catalina_start.bat` and `E:\xampp\tomcat6\catalina_stop.bat` into `E:\xampp\tomcat\` as these batch scripts are used by the XAMPP control panel to start and stop Tomcat and will work for any tomcat version.

7. Start XAMPP.

   Start the XAMPP control panel by executing `E:\xampp\xampp-control-3-beta.exe`. If Tomcat is set to automatically start, then after a few seconds, the Tomcat status will turn green:

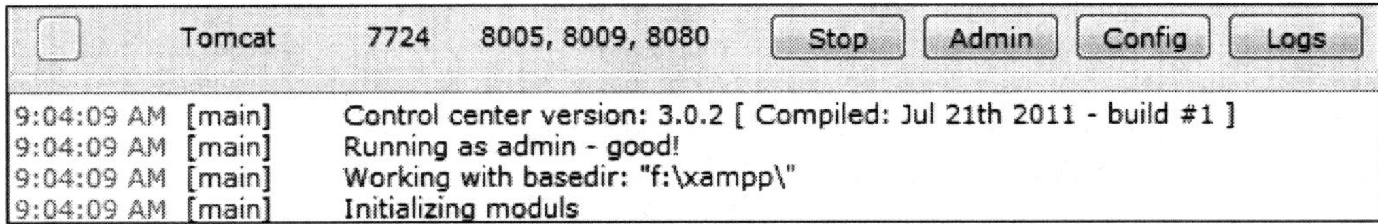

To verify, you are now running version 7, open any web browser and navigate to `http://localhost:8080/` and you should see a default splash screen like this:

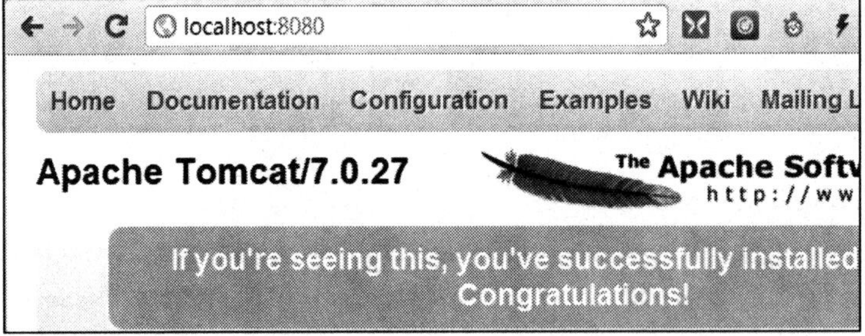

That is all that is required for upgrading to Tomcat 7 with XAMPP.

Accessing Tomcat applications through Apache

Another great feature of XAMPP is that Apache is pre-configured to access Tomcat applications with the Apache JServ Protocol version 1.3 (AJP13), so any web applications deployed to Tomcat can be accessed on port 80:

1. Deploy the Tomcat application.

   The first step is to deploy an application to Tomcat which will be used for this recipe.

   For this example, we will assume that we are deploying `ch06-web-mobile.war` to Tomcat which deploys the application and is accessible in a web browser at `http://127.0.0.1:8080/ch06-web-mobile/`.

2. Add AJP application entries.

   To begin, open `E:\xampp\apache\conf\extra\httpd-ajp.conf` in a text editor.

   We want to add our configuration just below the following proxy directives:

   ```
   <Proxy *>
   Order deny,allow
   allow from all
   </Proxy>
   ```

   The configuration for each application mapping is simply adding a single `ProxyPass` directive for each application mapping required. To map `ch06-web-mobile`, we need to add the following directive:

   ```
   ProxyPass /ch06-web-mobile ajp://127.0.0.1:8009/ch06-web-mobile
   ```

   We can also change the context name Apache will associate with the deployed application to anything we want. In this listing we will add another entry for `/javaee6` as the Apache context:

   ```
   ProxyPass /javaee6 ajp://127.0.0.1:8009/ch06-web-mobile
   ```

3. Restart Apache.

   In order for this change to take effect, we need to restart Apache.

   - Open the XAMPP control panel and click the stop action
   - Wait for Apache to completely stop
   - Click the start action button to start Apache.

4. Verifying Apache AJP configuration.

   To verify the AJP connection is working correctly, open a web browser and navigate to the corresponding URL for your mapping. The first mapping would be:

   `http://127.0.0.1/ch06-web-mobile/`

We should also be able to access the same application with the alternative mapping:

```
http://127.0.0.1/javaee6/
```

And because XAMPP is pre-configured with SSL, we can now access the application on HTTPS (port 443):

```
https://127.0.0.1/javaee6/
```

Now we have a mobile development solution to use Apache and Tomcat in a variety of architectural configurations.

Changing the installation PATH

If you are installing XAMPP on a USB drive, or if you want to move the physical drive, or even directory where XAMPP is installed, you cannot just move the directory. This is more problematic with USB installations as the drive letter can change between drive mountings.

XAMPP comes with a setup script that edits the various configuration files to adjust the PATH where XAMPP is installed.

1. Shutdown XAMPP.

   First stop all running services, and then shutdown the XAMPP control panel.

2. Move XAMPP.

   Next, move the `xampp` directory to the desired location, let's say from `F:\xampp` to `C:\xampp`.

3. Run XAMPP setup script.

   Execute `C:\xampp\setup_xampp.bat` which will result in a command window asking about refreshing the XAMPP installation:

   ```
   Do you want to refresh the XAMPP installation?
   Soll die XAMPP Installation jetzt aktualisiert werden?

   1) Refresh now! (Jetzt aktualisieren!)
   x) Exit (Beenden)
   ```

   Here we are prompted to enter 1 to refresh the installation, or x to exit this script without any action.

Type 1 then hit the *Enter* key, which will refresh the installation:

```
Do you want to refresh the XAMPP installation?
Soll die XAMPP Installation jetzt aktualisiert werden?

1) Refresh now! (Jetzt aktualisieren!)
x) Exit (Beenden)

XAMPP is refreshing now ...
XAMPP wird nun aktualisiert ...

Refreshing all paths in config files ...

Configure XAMPP with awk for 'Windows_NT'
Please wait ...  DONE!

##### Have fun with ApacheFriends XAMPP! #####

Press any key to continue . . .
```

You now have successfully relocated the XAMPP installation.

See also

- *XAMPP on Apache Friends*: `http://www.apachefriends.org/en/index.html`
- *Cross-Origin Resource Sharing (CORS)*: `http://en.wikipedia.org/wiki/Cross-Origin_Resource_Sharing`
- *JSONP*: `http://en.wikipedia.org/wiki/JSONP`
- *Apache JServ Protocol*: `http://en.wikipedia.org/wiki/Apache_JServ_Protocol`
- *Apache AJP Module*: `http://httpd.apache.org/docs/2.2/mod/mod_proxy_ajp.html`
- *Tomcat AJP Configuration*: `http://tomcat.apache.org/tomcat-7.0-doc/config/ajp.html`
- *Java EE 6 Cookbook Project files*: `https://github.com/mickknutson/javaeecookbook`

Native SDK development considerations

There are several considerations that need to be taken when going to develop applications with native SDKs. In enterprise topography, the main considerations are going to be the IDE developers to use and build management strategies that are used for configuration and release management. Mobile development is still a fairly new feature offering for tool manufacturers compared to more seasoned offerings such as Java, XML, and other technologies. The use of build automation tools has also become an essential part of a cohesive continuous automation system but comes with their own set of challenges when considering the integration of mobile application development.

IDE considerations

We first want to review some of the IDEs that will be used in a Java EE development team for mobile application development.

Eclipse IDE

Eclipse has long been an initial choice based on the large community and cost because it is open source. There has been great support for Android development with plugins that makes starting an Android application fairly quick. However, in my experience, I have found that the Eclipse plugin has strong constraints on the directory structure and uses Ant as the build automation tool by default.

I also found it difficult for new Android developers to modify project attributes of a standard Eclipse-generated project. The Eclipse project files would become out-of-sync and would instantly confuse developers. I think this was an interesting point because if developers on desperate teams have issues modifying project files that cause issues with their IDE, then disruptions are inevitable.

IntelliJ IDEA

Intellij IDEA from Jetbrains has released a community edition of their popular commercial IDE that has exceptional Android development support. When creating an Android application through the IDE, I found that the same non-standard directory structure and Ant support was created as with Eclipse. However, I created a Maven-based Android application and imported it into IDEA and was pleasantly surprised how easy IDEA was to adapt to the new structure and absence of Ant. When I tried to integrate the same Maven Android project into Eclipse, I was confronted with many more errors and the learning curve increased.

AppCode

AppCode is an Objective-C IDE from JetBrains that builds on the functionality and foundation of the award-winning IntelliJ J-IDEA editor. Not only does this IDE have the same great features as IDEA that helps rapid code development, brief factoring, and version control to all the major vendors, but this IDE also has several other great features.

There is only a Mac OS X version of *AppCode* because Object-C for iOS development, at the time this book was written, does not have support for Windows. Objective-C applications for iOS devices such as iPhone and iPad run on Mac OS X, a Linux-based operating system, and are very different than the Windows operating system.

Build management considerations

Build management in the enterprise landscape takes many forms. Sometimes each team or project is allowed to use the build management tool they choose. Other times, standardization dictates what tool will be used to build, test, and deploy applications. While many companies allow teams or projects to build, deploy, and manage their applications, many times there are dedicated teams that are solely responsible for building and deploying applications.

In my experience, more and more teams are taking on additional tasks which lead management to consolidate and automate build and deployment tasks for teams. This usually leads teams to choose a tool for build automation and the choice of tools is typically Maven or Ant.

Ant

Ant has long been a great choice for build automation. I find you are able to easily perform low-level file operations that aid in complex build-related tasks. This is undoubtedly the reason that the Google team decided to standardize on Ant as the build management tool for their team. The Android SDK comes with many Ant tasks to aid your Android development and deployment to a local emulator.

One of the biggest issues I find is the use of a non-standard directory structure for a default Android application. While this might work well for the packaging of an application set to be deployed on an Android device, this poses an issue with the team learning curve. This issue has plagued many teams and causes endless debates about how to shorten ramp-up time and lower the learning curve for a team member. I feel this is an important issue that should be addressed as when I confronted this new directory structure for the book, I had some issues getting used to where to find or create artefacts.

The support for building Objective-C iOS applications is very limited, but creating custom Ant tasks to run external Objective-C compilers is possible if iOS build automation is needed.

Maven

Maven has become a prominent choice for build automation in the enterprise. This can be attributed to the theory to choose 'convention over configuration', which reduces project to project changes in the build lifecycle, directory structure, and build hierarchy. Many teams have found great success with very large teams, projects, and global deployment using the foundation of Maven with its endless supply of plugins and the ability to use Ant for specific tasks, Groovy for inline scripting, and JRuby for creating reusable plugins.

While Maven is my choice for enterprise build automation, when attempting to integrate an Android application into an existing build hierarchy, I found several challenges in order to create a cohesive build. Luckily, I did not find issues that precluded the integration of an Android application into any Maven build, although there are some specific considerations that need to be taken in order to complete the integration. In the recipe 'Integrating Android into an Enterprise build system', we will review these issues as well as resolutions in order to integrate your Android application into an existing Maven build.

The support for building Objective-C iOS applications is very limited, but creating custom Maven plugins or Ant tasks to run external Objective-C compilers is possible if iOS build automation is needed.

Other build tools

There are many other build tools available on the market.

Gradle is a build tool based on the Groovy language that allows advanced scripting for people who want more control over the build process. Builder is another build management tool very similar to Gradle and uses the Ruby language to provide syntax and scripting capabilities.

Jenkins is a powerful continuous integration server that has countless modules for performing almost any task the CM team would need. Jenkins also comes with Android as well as Objective-C support.

See also

- *Eclipse*: `http://www.eclipse.org/`
- *Intellij*: `http://www.jetbrains.com/idea/`
- *AppCode*: `http://www.jetbrains.com/objc/`
- *Xcode*: `http://developer.apple.com/xcode/`
- *Ant*: `http://ant.apache.org/`
- *Maven*: `http://maven.apache.org/`
- *Gradle*: `http://gradle.org/`
- *Buildr*: `http://buildr.apache.org/`
- *Jenkins*: `http://jenkins-ci.org/`

7 Deployment and Configuration

In this chapter, we will cover:

- Java EE configuration with CDI
- Java EE configuration with Groovy
- Enabling remote JMX on Tomcat server
- Enabling JMX over SSL on Tomcat server
- Enabling remote JMX on GlassFish server
- Enabling JMX over SSL on GlassFish server
- Using JRebel for rapid redeployment
- Managing VisualVM application repository configuration

Introduction

In this chapter we will cover issues and solutions to application configuration. The solutions described will cover the use of standard Java EE APIs to access external properties files, as well as Groovy-based configuration scripts.

Advanced configuration topics will be covered using the **Java Management Extensions** (**JMX**) including detailed configuration and recipes explaining the use of tools to connect to a JMX service.

This chapter will also cover tools to aid in rapid and hot-deployment of Java EE applications through a development IDE or existing build tool such as Apache Ant or Apache Maven.

This chapter begins with a brief overview of JMX as a primer for JMX-related recipes later in this chapter and additional recipes in *Chapter 8, Performance and Debugging*.

The Java Management Extensions

The **Java Management Extensions** (**JMX**) is one of the most robust configuration options in the Java SE platform. It can allow you to configure one application as well as configure a group of applications.

In many production scenarios, groupings of servers can be between 2 to 200. In this type of production topography, configuration becomes a complex task. Typical property files or JVM scripts still have limitations if an operation needs to make edits to a running environment consisting of more than a couple of servers. The potential risk of mistakes in editing the configuration, due to human error, can be fairly high. The risk increases exponentially based on the number of configuration files that require editing.

JMX management applications can be generic terminals such as jConsole or jVisualVM which are distributed with Java SE, external applications such as VisualVM, or custom JMX management applications. The JMX recipes in this chapter are based on JDK 1.6 and VisualVM 1.3.3.

Java EE configuration with CDI

The easiest approach to externalizing configuration within your application is to use property files to store key value pairs that are imported on start up for the application. This solution is fairly simple to implement and allows for simple properties to be set.

One of the major drawbacks to this solution is the need to stop and start the server in the event a property needs to be changed before it can be used in a running application. Another drawback to this situation is the flat nature of properties.

Property files do not allow for nested property collections or data types other than Strings. Most teams that start with this approach create wrapper classes that convert Strings to other datatypes, and in some situations allow for collections to be created. This work needs additional coding that from a logical standpoint requires additional unit testing as well as QA testing.

Another issue that teams will face using property files is property name conflicts. These conflicts can only be realized at runtime and in some cases will not raise a distinct error.

In this recipe we will examine how to implement application configuration with property files using the **Contexts and Dependency Injection** (**CDI**) APIs defined in the JSR-299 specification which includes the JSR-330 specification for **Dependency Injection for Java** (**DI**) APIs.

Getting ready

Typically with CDI, you use the `@Inject` annotation to inject elements where you would like. With the `@inject` annotation the container does not know exactly what you're interested in injecting, so we must create a qualifier that will tell the container exactly what you're interested in using. To begin we first need to create a `@Qualifier` annotation which was used to decorate our classes to provide property injection:

```
@Qualifier
@Retention(RetentionPolicy.RUNTIME)
@Target({ElementType.TYPE, ElementType.METHOD, ElementType.FIELD,
ElementType.PARAMETER})
public @interface Config {
}
```

We next need to create a configuration factory that will pull in a properties file and load those properties into context in order to make them available for subsequent requests:

```
public class ConfigurationFactory {

    private volatile static Properties configProperties;
    public static final String propertiesFilePath =
      "/config/application.properties";

    public synchronized static Properties getProperties() {

        // If properties have already been loaded, do not
             re-load them.
        if (configProperties == null) {
            configProperties = new Properties();
            try {
                configProperties.load(
                  new FileInputStream(propertiesFilePath));
            } catch (IOException ex) {
                logger.error(ex.getMessage(), ex);
                throw new RuntimeException(ex);
            }
        }

        return configProperties;
    }
...
```

Now that we have the properties loaded, we can create injection point cuts that are called from our `config` annotation which will get its string property by the property name that was decorated by our point cuts annotation:

```
public @Produces @Config String getConfiguration(InjectionPoint p) {

        String configKey = p.getMember().
          getDeclaringClass().getName() + "." +
          p.getMember().getName();
        Properties config = getProperties();
        if (config.getProperty(configKey) == null) {
            configKey = p.getMember().
              getDeclaringClass().getSimpleName() + "." +
              p.getMember().getName();
            if (config.getProperty(configKey) == null)
                configKey = p.getMember().getName();
        }
        logger.error("Config key= {} value = {}",
          configKey, config.getProperty(configKey));

        return config.getProperty(configKey);
    }
```

We now need to create an external `application.properties` to hold the properties we want to inject and for this recipe we created them in a root directory called `/config`.

At this point we have the two required classes and `application.properties` created and can work on injecting properties into our target classes.

How to do it...

In order to inject configuration properties, we need to create a key value pair in our `application.properties` file as follows:

```
webserviceAddress=http://baselogic.com/blog/someWebserviceUrl?wsdl
```

Here we have defined a property key named `webserviceAddress` and assigned a value of `http://baselogic.com/blog/someWebserviceUrl?wsdl` to that key.

The only thing left at this point to use as a registered property is to add a member variable for our property with the same name as the property key in our `application.properties` file, and include our annotation declarations for injecting our custom configuration:

```
@Inject
@Config
private String webserviceAddress;
```

Once we have injected this property into our class, it will be available globally to the class:

```
protected void doGet(HttpServletRequest request,
  HttpServletResponse response)
  throws ServletException, IOException {
      response.getWriter().println(
        "<b>webserviceAddress: </b>" + webserviceAddress);
  }
```

There's more...

Another useful feature of this approach is the ability to have automatic typecasting of certain properties. For example, if we decide we want to add a `Double` value in the `application.properties` file, we can simply add it just as another key value pair:

```
doubleKeyProperty=123.456
```

Then add a new method in our configuration factory which returns a `Double` object:

```
public @Produces @Config Double
    getConfigurationDouble(InjectionPoint p) {
        String val = getConfiguration(p);
        return Double.parseDouble(val);
    }
```

Now to access this property as a `Double` object instead of the stream used previously, simply create a member variable of type `Double`:

```
@Inject
@Config
private Double doubleKeyProperty;
```

You can use this same approach for other automatic type conversions you wish to support.

See also

- **JSR-299**: `http://jcp.org/en/jsr/detail?id=299`
- **JSR-330**: `http://jcp.org/en/jsr/detail?id=330`

Java EE configuration with Groovy

In a Java project as seen in the section *Integrating Groovy into Enterprise Applications* in *Chapter 5, Extending Enterprise Applications*, you can use JVM scripting languages to augment the Java language. This is true for being able to utilize a JVM scripting language for configuration. In this scenario, the Groovy language allows you to pull in a Groovy script and treat it as configuration-based Objects in your Java application.

This solution allows for more descriptive configuration descriptors; it also enables configuration files to be unit tested and is easy to integrate into a Java / Java EE application. This solution gives you access to the features of the Groovy language, including automatic datatype mapping for configuration values, which make it a more robust solution compared to using property files.

This solution still requires manual editing of the configuration file to change configuration values. If configuration values are changed, the application must be reloaded for the new values to take effect if the configuration object does not implement a function to reload the configuration at runtime versus load time.

This technique can also be used in conjunction with Contexts and Dependency Injection (CDI) as shown earlier in this chapter.

Getting ready

To begin we first need to add Groovy dependencies into our application. Using Maven we can import the groovy-all dependency which will add everything we need for this recipe:

```
<dependency>
    <groupId>org.codehaus.groovy</groupId>
    <artifactId>groovy-all</artifactId>
    <version>${groovy.version}</version>
</dependency>
```

It's important to note at this point we have not added a groovy compilation step because we are not compiling groovy scripts into Java class files. The groovy language will allow us to import a groovy script directly into a Java object at runtime which is where the magic for this recipe happens.

How to do it...

Now that we have groovy support in our application, we can focus on our configuration. The next step is creating unit tests to help drive the functionality we are looking to implement. Let's first start by defining the external configuration groovy script:

```
private static String file = "ch05/src/test/
    resources/ExternalConfiguration.groovy";
```

Next we want a unit test to initialize our configuration script into a groovy `ConfigObject` that we can get property objects from:

```
@Test
    public void testInitializeDefaultConfiguration() {
        ConfigObject config = ConfigurationFactory.init(file);
    }
```

Now we need to create a factory to instantiate a single instance of a `ConfigObject`:

```
public static ConfigObject init(String file, String environment){
        try{
            if(config == null || isReloadable){
                synchronized (ConfigObject.class){
                    config = new ConfigSlurper(environment).
                      parse(new File(file).toURL());
                }
            }
        } catch(IOException e){
            throw new RuntimeException(
              "IOException initializing Groovy
              ConfigObject: " + e.getMessage(), e);
        }

        return config;
    }
```

Most of the magic happens by creating an instance of the `ConfigSlurper` and parsing the groovy configuration file.

Next in our unit test we can add assertions where we want to have properties. If we were to create this in pure groovy language, it would give us support for dot (.) notation for nested objects. In this case, we have an example object with a key named foo and the property set to `default_foo`:

```
        assert config.example.foo == "default_foo"
```

Java does not support the dot (.) notation as with groovy, so getting the `foo` property means we must first get the example `ConfigObject` from our base `ConfigObject` and then get the `foo` property and typecast it to a String:

```
        String result = (String)((ConfigObject)
          config.get("example")).get("foo");
        assertThat(result, is("default_foo"));
```

This makes it easier for getting properties out of Java from a build standpoint because we do not need to add an additional groovy compilation step. But referring back to *Chapter 5, Extending Enterprise Applications* this may be an added benefit that can also be incorporated into this recipe.

The final unit test for initializing default configuration looks something like this:

```
@Test
public void testInitializeDefaultConfiguration() {

    ConfigObject config = ConfigurationFactory.init(file);

    String result = (String)((ConfigObject)
      config.get("example")).get("foo");
    assertThat(result, is("default_foo"));

    result = (String)((ConfigObject)
      config.get("example")).get("bar");
    assertThat(result, is("default_bar"));
}
```

Now we can create the configuration enclosures which will match this unit test.

A few of the things I especially like about Groovy is the ability to create nested objects and also the ability to have automatic datatype conversions, so properties are not always strings, they can also be numeric or Boolean values:

```
example {
    foo = "default_foo"
    bar = "default_bar"
    baz = 1234L
    reloadable = false
}
```

All-in-all this is all that is needed to pull in default configuration.

How it works...

The `ConfigSlurper` object performs all of the magic importing a groovy script and creating recursive `ConfigObjects` based on the enclosures to create in your configuration. The `ConfigObjects` will also perform datatype conversions at load time; of course if you're using Java you will have to typecast the object manually.

There's more...

You can also change the configuration environment level at load time. This allows you to have one configuration file with all the values needed, instead of using different files for every environment as you would have to do with property files.

The `ConfigSlurper` has a default constructor but also has a constructor which takes a String. This string can be the name of an environment enclosure within the Groovy script that is being parsed:

```
config = new ConfigSlurper("development").
    parse(new File(file).toURL());
```

We can reconstruct the `ConfigSlurper` constructor to only parse the objects in our development environment enclosure, with the following:

```
environments {
    development{
        example{
            foo = "development_foo"
            bar = "development_bar"
            baz = 5678L
            reloadable = true
        }
    }
}
```

Isn't it good practice to have a default version of the properties than have different ones for each given environment?

This override can be tested by initializing the `ConfigSlurper` with `development` as the constructor and perform the same assertions as we did in the previous unit test:

```
@Test
public void testInitializeDevelopmentConfiguration() {

    ConfigObject config = ConfigurationFactory.
      init(file, "development");

    String result = (String)((ConfigObject)
      config.get("example")).get("foo");
    assertThat(result, is("development_foo"));

    result = (String)((ConfigObject)
      config.get("example")).get("bar");
    assertThat(result, is("development_bar"));
```

```
        assertThat((Long)((ConfigObject)
          config.get("example")).get("baz"), is(5678L));

        assertThat((Boolean)((ConfigObject)
          config.get("example")).get("reloadable"),
          is(true));
    }
```

Switch statements

In addition to the `environment` constructor notation, the `ConfigSlurper` also supports `switch` statements to achieve the same hierarchy:

```
switch (environment) {
    case 'development':
        example {
            foo = "development_foo"
            bar = "development_bar"
            baz = 5678L
            reloadable = true
        }
}
```

See also

- The *Java EE configuration with CDI* section in this chapter
- *Groovy*: `http://groovy.org`
- *Factory Pattern*: `http://en.wikipedia.org/wiki/Factory_pattern`

Enabling remote JMX on Tomcat server

The Apache Tomcat application server supports local JMX capabilities, which allow connections anonymously to a local process with a jvmstat connection to interact with the exposed application objects.

There are several terminal applications freely available for JMX management. The **Java Development Kit** (**JDK**) is distributed with a terminal called `jConsole` (`%JAVA_HOME%\bin\jconsole.exe`). The release of `JDK 1.6_07` also includes `jVisualVM` (`%JAVA_HOME%\bin\jvisualvm.exe`) which is a newer and more robust terminal application based on the Java.NET project called VisualVM which can be found at `http://visualvm.java.net/`.

When VisualVM is started, local applications which are available for connection will be automatically discovered. A connection from VisualVM to the running process can be established by double-clicking on the application. Each connection will open in a new tab and will contain several child tabs associated with it. In the following screenshot, a connection to Tomcat was established:

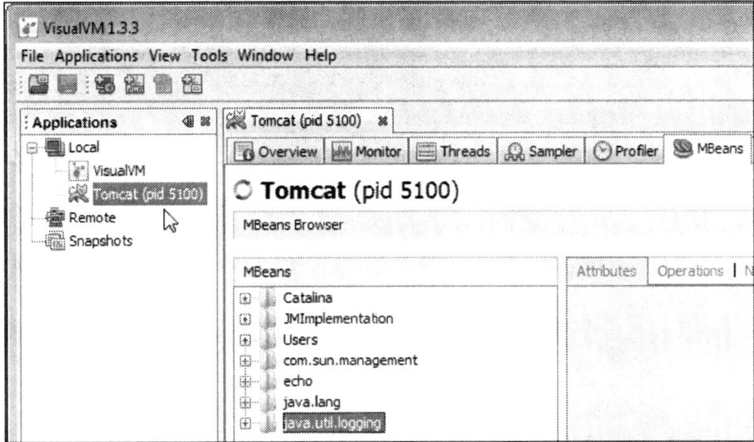

By opening the properties dialog for the local Tomcat application, the connection can be verified as a local **jvmstat** as seen in the following listing:

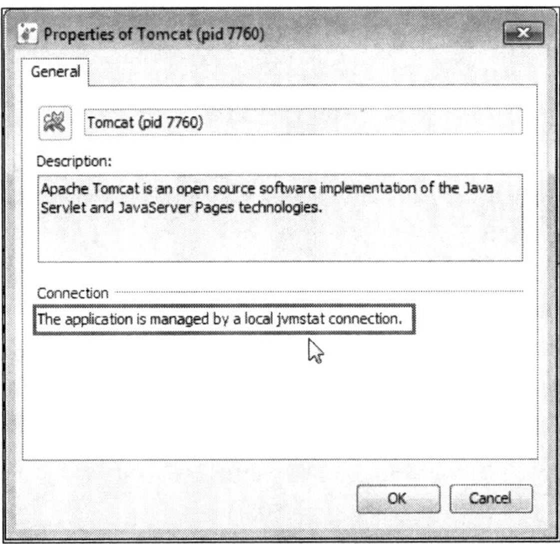

There are several issues with a local JMX approach, most notably this does not allow for remote access outside of the server to be managed. Secondly, this allows anyone to connect, not requiring security credentials.

Getting ready

In order to allow remote JMX access, there are a few steps you need to take to prepare a standard Tomcat installation.

JMX library

Tomcat needs additional Java libraries to support JMX and these libraries can be found in the extras section at `http://tomcat.apache.org/download-70.cgi`. Once downloaded, move `catalina-jmx-remote.jar` into the `%CATALINA_BASE%\lib` directory.

JMX listener

Next, Tomcat needs to be configured to expose an RMI listener to broker JMX communications. This is accomplished by adding a listener declaration to the `conf/server.xml` as seen in the following listing:

```
<Server port="8005" shutdown="SHUTDOWN">
    ...
  <Listener className="org.apache.catalina.mbeans.
    JmxRemoteLifecycleListener"
    rmiRegistryPortPlatform="10001"
    rmiServerPortPlatform="10002" />
   ...
  <Listener className="org.apache.catalina.core.
    JreMemoryLeakPreventionListener" />
  ...
```

At this point, Tomcat is ready to expose JMX services via RMI. Now we only need to configure `CATALINA_OPTS` to add the required settings.

How to do it...

Tomcat is now ready to allow anonymous connections to JMX on port 1001.

Linux / OS X / Unix configuration

Linux, OS X, and Unix are all configured in a similar manner, by setting `CATALINA_OPTS` as system properties on the user profile, or in other ways such as `setenv.sh`:

```
set CATALINA_OPTS=-Dcom.sun.management.jmxremote \
    -Dcom.sun.management.jmxremote.port=1001 \
    -Dcom.sun.management.jmxremote.ssl=false \
    -Dcom.sun.management.jmxremote.authenticate=false
```

This will expose JMX on port 1001 without the use of SSL or authentication. This is the first step in exposing JMX and is the simplest implementation. We will revisit it later in this recipe and see how to enhance the settings to make it more secure.

Windows configuration

When Tomcat is running on Windows, `CATALINA_OPS` can be set using a wrapper start-up script, or directly in the Windows service configuration if Tomcat is running as a Windows service.

To create a wrapper start-up script, create a new batch file with a unique name to distinguish which mode options you would like to start tomcat up with, such as `startup_with_JMX.bat`. In the batch script, set required `CATALINA_OPS` and then call the existing Tomcat `startup.bat` to start the server:

```
set CATALINA_OPTS=-Dcom.sun.management.jmxremote ^
    -Dcom.sun.management.jmxremote.port=1001 ^
    -Dcom.sun.management.jmxremote.ssl=false ^
    -Dcom.sun.management.jmxremote.authenticate=false
@call startup.bat
```

To configure `CATALINA_OPS` within a Windows service, the `-D` properties can be added to the Windows service **Java Options** as seen in the following listing:

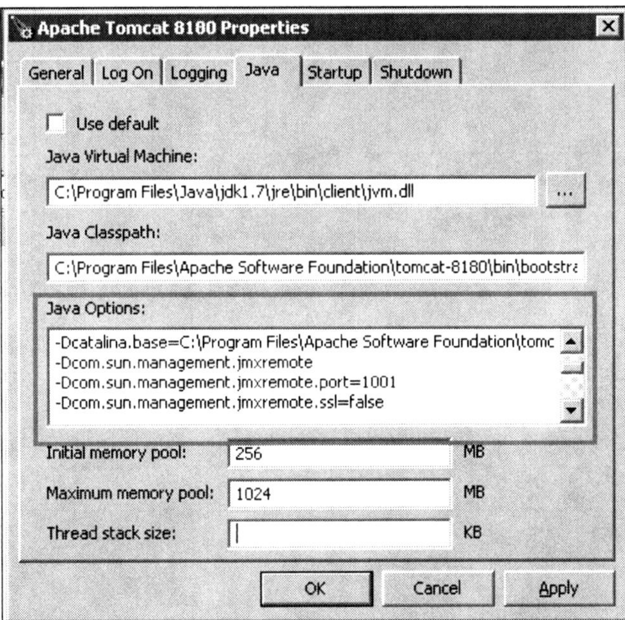

At this point, Tomcat needs to be restarted with the new `CATALINA_OPS` set, in order for JMX to be available.

How it works...

Opening VisualVM again, we can now attempt to connect to Tomcat by adding a JMX connection with ports 10001 (RMI Registry) and 10002 (JMX/RMI Server) which would allow remote connection through a firewall if using the following form:

```
service:jmx:rmi://<hostname>:<port>/jndi/rmi://
  <hostname>:<port>/jmxrmi
```

We can still connect to our local machine for testing the new connection with the connect string:

```
service:jmx:rmi://127.0.0.1:10002/jndi/rmi:// 127.0.0.1:10001/jmxrmi
```

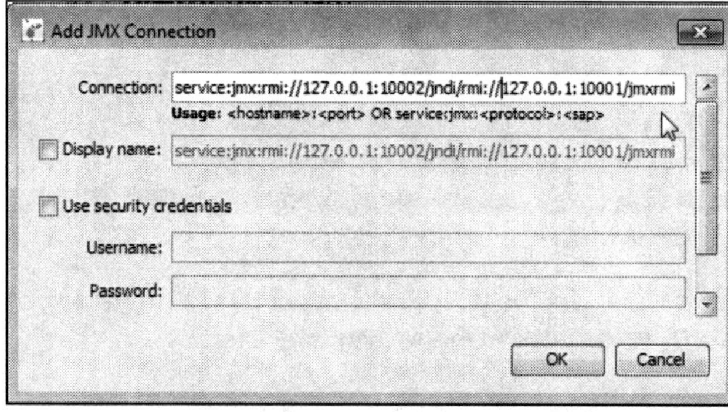

This application connection is managed by a **JMX connection** instead of a jvmstat connection as seen earlier:

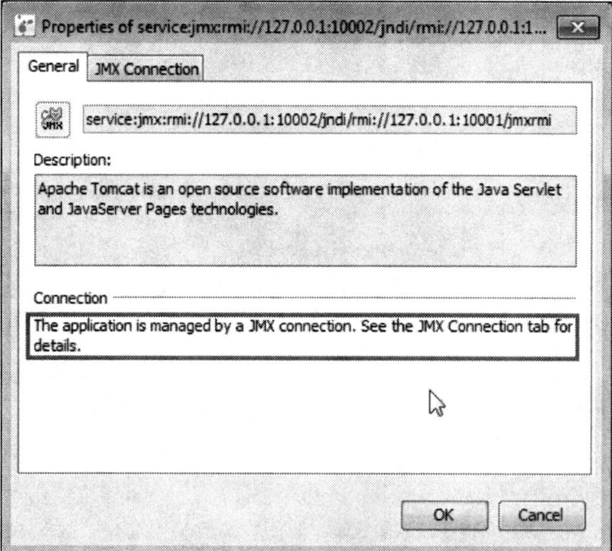

Running locally over a JMX connection versus a jvmstat connection does not give much advantage. The advantage with the JMX connection is the ability to connect remotely and to add security constraints.

There's more...

Up to this point we've seen how to connect locally and remotely via RMI to a JMX-based service. At this point we want to secure the JMX service with authentication as well as authorization rights.

The next step is to enable security authentication to the JMX connection to ensure only trusted users can connect. In order to enforce security, Tomcat needs to be configured to validate user security credentials against a password file.

So to begin, let's create a password file which will be used in server configuration later.

Password file

Create a file called `%CATALINA_BASE%\conf\jmxremote.password` with the following contents:

```
admin secretPassword
```

On Windows systems using NTFS, the permissions must be set so that only the owner has the write permission to this file. There are several ways to accomplish this with the Windows User Interface based on the version of Windows that is running. Another way is to open the command line and use the `cacls` command to manage the **Access Control List** (**ACL**) information.

Running `cacls` on the password file displays each of the users with the permissions they have on this file. *Administrators:F* shows the Administrator that the user has full access to the file, and *Users:R* and *Everyone:R* indicates read-only access. The commands are:

```
C:\usr\bin \bin>cacls %CATALINA_HOME%\conf\jmxremote.password

C:\usr\bin\conf\jmxremote.password BUILTIN\Administrators:F
C:\usr\bin\conf\jmxremote.password BUILTIN\Users:R
C:\usr\bin\conf\jmxremote.password BUILTIN\Everyone:R
```

Only the user that Tomcat is running as can have any permissions on the password file. Assuming Tomcat is running as Administrators on the local machine, we need to remove all other user permissions to the password file, and give Administrator users read-only permissions:

```
cacls %CATALINA_HOME%\conf\jmxremote.password /P Administrators:R
```

You will be prompted to confirm the change:

```
Are you sure (Y/N)? Y
```

Then the status of the file being processed will be displayed, if successful:

```
processed file: C:\usr\bin\conf\jmxremote.password
```

Now rerunning `cacls` on the password file will show only one read-only account permission:

```
C:\usr\bin\bin>cacls %CATALINA_HOME%\conf\jmxremote.password
C:\usr\bin\conf\jmxremote.password BUILTIN\Administrators:R
```

If this step is not completed, Tomcat will not start up and may or may not actually throw a security violation error. However, if it is not correct, secured JMX connections from a terminal will fail. If an error occurs, start the process again.

On Linux and Unix, the password file permissions need to be set to 600:

```
$ chmod 600 $CATALINA_HOME/conf/jmxremote.access
```

Access file

Next, create `%CATALINA_BASE%\conf\jmxremote.access` to define the access rights for the admin connection with the following content:

```
admin readwrite
```

Startup script

The `CATALINA_OPTS` need to be modified to force authentication, and to define the location of the password and access files used by Tomcat for the authentication:

```
@echo off
set CATALINA_OPTS=-Dcom.sun.management.jmxremote ^
     -Dcom.sun.management.jmxremote.port=8686 ^
     -Dcom.sun.management.jmxremote.ssl=false ^
     -Dcom.sun.management.jmxremote.authenticate=true ^
     -Dcom.sun.management.jmxremote.password.file=
       %CATALINA_BASE%/conf/jmxremote.password ^
     -Dcom.sun.management.jmxremote.access.file=
       %CATALINA_BASE%/conf/jmxremote.access
@call startup.bat
```

At this point the JMX console connection configuration must be set to use the new authentication by checking the box for **Use security credentials** and then add the **Username** and **Password** as created in the password file:

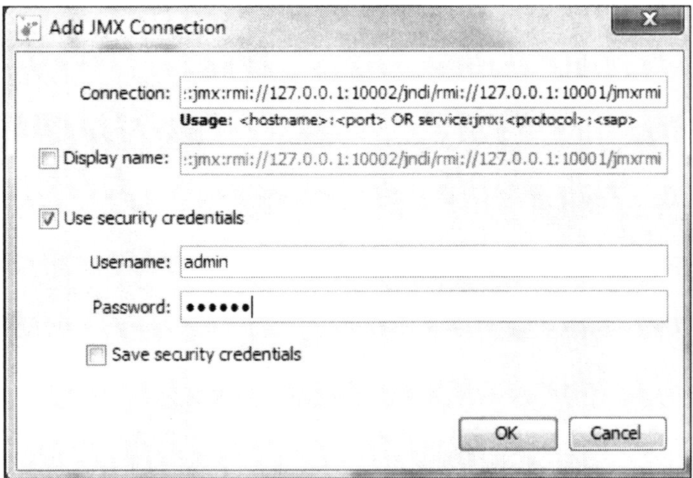

After connecting to the Tomcat JMX remote connection, the newly added JVM arguments can be reviewed to ensure the values are correct as expected.

Cacls Windows utility

The `cacls` utility was introduced with Windows 2000 and may be distributed with newer versions of Windows. This utility can usually be found at `%SystemRoot%\System32\cacls.exe` for 32-bit operating systems, and `%SystemRoot%\SysWOW64\cacls.exe` for 64-bit operating systems. Windows Server 2003 Service Pack 2 introduced a newer version of the utility called `icacls.exe` which can be used if `cacls.exe` is not present. This utility can usually be found at `%SystemRoot%\System32\icacls.exe` for 32-bit operating systems, and `%SystemRoot%\SysWOW64\icacls.exe` for 64-bit operating systems.

See also

- The *Profiling memory with jVisualVM* section in *Chapter 8, Performance and Debugging*
- The *Using jstatd to enable VisualGC* in *Chapter 8, Performance and Debugging*
- *Apache Tomcat*: `http://tomcat.apache.org/`
- *JMX*: `http://www.oracle.com/technetwork/java/javase/tech/javamanagement-140525.html`
- *Oracle Security Appendix*: `http://docs.oracle.com/javase/6/docs/technotes/guides/management/security-windows.html`

- *Cacls Command*: `http://en.wikipedia.org/wiki/Cacls`
- *SecureCRT*: `http://www.vandyke.com/products/securecrt/index.html`

Enabling JMX over SSL on Tomcat server

Tomcat has the ability to allow connections to JMX over SSL. This is an easy change to make and it is a great security benefit, so in this recipe we will go through the steps to add SSL support to Tomcat and VisualVM to connect over SSL.

Getting ready

To enable an SSL-encrypted connection for JMX, a few configuration items as well as SSL keystore preparation must be completed first.

SSL keystore

Tomcat is not distributed with an SSL keystore, so one must be created or supplied to the server installation to use for this recipe.

Java SE has a command called `keytool` that will create a `keystore` with a self-signed certificate called `.keystore`, by executing the following command from a console terminal in the current user's home directory:

```
%JAVA_HOME%\bin\keytool -genkey -alias tomcat -keyalg RSA
```

The `keytool` command will prompt for answers to a series of questions that will be used to create and sign the certificate:

```
[mickknutson@/ usr/bin]$ %JAVA_HOME%\bin\keytool -genkey -alias tomcat
-keyalg RSA


Enter keystore password: secret
Re-enter new password: secret
What is your first and last name?
  [Unknown]:  Mick Knutson
What is the name of your organizational unit?
  [Unknown]:  baselogic.com
What is the name of your organization?
  [Unknown]:  BASE Logic, Inc.
What is the name of your City or Locality?
  [Unknown]:  Reno
What is the name of your State or Province?
```

```
  [Unknown]:  Nevada
What is the two-letter country code for this unit?
  [Unknown]:  us
Is CN=Mick Knutson, OU=baselogic.com, O="BASE Logic, Inc.", L="Reno",
ST=Nevada, C=us correct?
  [no]:  yes

Enter key password for <baselogic.com>
        (RETURN if same as keystore password): secret
Re-enter new password: secret
```

After the command has completed, a new keystore will be located at `%HOMEPATH%\.keystore` which can be used as the SSL certificate for this recipe.

SSL JMX configuration

Now that a valid keystore has been created, Tomcat must be configured to use these new values. SSL can be enabled by setting `ssl=true`, specifying the `keystore` password set during the certificate creation, and the full path to the newly created `keystore`:

```
set CATALINA_OPTS=-Dcom.sun.management.jmxremote ^
    -Dcom.sun.management.jmxremote.port=8686 ^
    -Dcom.sun.management.jmxremote.authenticate=false ^
    -Dcom.sun.management.jmxremote.ssl=true ^
    -Djavax.net.ssl.keyStorePassword=secret ^
    -Djavax.net.ssl.keyStore="%HOMEPATH%\.keystore"
```

At this point, Tomcat needs to be restarted with the new `CATALINA_OPS` set in order for the new SSL JMX settings to take effect.

How to do it...

Now that Tomcat has been restarted with the new SSL settings configured, connecting to Tomcat with a generic terminal will result in a failed connection as seen in this dialog:

The reason for the failure results from the terminal not finding a trusted keystore to connect to Tomcat and that unsecured connections are not allowed with the new configuration. This can be solved by telling the terminal which trusted store to run with. The terminal should be started with the newly created `.keystore` as a start-up parameter, as depicted in the following listing:

```
%VISUALVM_HOME%\bin\visualvm.exe -J-
  Djavax.net.ssl.trustStore="%HOMEPATH%\.keystore"
```

With the terminal started using the new trusted store parameter, a secured connection to `127.0.0.1:8686` can be made without error.

Enabling VisualVM logging

If VisualVM encounters issues while attempting to connect, enabling management logging (`-J-Djavax.management.level=ALL`) and network debugging (`-J-Djavax.net.debug=all`) can aid in debugging these issues. To enable logging, VisualVM should be started with the following start-up parameters:

```
%VISUALVM_HOME%\bin\visualvm.exe -J-
  Djavax.net.ssl.trustStore="%HOMEPATH%\.asadmintruststore" -J-
  Djavax.management.level=ALL -J-Djavax.net.debug=all
```

To view the logs in VisualVM, navigate to **Help | About**:

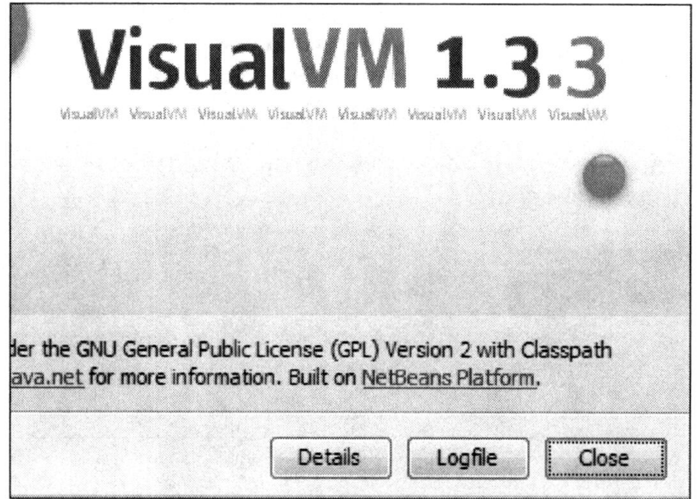

Then by clicking the **Logfile** button, the `messages.log` file will be opened as read-only:

```
Logfile Viewer (C:\Users\mknuts6173c\AppData\Roaming\.visualvm\1.3.3\var\log\messages.log)
FINER [javax.management.remote.rmi]: [javax.management.remote.rmi.RMIConnector: jr
FINER [javax.management.remote.rmi]: [javax.management.remote.rmi.RMIConnector: jr
FINER [javax.management.remote.rmi]: [javax.management.remote.rmi.RMIConnector: jr
FINER [javax.management.remote.rmi]: [javax.management.remote.rmi.RMIConnector: jr
FINER [javax.management.remote.rmi]: [javax.management.remote.rmi.RMIConnector: jr
FINER [javax.management.remote.rmi]: [javax.management.remote.rmi.RMIConnector: jr
FINEST [javax.management.remote.rmi]: name=java.lang:type=Runtime, className=java.
FINEST [javax.management.remote.rmi]: name=java.lang:type=Runtime, className=java:
FINEST [javax.management.remote.rmi]: name=java.lang:type=Runtime, attribute=Input
Diagnostic information
Input arguments:
        -Xms24m
        -Xmx256m
        -Dnetbeans.accept_license_class=com.sun.tools.visualvm.modules.startup.Ac
        -Dsun.jvmstat.perdata.syncWaitMs=10000
        -Dsun.java2d.noddraw=true
        -Dsun.java2d.d3d=false
        -Djavax.net.ssl.trustStore=\Users\mknuts6173c\.asadmintruststore
        -Djavax.management.level=ALL
Save to File                                                              Close
```

The file is located at `%HOMEPATH%\AppData\Roaming\.visualvm\[version]\var\log\messages.log`, in case direct access to the log file is needed.

See also

- The *Enabling remote JMX on Tomcat server* section in this chapter
- The *Profiling memory with jVisualVM* section in *Chapter 8, Performance and Debugging*
- The *Using jstatd to enable VisualGC* section in *Chapter 8, Performance and Debugging*
- *Glassfish*: `http://glassfish.java.net/`
- *JMX*: `http://www.oracle.com/technetwork/java/javase/tech/javamanagement-140525.html`
- *Oracle Security Appendix*: `http://docs.oracle.com/javase/6/docs/technotes/guides/management/security-windows.html`
- *SSL*: `http://en.wikipedia.org/wiki/Secure_Sockets_Layer`
- *SecureCRT*: `http://www.vandyke.com/products/securecrt/index.html`

Enabling remote JMX on GlassFish server

The GlassFish application server supports local JMX capabilities, which allow connections anonymously to a local process with a 'jvmstat' connection to interact with the exposed application Objects.

If GlassFish is running, then by starting a terminal console application such as VisualVM on the same machine, VisualVM will automatically discover the JMX-enabled service as seen in the following screenshot:

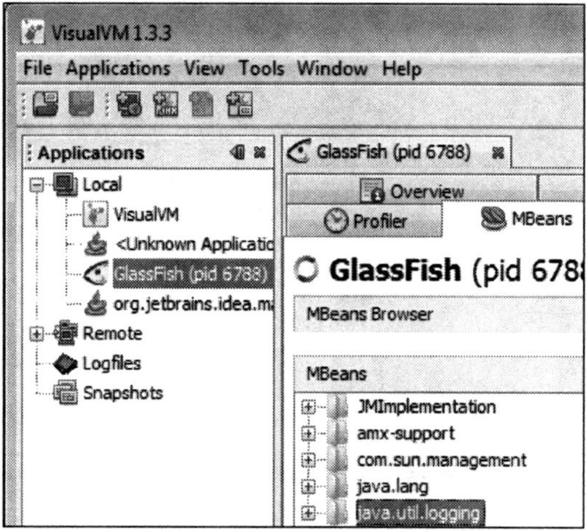

By opening the properties dialog for the local GlassFish application, the connection can be verified as a **local jvmstat** as seen in the following screenshot:

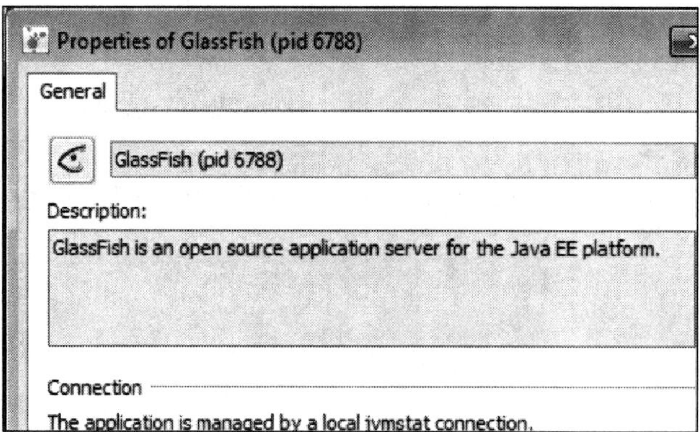

There are several issues with a local JMX approach. Most notably, this does not allow for remote access outside of the server to be managed. Secondly, this allows anyone to connect, not requiring security credentials.

Getting ready

GlassFish does not need any additional Java libraries to support JMX, but does require some configuration to allow remote JMX connections.

JMX configuration

Add the required `<jvm-options>` to the `%GLASSFISH_HOME%\glassfish\domains\domain1\config\domain.xml` configuration file as seen in the following listing:

```
<configs>
    <config name="server-config">
      ...
      <java-config ...>
        ...
          <jvm-options>-Dcom.sun.management.jmxremote
          </jvm-options>
          <jvm-options>-Dcom.sun.management.jmxremote.port=8686
          </jvm-options>
          <jvm-options>-Dcom.sun.management.jmxremote.ssl=false
          </jvm-options>
          <jvm-options>
            -Dcom.sun.management.jmxremote.authenticate=false
          </jvm-options>
            ...
```

The JVM options can also be set in the GlassFish web administration page located at `http://localhost:4848/common/javaConfig/serverJvmOptions.jsf?configName=server-config`:

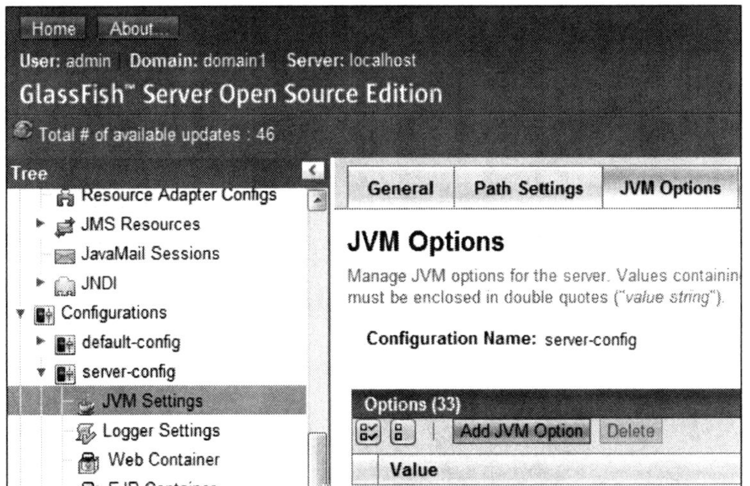

This will expose JMX on port 8686 without the use of SSL or authentication. This is the first step in exposing JMX and is the simplest implementation. We will revisit it later in this recipe and see how to enhance the settings to make it more secure.

At this point, the GlassFish domain needs to be restarted with the new `<java-options>` set in order for JMX to be available.

How it works...

Opening VisualVM again, we can now attempt to connect to Tomcat by adding a JMX connection with ports 10001 (RMI Registry) and 10002 (JMX/RMI Server) which would allow remote connection through a firewall if using the following short form: `<hostname>:<port>`.

We can still connect to our local machine for testing the new connection with the connect string **127.0.0.1:8686**:

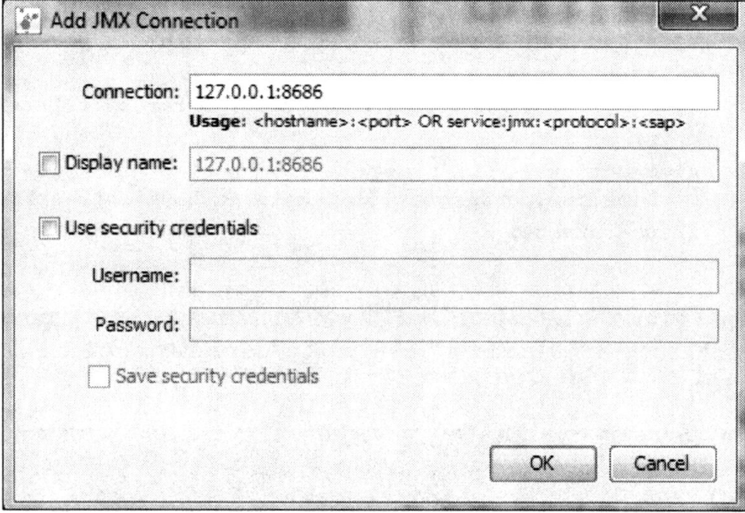

This application connection is managed by a **JMX connection** instead of a jvmstat connection as seen earlier:

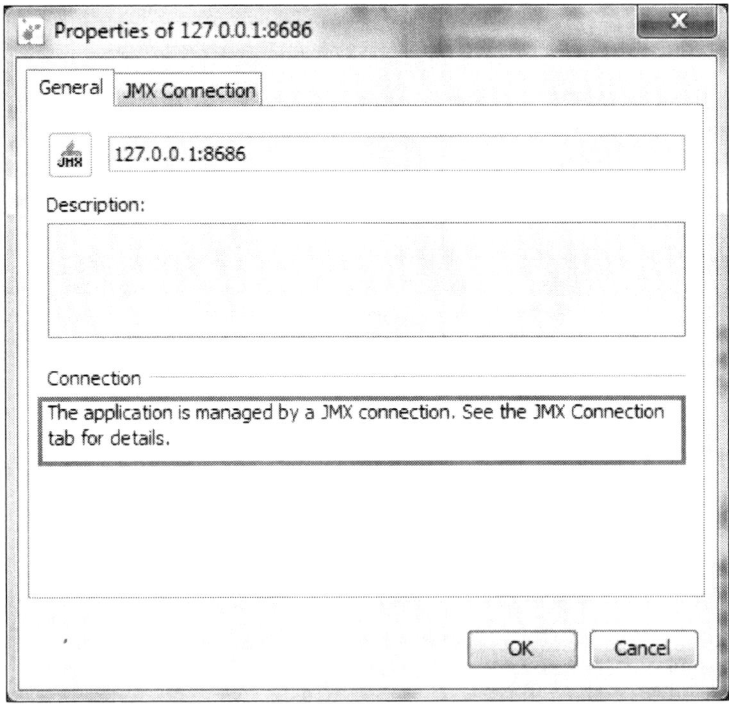

Running locally over a JMX connection versus a jvmstat connection does not give much advantage. The advantage with the JMX connection is the ability to connect remotely and to add security constraints.

There's more...

Up to this point we've seen how to connect locally and remotely via RMI to a JMX-based service. At this point we want to secure the JMX service with authentication as well as authorization rights.

The next step is to enable security authentication to the JMX connection to ensure only trusted users can connect. In order to enforce security, Glassfish needs to be configured to validate user security credentials against a password file.

So to begin, let's create a password file which will be used in server configuration later.

Password file

Create a file called `%GLASSFISH_HOME%\glassfish\domains\domain1\config\jmxremote.password` with the following contents:

```
admin secretPassword
```

On Windows systems using NTFS, the permissions must be set so that only the owner has the write permissions to this file. There are several ways to accomplish this with the Windows User Interface based on the version of Windows that is running. Another way is to open the command line and use the `cacls` command to manage the **Access Control List** (**ACL**) information.

Running `cacls` on the password file displays each of the users with the permissions they have on this file. *Administrators:F* shows the Administrator that the user has full access to the file, and *Users:R* and *Everyone:R* indicates read-only access. The commands are:

```
C:\usr\bin\>cacls

%GLASSFISH_HOME%\glassfish\domains\domain1\config\
  jmxremote.password

%GLASSFISH_HOME%\glassfish\domains\domain1\config\
  jmxremote.password BUILTIN\Administrators:F
%GLASSFISH_HOME%\glassfish\domains\domain1\config\
  jmxremote.password BUILTIN\Users:R
%GLASSFISH_HOME%\glassfish\domains\domain1\config\
  jmxremote.password BUILTIN\Everyone:R
```

Only the user that Tomcat is running as can have any permissions on the password file. Assuming Tomcat is running as `Administrators` on the local machine, we need to remove all other user permissions to the password file, and give Administrators read-only permissions:

```
cacls %GLASSFISH_HOME%\glassfish\domains\
  domain1\config\jmxremote.password /P Administrators:R
```

You will be prompted to confirm the change:

```
Are you sure (Y/N)? Y
```

Then the status of the file being processed will be displayed, if successful:

```
processed file:
  %GLASSFISH_HOME%\glassfish\domains\domain1\config\
  jmxremote.password
```

Now rerunning `cacls` on the password file will show only one read-only account permission:

```
C:\usr\bin >cacls
%GLASSFISH_HOME%\glassfish\domains\domain1\config\
  jmxremote.password


%GLASSFISH_HOME%\glassfish\domains\domain1\config\
  jmxremote.password BUILTIN\Administrators:R
```

If this step is not completed, GlassFish will not start up and may or may not actually throw a security violation error. However, if it is not correct, secured JMX connections from a terminal will fail. If an error occurs, start the process again.

On Linux and Unix, the password file permissions need to be set to 600:

```
$ chmod 600 $GLASSFISH_HOME/glassfish/domains/domain1/config/jmxremote.
access
```

Access file

Next, create `%GLASSFISH_HOME%\glassfish\domains\domain1\config\jmxremote.access` to define the access rights for the admin connection with the following contents:

```
admin readwrite
```

JVM options

The `<jvm-options>` need to be modified to force authentication and to define the location of the password and access files used by Glassfish for the authentication.

In the `%GLASSFISH_HOME%\glassfish\domains\domain1\config\domain.xml` configuration file, change the `<jvm-options>` for `com.sun.management.jmxremote.authenticate` to be `true`:

```
<config name="server-config">
  ...
  <java-config ...>
    ...
      <jvm-options>
        -Dcom.sun.management.jmxremote.authenticate=true
      </jvm-options>
        ...
```

Next, a `<jvm-opitons>` entry needs to be added for the password and access file:

```
<config name="server-config">
  ...
  <java-config ...>
        ...
    <jvm-options>
      -Dcom.sun.management.jmxremote.password.file=${
      com.sun.aas.instanceRoot}/config/jmxremote.password
    </jvm-options>
    <jvm-options>
      -Dcom.sun.management.jmxremote.access.file=${
      com.sun.aas.instanceRoot}/config/jmxremote.access
    </jvm-options>
```

After making these edits, we will want to restart the GlassFish server for these changes to take effect.

How it works...

Open VisualVM and add a JMX connection to the remote JMX service with the `<host>:<port>` like this:

127.0.0.1:8686

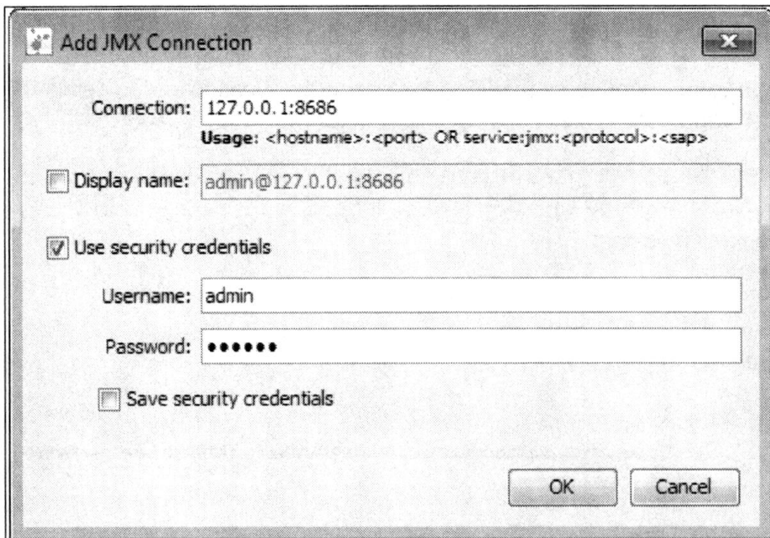

Check the box for **Use security credentials** and then add the **Username** and **Password** as created in the password file.

Now when you connect to the JMX remote connection, you can see the JVM arguments used in connecting securely:

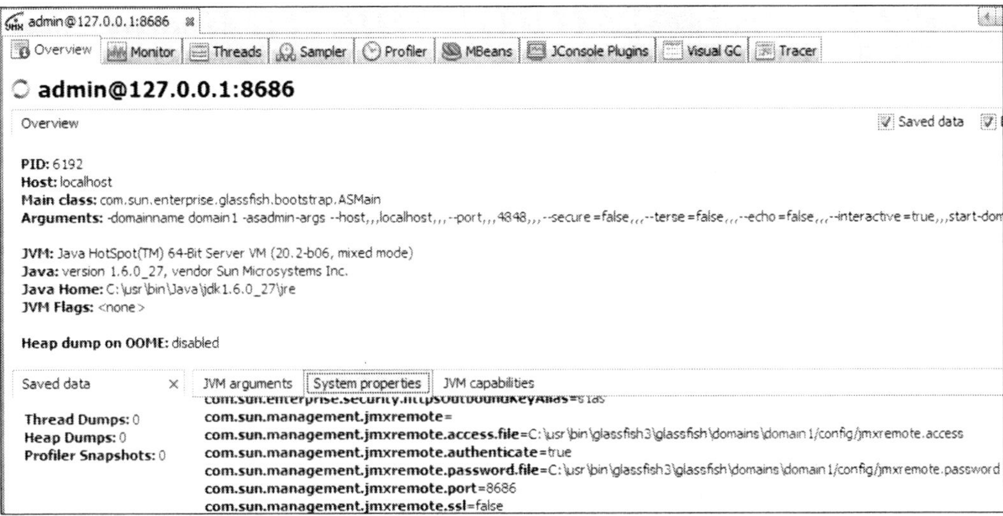

After connecting to the GlassFish JMX remote connection, the newly added JVM arguments can be reviewed to ensure the values are correct as expected.

See also

- The *Profiling memory with jVisualVM* section in *Chapter 8, Performance and Debugging*
- The *Using jstatd to enable VisualGC* section in *Chapter 8, Performance and Debugging*
- *GlassFish*: `http://glassfish.java.net/`
- *JMX*: `http://www.oracle.com/technetwork/java/javase/tech/javamanagement-140525.html`
- *Oracle Security Appendix*: `http://docs.oracle.com/javase/6/docs/technotes/guides/management/security-windows.html`
- *Cacls Command*: `http://en.wikipedia.org/wiki/Cacls`
- *SecureCRT*: `http://www.vandyke.com/products/securecrt/index.html`

Enabling JMX over SSL on GlassFish server

GlassFish has the ability to allow connections to JMX over SSL. This is an easy change to make and it is a great security benefit, so in this recipe we will go through the steps to add SSL support to GlassFish and VisualVM to connect over SSL.

Getting ready

To enable SSL-encrypted connection for JMX, a few configuration items as well as SSL keystore preparation must be completed first.

SSL keystore

The GlassFish server is distributed with a self-signed SSL keystore located at `$GLASSFISH_HOME/glassfish/domains/domain1/config/keystore.jks` and will be used for this recipe.

SSL JMX configuration

This recipe will configure the JMX connection to leverage GlassFish authentication which will either set the `security-enabled` attribute in the `<jmx-connector>` element to `"true"`, or delete the property all together. The following listing is the `< jmx-connector>` element in `%GLASSFISH_HOME%\glassfish\domains\domain1\config\domain.xml`, which is set to `"false"` in the default GlassFish distribution:

```
<jmx-connector port="8686" address="0.0.0.0"
  security-enabled="false" auth-realm-name="admin-realm"
  name="system"></jmx-connector>
```

This change can be made by manually editing `%GLASSFISH_HOME%\glassfish\domains\domain1\config\domain.xml`. The GlassFish server includes an administration utility called *asadmin* that enables administrative commands to be executed from the command line instead of through the web administration console, or by manually editing configuration files.

JMX security can be enabled with the following command:

```
%GLASSFISH_HOME%\bin\asadmin.bat set configs.
  config.server-config.admin-service.jmx-connector.
  system.security-enabled=true
```

The result of the previous command will be to remove the `security-enabled` property in the `<jmx-connector>` element, which defaults `security-enabled` to `"true"` if the property is not present inside the `<jmx-connector>` element:

```
<jmx-connector port="8686" address="0.0.0.0"
  auth-realm-name="admin-realm" name="system">
</jmx-connector>
```

Next we need to create an `<ssl>` element for the `<jmx-connector>` to use by issuing the following command on the command line:

```
%GLASSFISH_HOME%\bin\asadmin.bat create-ssl --type
  jmx-connector --certname s1as system
```

The previous command will add an `<ssl>` element to the `<jmx-connector>` element. The certificate assigned was named *s1as*, which is the default SSL certificate that is distributed with the GlassFish server. The `<ssl>` element will be added to `%GLASSFISH_HOME%\glassfish\domains\domain1\config\domain.xml` as seen in the following listing:

```
<jmx-connector port="8686" address="0.0.0.0"
  auth-realm-name="admin-realm" name="system">
          <ssl classname="
            com.sun.enterprise.security.ssl.GlassfishSSLImpl"
            cert-nickname="s1as"></ssl>
        </jmx-connector>
```

This is the only configuration change required to allow secure connections to be established.

In order to connect a JMX console over an SSL connection, the console will need to have a trusted keystore local to the JMX console to use for the secured connection. The keystore can be generated from the GlassFish server by enabling security for the web administration console.

Enabling secure administration

Enabling security for the web administration console will disable the ability to access the web administration console with an unsecured connection over `http` and only allow connections over secured `https`. Using `asadmin`, security can be enabled with the following command:

```
%GLASSFISH_HOME%\bin\asadmin.bat enable-secure-admin
```

If this is the first time this command has been executed, you will be prompted to accept a certificate as depicted in the following listing:

```
  Key:  Sun RSA public key, 1024 bits
  modulus: 109550937519782703821555433651818462034774931149622614856753153
964920598193172568869694600014161286526049208984582847309541082187392718293
307833667170738380803922382723608453253310774808552647542250818959 4391
  public exponent: 65537
  Validity: [From: Tue Jul 19 21:42:35 EDT 2011,
               To: Fri Jul 16 21:42:35 EDT 2021]
  Issuer: CN=localhost, OU=GlassFish, O=Oracle Corporation, L=Santa Clara,
  SerialNumber: [    4e26328b]

Certificate Extensions: 1
[1]: ObjectId: 2.5.29.14 Criticality=false
SubjectKeyIdentifier [
KeyIdentifier [
0000: 77 F3 C5 C7 DA 1F B9 A7   9A D6 EC D7 07 09 64 D2  w.............d.
0010: 5F 30 AA AC                                        _0..
]
]

]
  Algorithm: [SHA1withRSA]
  Signature:
0000: 35 B8 BB 90 11 B3 44 8A   25 2E 21 2D BD 43 B7 16  5.....D.%.!-.C..
0010: 42 44 F0 6D 32 0A 76 34   E6 B8 E5 B0 43 15 70 29  BD.m2.v4....C.p)
0020: 51 7B 70 57 DA 98 1F DA   96 CE 0E 6D F2 A0 E4 8D  Q.pW.......m....
0030: 1B 43 F7 A2 30 25 79 B0   CF B2 44 0B 2F A5 36 09  .C..0%y...D./.6.
0040: 4C 6A D4 AC 4E B2 81 3F   94 F5 91 F8 2C 2E 79 6E  Lj..N..?....,.yn
0050: D8 EF AD C3 7F 8A 6E D1   0A EF F3 C8 2C E2 EE 0D  ......n.....,...
0060: 5A 6E E8 15 F3 63 5C 12   2D 62 7F E0 6D C8 C1 E5  Zn...c\.-b..m...
0070: BD D5 E3 34 B7 2D 50 A1   9E 66 C5 A1 A8 67 A8 CF  ...4.-P..f...g..

]
Do you trust the above certificate [y|N] -->
```

Enter *Y* to confirm the acceptance of the certificate which will then be stored in the home directory of the user that is executing the command which is located at `%HOMEPATH%\.asadmintruststore`.

Once the command is executed, GlassFish needs to be restarted for the new settings to take effect.

GlassFish can be stopped with the following `asadmin` command:

%GLASSFISH_HOME%\bin\asadmin.bat stop-domain domain1

Once GlassFish has been stopped, re-start the server with the following `asadmin` command:

%GLASSFISH_HOME%\bin\asadmin.bat start-domain domain1

The settings can be verified by looking in the server logs located at %GLASSFISH_HOME%\glassfish\domains\domain1\logs\server.log to validate whether port 8686 has been opened as an SSLServerSocket:

```
[#|2011-12-26T18:49:13.773-
  0500|INFO|glassfish3.1.1|javax.enterprise.system.tools.admin.org.
  glassfish.server|_ThreadID=16;_ThreadName=Thread-2;|SSLServerSocket
  /0.0.0.0:8686and [SSL:
  ServerSocket[addr=/0.0.0.0,port=0,localport=8686]] created|#]


[#|2011-12-26T18:49:13.944-
  0500|INFO|glassfish3.1.1|javax.enterprise.system.tools.admin.org.
  glassfish.server|_ThreadID=16;_ThreadName=Thread-2;|
  JMXStartupService: Started JMXConnector, JMXService URL =
  service:jmx:rmi://localMachineName:8686/jndi/rmi://
  localMachineName:8686/jmxrmi|#]
```

At this point GlassFish is ready to accept JMX connections over SSL.

How to do it...

Using a JMX console to connect to GlassFish will result in a failed connection as seen in this dialog:

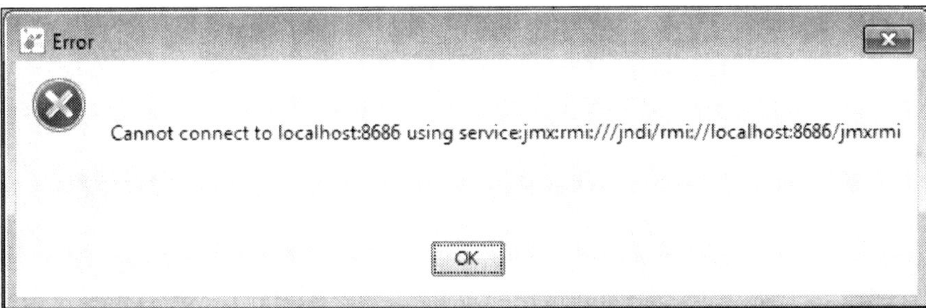

The reason for the failure results from the terminal not finding a trusted keystore to connect to GlassFish and unsecured connections are not allowed with the new configuration. This can be solved by telling the terminal which trusted store to run with. The terminal should be started with the newly created .keystore as a start-up parameter, as depicted in the following listing:

```
%VISUALVM_HOME%\bin\visualvm.exe -J-
  Djavax.net.ssl.trustStore="%HOMEPATH%\.asadmintruststore"
```

Now we can connect to 127.0.0.1:8686 without any connection error.

Enabling VisualVM logging

If VisualVM encounters issues while attempting to connect, enabling management logging (`-J-Djavax.management.level=ALL`) and network debugging (`-J-Djavax.net.debug=all`) can aid in debugging these issues. To enable logging, VisualVM should be started with the following start-up parameters:

```
%VISUALVM_HOME%\bin\visualvm.exe -J-
  Djavax.net.ssl.trustStore="%HOMEPATH%\.asadmintruststore" -J-
  Djavax.management.level=ALL -J-Djavax.net.debug=all
```

To view the logs in VisualVM, navigate to **Help | About** and then click the **Logfile** button. The `messages.log` file will then open as read-only:

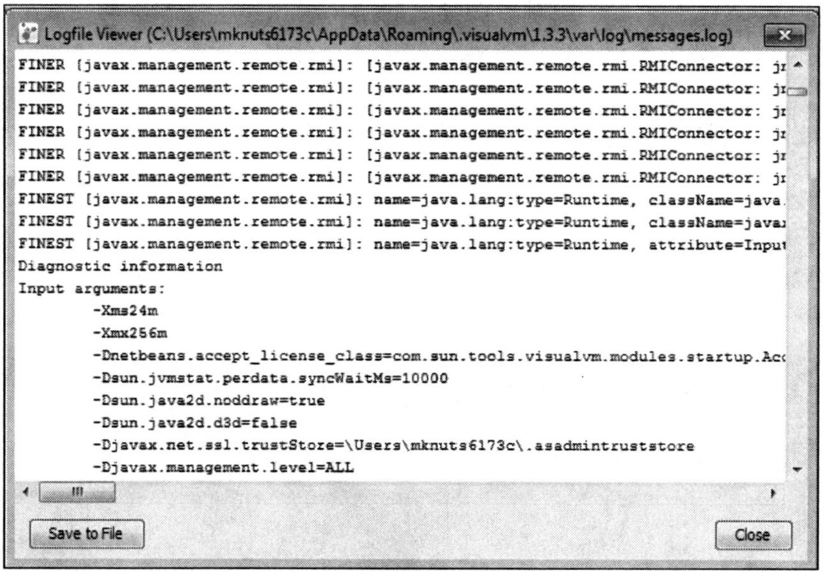

```
Logfile Viewer (C:\Users\mknuts6173c\AppData\Roaming\.visualvm\1.3.3\var\log\messages.log)
FINER [javax.management.remote.rmi]: [javax.management.remote.rmi.RMIConnector: jr
FINER [javax.management.remote.rmi]: [javax.management.remote.rmi.RMIConnector: jr
FINER [javax.management.remote.rmi]: [javax.management.remote.rmi.RMIConnector: jr
FINER [javax.management.remote.rmi]: [javax.management.remote.rmi.RMIConnector: jr
FINER [javax.management.remote.rmi]: [javax.management.remote.rmi.RMIConnector: jr
FINER [javax.management.remote.rmi]: [javax.management.remote.rmi.RMIConnector: jr
FINEST [javax.management.remote.rmi]: name=java.lang:type=Runtime, className=java.
FINEST [javax.management.remote.rmi]: name=java.lang:type=Runtime, className=java
FINEST [javax.management.remote.rmi]: name=java.lang:type=Runtime, attribute=Input
Diagnostic information
Input arguments:
        -Xms24m
        -Xmx256m
        -Dnetbeans.accept_license_class=com.sun.tools.visualvm.modules.startup.Acc
        -Dsun.jvmstat.perdata.syncWaitMs=10000
        -Dsun.java2d.noddraw=true
        -Dsun.java2d.d3d=false
        -Djavax.net.ssl.trustStore=\Users\mknuts6173c\.asadmintruststore
        -Djavax.management.level=ALL
Save to File                                                       Close
```

The file is located at `%HOMEPATH%\AppData\Roaming\.visualvm\[version]\var\log\messages.log`, in case direct access to the log file is needed.

See also

- The *Enabling remote JMX on GlassFish server* section in this chapter
- The *Profiling memory with jVisualVM* section in *Chapter 8, Performance and Debugging*
- The *Using jstatd to enable VisualGC* section in *Chapter 8, Performance and Debugging*
- *GlassFish*: `http://glassfish.java.net/`

- *GlassFish Asadmin*: `https://wikis.oracle.com/display/GlassFish/GlassFish+Server+3.1+asadmin+Subcommands`
- *JMX*: `http://www.oracle.com/technetwork/java/javase/tech/javamanagement-140525.html`
- *Oracle Security Appendix*: `http://docs.oracle.com/javase/6/docs/technotes/guides/management/security-windows.html`
- *SecureCRT*: `http://www.vandyke.com/products/securecrt/index.html`

Using JRebel for rapid redeployment

One persistent issue with developing Enterprise Applications is the time it takes to recompile and redeploy them in a continuous build or test-driven development fashion. JRebel is a continuous build and deploy tool that can drastically speed up this cycle.

What is JRebel? **JRebel** is a Java agent (`-javaagent`) that monitors the classes and resources in the workspace and propagates their changes to the running application. Several types of changes are above the standard JVM HotSwap capabilities. This includes adding and removing constructors, fields, and annotations to name a few. JRebel will also monitor various framework configuration changes (for example, Spring XML files and annotations, Struts mappings, and so on) and changes to static resources (for example, JSPs, HTMLs, CSSs, XMLs, .properties, and so on).

If the average developer redeploys and restarts a server four times per hour and it takes 3.1 minutes for the complete server turnaround, this consumes approximately 59 minutes per day. This is based on a developer working 4.75 hours on development and the rest of the time on other project-related activities.

JRebel has several different licensing options available, but if you consider that each developer can save approximately 59 minutes per day that would be otherwise spent idle, this tool can pay for itself in a matter of days.

JRebel works with many containers on the market, including Tomcat, GlassFish, and JBoss just to name a few. It also works with almost any framework your team is using including Java EE, Struts, and the Spring framework just to name a few.

JRebel can also be integrated into many popular IDEs including Eclipse, IntelliJ, NetBeans, and others. However, you can also use build automation tools such as Apache Ant and Apache Maven to run JRebel, so there are many options to suit almost any project you are working on.

Getting ready

To begin, JRebel needs to be installed and configured using the appropriate JRebel installer based on the type of machine JRebel is to be installed on. The available installers are a *Generic Windows Installer* or a *Generic JAR Installer*; a zipped archive is also available that does not have an automated installer.

The installation process will configure the required JRebel settings and license, and once the installation is complete, JRebel is ready to integrate into an IDE or build tool.

How to do it...

JRebel IDE integration plugins are available for Eclipse, IntelliJ IDEA, and NetBeans and can be downloaded directly from the target IDE.

For this recipe we will be integrating JRebel into IntelliJ IDEA IDE, and the plugin needs to be installed from the plugins settings.

Open the IntelliJ settings for **Plugins**, located at **File** | **Settings** | **Plugins** and **Browse repositories** for new plugins to install, as depicted in the following screenshot:

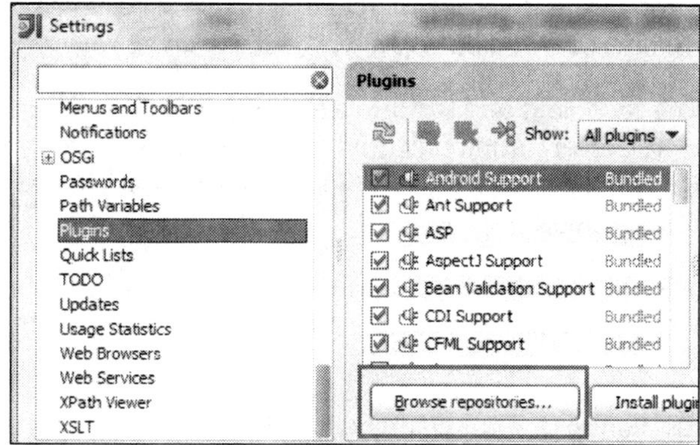

Then download and install the plugin, as depicted in the following screenshot:

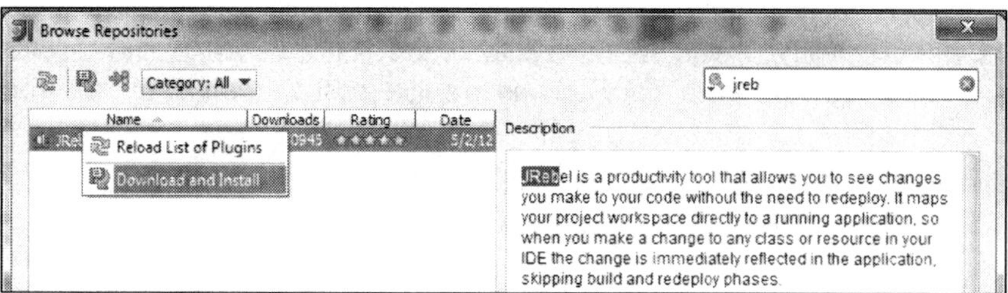

After installing the plugin, IntelliJ will need to be restarted to activate the plugin.

JRebel plugin configuration

After the JRebel plugin has been installed and IntelliJ restarted, the plugin will require configuration to point to the JRebel installation.

To configure the plugin, open the IntelliJ settings for JRebel located at **File** | **Settings** | **JRebel**. The plugin defaults to using an embedded JRebel version, but we will want to use the version installed previously, so this option should be deselected.

Next, change the JRebel location by clicking the **Browse** button and choosing where `jrebel.jar` is installed on the file system such as `%JREBEL_HOME%\jrebel.jar`, as depicted in the following screenshot:

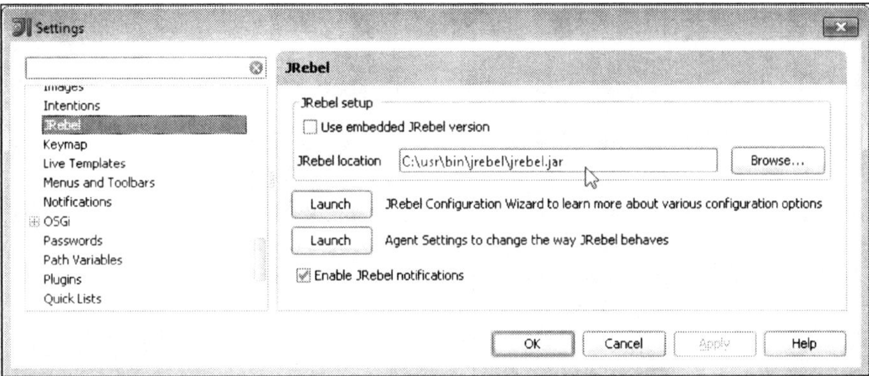

There are also a few configuration changes to be done in the debugger settings. Open the debugger properties located at **File** | **Settings** | **Debugger** | **Stepping** and check the **Skip synthetic methods** checkbox:

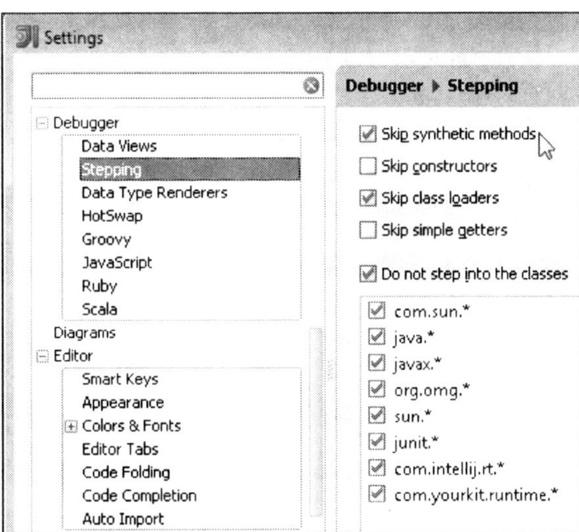

Next open the debugger properties located at **File** | **Settings** | **Debugger** | **HotSwap** and ensure that **Reload classes after compilation** is set either to **Always** or **Ask**:

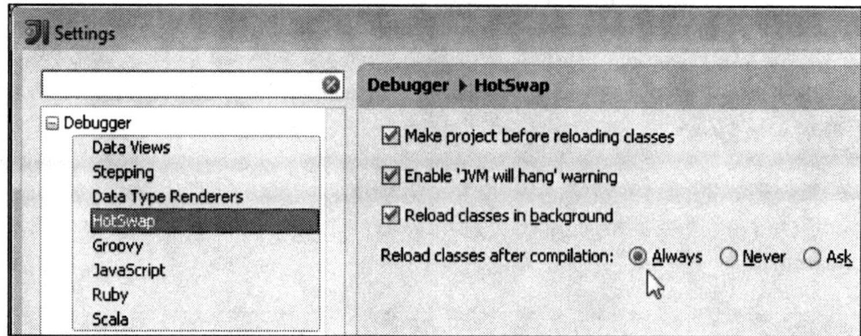

Next open the debugger properties located at **File** | **Settings** | **Debugger** | **Data Views** and uncheck the **Synthetic fields** checkbox:

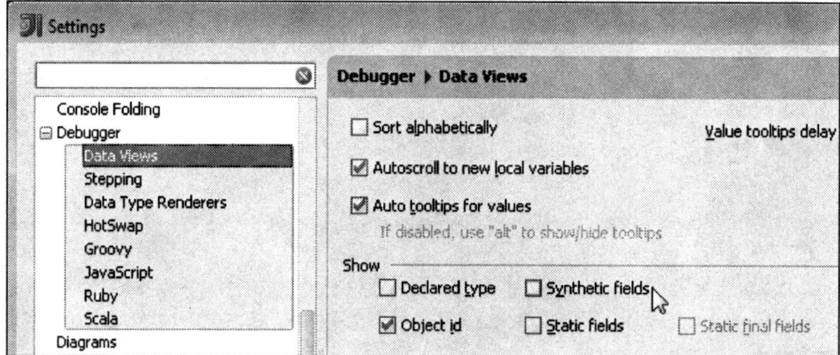

Now JRebel and IntelliJ are configured and ready to use in a project. The next step is to create a container run configuration that is configured specifically for JRebel.

IntelliJ Tomcat run configuration

Create a new Tomcat run configuration located at **File** | **Run** | **Edit Configurations** and then click the yellow plus sign (+) to add a new Tomcat configuration.

Select a **Local** server configuration as the type of Tomcat server configuration:

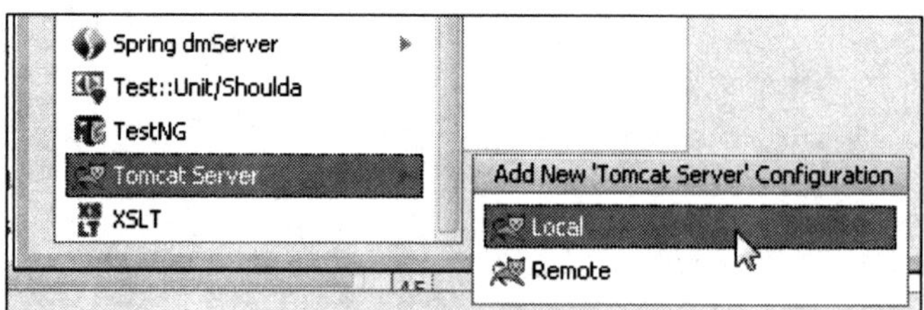

On the **Server** tab, most of the defaults for Tomcat will stay the same for JRebel, but we must define a **Before Launch** action to prepare JRebel and Tomcat to begin running when this configuration is started. The build tool being used will dictate the action that must occur. As shown in the following screenshot, Apache Maven is being used to build this project, so this configuration should run the package goal from Maven before starting Tomcat:

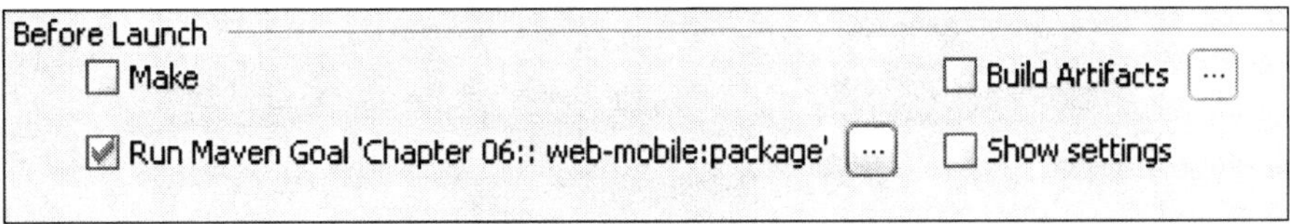

Essentially, you want to compile and aggregate the contents of the web application into the target or build directories, so Tomcat can access them as an exploded WAR file. IntelliJ automatically saves files in place, but does not automatically build and compile files to make them available in the target or build directories. Eclipse IDE does have a Build Automatically option which will accomplish the same function, but with IntelliJ we need to set up an option to do this first before Tomcat starts, and then again after modifications are made to application files.

We next want to add an **Artifact** to run with this configuration:

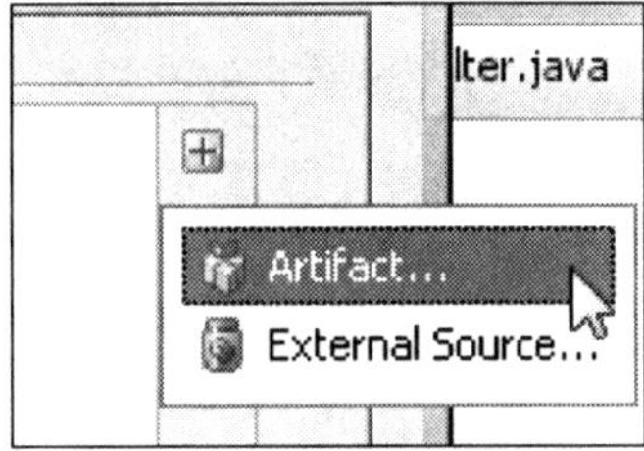

We need to select the exploded version of the web application which will allow JRebel to hot re-deploy individual items as they are updated:

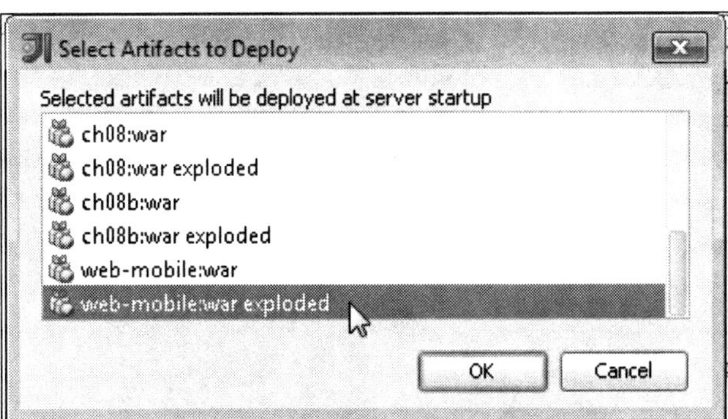

We can also change the default context for the deployed application if it is something other than the root context. If you are attempting to use this Run Configuration for standard Tomcat deployments, you can add additional artifacts, but they must all have unique contexts:

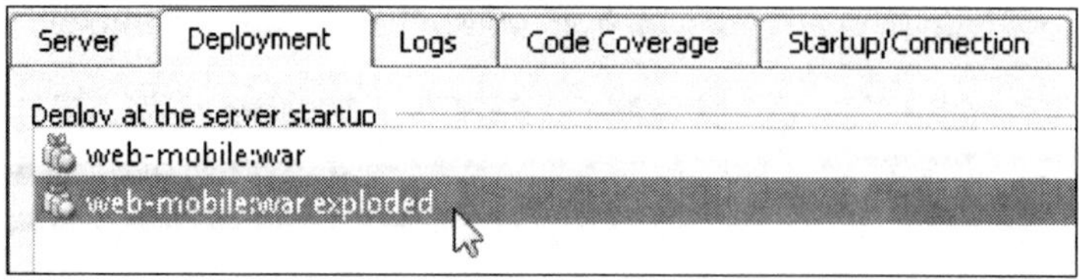

On the **Startup/Connection** tab, the predefined defaults can be changed if there is a need to change how Tomcat is started. Tomcat can be started in either **JavaRebel** or **JavaRebel Debug** mode:

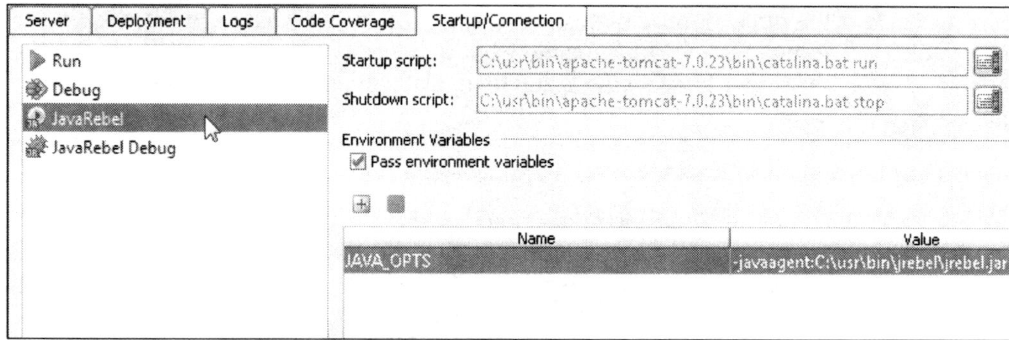

Click **Apply** and then **Ok** to save this run configuration.

Intellij keymap

At this point we are able to run the application as an exploded WAR file in Tomcat using the JRebel agent. The last item we need to configure is a way to recompile Java files after editing them as IntelliJ does not have a *Build Automatically* function. Files that do not require compilation such as XML, properties, and even JSPs will be updated in-place, but Java, Groovy, Scala, and other files that require compilation will need to be built in order for JRebel to re-deploy the changes. There are some existing keymaps such as **Make Project** (*Ctrl* + *F9*) and **Compile** (*Ctrl* + *Shift* + *F9*), but if you want to build just a specific section of your application or want a different mapping, they can be changed with a key mapping configuration located at **File** | **Settings** | **Keymap**:

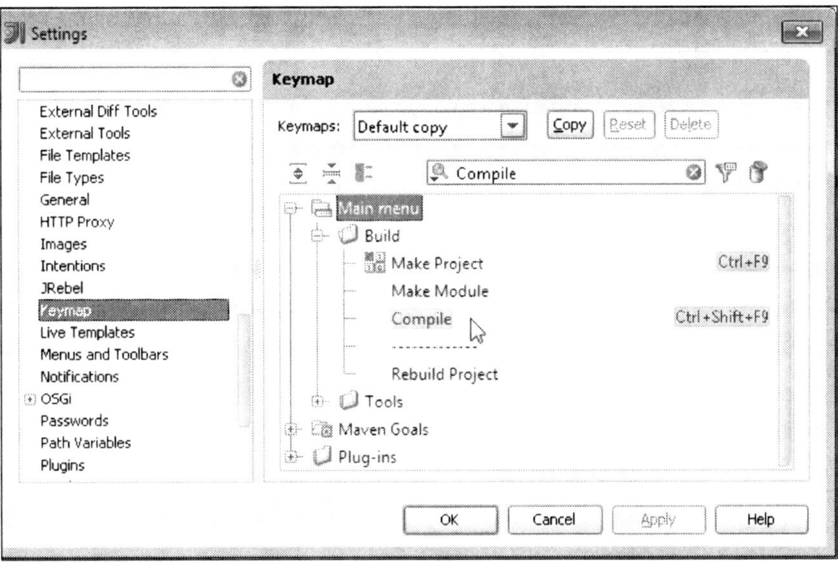

We can now run the newly created run configuration and click the **Run with JRebel** icon to start Tomcat and JRebel:

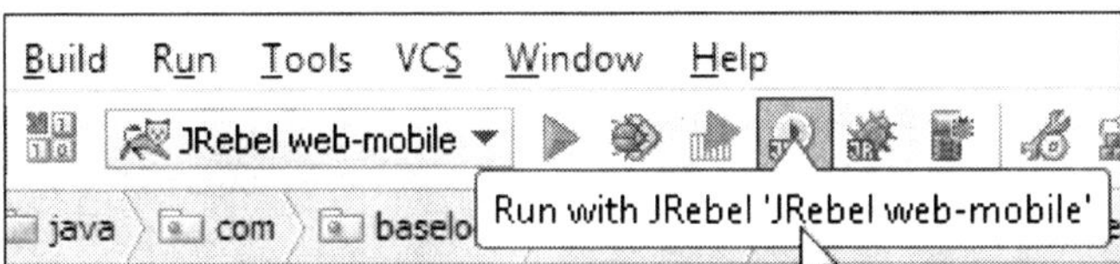

When editing non-compiled files such as JSPs, IntelliJ automatically saves files when they are modified and there will not be any console output eluding file updates, but JRebel will propagate the changes and should be available in Tomcat without hesitation.

For files that require recompilation, IntelliJ will need to be forced to rebuild the project before the changes are picked up by the JRebel agent for redeploying. This can be accomplished using the keymap *Ctrl* + *Shift* + *F9* to start compiling a project.

How it works...

JRebel integrates with the JVM and application servers such as Tomcat at the class loader level. JRebel does not create any new class loaders; instead, it extends the existing ones with the ability to manage reloaded classes.

When a class is loaded JRebel will try to find a corresponding `.class` file for it. JRebel will search from the classpath and from the locations specified in the `rebel.xml` configuration file. If it finds a `.class` file, JRebel instruments the loaded class and associates it with the found `.class` file. The `.class` file timestamp is then monitored for changes in the loaded class and updates are propagated through the extended class loader, to your application. JRebel can also monitor `.class` files in JARs if they are specified in `rebel.xml`.

There's more...

In addition to the JRebel agent, ZeroTurnaround has another product called LiveRebel which allows deployment teams to have the same advantages as development teams with rapid hot-deployment capabilities.

LiveRebel incorporates hot-patching and rolling restart strategies for online updates of Java EE applications. Hot-patching allows applications' code and resources to be changed while the application is still running. Rolling restarts will stop, update, and restart one server at a time. Requests and sessions for the server being updated will be automatically redirected during the update to ensure there is no service disruption to users.

LiveRebel is out of the scope of this recipe, but is a valuable extension to teams wanting to integrate continuous delivery methodology into their projects.

Manual configuration

JRebel can also be configured manually using the property file in `$REBEL_HOME/conf/jrebel.properties`, which can be overridden by Java system properties. A description of available properties can be found at `http://zeroturnaround.com/reference-manual/agent.html`.

Plugins

When working with frameworks that require configuration files such as EclipseLink, Log4j, and JAXB (to name a few), JRebel offers plugins that assist with the reloading of those framework configuration files so you don't have to redeploy after editing those files. You can enable the plugins using a system property in Configuration Wizard or in the Agent Configuration UI.

See also

- **JRebel**: `http://zeroturnaround.com/jrebel/`
- **Live Rebel**: `http://zeroturnaround.com/liverebel/`

Managing VisualVM application repository configuration

VisualVM and jVisualVM are incredible assets for any Java developer. Every time we install a new JDK, there is a new version of jVisualVM. Apart from the JDK, there are updates to VisualVM that developers might want to follow. Not to mention the issue of a developer changing machines or working on multiple machines.

VisualVM and jVisualVM are easy enough to install and run. Connecting to remote jstat and JMX servers is very quick and it's easy to create dozens of connections that are used on a daily basis.

The tricky part is sharing the Remote Application configurations created on one installation of VisualVM with another installation.

This recipe will explain how to back up and move remote application configuration for VisualVM or jVisualVM.

Getting ready

To begin, we need to open an instance of VisualVM which will be located on Windows at:

```
%VISUALVM_HOME%\bin\visualvm.exe
```

jVisualVM will be located at:

```
%JAVA_HOME%\bin\jvisualvm.exe
```

Once the application is opened, navigate to **Help | About** and click the **Details** button on the **About** dialog which will have the details for the `Userdir` for this application:

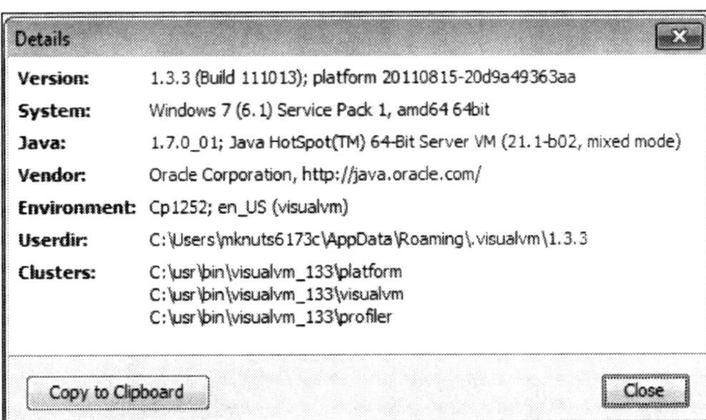

In the case of this installation, the `Userdir` is located at `%HOMEPATH%\AppData\Roaming\.visualvm\1.3.3`.

How to do it...

Now that we have the location where VisualVM stores its application data, we can begin with backing up the data.

The `Userdir` directory will contain a child directory called `.\repository\` that contains the entire host and JMX configuration for this user's installation.

Backup

The entire `.\repository\` directory can be saved to another location as a manual backup. For this recipe, copy `.\repository\` into `C:\backup\visualvm\`.

Restore

To restore the VisualVM repository on the same or another installation, copy the `.\repository\` directory from `C:\backup\visualvm\` to the `Userdir` directory of the target installation, overwriting the existing `.\repository\` directory.

How it works...

VisualVM and jVisualVM both use a similar `Userdir` to store application data and their repository. This makes it easy to backup and restore these repositories and share these with as many installations as needed.

There's more...

Another possible solution instead of backing up and restoring the repository directory is moving the repository directory to a shared location and then creating a `symlink` in the `Userdir` to the shared repository.

Windows

On Windows Vista and later, a new command called `mklink` was introduced to allow for proper `symlinks`, not just shortcuts. If you create a shortcut from Windows Explorer, VisualVM will not be able to access the shortcut and not load any repository entries. The issue is that, in Windows Explorer, `symlinks` and shortcuts look the same as seen here:

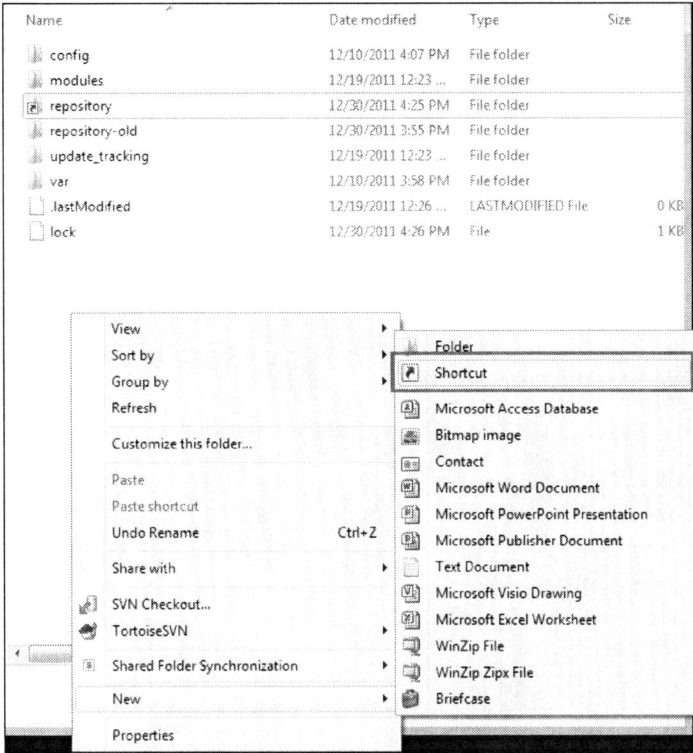

To create a shared repository at `C:\usr\share\repository`, copy the contents of the VisualVM repository that was previously backed up into that shared directory. Then open a command prompt window to the `Userdir`: `%HOMEPATH%\AppData\Roaming\.visualvm\1.3.3`.

The existing `.\repository\` directory in the installation `Userdir` needs to be deleted with the following command:

```
DELTREE repository
```

This will delete the repository directory and all the contents of that directory.

The next step is to create a symbolic link in the `%HOMEPATH%\AppData\Roaming\.visualvm\1.3.3` directory called `repository` pointing to the new shared repository directory. Using a Windows shortcut will not work for this link, so a link can be created with the `mklink` command:

```
mklink /D repository C:\usr\share\repository
```

The previous command will create a symbolic link and will appear as a standard shortcut in Windows Explorer.

Linux / OS X

If you are running Linux, or Mac OS X, the procedure is very similar, the main difference is that instead of using the `mklink` command, we can use the `link` command as follows:

```
ln -s repository /usr/share/repository
```

At this point, VisualVM will have the entire repository of remote application configurations available.

See also

- The *Profiling memory with jVisualVM* section in *Chapter 8, Performance and Debugging*
- The *Using jstatd to enable VisualGC* section in *Chapter 8, Performance and Debugging*
- **VisualVM:** `http://visualvm.java.net`
- **jVisualVM:** `http://download.oracle.com/javase/6/docs/technotes/tools/share/jvisualvm.html`

8
Performance and Debugging

In this chapter, we will cover:

- Profiling memory with jVisualVM
- Using jstatd to enable Visual GC
- Profiling applications with Netstat
- Profiling TCP connections with TCPMon
- Monitoring application and server performance with Munin
- Debugging HTTP connections with HTTP Debugger

Introduction

This chapter consists of recipes used to solve issues related to the performance and debugging of Java EE applications. The solutions described will help in understanding performance-related issues in a Java EE application and ways to identify the cause. Performance topics that will be covered include profiling application memory, TCP connections, server sockets, and threading-related problems that can face any Java application.

This chapter will also cover how to leverage tools for debugging web service payloads as well as ways to extend the capabilities of those tools. Additionally, we will cover leveraging tools to debug network-related issues, including profiling TCP, HTTP, and HTTPS-based connections. We finish the chapter by leveraging tools for application server monitoring to get a better understanding of the health and performance of a live application and the server it runs on.

Profiling memory with jVisualVM

There are several terminal applications freely available to monitor memory, CPU, application threads, classes, and to manage JMX services exposed by a running application. The **Java Development Kit** (**JDK**) is distributed with a terminal called jConsole (`%JAVA_HOME%\bin\jconsole.exe`). Since the release of `JDK 1.6_07`, it also includes jVisualVM (`%JAVA_HOME%\bin\jvisualvm.exe`) which is a newer and more robust terminal application based on the Java.NET project called VisualVM, which can be found at `http://visualvm.java.net/`.

This recipe will first cover running and configuring jVisualVM, and will then show you how to leverage jVisualVM to profile memory of a running Java application with additional plugins in order to provide a deeper view into memory usage of an application.

Getting ready

jVisualVM is distributed with JDK version 1.6_07 and newer versions including JDK 1.7. However, several plugins have not been ported to use Java 1.7 at the time of writing this book, so this recipe is based on Java 1.6.

jVisualVM can be started by executing `%JAVA_HOME%\bin\jvisualvm.exe` and once the terminal is started, it will anonymously connect to available Java applications on the machine where the terminal is running. The available local and remote applications are located on the left-hand side of the terminal, under **Applications**.

Double-clicking on an application under **Applications** will connect to the process and open a new tab.

The **Overview** tab contains useful information about the Java process and various configuration properties that can be reviewed when debugging issues.

Click on the **Monitor** tab and then uncheck the **CPU**, **classes**, and **threads** check boxes to allow the **Heap** memory graph to expand, as seen in the following screenshot:

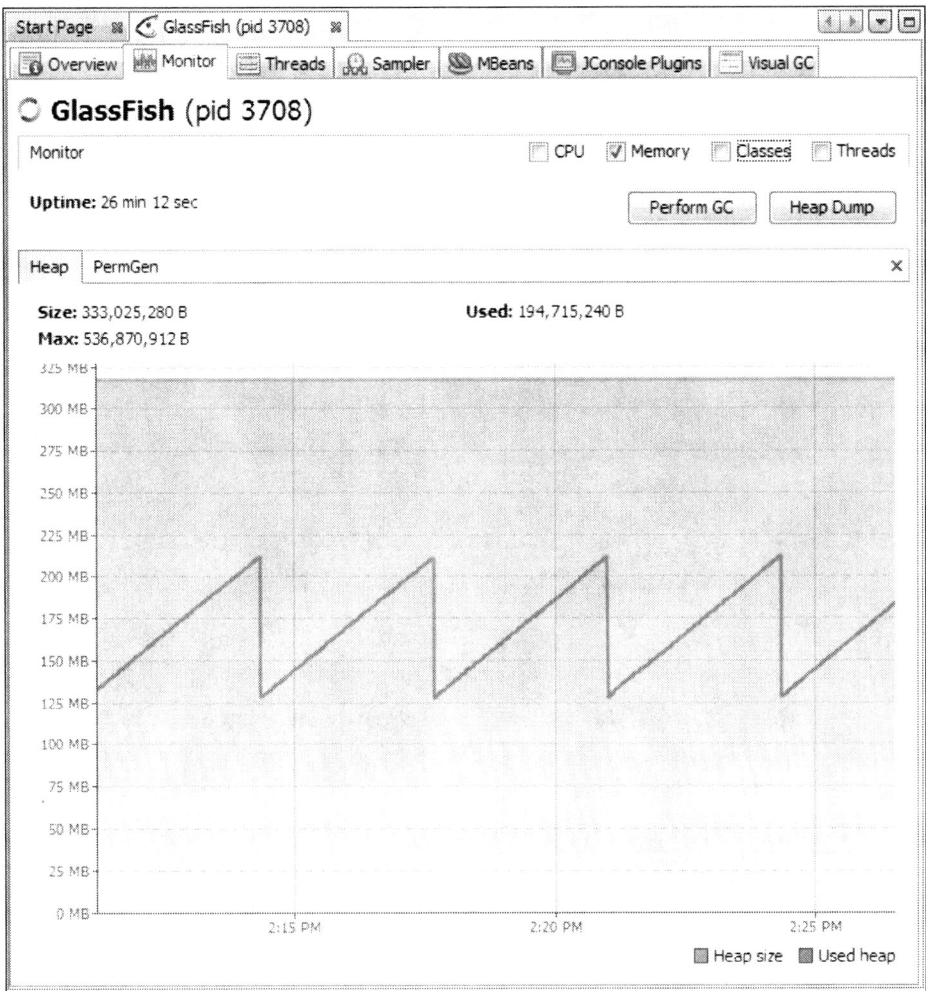

The default Heap graph in jVisualVM only reports the total heap available and total heap size. The more details available about the memory usage and consumption of an application, the easier it is to determine and correct issues. The following screenshot shows a plugin called Visual GC which displays a more detailed profile of a Java application:

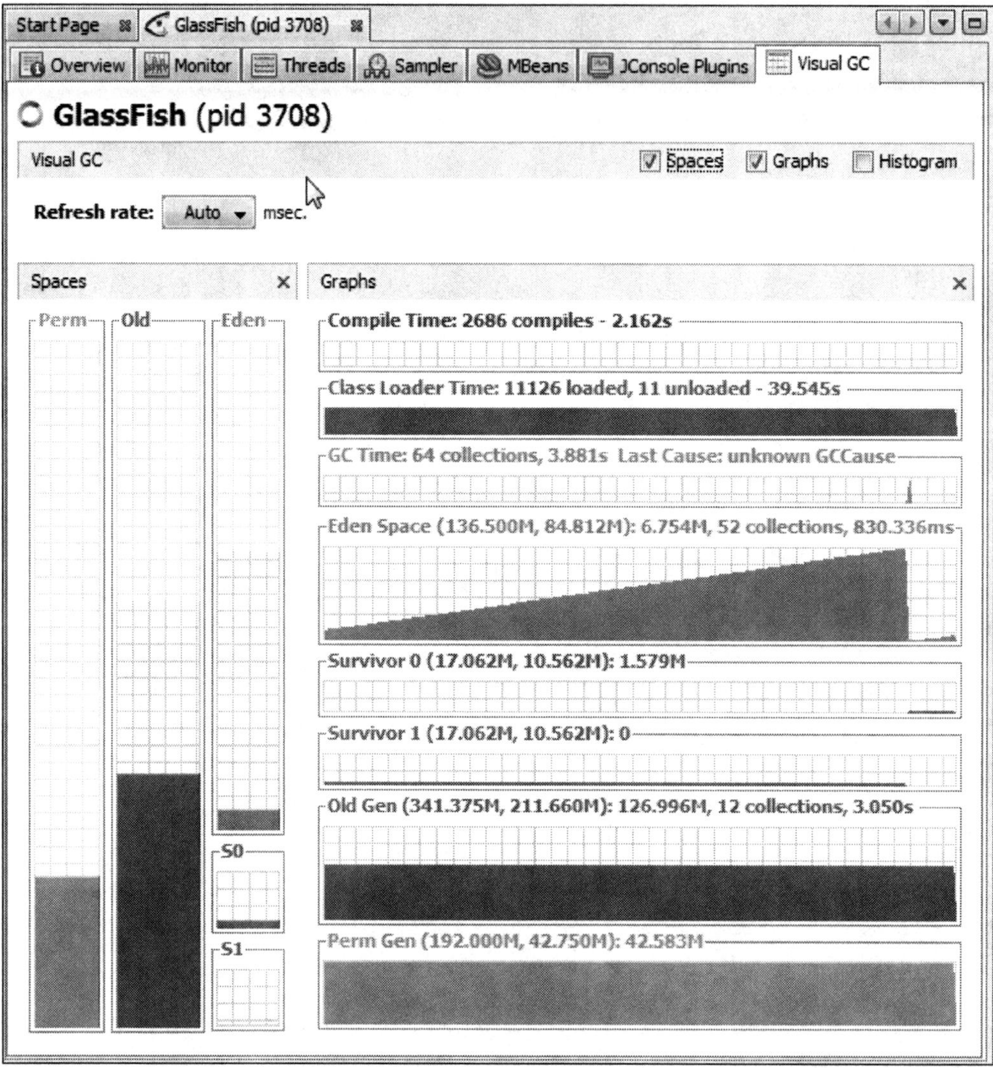

The Visual GC plugin displays a detailed memory profile including Eden Space, Survivor, Old generation, and permanent generation memory. Visual GC also profiles class compile time, class loader details, and garbage collection cycles.

How to do it...

Plugins can be installed directly from the jVisualVM console by navigating to the context menu located at **Tools** | **Plugins** and then selecting the **Available Plugins** tab as depicted in the following screenshot:

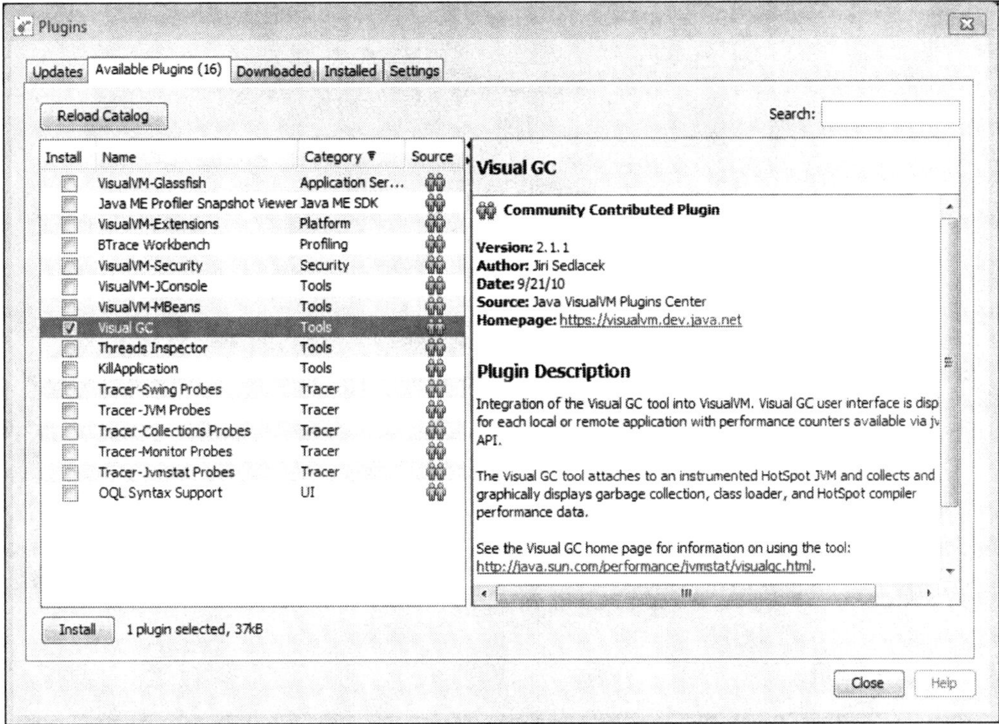

There are several plugins that can be installed into jVisualVM, but for this recipe we will be describing the Visual GC plugin.

Install the **Visual GC** plugin by selecting it and clicking the **Install** button.

The installation process requires acceptance of the plugin's *GNU General Public License (GPL) Version 2* agreement, before downloading the plugin. The installation process will confirm the installation was successful or whether any errors occurred. Some plugins require jVisualVM to be restarted after installation which is considered to be a good practice to perform after installing any plugin.

After the installation has successfully completed, restart jVisualVM. This recipe is based on a local GlassFish server running jVisualVM, which can connect automatically on startup and should look similar to the following screenshot:

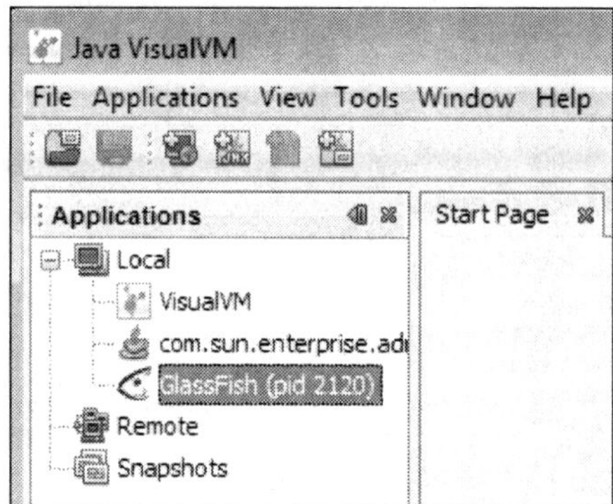

Now that the Visual GC plugin has been installed, double click on the **GlassFish** service to establish a connection between jVisualVM and the running server process. Each connection will open in a new tab and will contain several child tabs associated with each connection. Select the **Visual GC** child tab for the GlassFish connection as depicted in the following screenshot:

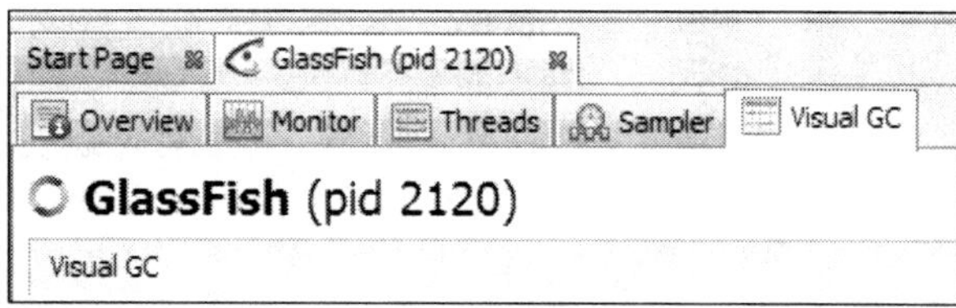

The Visual GC plugin is now installed and will provide greater insight into how memory is being used by an application.

How it works...

The Visual GC plugin displays a detailed memory profile, class compile time, class loader details, and garbage collection cycles that can provide fine-grained details of a Java application.

In order to understand the information being collected, we need to examine the types of data being collected and how each type is being used in a Java application.

Java memory types

When a Java application is started, the Java process pre-allocates a given block of memory from the underlying operating system which is dedicated to that Java process. Addressable Java memory consists of a heap, permanent generation, and other memory spaces. The other memory space includes variables for JNI, Stack space, and the running **Java Virtual Machine** (**JVM**). A Java application can store variables in either the stack or heap spaces, depending upon the type and scope of the variable being stored.

Java stack

The Java stack space consists of local variables, method calls, arguments, reference variables, intermediate computations, and return values if any, corresponding to the method invoked. Primitive data type variables such as `int`, `long`, `float` and `double` are also stored in the stack space.

Every thread, including the main thread and daemon threads, get their own stack space but will share the same heap space.

The memory for stack space does not need to be contiguous and follows a **Last In**, **First Out** (**LIFO**) algorithm.

Java permanent generation

The Java permanent generation space, or permGen, consists of reflective data of the virtual machine such as Class and Method objects. When new Class or Method types are created at runtime, new space is allocated in the permGen space for these types.

The default maximum Java permGen space size is 64 MB but is controlled by the JVM's Java permanent generation setting: `-XX:MaxPermSize` to set the maximum Java permanent generation size.

Java heap

The Java heap spaces consist of instances of Objects, instance variables, and instance-level references to Objects.

The default maximum Java heap space size is 64 MB but is controlled by the JVM's Java heap settings: `-Xms` and `-Xmx` to set the minimum and maximum Java heap size, respectively.

The Java heap space consists of three different memory regions or spaces. The JVM allocates each space its own memory pool based on the available Java heap allocation of the running virtual machine:

1. **Eden space**: Memory pool allocation for most newly created Objects. The Eden space heap contains young generation memory allocations that can be reclaimed during a minor garbage collection cycle if allocations are eligible.

2. **Survivor space**: The survivor space consists of two identical pools for Objects that existed in the Eden space after some time and still contain references making them ineligible for reclamation. The two identical spaces copy their collection of live Objects from one space to the other in short cycles allowing for minor garbage collections. Objects remain in this space until they are old enough to be copied into the tenured space, or until the Objects are reclaimed during a minor garbage collection.
3. **Tenured space**: Memory pool allocation containing Objects that existed in the survivor spaces for some time and still contain references making them ineligible for reclamation. The tenured space heap contains old generation memory allocations that can usually require a major garbage collection cycle to reclaim.

Running jVisualVM from anywhere

This recipe refers to executing jVisualVM with the full path to the executable, as follows:

```
C:\>%JAVA_HOME%\bin\jvisualvm.exe
```

If `%JAVA_HOME%` is set as a system property pointing to a Java 1.6_07 + installation and `%JAVA_HOME%\bin` is added to the system `%PATH%`, then jVisualVM can be executed from any location without the full path to the executable, as follows:

```
C:\>jvisualvm.exe
```

See also

- The *Enable remote JMX on Tomcat server* section in *Chapter 7, Deployment and Configuration*
- The *Enable remote JMX on Glassfish server* section in *Chapter 7, Deployment and Configuration*
- The *Managing VisualVM application repository configuration* section in *Chapter 7, Deployment and Configuration*
- The *Using jstatd to enable VisualGC* section in this chapter
- **VisualVM**: `http://visualvm.java.net`
- **VisualGC**: `http://visualvm.java.net/plugins.html`
- **JConsole**: `http://download.oracle.com/javase/6/docs/technotes/guides/management/jconsole.html`
- **Java Monitoring**: `http://docs.oracle.com/javase/7/docs/technotes/tools/index.html#monitor`
- **SecureCRT**: `http://www.vandyke.com/products/securecrt/index.html`

Using jstatd to enable Visual GC

In this recipe we will configure jVisualVM to make a remote connection to enable Visual GC memory profiling.

The 'jstatd' tool is an RMI server application that makes 'jstat' instrumentation statistics available over a remote RMI connection. The 'jstat' technology adds lightweight performance and configuration instrumentation to JVMs running on the host machine which is required by the Visual GC plugin. If a 'jstatd' connection is not available, Visual GC will display an error as shown in the following screenshot:

A JMX connection is required to access remote JMX MBeans. If JMX is enabled on the target server, jVisualVM will automatically detect the JMX services and 'jstat' data over the 'jstatd' connection.

Getting ready

To prepare for this recipe, the 'jstatd' daemon needs to be configured and started on the target server.

In order for 'jstatd' to function, the full Java Development Kit (JDK) must be installed on the target machine. The **Java Runtime Engine** (**JRE**) is not distributed with `%JAVA_HOME%\lib\tools.jar` and 'jstatd' requires this library.

Next, we need to create a security policy file `*.policy` for running the 'jstatd' daemon and, for this recipe we are going to call this file `tools.policy` because we are granting `AllPermission` on `tools.jar` from the installed JDK on the target machine:

```
grant codebase "file:${java.home}/../lib/tools.jar" {
   permission java.security.AllPermission;
};
```

This file should be placed in an accessible location such as:

```
%HOMEPATH%\jstatd\bin\tools.policy
```

The 'jstatd' daemon can be started with the following command:

```
"%JAVA_HOME%\bin\jstatd" -p 1099-J-Xrs -J-Djava.security.
policy=%HOMEPATH%\jstatd\bin\tools.policy
```

The 'jstatd' daemon process can be verified using the `netstat` command and using the `grep` command to find a TCP connection on port `1099`, and to ensure the port is `LISTENING` for connections:

```
C:\tmp>netstat -na | grep 1099
  TCP    0.0.0.0:1099           0.0.0.0:0              LISTENING
  TCP    24.40.31.85:2825       24.40.31.85:1099       TIME_WAIT
```

Now that the 'jstatd' daemon is running and the connection has been verified, the next step is to configure jVisualVM.

How to do it...

To configure jVisualVM using the 'jstatd' connection, add a new remote host entry with the setting located at **File** | **Add Remote Host...**. The host can also be added by right-clicking on the **Remote** application which will bring up a context menu as shown in the following screenshot:

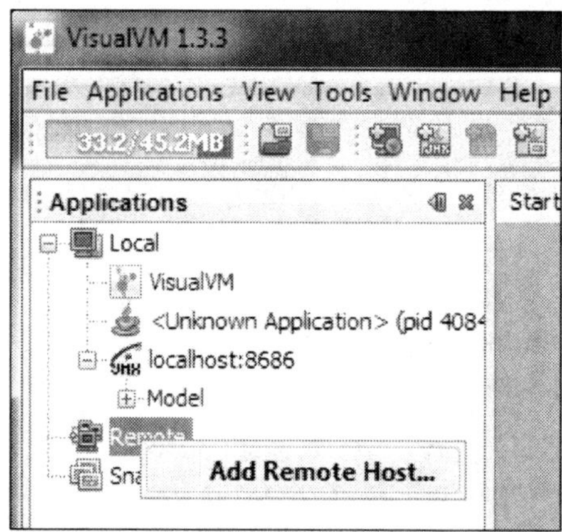

Enter the host name and an optional display name for this remote server.

Next, right-click on the newly created host and select the option to add a **jstatd** connection.

Enter the correct remote 'jstatd' connection port configured earlier, and then click the **Ok** button.

jVisualVM will display all Java processes available on the 'jstatd' connection as seen in the following screenshot depicting three 'jstatd' connections and one JMX connection:

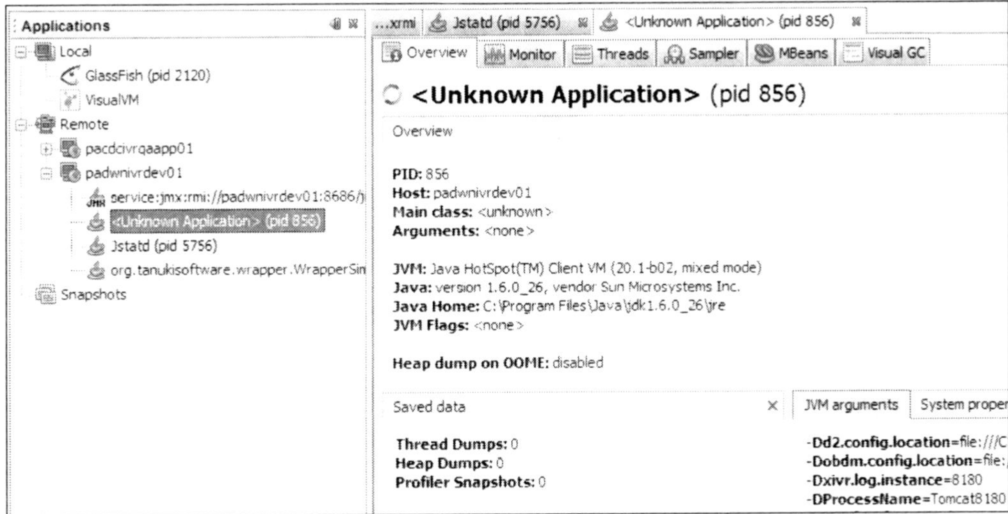

A separate JMX connection is not required when connecting using the 'jstatd' daemon because 'jstatd' will allow JMX as well as 'jstat' communication with all of the Java processes on the target host.

Now when jVisualVM connects to the remote host using the 'jstatd' connection, the previous error with Visual GC is resolved and will display a detailed memory profile, as shown in the following screenshot:

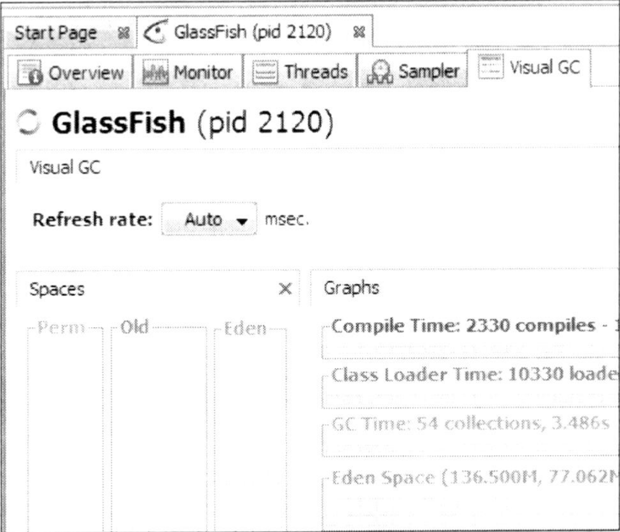

Running jstatd as a Windows service

In order for the 'jstatd' daemon to automatically restart on a Windows machine, a Windows service must be created that is set to automatically start up.

The Windows Server 2003 Resource Kit Tools includes two utilities to allow any executable to be run as a Windows service, which are `instsrv.exe` and `srvany.exe`, respectively.

1. **Windows Server 2003 Resource Kit Tools**

   Download Windows Server 2003 Resource Kit Tools from `http://www.microsoft.com/download/en/details.aspx?id=17657` and run the installer program which will install necessary files to the `%Program Files%\Windows Resource Kits\Tools` directory.

2. **Create Windows service**

   Create a Windows service called `jstatd` by opening a command-prompt terminal and executing the following command:

   ```
   %Program Files%\Windows Resource Kits\Tools\instsrv.exe jstatd
   %Program Files%\Windows Resource Kits\Tools\srvany.exe
   ```

3. **Add service parameters**

   The steps are as follows:

   - Open Regedit to edit the registry entries for the `jstatd` service located at **Start Menu | run | regedit**.
   - Navigate to the **jstatd** entry located at `HKEY_LOCAL_MACHINE\SYSTEM\CurrentControlSet\Services\jstatd` as shown in the following screenshot:

- Create a key for the `jstatd` service named **Parameters**.
- Create a new String value (`REG_SZ`) for the `Parameters` key named **Application** and enter `"%JAVA_HOME%\bin\jstatd" -p 1099 -J-Djava.security.policy=%HOMEPATH%\jstatd\bin\tools.policy` as the **Value** data entry.

4. **Configure service**

   Open **Windows Services Manager** located at **Start Menu | run | services**, and navigate to the **jstatd** service.

   Right-click on the **jstatd** service, select **Properties**, change the start-up type to **Automatic**, and then click **Ok**.

5. **Start service**

   Finally, in the **Windows Services Manager**, start the new **jstatd** service.

The 'jstatd' service is now running as a Windows service and will automatically start up when Windows starts.

Windows service wrappers

Adding Windows services with Srvany is a tried and tested way to run various applications as a Windows service, but there are several other alternatives available, both open source and commercially:

1. Open source alternatives:
   - `http://nssm.cc`
   - `http://yajsw.sourceforge.net`
   - `http://launch4j.sourceforge.net`
   - `http://commons.apache.org/daemon/`
   - `http://winrun4j.sourceforge.net`
2. Commercial alternatives:
   - `http://coretechnologies.com/products/AlwaysUp/`
   - `http://firedaemon.com`
   - `http://wrapper.tanukisoftware.com`

The advantage of these alternative service wrappers is configurability of the service to be run and the ability to run Java applications directly. The specific advantages of each tool vary, but one advantage we can cover is the ability for a service to recover after application failure. If the application terminates unexpectedly, Srvany will not receive the termination notification and will continue to run, giving the false impression that the application is running. These alternative service wrappers have the ability to detect application failure notifications and restart the application if desired.

We will briefly cover an open source alternative called the **Non-Sucking Service Manager** (**NSSM**). NSSM is available in a 32-bit and 64-bit version depending upon the Windows installation NSSM is running on. To install the 'jstatd' service on a 32-bit Windows machine, open a command terminal and execute the following command:

```
%NSSM_HOME%\nssm install jstatd
```

This will bring up the following window to add the path to 'jstatd', command options, and service name:

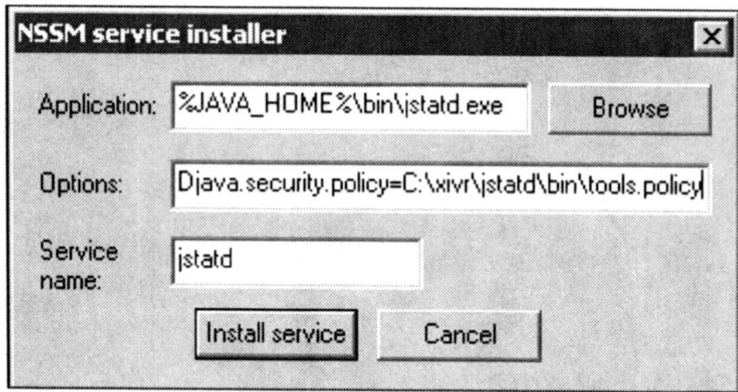

After installing the 'jstatd' service, navigate to the registry entry located at `HKEY_LOCAL_MACHINE\SYSTEM\CurrentControlSet\Services\jstatd` to review the new service, as shown in the following screenshot:

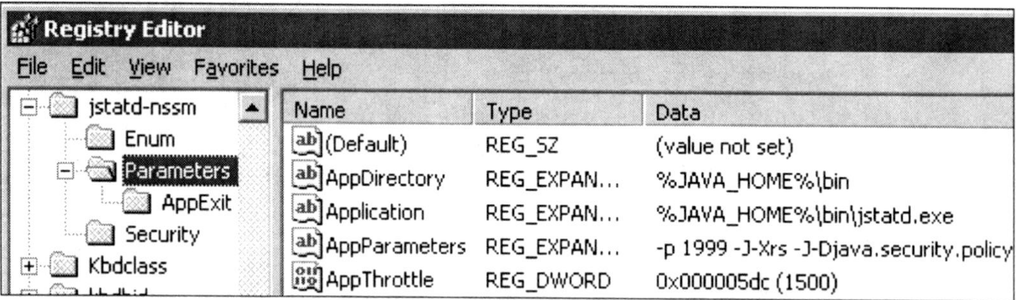

The default action for this service is to restart the application when NSSM receives an application exit.

Installing a Windows service with NSSM is now complete, and was much easier than Srvany, and will now restart the application automatically.

Preventing JVM process termination

Adding the option `-Xrs` to the 'jstatd' process reduces its usage of operating system signals that can occur when the user logs out of a Windows session. Using this parameter to start 'jstatd' will enable the process to continue to run after logging out of the session, if the server is still running.

See also

- **VisualVM**: `http://visualvm.java.net`
- **VisualGC**: `http://visualvm.java.net/plugins.html`
- **Java Monitoring**: `http://docs.oracle.com/javase/7/docs/technotes/tools/index.html#monitor`
- **Windows Server 2003 Resource Kit Tools**: `http://www.microsoft.com/download/en/details.aspx?id=17657`
- **NSSM**: `http://nssm.cc`
- **Netstat**: `http://en.wikipedia.org/wiki/Netstat`

Profiling applications with Netstat

Enterprise web application development is becoming more complex by the day. The demand on a web application today extends far beyond serving simple web pages. Applications must support extensive AJAX requests, static content, and web service requests from various clients. In addition to serving content to clients, web applications must interact with other databases and request additional content from other remote web services.

Java applications and Java EE applications for that matter have extensive threading capabilities available to solve a multitude of integration and performance issues.

Concurrency is the ability to run multiple instructions in a program or several programs in parallel. The Java SE has extensive collection services running concurrently that allow applications to run certain tasks asynchronously or in parallel. Java EE builds on this collection of services to support technologies such as the EJB and JMS APIs.

In this recipe we will investigate concurrency issues resulting from creating TCP connections to external systems.

Getting ready

In order to understand concurrency issues facing TCP connections and how these connections affect the server they run on, we want to define the difference between a process and a thread.

Process

A process runs in isolation and cannot access data in another process. Resources for a process are managed by the operating system such as memory CPU and I/O.

Thread

A thread is a lightweight process that has its own call stack and can access shared data. Application threads are managed by the Java process that created them.

A thread connects to a process when a TCP connection is established using a socket that is bound to an I/O port.

Considerations

The following are considerations based on the basic definition characteristics of processes versus threads:

- A single thread will execute tasks in serial, and using multiple threads simultaneously in an application will enable those tasks to be executed in parallel
- A socket is an inter-process communication between computer networks which are used to connect a client to a web application using the HTTP application protocol over a TCP-based socket connection
- A thread connects to a process when a socket connection is established which is bound to an I/O port
- An HTTP connection which is used to connect to a remote web service uses a socket bound to an I/O port, to establish the connection to a remote computer
- Each socket connecting to an I/O port becomes a resource that can be shared between many threads within the process the resource is bound to

Considering the relationship between threads bound to I/O resources by sockets, we can now explore how this relationship can affect the Enterprise Application ecosystem.

Client problem space

Now that we understand the relationship between threads, processes, and sockets, we can now begin to describe the problem space with this relationship in a multi-threaded application.

Two threads cannot share a single socket resource at the same time. Threads must coordinate their efforts to ensure the socket resource can complete the conversation in full before processing another request. Unless the entire response is read in a single operation by a single thread, then one thread may only get part of the response, and the other thread gets the other part:

1. Thread-1 connects to peer with socket-1 and sends a request.
2. Thread-2 connects to peer with socket-1 and sends a request.

3. Peer begins sending a response to thread-1 on socket-1.
4. Thread-1 begins to read the response from the peer on socket-1.
5. Thread-1 reads the first half of the response data from socket-1.
6. Thread-2 begins to read the response from the peer on socket-1.
7. Thread-2 reads the second half of the response data from socket-1.
8. Thread-2 cannot parse the response from socket-1 and throws an exception.
9. Thread-1 is waiting to receive the second half of the response from the peer on socket-1.
10. Thread-1 throws a read timeout exception after five minutes.

If socket-1 was shared between thread-1 and thread-2 and was not synchronized, then thread-2 can interrupt the response thread-1 was receiving, and read the remaining bytes of data from socket-1.

Thread-2 fails to parse the incomplete response from socket-1 resulting in an application error.

Thread-1 will continue to listen on socket-1 until it receives the expected number of bytes. However, thread-2 intercepted the remaining bytes and thread-1 continues to listen until it throws a read timeout which is usually five minutes. The socket will be in a state known as `ESTABLISHED` and appear to be operating normally. Thread-1 will not be available to use for approximately five minutes and will still tie up resources available to the application.

This socket hijacking paradigm is more prevalent when the load on the application is higher. This is especially problematic considering the load needed to create the situation may only be sufficient in a production environment, not in development or QA.

Server problem space

The client problem space is a result of threads opening socket connections to a peer to initiate requests. An application can also participate as the server for a connection:

1. Client-1 connects to a server on socket-1 and sends a request.
2. Client-2 connects to a server on socket-1 and sends a request.
3. Client-1 connects and initiates a connection closure to the server.
4. Socket-1 sends `FIN` bit to the server.
5. Server receives the closure request and enters a `CLOSE_WAIT` state.
6. Server sends an `ACK` response to socket-1.
7. Socket-1 encounters an error from client hijacking.
8. Socket-1 does not initiate `close()` to the server.

When a server TCP socket connection does receives a request to close the connection but does not receive the final `close()` from the connected socket, the server socket can be left in the `CLOSE_WAIT` state until the socket times out.

Socket states

We now understand how client and server sockets can become unavailable and wait for a timeout to occur before becoming available for additional connections. The following table is a list of the TCP states that a socket can be in, and the timeout values associated with each state:

State	Timeout value	Description
`LISTEN`	2 minutes	Waiting to receive connection requests.
`ESTABLISHED`	5 days	Connection is established. Normal data transfer can occur.
`CLOSE_WAIT`	12 hours	Waiting for connection termination request from client.
`FIN_WAIT_1`	2 minutes	Received connection termination request from the server.
`FIN_WAIT_2`	2 minutes	Received connection termination request acknowledgement from the server.
`TIME_WAIT`	4 minutes	Waiting to ensure the server received an acknowledgment of connection termination request.
`CLOSED`	n/a	Represents no connection.

Now that we have a better understanding of how socket resources can be left in a non-recoverable state, the next step is to detect when this is occurring.

How to do it...

The situation discussed earlier is when the client or server sockets become unusable by the server. If sockets continue to become non-recoverable, eventually the server will run out of available resources which can lead to application failure.

Consider the following implications on sockets:

- Sockets in the `CLOSE_WAIT` state are unusable
- Sockets in the `ESTABLISHED` state in a conversation
- Sockets in the `TIME_WAIT` state are finishing a conversation
- Sockets in the `LISTEN` state are available for new conversation

Essentially if there are not enough sockets available in the `LISTEN` state, the application will not be able to initiate or handle requests.

Open VisualVM and connect to the target server to profile, and navigate to the **Threads** tab as shown in the following screenshot:

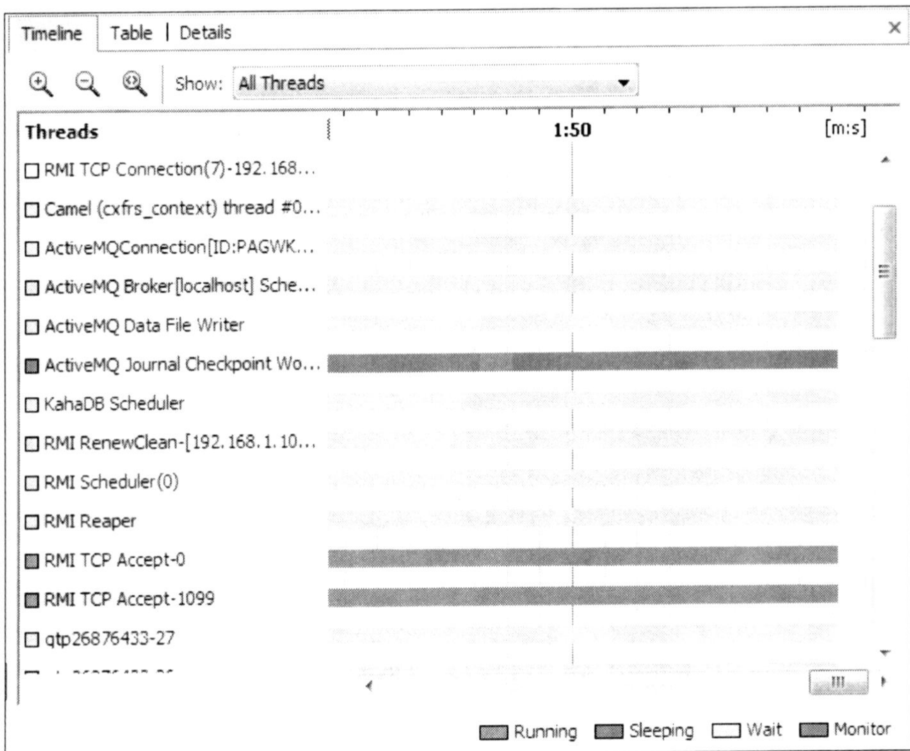

Threads can be created by the application and appear available, or in `Wait` state giving the impression that the threads are ready to process requests. If socket resources are not available for the threads to process a request, they will throw exceptions but continue to appear as available.

Profiling server threads will not help identify socket-related issues on a server. The specific socket issues that web applications encounter are TCP-based connections. The TCP connections and the state those connections are in are available through the `netstat` command on Windows and Linux. The following command will list all sockets on the current machine:

```
netstat -an
```

The previous command can result in a large list of sockets which will look similar to the following:

```
Active Connections

  Proto  Local Address          Foreign Address        State
  TCP    0.0.0.0:41359          0.0.0.0:0              LISTENING
  TCP    10.21.176.89:139       0.0.0.0:0              LISTENING
  TCP    10.21.176.89:1317      24.40.71.19:3122       ESTABLISHED
```

The previous command might return too many results to determine a specific issue.

The results can be piped into a `find` command only returning results of sockets that are in the `LISTENING` state:

```
netstat -an |find /i "listening"
```

The previous command will result in a list of sockets that are currently in the `LISTENING` state, as follows:

```
TCP    0.0.0.0:80             0.0.0.0:0              LISTENING
```

We can determine how many sockets are in the `TIME_WAIT` state with the following command:

```
netstat -an |find /i "TIME_WAIT"
```

The previous command will result in a list of sockets that are currently in the `TIME_WAIT` state, as follows:

```
TCP    192.168.1.103:5357     192.168.1.100:57788    TIME_WAIT
```

We can determine how many sockets are in the `CLOSE_WAIT` state with the following command:

```
netstat -an |find /i "CLOSE_WAIT"
```

The previous command will result in a list of sockets that are currently in the `CLOSE_WAIT` state, as follows:

```
TCP    192.168.1.103:62204    60.48.190.47:42233     CLOSE_WAIT
```

Netstat is a valuable tool that can aid debugging socket-level issues with any TCP socket connections. When debugging applications, profiling low-level sockets can provide invaluable information.

Netstat tools

In addition to profiling socket connections in terminal windows, several other products are available both commercially and open source.

NetStat Agent

NetStat Agent (`http://netstatagent.com`) is a commercially available Windows application that can profile all active TCP and UDP connections. NetStat Agent is also bundled with several other networking tools such as `ping`, `ipconfig`, `traceroute`, and `whois` just to name a few. The following screenshot shows how connections can be sortable by status:

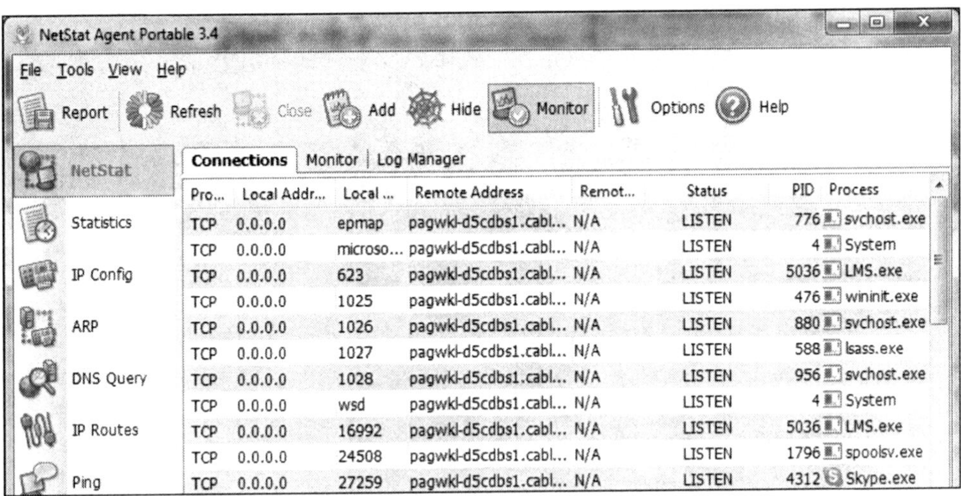

NetStat Agent can also monitor for specific rules based on various connection characteristics as depicted in the following screenshot:

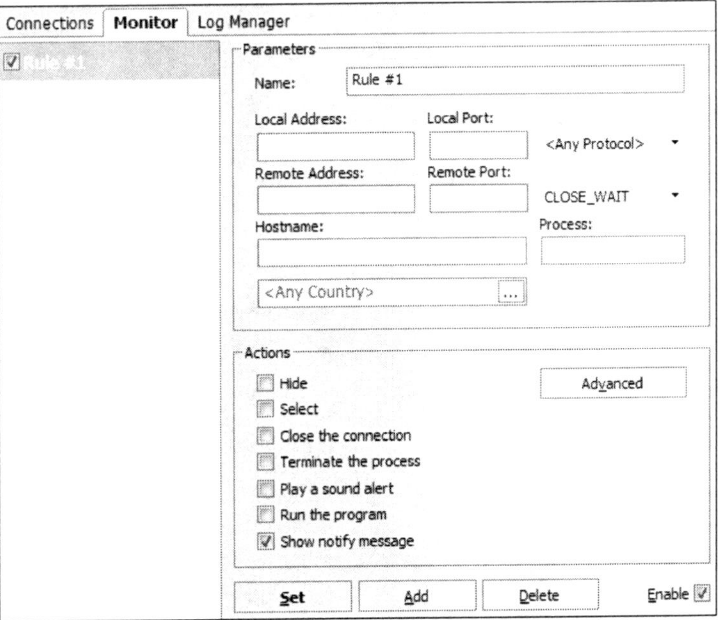

A rule can be created to show a notification every time a connection from a specific address enters the `CLOSE_WAIT` state.

TCPView

The Sysinternals website was created in 1996 by Mark Russinovich and Bryce Cogswell to host advanced system utilities and technical information but is now hosted by Microsoft. The Sysinternals suite contains many tools for various system administration tasks. One specific tool is called TCPView (`http://technet.microsoft.com/en-US/sysinternals`) as shown in the following screenshot:

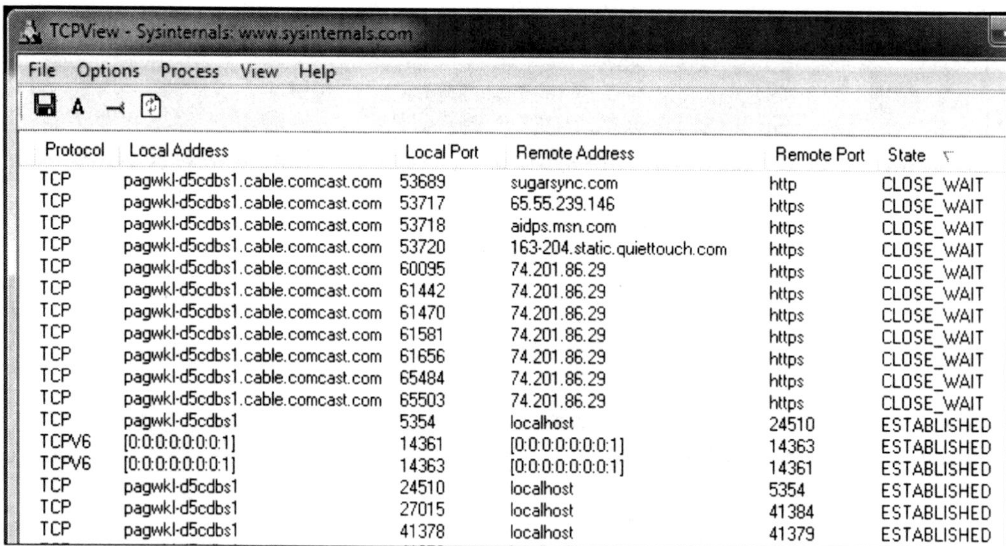

Protocol	Local Address	Local Port	Remote Address	Remote Port	State
TCP	pagwkl-d5cdbs1.cable.comcast.com	53689	sugarsync.com	http	CLOSE_WAIT
TCP	pagwkl-d5cdbs1.cable.comcast.com	53717	65.55.239.146	https	CLOSE_WAIT
TCP	pagwkl-d5cdbs1.cable.comcast.com	53718	aidps.msn.com	https	CLOSE_WAIT
TCP	pagwkl-d5cdbs1.cable.comcast.com	53720	163-204.static.quiettouch.com	https	CLOSE_WAIT
TCP	pagwkl-d5cdbs1.cable.comcast.com	60095	74.201.86.29	https	CLOSE_WAIT
TCP	pagwkl-d5cdbs1.cable.comcast.com	61442	74.201.86.29	https	CLOSE_WAIT
TCP	pagwkl-d5cdbs1.cable.comcast.com	61470	74.201.86.29	https	CLOSE_WAIT
TCP	pagwkl-d5cdbs1.cable.comcast.com	61581	74.201.86.29	https	CLOSE_WAIT
TCP	pagwkl-d5cdbs1.cable.comcast.com	61656	74.201.86.29	https	CLOSE_WAIT
TCP	pagwkl-d5cdbs1.cable.comcast.com	65484	74.201.86.29	https	CLOSE_WAIT
TCP	pagwkl-d5cdbs1.cable.comcast.com	65503	74.201.86.29	https	CLOSE_WAIT
TCP	pagwkl-d5cdbs1	5354	localhost	24510	ESTABLISHED
TCPV6	[0:0:0:0:0:0:0:1]	14361	[0:0:0:0:0:0:0:1]	14363	ESTABLISHED
TCPV6	[0:0:0:0:0:0:0:1]	14363	[0:0:0:0:0:0:0:1]	14361	ESTABLISHED
TCP	pagwkl-d5cdbs1	24510	localhost	5354	ESTABLISHED
TCP	pagwkl-d5cdbs1	27015	localhost	41384	ESTABLISHED
TCP	pagwkl-d5cdbs1	41378	localhost	41379	ESTABLISHED

See also

- *The Testing JAX-WS and JAX-RS with soapUI* section in *Chapter 4, Enterprise Testing Strategies*
- *TCP*: `http://en.wikipedia.org/wiki/Transmission_Control_Protocol`
- *RFC 793 TCP Connection states*: `http://tools.ietf.org/html/rfc793`
- *NetStat*: `http://en.wikipedia.org/wiki/Netstat`
- *SecureCRT*: `http://www.vandyke.com/products/securecrt/index.html`

Profiling TCP connections with TCPMon

TCPMon is an open source utility for monitoring the data flowing on a TCP connection.

TCPMon is used by configuring the tool to listen on one TCP port as a proxy to a client and delegating the request to another port on the target server.

There are many tools similar to TCPMon available including standalone application and browser plugins for Firefox and Google Chrome. One nice feature of TCPMon is the ability to integrate the tool directly into Eclipse and IntelliJ IDEs.

In this recipe we are going to learn how to leverage TCPMon to debug TCP connections.

Getting ready

TCPMon is distributed as an executable JAR and can be downloaded from `http://code.google.com/p/tcpmon/`.

TCPMon can be started by either double-clicking the **executable JAR**, or by executing the following command on a terminal console:

```
java -jar %TCPMON_HOME%\tcpmon.jar
```

TCPMon displays the following splash screen when the tool is first started:

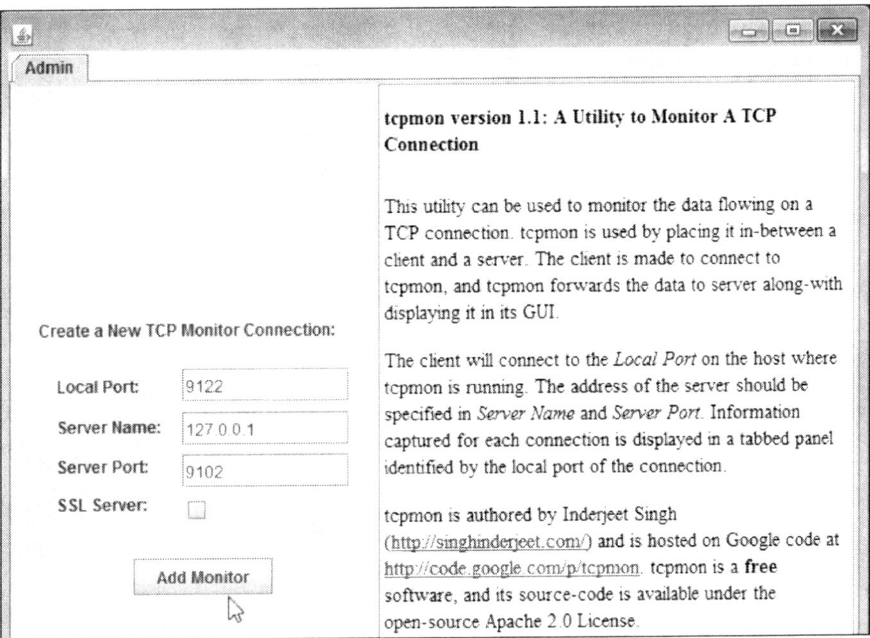

TCPMon is going to act as a proxy to a client TCP request and then delegate the requests to a target server and port.

We begin by creating a new TCP monitor connection by entering a local port that the client is sending requests to. Then enter the target server name or IP address and port number to send the request to. Next, click on the **Add Monitor** button and a new tab will be created for every connection.

TCPMon is now listening on port 9122 for client requests and will delegate those requests to 127.0.0.1 on port 9102.

How to do it...

Now that TCPMon is monitoring for client TCP requests, we can send requests to port 9122 and they should be logged into TCPMon as shown in the following screenshot:

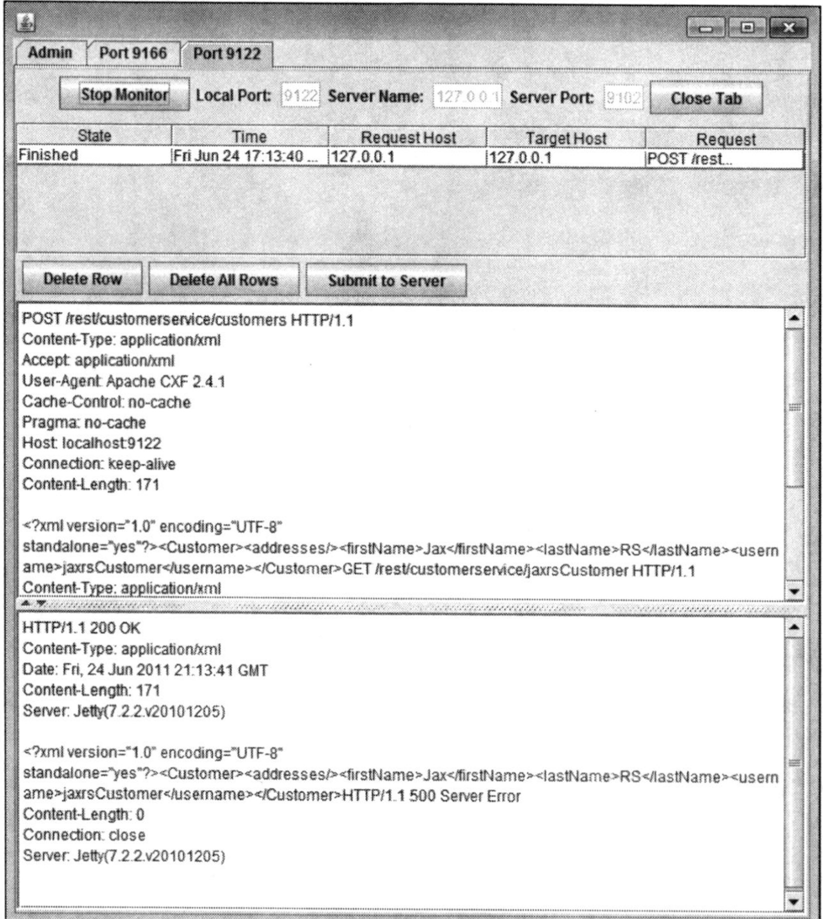

TCPMon will log every request to the port being monitored. Each request log will contain the header and payload information that can be used to track down request or response issues.

There's more...

Valid request and response test data is required when writing unit tests for web services. The request and response body being logged in TCPMon can be used to create this test data without the need to create the data manually.

The following listing is a SOAP response logged by TCPMon:

```
<soap:Envelope xmlns:
  soap="http://schemas.xmlsoap.org/soap/envelope/">
  <soap:Body>
    <ns2:addCustomer xmlns:
      ns2="http://resources.jaxrs.javaee6.baselogic.com/">
      <customer>
      <addresses/>
        <firstName>Jax</firstName>
        <lastName>WS</lastName>
        <username>jaxWSCustomer</username>
      </customer>
    </ns2:addCustomer>
  </soap:Body>
</soap:Envelope>
```

This SOAP request data can be saved in a file named `response.xml` and made available to unit testing tools including soapUI as seen in the *Testing JAX-WS and JAX-RS with soapUI* section in *Chapter 4, Enterprise Testing Strategies*.

This recipe demonstrates the flexibility of TCPMon as a simple yet powerful tool when working with TCP-based applications that require monitoring or debugging.

See also

- *The Testing JAX-WS and JAX-RS with soapUI* section in *Chapter 4, Enterprise Testing Strategies*
- *TCPMon*: `http://code.google.com/p/tcpmon/`
- *XMLUnit*: `http://xmlunit.sourceforge.net`

Monitoring application and server performance with Munin

Staying ahead of problems on your server can often be more valuable than fixing them after the fact. Server monitoring tools can give valuable insight about the performance of a computer, networks, applications, and other information that might be valuable. Monitoring tools will graph an ongoing trend that makes it easy to determine "what's different today" when a performance problem crops up. These graphs can be used to determine when to add additional resources or alert you of potential issues before they cause downtime or bandwidth overages.

In this recipe, we will cover how to install and configure Munin to monitor computer resources and a Tomcat application server. Munin is available for various distributions of Linux, Mac OS X, and Solaris but there is also a Windows port available which is located at `http://code.google.com/p/munin-node-win32/`. This recipe will focus on installation on a Linux-based server.

Munin can monitor one or more computers and presents the information in graphs displayed in a web interface. Munin uses RRDTool, which is an open source data logging and graphing system for time series data and the framework is written in Perl, while plugins may be written in any language.

Munin has a master/node architecture in which the master connects to all the nodes at regular intervals and asks them for data. One of the main goals of Munin has been the ease of creating new plugins (graphs).

Getting ready

In order to begin, we need to ensure that the server which Munin will be installed onto is accessible through SSH and be able to connect with a user account that has `sudo` privileges.

The installation procedures described in this recipe are based on using a Linux package tool such as Apt-get and YUM. It is also possible to install Munin using RPM Package Manager or from source code, but is out of the scope of this recipe.

An HTTP web server such as *Apache Server* or *Nginx* should also be installed and configured in order to view the graphs displayed in a web interface.

How to do it...

The first step to this recipe is to install the Munin master and Munin node packages.

Begin by opening an SSH client and connecting to the server to begin the installation.

There are two different package tools we will cover. The first is called **Yellowdog Updater, Modified** (**YUM**) executed by the command `yum`. The other is called **Advanced Packaging Tool** (**Apt-get**) and is executed by the command `apt-get`.

Red Hat and CentOS Linux distributions use YUM while the Ubuntu distribution uses Apt-get.

Munin master and node can be installed using YUM with the following command:

```
yum -q -y install munin munin-node
```

The `-q` parameter tells YUM to install quietly, and the `-y` parameter tells YUM to automatically confirm the installation.

Munin master and node can be installed using Apt-get with the following command:

```
apt-get -qq install munin munin-node
```

The `-qq` parameter tells Apt-get to install without displaying the dependencies being installed as shown in the following screenshot:

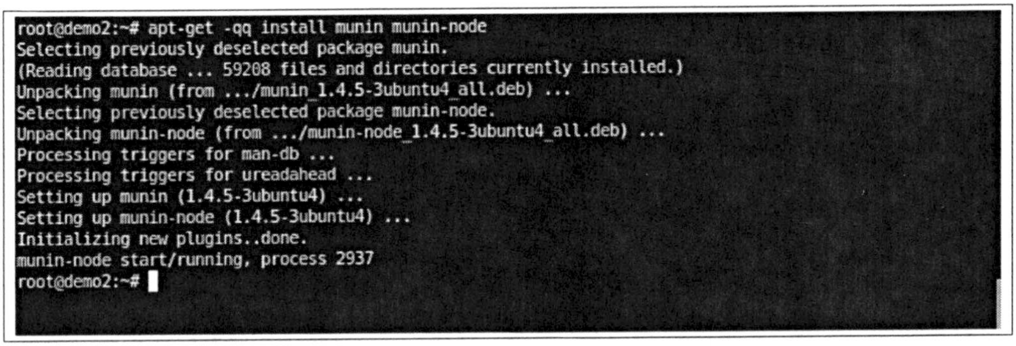

```
root@demo2:~# apt-get -qq install munin munin-node
Selecting previously deselected package munin.
(Reading database ... 59208 files and directories currently installed.)
Unpacking munin (from .../munin_1.4.5-3ubuntu4_all.deb) ...
Selecting previously deselected package munin-node.
Unpacking munin-node (from .../munin-node_1.4.5-3ubuntu4_all.deb) ...
Processing triggers for man-db ...
Processing triggers for ureadahead ...
Setting up munin (1.4.5-3ubuntu4) ...
Setting up munin-node (1.4.5-3ubuntu4) ...
Initializing new plugins..done.
munin-node start/running, process 2937
root@demo2:~#
```

Additional dependencies and package updates might be required during the installation process and should be considered based on the target installation operating system which is out of the scope of this recipe. At this point, it is assumed that Munin master and node packages were successfully installed.

Configuration

Now that Munin is installed, the next step is to configure the master and node.

The Munin master server is configured by a file called `munin.conf` that will be located at `/etc/munin/`. Open `munin.conf` in edit mode using a system editor such as VI or NANO. The first thing to search for is the location of the property where Munin stores the HTML graphs which will look similar to the following:

```
dbdir      /var/lib/munin/
htmldir    /var/www/munin/
logdir     /var/log/munin
rundir     /var/run/munin/
```

The property `htmldir` is set to a default location, but should be changed to the location of the public document's folder of the server's web server.

The next change required in the `munin.conf` file is to set the hostname and address for the master server. First search for the default host entry which will be inside square brackets as depicted in the following listing:

```
[localhost.localdomain]
  address 127.0.0.1
  use_node_name yes
```

Change this entry to the hostname of the server where the Munin master server is being installed on. This will register the hostname with a given IP address, which in the following listing, points to localhost:

```
[demo1.home.network]
  address 127.0.0.1
  use_node_name yes
```

The Munin nodes are configured by a file called `munin-node.conf` that will be located at `/etc/munin/`. Open `munin-node.conf` in edit mode using a system editor such as VI or NANO. The first thing to search for is a property that configures the hostname of the Munin master server which will look similar to the following listing:

```
#host_name localhost.localdomain
```

First, remove the preceding hash character (#), which will make the configuration property active. Next, change the hostname to the value set earlier in the Munin master configuration. The resulting configuration change should look similar to the following listing:

```
host_name demo1.home.network
```

Basic configuration for a master server and single node are complete.

Restart service

Now that we have completed the configuration of the master server and node, each service must be restarted for the change to take effect. Begin by restarting the Munin master server with the following command:

```
[mick@/etc/munin ]$ service munin restart
[mick@/etc/munin ]$ Starting Munin:             [ ok ]
```

After the Munin master server service has successfully started, execute the following command to restart the Munin node:

```
[mick@/etc/munin ]$ service munin-node restart
[mick@/etc/munin ]$ Starting Munin Node:             [ ok ]
```

When the master server and node are started, the Munin graphs should be accessible and collecting data about the server. The web console will be available at the location the web server is configured to serve the graphs that was set up earlier in the Munin master server configuration. Assuming the web server is configured to serve web documents for an internal hostname of `demo1.home.network`, opening a web browser to `http://demo1.home.network` should result in the Munin overview page.

Now Munin is collecting data for many aspects of your server including CPU, disk, and memory profiles just to name a few. The following screenshot shows a detailed history of different server characteristics being collected:

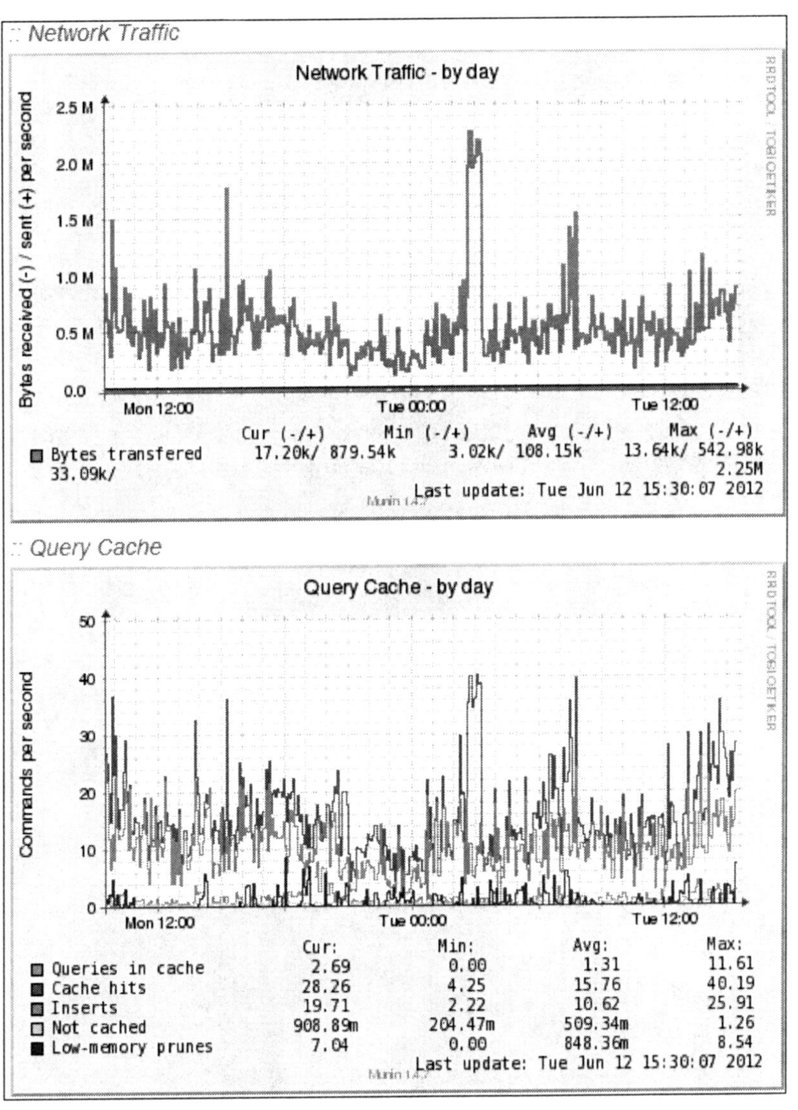

There's more...

Tomcat server can be configured to be displayed from any web application by using the CGIServlet that is distributed with the Tomcat server. The CGIServlet is a standard servlet that can be mapped to any `url-pattern` and points the requests to a `real-path` which contains the graphs generated by Munin as shown in the following example `web.xml` configuration:

```
<web-app>
...
  <servlet servlet-name="cgiservlet"
    servlet-class="org.apache.catalina.
      servlets.CGIServlet" />
  <servlet-mapping url-pattern="/cgi/munin"
    servlet-name="cgiservlet" />
  <path-mapping url-pattern="/*"
    real-path="/var/www/munin" />
...
</web-app>
```

This will configure Tomcat to serve the graphs for Munin located at `http://demo1.home.network:8080/cgi/munin`.

Monitoring Tomcat

Munin is distributed with a plugin to collect data on a Tomcat server by the Munin node and can be configured with the `munin-node-configure` command.

The `munin-node-configure` command can suggest plugins to be installed based on the server's configuration by running the following command:

```
[mick@/etc/munin ]$ munin-node-configure --suggest
```

This command will display all of the plugins available for the current Munin installation. The result will be displayed if a plugin is used, or not, as seen in the following listing:

```
Plugin                          | Used | Suggestions
...
swap                            | yes  | yes
threads                         | yes  | yes
tomcat_                         | no   | yes (access avgtime jvm maxtime
threads volume)
uptime                          | yes  | yes
users                           | yes  | yes
...
```

The Tomcat plugin has not been enabled by default, as seen in the previous listing. A plugin can be enabled in Munin by creating a symbolic link from the plugin file located in the /usr/share/munin/plugins directory to the /etc/munin/plugins directory which is as shown in the following listing:

```
ln -s /usr/share/munin/plugins/tomcat_access /etc/munin/plugins/tomcat_
access
ln -s /usr/share/munin/plugins/tomcat_jvm /etc/munin/plugins/tomcat_jvm
ln -s /usr/share/munin/plugins/tomcat_threads /etc/munin/plugins/tomcat_
threads
ln -s /usr/share/munin/plugins/tomcat_volume /etc/munin/plugins/tomcat_
volume
```

This will enable access, JVM, thread, and volume statistics to be tracked from the Tomcat server.

Next we need to configure the Munin node to connect to Tomcat, by opening /etc/munin/plugin-conf.d/munin-node in edit mode using a system editor such as VI or NANO. Next, append the following configuration block to the end, changing the values to match the Tomcat installation:

```
[tomcat_*]
env.host 127.0.0.1
env.ports 8080
env.request /manager/status?XML=true
env.user munin
env.password secretPassword
enc.connector jk-8009
```

The next step is to add a new user to access Tomcat. This can be accomplished by opening $TOMCAT_HOME/conf/tomcat-users.xml and adding a status role and the Munin user we configured in the Munin node as depicted in the following listing:

```
<tomcat-users>
<role rolename="manager-status"/>
<user username="munin" password="secretPassword" roles="manager-
status"/>
</tomcat-users>
```

After adding the new user configuration, the Tomcat server will need to be restarted for the configuration to take effect.

After the Tomcat server has been successfully restarted, execute the following command to restart the Munin node:

```
[mick@/etc/munin ]$ service munin-node restart
[mick@/etc/munin ]$ Starting Munin Node:             [ ok ]
```

At this point Munin is now collecting statistics from Tomcat and will be available in the web console.

See also

- *Munin*: `http://munin-monitoring.org/`
- *Munin Windows*: `http://code.google.com/p/munin-node-win32/`
- *RRDTool*: `http://oss.oetiker.ch/rrdtool/`
- *YUM*: `http://en.wikipedia.org/wiki/Yellow_dog_Updater_Modified`
- *Advanced Packaging Tool*: `http://en.wikipedia.org/wiki/Apt-get`
- *RPM Package Manager*: `http://en.wikipedia.org/wiki/RPM_Package_Manager`
- *RedHat*: `http://en.wikipedia.org/wiki/RedHat`
- *CentOS*: `http://en.wikipedia.org/wiki/Centos`
- *Ubuntu*: `http://en.wikipedia.org/wiki/Ubuntu_(operating_system)`
- *Apache Server*: `http://httpd.apache.org`
- *Nginx*: `http://wiki.nginx.org`

Debugging HTTP connections with HTTP Debugger

A common issue with developing web applications is debugging HTTP connections from client as well as server perspectives. Clients are sending and receiving content in the form of content pages, AJAX requests, and FORM submissions. Servers are receiving requests in the form of HTTP GET and HTTP POST requests from content pages and from web service clients. Debugging requests and responses for an application to determine a specific issue can become quite complex.

In this recipe we will leverage HTTP Debugger to trace client and server-based requests and responses.

HTTP Debugger is a feature-rich Windows-based application used for intercepting, viewing, and analyzing traffic between clients using the HTTP/HTTPS protocol and a web server.

Getting ready

HTTP Debugger is a commercial product and offers a 14-day trial download. We begin this recipe by downloading HTTP Debugger from `http://httpdebugger.com/download.html` which is available in 32-bit and 64-bit distributions.

After HTTP Debugger has been installed, start the application to access the main dashboard as shown in the following screenshot:

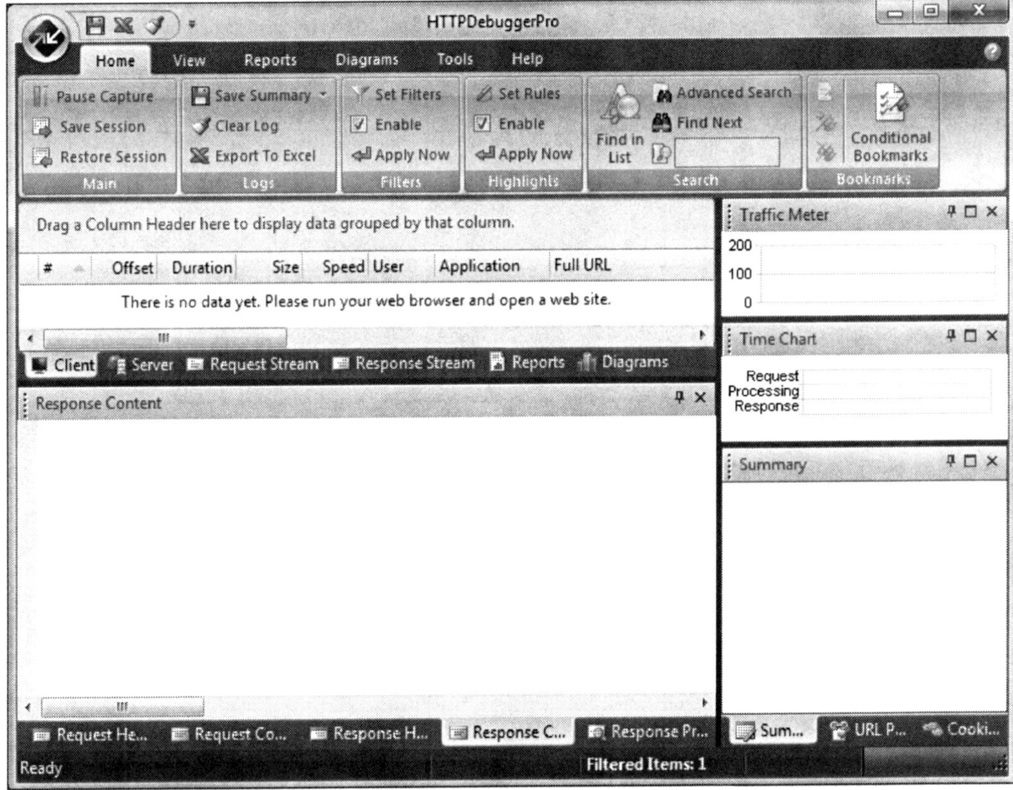

Before we begin using HTTP Debugger, select the **Tools** tab. Next, click **Networking Mode** and set to use **Advanced Mode**.

The advanced networking mode allows HTTP Debugger to intercept client traffic from a web browser and also intercept server traffic from Apache Tomcat, GlassFish, or other application servers.

After setting HTTP Debugger to advanced network mode, the computer will need to be rebooted for the change to take effect.

How to do it...

To begin debugging with HTTP Debugger, start the application. At this point HTTP Debugger will intercept all HTTP/HTTPS traffic incrementally and will display the client requests as depicted here:

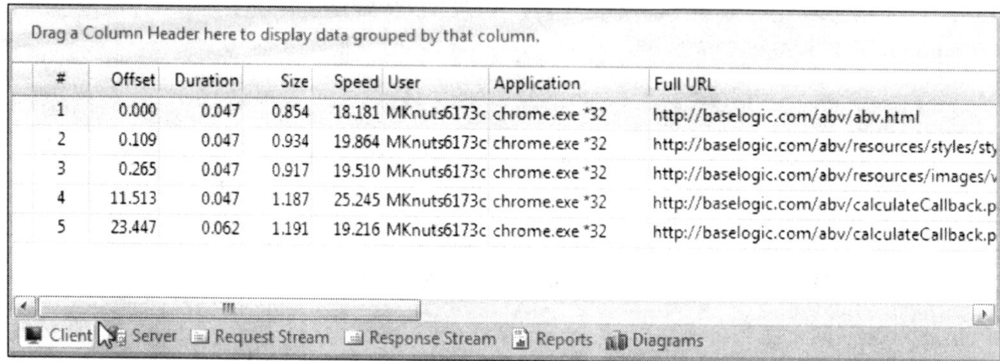

Each client request is captured to include the requested URL, method, headers, and body. The client response that is captured includes content type, status code, headers, and body. The following listing depicts both the request and response header for a given transaction:

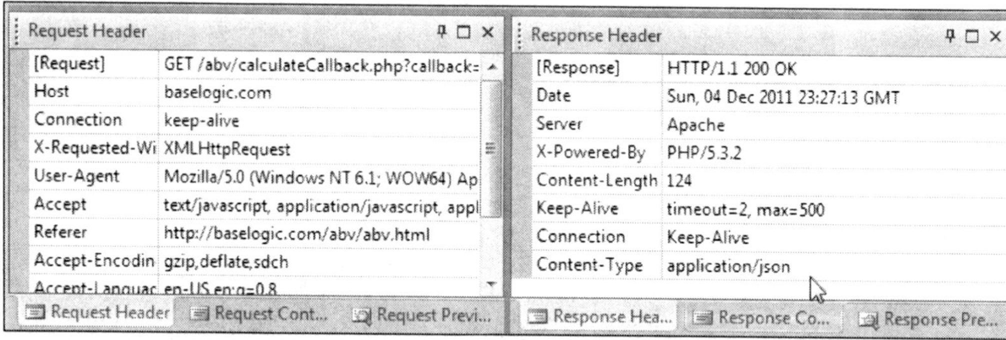

Each transaction captured also contains request and response content. The following listing depicts a JSONP response content body that can be used to validate issues with AJAX applications:

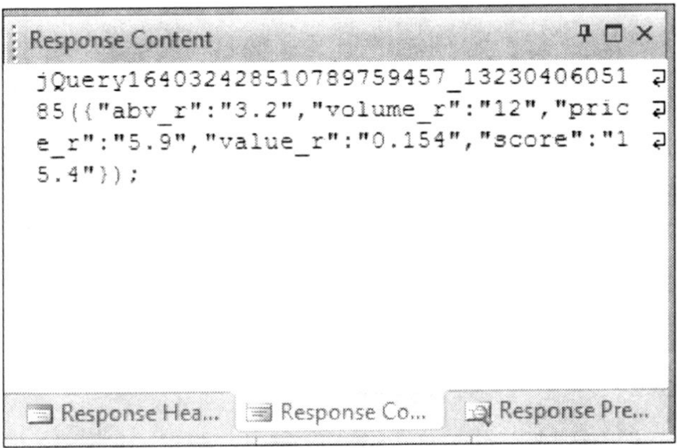

The ability to see both the request and response can help determine specific points where a transaction is failing. Client and server transactions are divided into separate tabs to delineate the connections being captured. It provides the ability to compare the transaction the client is involved in with the transaction the server is involved in. The following screenshot shows that the server connections have the same data available per (each) connection as the client tab contains:

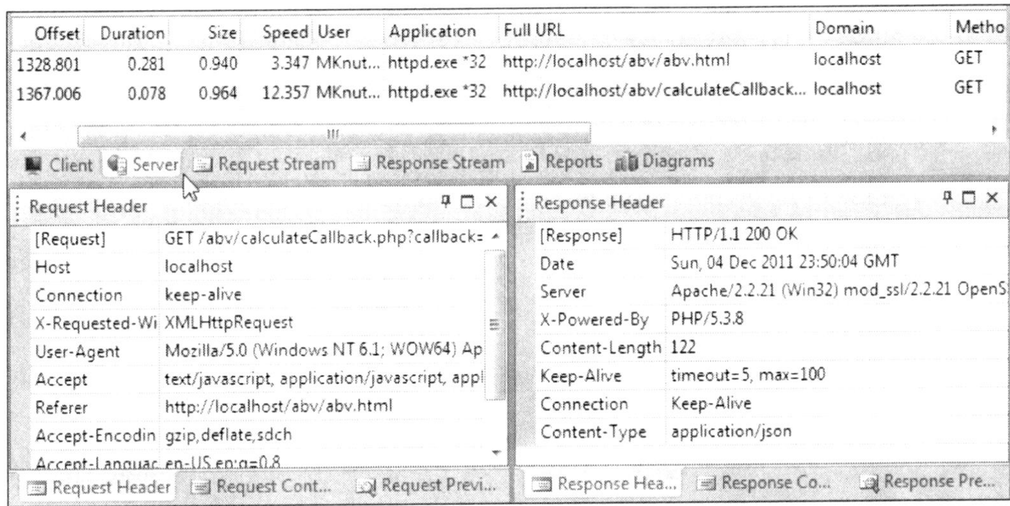

There's more...

HTTP Debugger can also generate summarized reports based on various attributes. The following screenshot shows a report detailing all requests from **localhost** including the duration and speed of the transaction:

#	Domain	Method	Status	Duration	Speed	Request: Host
1	localhost	GET		0.000	0.000	localhost
2	localhost	GET	200 OK	0.078	139.223	localhost
3	localhost	GET		0.000	0.000	localhost
4	localhost	GET	200 OK	0.015	64.518	localhost
5	localhost	GET	200 OK	0.015	64.518	localhost

Application	HTTP Debugger Pro 4.0.0.6
Browser	Internet Explorer 8.0.7601.17514 Mozilla Firefox 8.0 (en-US)
Hardware	Intel(R) Core(TM) i5-2520M CPU @ 2.50GHz RAM 710Mb/4170Mb HDD 78139Mb/250057Mb
OS	Windows 7 Enterprise,

HTTP Debugger can also generate various diagrams which can be useful when depicting attribute distribution of dozens or even thousands of transactions. The following listing depicts a pie chart showing the status response code distribution from the current transactions:

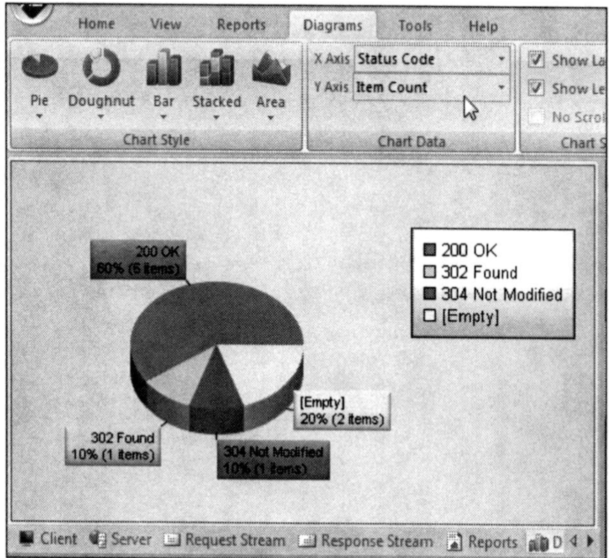

Hopefully this overview of the capabilities of HTTP Debugger has demonstrated the benefits this tool can provide.

See also

- *HTTP Debugger*: `http://www.httpdebugger.com`

Index

Symbols

A

B

C

D

J

K

L

N

O

Thank you for buying
Java EE 6 Cookbook for Securing, Tuning, and Extending Enterprise Applications

About Packt Publishing

Packt, pronounced 'packed', published its first book "*Mastering phpMyAdmin for Effective MySQL Management*" in April 2004 and subsequently continued to specialize in publishing highly focused books on specific technologies and solutions.

Our books and publications share the experiences of your fellow IT professionals in adapting and customizing today's systems, applications, and frameworks. Our solution-based books give you the knowledge and power to customize the software and technologies you're using to get the job done. Packt books are more specific and less general than the IT books you have seen in the past. Our unique business model allows us to bring you more focused information, giving you more of what you need to know, and less of what you don't.

Packt is a modern, yet unique publishing company, which focuses on producing quality, cutting-edge books for communities of developers, administrators, and newbies alike. For more information, please visit our website: `www.PacktPub.com`.

About Packt Enterprise

In 2010, Packt launched two new brands, Packt Enterprise and Packt Open Source, in order to continue its focus on specialization. This book is part of the Packt Enterprise brand, home to books published on enterprise software - software created by major vendors, including (but not limited to) IBM, Microsoft and Oracle, often for use in other corporations. Its titles will offer information relevant to a range of users of this software, including administrators, developers, architects, and end users.

Writing for Packt

We welcome all inquiries from people who are interested in authoring. Book proposals should be sent to `author@packtpub.com`. If your book idea is still at an early stage and you would like to discuss it first before writing a formal book proposal, contact us; one of our commissioning editors will get in touch with you.

We're not just looking for published authors; if you have strong technical skills but no writing experience, our experienced editors can help you develop a writing career, or simply get some additional reward for your expertise.

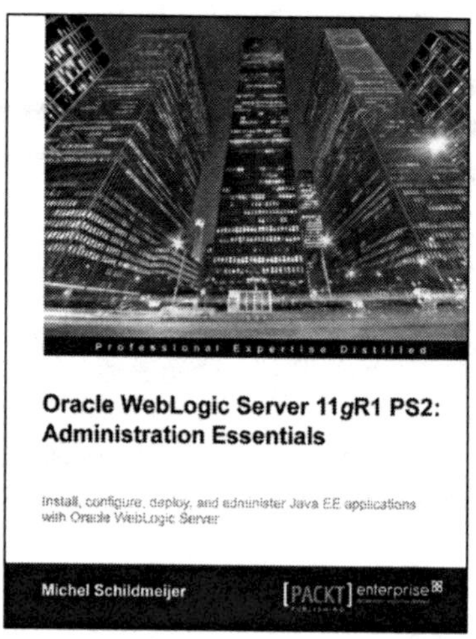

Oracle Weblogic Server 11gR1 PS2: Administration Essentials

ISBN: 978-1-849683-02-9 Paperback: 304 pages

Install, configure, deploy, and administer Java EE applications with Oracle WebLogic Server

1. A practical book with step-by-step instructions for admins in real-time company environments
2. Create, commit, undo, and monitor a change session using the Administration Console
3. Create basic automated tooling with WLST
4. Access advanced resource attributes in the Administration Console

---

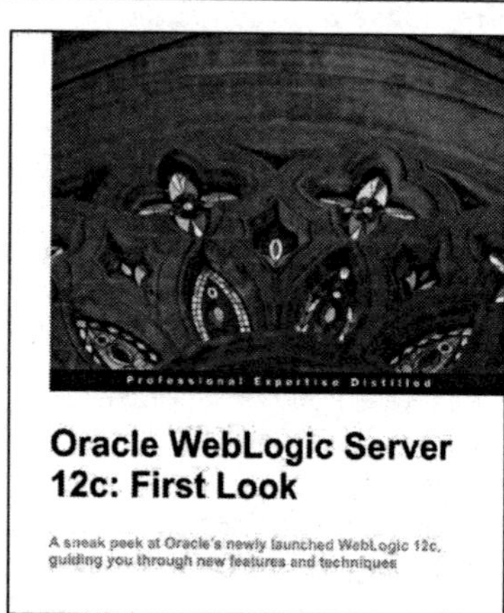

Oracle WebLogic Server 12c: First Look

ISBN: 978-1-849687-18-8 Paperback: 200 pages

A sneak peek at Oracle's newly launched WebLogic 12c, guiding you through new features and techniques

1. A concise and practical first look to immediately get you started with Oracle Weblogic 12c
2. Understand the position and use of Oracle WebLogic 12c in Exalogic and the Cloud

Please check **www.PacktPub.com** for information on our titles

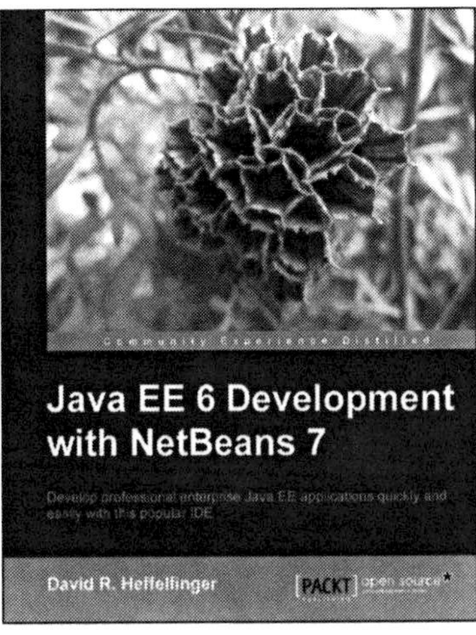

Java EE 6 Development with NetBeans 7

ISBN: 978-1-849512-70-1 Paperback: 392 pages

Deploy professional enterprise Java EE applications quickly and easily with this popular IDE

1. Use features of the popular NetBeans IDE to accelerate development of Java EE applications
2. Develop JavaServer Pages (JSPs) to display both static and dynamic content in a web browser
3. Covers the latest versions of major Java EE APIs such as JSF 2.0, EJB 3.1, and JPA 2.0, and new additions to Java EE such as CDI and JAX-RS
4. Learn development with the popular PrimeFaces JSF 2.0 component library

---

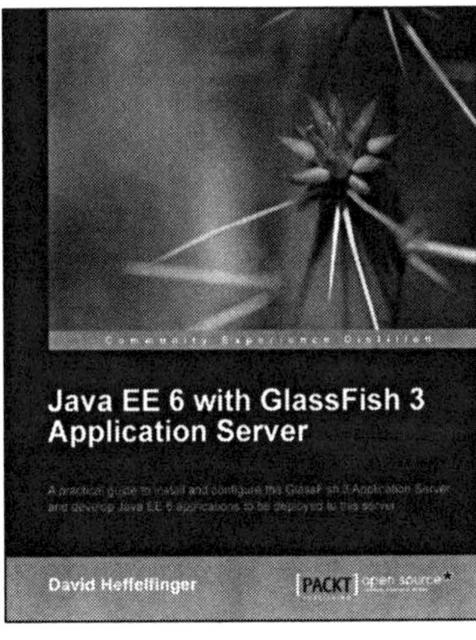

Java EE 6 with GlassFish 3 Application Server

ISBN: 978-1-849510-36-3 Paperback: 488 pages

A practical guide to install and configure the GlassFish 3 Application Server and develop Java EE 6 applications to be deployed to this server

1. Install and configure the GlassFish 3 Application Server and develop Java EE 6 applications to be deployed to this server
2. Specialize in all major Java EE 6 APIs, including new additions to the specification such as CDI and JAX-RS
3. Use GlassFish v3 application server and gain enterprise reliability and performance with less complexity

Please check **www.PacktPub.com** for information on our titles

CPSIA information can be obtained at www.ICGtesting.com
Printed in the USA
BVOW051307120912

300138BV00003B/6/P